To Bernard, with much love and all good wishes on your Birthday — Mary (February 2013.)

The author of this [illegible] the wines for your wedding... [illegible] hope you enjoy!

D0297607

A Matter of Taste

A HISTORY OF WINE DRINKING IN BRITAIN

'In the matter of wine you must go by the taste
and let everything else go hang'
Hilaire Belloc

A Matter of Taste

A HISTORY OF WINE DRINKING IN BRITAIN

JON HURLEY

TEMPUS

To my wife Heather, with whom I have shared much, including wine.

First published 2005

Tempus Publishing Limited
The Mill, Brimscombe Port,
Stroud, Gloucestershire, GL5 2QG
www.tempus-publishing.com

© Jon Hurley, 2005

The right of Jon Hurley to be identified as the Author
of this work has been asserted in accordance with the
Copyrights, Designs and Patents Act 1988.

British Library Cataloguing in Publication Data.
A catalogue record for this book is available from the British Library.

ISBN 0 7524 3402 0
Typesetting and origination by Tempus Publishing Limited
Printed in Great Britain

CONTENTS

Introduction

As a downy-chinned, carefree wine trainee in the early 1960s, I wheeled through sunny Richmond Park, scattering the deer on my way to my first managerial post as a relief manager at an off-licence in Clapham. I was to mind the store for a fortnight while the regular fellow was on holiday. I parked my BSA outside and barely had time to undo the locks and bolts and wriggle out of my Belstaff and pudding basin helmet before I was ambushed by a pongy scrum of alkies drooling for their early morning hit of Gaymer's Cider.

The shop was the grimmest outpost of my Richmond-based employers. As I gazed around me with the spoor and echoing boots of the departing alkies still in the air, and saw the towers of Watney's Red Barrel, crates of Sanatogen, boxes of crisps, tiers of Craven A, Senior Services, Park Drive, Woodbine, Rizlas, Smarties and Panatella, any romance associated with wine vanished. Gloomily I checked the float, made a cup of instant and, after noticing a brass ring in the floor, I pulled it and descended.

The cellar was clearly a part of the premises the manager, a former bus conductor, never explored. It was dingy. Rosy-cheeked girls in Buckfast posters smiled through the cobwebs, their eyelashes great black spiders. Mice had long deserted their nests in the piles of dirty straw. Bunches of plastic grapes dangled flaccidly; there were tarnished brass funnels, discarded spigots, an old bar table and heaps of empty flagons.

Then I noticed the wine bins. They were packed with bottles, their labels torn, faded and pocked with little spots of manure dropped by dead bluebottles. There were brown fluted bottles ullaged with Lutomer Riesling and Schloss Bockelheimer. There was Graves the colour of Red Rum's pee. I found Chablis, London bottled and London blended, Blue Nun, raffia-entwined Chianti, Aussie Emus in flat-sided bottles. I smiled in the moted haze I had created when I uncovered several old Clarets sleeping in their dusty beds, village Burgundies, a small cache of white-splashed port. I hauled everything upstairs and cleared the big old-fashioned window of dead bumblebees, beer, porcelain toucans, VP Ruby and sunburnt Emva Cream.

I paused to serve my first customer in an hour – a quarter-bottle of Bells to a broken down aristocrat with twitching hands – then laid out the straw, strung the grapes, and made bottles cleverly spill from old wooden crates. I polished generations of cider drinkers' breath from the windowpane. I spent the afternoon reading the TT edition of the *Motor Cycling News*. At the time motorcycle racing around the Isle of Man took first place, by a long way, to my new career.

I measured the day in Nescafé-stained spoons; then, as dusk set in, a large car cruised up. 'Kerb crawler,' I muttered as I lurked behind a huge cash register, brassy and embossed as a tinker's caravan. I saw a well-dressed man peering in the window. Like a spider with a fat fly in its sights, I waited. Come on, come on. He did, and bought everything – the port, Claret and the Burgundies, and even an eight-and-six bottle of London Chablis. Next morning, after refuelling the bomb site habitués, I rang head office to order more wine. 'But the Clapham branch never sells wine,' I was told. 'It does now,' I said. 'Oh, would you like to take it over?' 'No thanks,' I said.

That Clapham off-licence was typical of the time. The companies who owned such emporiums, often big breweries, could see no future in wine unless it was cheap and gaudily labelled. No-one had a clue about wine, least of all the staff, who were poorly motivated, ill-educated and, if married, more interested in the flat above the shop. Money spent on training staff was a waste of time. Make it easy for the customer instead. Not too many choices, easy-to-remember names, and don't give up on the sweets and tobacco. It was only with the advent of the supermarkets that sales really took off. They offered variety, bright stores, muzak, staff with acne who knew nothing. The few independents who had hitherto concentrated on supplying well-cushioned farmers and accountants had to become more adventurous. Off-licences closed in droves and the survivors were forced to develop more exciting ranges. Some actually trained their staff. Wine drinking gradually became part of the British way of life.

But a recent article by Andrew Jefford proves the wine drinker has much to fear. 'The windows of my local branch of Thresher and Victoria Wine are full of cans of lager,' writes Jefford. 'Sellotaped posters shout mega deals. Selection is once again shrinking on the high street. Customers aren't getting any savvier, says a spokesperson. They want things made simpler. It's a nice idea.' Help! It's back to the future. Wine drinkers who cherish diversification in wine must rush to hug their crusty old independents, support the eejit who on a wing and a prayer has launched a range of Swiss reds in Cwmbran, or the ex-dentist who is desperate to show you the delights of Ecuador.

Britain has always been a wine-drinking democracy. Inky reds from Stalinist Russia, whey-faced Hocks from fascist Germany, fake 'sherry' from Apartheid-shackled South Africa. From junta-ruled Portugal came port and Mateus – a favourite tipple of Her Majesty, Sir Cliff and Saddam. Silky Riojas from Franco's Spain, Merlots and Malbecs from dictators in bus conductor's hats in Chile and Argentina.

Unlike the Frenchman, the Briton has no loyalty. He sips here and there, willing to try everything from Ausone to Zilavka. But, considering the Englishman's centuries-old reputation for connoisseurship, the 1960s wine list was awash with poor wines: cabbagey Entre Deux Mers, sulphuric Graves and Spanish 'Sauternes', 'Burgundy' and 'Claret', all garishly labelled to catch the jaundiced eye of the head-scarved housewife discovering wine for the first time. Tarragona had replaced port. It was a sleep-inducing aphrodisiac used to deadly effect by Aussies is Earl's Court, where every crumbling and catacombed mansion in the Cromwell Road rocked.

Branded wines were hugely popular. Always bland and often semi-sweet, they went with everything from spam to faggots. It is easy to sneer at Mateus Rose and Blue Nun but pre-supermarkets, pre-*Which Wine Guide*, pre-small independent wine merchants operating out of places with Mews in the title, pre-family holidays in the Dordogne, Blue Nun, Mateus Rose and a host of imitators, took the nervous wine drinker by the hand and led, via many a cul de sac, to the current Aladdin's cave of vinous delights. Ask any English wine drinker of a certain age – they are all bus pass holders now – what they first apprehensively sipped and they will say with head bowed, and much shifting of feet, Mateus Rose. And they will add with a fetching blue-rinsed smile, 'and I still have the bottle somewhere'. Those innocent wine-drinking days seem prehistoric, an age or two away from the modern Surrey Champagne-spattered alfresco lunch, speckled with little pipings of, 'Dahling, you must try this lusty little Italian Waitrose are flogging.' All levels of the British wine trade owe a debt of gratitude to the famous brands.

Sherry, without which the vicar's hand shook and no Home Counties church wedding could be blessed, or a new baby's head wetted, bore reassuringly English names like Dry Sack, Dry Fly, Double Century and Winter's Tale. The best of it came from Spain but plenty of sweet dark treacle came from Australia and South Africa. Cyprus scrambled onto the sherry bandwagon and launched a host of thin, oxidised wines onto the British market. Oxidised white wine was shipped with the word 'cream' printed on the label. It sold by the tankerful. Emva Cream carved out a small niche among the working classes and old ladies spreadeagled on their sofas.

A British sherry was spawned in 1905 when Mitsotakis, a Greek, sent duty-free concentrated grape juice to England to be turned into 'wine' by the simple expedient of adding yeast and water and fortifying it with industrial alcohol. It was cheap and strong, and it caught on. Sherry shippers consulted their lawyers and a law was passed in 1933 to protect the Spanish original. In various guises, British wine still sells in volume, especially around Christmas when television commercials featuring top-hatted, bullwhip-whirling stagecoach drivers cheerfully battling snowstorms to reach chocolate-box inns, to be greeted by aproned landlords, their ample rears warmed by fake log fires. British sherry was often pitted against the genuine Spanish article in blind tastings. Many a Woodbine-puffing off-licence manager sloshed it back and thought it better.

Lesley Phillips types from Oxshott drank 'fine' wine: something French and expensive. Even if bottled at source, it was unlikely to be either French or fine. If the label said Meursault or Chassagne-Montrachet it often came from the same vat. Nuits St George Beaune, Pommard, Volnay were all interchangeable, as were simple St Julien, Margaux, Saint-Emilion and St Estephe. They were 'generic'. Later, while working in a North London wine cellar with all the rustic charm of Merthyr Tydfil bus station, I plucked up the courage to ask one of our five Masters of Wine to explain 'generic'. Wearily he intoned: 'It's perfectly straightforward. These are names simply to indicate a type of wine.'

It has taken historians, archaeologists and botanists centuries to trace the mysterious journey made by the grape. Rock-loving or riverbank-hugging, the vine is a tenacious shrub. It thrives where other plants curl up and die. If it needs water in a barren land it fingers the arid soil until it finds it. Exploratory roots lap up every tear trapped in every stony crevice. Chop off its limbs, burn it, decapitate it, flood it and poison it with chemicals, like some terrifying Triffid it will quietly creep back. Its flailing tendrils can tear down gutters, shade the light from windows, bind outside taps and block drains. If left unhacked it will wrestle a henhouse to the ground or engulf a Surbiton tennis court. No-one knows where and when the fruit was first plucked by some peasant hunting his dessert in the hedgerows.

The vine adapts easily: it is at home in arid Iran or icy Germany. A handful of berries can quench a thirst; a few raisins take a traveller miles. And, unlike the thorny bramble, the vine's fruit is given up easily, its pendulous bunches dangling so low a naked and helpless cherub could feed himself.

Professor J.G. Carr writes: 'Knowing how easily things ferment, wine was probably discovered in several places at various times by different people. The Georgians say it was made there by some hirsute genius who lived in a stone hovel with a wife and a goat 7,000 years ago. But it may been in a remote, spring-watered valley in the Zagros Mountains in Iran, or the Taurus in Turkey. It could just as easily been in Syria, Lebanon or Jordan. The first wine maker may have been Gestin, the Sumerian goddess of the vine. Or could it have been Pagat, whose father was a God and in his spare time a vine grower in Syria? It might have been King Jemsheed, a Persian, who stored grapes in a stone jar where they split and produced a cloudy, fizzy juice. When he tasted the liquid he labelled it 'poison'. One of his harem attempted suicide by drinking it, but the wine had by now finished its fermentation and was delightful. Instead of killing herself the woman leapt onto a marble table and break-danced.

The Sumerian epic *Gilgamesh*, dating from 1800 BC, tells how Gilgamesh set off with an arkful of animals to find himself. Instead he located a dreamy vineyard, whose 'lapis lazuli branches' sparkled with 'rubies for fruit'. Siduri, a beautiful goddess, was invitingly draped on a bed of cool green vine leaves. Anyone who has visited a quiet vineyard at midnight after an alcohol-fuelled dinner can vouch for similar imagery. Gilgamesh's friend Enkidu was a wild man of the woods who ate wild plants and drank nought but ditchwater. Enkidu's life was blameless, if dull, until he met a harlot who poured him a beaker of date wine. After draining seven cups, Enkidu's 'thoughts wandered, he became hilarious, his heart overflowed with joy, and his face shone.' It led to the first recorded incident of date rape.

Noah built the most famous ark in history and sailed off with his giraffes standing proud about the waves. When the deluge ceased he found his dung-encrusted craft aground on Mount Ararat. He released his zoo and cleared a patch of ground to plant vines. He built a watchtower to keep an eye on his enterprise and flung pebbles at the birds, beasts and children who came to nibble his clusters. The wine he made was sweet and prickly. The sun was high and he perspired and the flies were bothering him. Knuckling the drops off his beard Noah quaffed and slurped until he felt the desire to fling off his clothes. Naked and befuddled he was found by his son Ham. Noah overreacted as drunks do and condemned Ham 'to sire nothing but inferior beings'.

From earliest times wine was as revered for its sociability as tea still is in Connemara. A hovel without it was considered unblessed. With its thought-scattering effects, wine was an essential aid for self-styled gods, who gave their followers the rubbish they could find. Communion wine is still more likely to be stale Vino Sacro than Taylor's '45. In crypts and caves Psalmists raised their eyes to Heaven. 'Wine maketh glad the heart of man, oil to make his face shine, and bread which strengtheneth his heart.'

Wine was eventually accepted. The educated recruited botanists and gardeners to find new and better wines. With new grapes, and new ways of making it, wine tasted better and kept longer. Kings employed cupbearers, not to detect that elusive cigar-box nuance, but to see if poison had been added. If the taster keeled over screaming and clutching his guts, the king drank water.

Soldiers drunk wine to deaden their senses. In the eighth century BC an Assyrian army officer purchased 'two homers' – about 20,000 litres – of weak wine to keep the guards alert while he and his brother officers, who drank the strongest and the best, staggered about in the sun, their swords clanging uselessly by his sides. When a battle was fought, and 'the bone gatherer from Sepphoris collected his grisly armful, black bones belonged to the water drinker, red bones to the man who loved his wine.'

The Talmud insists that at least sixty types of wine were known in ancient times. It included those made from dates, palms, figs and pomegranates. Sweetness was essential but Sharon wine was reputed to be pleasantly off-dry, Carmel strong and Ammonite 'so powerful it induced the body to sin'. Temed, a watery concoction, was made by pouring water over pressed stalks, skins and pips. It was given to labourers and women. When halfway to vinegar, it was delicious for dipping bagels in.

Strabo (*c.*63 BC–AD 25), who traveled widely in Greece, Italy, Egypt, Sardinia and Ethiopia, knew of 130 different vine types. Wine came in many colours, from crystal clear to bathwater grey, from honey yellow to burnished gold, from alcoholic and earthy to scarlet and pink. Tirosh, an unfermented grape juice, was approved by the Bible for giving to virgins. It was pink and sparkly – the first Mateus.

Persia received the vine as it trailed across deserts. Omar Khayyam, a Persian astronomer and the world's first marketing man, wrote:

'And lately, by the Tavern Door agape,
Came stealing through the Dusk an Angel Shape,
Bearing a Vessel on his Shoulder; and
He bid me taste of it; and 'twas – the Grape'

His poetry failed to wean his compatriots off kokemaar, a drug made from boiled poppy seeds. The addicted quarrelled, swore and capsied into snoring heaps. Wine was bartered and sold. Lumbering waggons, piled high with camel skins of wine and tormented by the vinegar fly, delivered salted meat, tobacco and dried fruit. Before wooden casks, animal hides were indestructible and easy to stash on waggons and boats, and they didn't explode when filled with fermenting wine. The skins of goats and sheep were used by the Greeks and Romans until the latter embraced the wooden cask in the third century BC. Bulk wine was then delivered in wooden wine 'tankers' drawn by oxen. Pliny noticed how wine deteriorated when sent on long journeys.

Pilgrims travelling on foot to the Holy Land brought with them bags of money and a taste for good wine. The wine makers of Ashkelon and Gaza helped satisfy their need. Ashkelon would eventually make its way to Germany and London. There is no evidence of what were grown. A one-dimensional sweetness suited most palates. King Solomon (d. 953 BC) drank wine with milk.

Pressing with warty feet, weak in boiling sun, add bacteria, animal droppings, diseased grapes and filthy utensils – all meant ancient wine was so unattractive and bitter that some preferred it spiced and sweetened with honey. Growers devised methods to make rank wine acceptable. They poured oil into troubled cask or added a paste made from mustard seed. Some tried cow, goat or camel milk.

Though the *Arabian Nights* spoke highly of wine – 'It digesteth food, disperseth care and flatulence, clarifieth the blood, cleareth the complexion, and fortifieth the sexual power in man' – in the seventh century AD, Mohammad (d. 632) 'set his canon against wine'. But wine drinking continued, especially among the better off, and four centuries later a physician to the Caliph in Baghdad wrote: 'The melted marrow of camel's shin bones taken with date wine four times will help epilepsy and cure diphtheria.' Alec Waugh, who enjoyed the company of Muslims and found them to be unhurried, dignified and impeccably mannered, wrote: 'Normally I dislike a meal without beer or wine, but I felt no need for alcohol during those long hot days when the sun beat down out of a cloudless sky and the glare of the parched earth dazzled me.'

The Pharaohs, Inventors of Fine Wine

The Egyptian wine makers dedicated special areas for vine planting and employed skilled men, women and children in the vineyards. Hugh Johnson writes: 'There are signs of technical ingenuity which was not to be reproduced by any other civilization until modern times. The labeling of wine jars was almost as precise as Californian is today. They specified the year, the vineyard, the owner and the vintner.' While the names of the grapes are lost in the dust of time, they were fussily tended and picked at optimum ripeness.

The vine shared the soil with bananas and figs, cabbages and potatoes, as it still does in Madeira. Fertilised with pigeon droppings, vines stretched over pergolas, climbed walls and trees and flopped over raffia frames to protect Egyptian royals from the heat. The vineyards of Tyre and Laodicea made wine from grapes, figs and pomegranates. Grape wine cost six times the price of beer and was reserved for the rich, who drank it sweetened with honey. Egyptians linked wine with man's struggle to exist and be happy. While the poor sat in shady ale houses to talk and drink, their children stood in vineyards employed as scarecrows.

The larger Muscatel grape, the Alexandrian, with its perfumed flesh and oblong pips, named 'the grape of the bees' by Pliny the Elder, flourished in the hot sun until its rubbery skin unzipped and thick juice slithered down the vine to feed the bees and the lapping mice below.

Egyptian growers allowed their vines to 'grow rampant at their own sweet will'. Grapes as big as golf balls formed weighty clusters, which legend has it took two men to carry a single bunch. Picking was messy and dangerous, with the tranquillity of the harvest often interrupted by terrified shrieks as some poor plucker lost his footing on the juice-smeared branches.

On the King's estates, after a prayer thanking the Snake God for the harvest, the grapes were gathered and placed in stone lagars to be foot pressed, as some of the growers still do today in the Douro. The action was violent and sweaty, as men stamped, sang and held onto each other like drunken lovers, making the floor slippery with their splashes. With the grapes harvested and the juice bubbling, pickers roamed among the stripped vines looking for love. Girls wore white to be noticed.

Juice from the oldest vines was fermented separately. The best wine was stored for longer in amphorae stamped with the owner's name. A leather label was affixed indicating the style of wine and the vintage. Frescoes record as vividly as a video, wine being fermented, stored and matured in conical, twin-handled jars big enough to house a woman and twins.

The overseer, or 'bearer of secrets', was in total control of the king's cellars. He was qualified in all aspects of grape growing and winemaking and was held in awe by all, including the King. The finest Egyptian wines were as carefully crafted as Grand Cru Claret is today. Every effort was made to make a wine that could resist the passing of the years. Sadly, its ability to improve and develop the exquisite flavours of a 1929 Château Latour, while stored in a leaking amphora buried in what amounted to a charnel house remains unproven.

On ordinary farms the wine was run into jars to ferment slowly. Amphorae were sealed with straw, mud or caps made from animal hide, leaving a hole for the carbon dioxide to escape. The dregs, with herbs, spices, animal dung and asses' hair added for 'flavour', were given to the workers as a tonic. In the poorest estates the vine dresser, often an immigrant, worked in chains and was beaten and made to drink vinegar.

When a jar was deemed ready to breach, the contents were decanted into decorated jugs and strained before serving. Libations were offered to the gods, and at the arrival of a new moon more wine was disposed of in the Egyptian Delta than at any other time in the year. Drunkenness 'created a bond between man and God, liberating the divinity hidden within every human soul in ecstasy.' By the fifth dynasty (*c*.2470 BC) vineyard names were designated. The twentieth-dynasty ruler Pharaoh Rameses III named one of his vineyards Kahn-Komet. According to Horace (65–8 BC), Anthylla from Lake Mareotis was Cleopatra's favorite wine. Hugh Johnson says that the Egyptians 'discriminated between qualities of wine as confidently and professionally as a sherry shipper or a Bordeaux broker of the twentieth century'.

Early Egyptians kept records of their tastings and their notes were models of brevity. 'Very good new wine of the House of Akhenaten' was quite sufficient. Scented and garlanded men gathered to taste. Unlike the modern enthusiast with his pebble spectacles and thumbed books, his Egyptian counterpart caroused and fondled overwrought girls as he sipped, cradling their pretty heads while the maidens vomited. If a man had a problem retching, a girl tickled his throat with a feather. Farting was enthusiastically encouraged. When it was time to eat, goose, beef, fish and fruit were offered, all accompanied by wine as sweet as Sauternes.

Pretty females played in the background. Children and grandparents attended, even though the party swiftly sank into depravity, with men and women vying to see who got drunk first. One cross-eyed woman who features in a wall painting in Paheri's tomb is captured slurring: 'Bring me eighteen cups of wine, I wish to get drunk.' In a Theban drawing an emotional female is captured vomiting as spectacularly as any Glaswegian labourer on any Saturday night after losing an Auld Firm game.

While the rich man enjoyed the fruits of paradise, his snaggle-toothed, permatanned vine dresser squinted and gurned as he swallowed his vapid beer and gnawed his heel of stale bread under a twisted olive bush in the white heat of the vineyard.

The Ancients were as keen on the latest health fads as our own troubled society. To cure constipation senna pods and the fruit of the colocynth (bitter cucumber) were dried, mixed with honey and eaten with sweet wine. The cure for male epilepsy was asses' testicles ground into a fine powder and mixed with wine. First you had to catch your ass, of course. A cure for 'watery ear' was to mix opium, calf's fat and milk with a few drops of wine. Quack cures were popular, but young doctors were warned that as 'the pain will stop immediately, do not administer this remedy until you have received your fee'. Goose grease, burnt frog, decaying flesh, pig's eyes, bat's blood, hippo's fat, snake parts, urine, the vulvas of dogs, crocodile dung and dragon's blood were all mentioned in the medical papyri. Some physicians added even more bizarre ingredients 'to add mystery and romance, and to discourage self-medication'.

When an Egyptian royal was close to death, physicians gathered and maidens with scented cloths mopped the royal brow and eased a spoonful of the finest wine between their parched lips. When the great ruler departed, a lavish party was thrown, featuring the most exotic foodstuffs and the finest vintages. Swathed and stiff, the corpse was accompanied by enough wine to toast Osiris, lord of the carouse. Tutankhamen, the boy king of the eighteenth dynasty, was interred with thirty-six amphorae of vintage wine. Twenty-three were from the royal estates. The sarcophagi of the mighty were adorned with friezes. In chilly, cavernous cellars the walls were emblazoned with cartoons, depicting the jolly gathering of grapes by naked nymphs, the foot pressing and the bubbling vats. Virgins cavorted engagingly with horned beasts. Even in the dusty, bricked-up hole into which the dead vine dresser was thrust, there were rudimentary sketches of tangled vines, their branches weighed down with fruit.

Wine was sacred, the sweat of the Sun God. Glorious imagery reminded the departed of the pleasures they were leaving behind. Under the Egyptians wine became sophisticated. They drank fine wine with discrimination, discussed it without raising their voices. They were the first wine connoisseurs.

Enter the Greeks

By 2000 BC Greek wine was well established. Grape pips, clay 'labels', shattered amphorae and excavated cellars point to a thriving industry. The gods sipped nectar, a 'low-strength sweet wine made by honey bees'. Rich merchants enjoyed the finest wines from their own vineyards, while the raggedy peasant who made his wine from the wizened fruit of the straggly vines that climbed his hovel slaked his thirst with grizzled pride.

'The Greeks were greedy for beauty in any form', asserts Warner Allen. Thucydides (c.464–c.404 BC), orator and gold mine owner, wrote that the Mediterranean emerged from barbarism only when its peoples learned to cultivate the vine. By picking bunches early and sun-burning them on mats or trellises, the juice was enriched and the wine became smoother. It is a technique still employed in Italy and elsewhere.

The Greeks were master viticulturists who knew how to plant to fifty rows of vines, each bearing fruit in succession, through the season. That way they avoided the attention of insects and infection. The grapes from each row were made into wine and stored in different containers so that 'the wines might retain their special bouquet and individual flavour'. A demand for complexity made the growers try harder. The wine makers of Bordeaux would follow their methods.

Thanks to Theophrastus of Eresus, who studied at Aristotle's feet and wrote *Enquiry into Plants*, we have an early glimpse into the complicated magic of ampelography. The Greeks identified new vines and made a variety of new styles that challenged an earlier addiction to sweetness. Vines were pruned hard, leading to an increase in flavour and quality. 'No vine grown today can be confidently traced back to any Greek variety,' says Jancis Robinson, author of *Vines, Grapes and Wines*. She concedes, however, that the Greco, Grechetto, Malvasia, Aglianico and Robola may be connected.

Greek viticulture was not always based on hard science. Pausanias, the celebrated second-century traveller, wrote of a ritual in Mathan in Troezen, in which two men took a cock with white feathers and tore it in two, then raced around the vineyard in opposite directions, each carrying half the bleeding bird. When they returned to the place they started from they buried both parts of the bird and on top of them planted the first vine. When Zeus, who was 'suckled on bees', defeated his father Kronos, he first got the old man drunk on mead, a drink made from honey and spices.

Greeks were unashamed guzzlers of dark, sweet wine with an alcoholic left hook. Delicate poets sipped their's watered down. There was a demand for better wines.

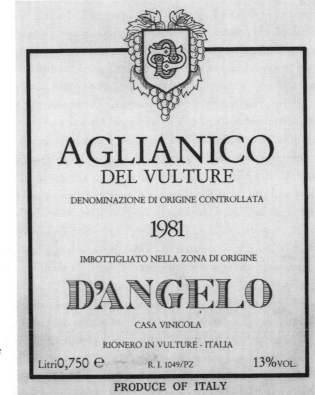

AGLIANICO
DEL VULTURE

DENOMINAZIONE DI ORIGINE CONTROLLATA

1981

IMBOTTIGLIATO NELLA ZONA DI ORIGINE

D'ANGELO

CASA VINICOLA

RIONERO IN VULTURE - ITALIA

Litri 0,750 e   R. I. 1049/PZ   13%VOL.

PRODUCE OF ITALY

Greek grape, volcanic soil and determined grower equals spicy, dark, full-flavoured wine that ought to be better known. Try it with goat stew and friends.

Plutarch reported Chian changing hands for up to 50 obols a jar, a price Socrates considered a rip-off. But the idea 'that taste might have its art as well as the senses of sight and hearing' would have to wait until the Greeks colonised southern Italy in around 800 BC.

The Greeks drank their wines with very hot food, which they ate with their bare hands. Philoxenus, an epicure, warmed his throat with scalding water and grew calluses on his fingers so that he could grab the juiciest titbit before the others. Another glutton, Pithyllus, had special leather 'finger guards' made. After greedily licking the last morsel of food from his platter, he cleaned his tongue by scrubbing it with a powder made from dried fish skin.

Greek boats ploughed the blue Aegean looking for someone to rob. They were, Warner Allen says, 'frankly pirates', preying on the flotillas of small sailing ships which ferried vast quantities of wine from island to island. Although the Greeks commanded an area less than 500 miles in size, their influence on modern wine is considerable.

Cyclops came to a gruesome end after he was tempted by Odysseus to taste Greek wine. His one eye gleaming, he drained several jars 'down to the lees' and keeled over. At this point Odysseus plunged his dagger into the giant's eye: as dramatic an end to a tasting as one could wish for. Theophrastus, in the fourth century, knew that by matching vines with appropriate soils they thrived and yielded superior fruit. A number of different methods of training and pruning were used, including the bush method still practised in the Rhône Valley. Some vines were allowed to spread. Like great spiders they covered the ground, planting their branches and throwing up bush and blossom like blackberries on a neglected English farm. It was the cheapest way, but the crops were small and the wine lacked body and flavour.

Slaves were put to work in vineyards owned by the wealthy. They were harshly treated and, if accused of a serious misdemeanour, tortured. It was 'the surest test of truth', as long as the accused were not so damaged they were unable to work.

The Minoans were capable of making wines that were surprisingly crisp, but also, says Warner Allen, 'capable of maturing to a fine old age'. The only fertilisers were goat and gull droppings. Bent and buckled by gales and refreshed by summer mists, the vines delicately blossomed and bore tiny, minerally berries. Canted hills are difficult to work and it was tempting to plant in the nitrogen-rich valleys, where the black soil was rich enough to clothe the vine in green leaf and yield large bunches. The Greeks knew, as the Romans did and the French do, that to achieve flavour and quality the vine has to forage.

Homer writes of 'delicious fruit carried in baskets by merry lads and girls. A boy skipped along behind playing sweet music on his lyre and singing a lovely song in clear and unfaltering treble.' Although a primitive screw press had been invented, it was considered too cumbersome for grapes and was used mainly for pulverising olives. Grapes were dumped into half-buried vats into which naked men disappeared like council workers inspecting sewers. There they stomped, stank and swore until juice and skins were reduced to pulp. The sweet mush was fermented for up to nine days.

Crete boasted sumptuous houses, culture and prosperity. The magnificent palace of Knossos still dominates the island, with its balconies, scarlet columns and fresco-covered walls. Wine was fermented in *pithoi* – huge, decorated jars like the open-mouthed *tinajas* still seen in Spain blooming with flowers outside touristy bars. At harvest time the fun went on into the warm, dark night. A few dollops of honey transformed the sour vintage and 'unskilled native people' danced. As Pindar (518–443 BC) wrote, 'wild men knew the scent of honeyed wine tames men's souls'. With the children abed, the strongest wines were poured and the adult entertainment began. It occasionally involved large, inebriated naked ladies doing unspeakable things with snakes.

The floppy-hatted, baggy-shorted tourist can still peer into the ruins of Knossos, which reveal chambers crowded with massive jars with 'relief decoration imitating the rope tied around the body for reinforcement'. They are mighty containers. When not holding wine they were used for cheese, salted meat or fish, olive oil or honey. If left unlidded they could be as dangerous as an unguarded manhole, as young Glaukos, son of Minos, discovered when he plunged head first into a jar of honey and was suffocated.

The tinted Cretan dream is still alive today, even though their modern wines are ordinary. Nikos Kazantzakis, author of *Zorba the Greek*, writes: 'We clinked glasses and tasted the wine, an exquisite Cretan wine, a rich red colour, like hare's blood. When you drank it you were in communion with the blood of the earth itself and you became a sort of ogre. Your veins overflowed with strength, your heart with goodness. If you were a lamb you turned into a lion. You forgot the pettiness of life, constraints all fell away. United man to man, beast and God, you felt that you were one with the universe.'

Greek wine kept better than Egyptian. Homer refers to vintages up to eleven years old stored in a jar with just a film of oil for protection. The fame of Chian wine spread and the shattered fragments of stamped amphora still lie beneath France. The Greeks added salt to wine to add piquancy and to brighten, preserve and purify. Fragrances from flowers and herbs were used for the same reason. Athanasius (*c.*AD 296–373) confirmed that salt made sour wine sweeter. It also made his bowels move. Cato (234–149 BC), the warrior son of a plebeian, teetotal smallholder, and author of a version of *De re rustica*, had little time for fine wine. He personally liked rustic. He 'gave his slaves young wine blended with vinegar, boiled must, and sea water, all stirred up together', and he prevented them from joining secret drinking societies for fear it should lead to plotting and revolution.

While historians find little evidence to suggest that the Greeks used the resin extracted from pine cones as a preservative, Rhianus is said to have tasted a wine in Alexandria that smelt and tasted of pine cone pitch. The wine was probably Egyptian. A jar sent to him by his friend Hippocrates (*c.*460–357 BC) was half wine and half pine cone pitch, a dark, sticky resin. Good wines were stored in resinated jars, the resin providing a better seal. The best Greek wines, including Chian, were resinated as far back as 430 BC. Much later in the Crimea solid resin was ground into powder and added to sometimes quite decent wine.

Sulphur was added by the islanders of Thrace. Growers also dropped bouquets of herbs into the vats to sweeten and perfume the wine. Insipid vintages were thickened and coloured by stirring in boiled musts. Pliny the Elder (AD 23–79) said the Greeks added potter's earth and powdered marble to their wines to clarify them.

Pramnian, Wine of the Gods

Pramnian, 'neither rich nor sweet, but dry, hard and unusually strong', was the most famous of all Greek wines. The playwright Aristophanes (c.450–385 BC), in *The Knights*, called it 'a god of a wine'. He used it as a laxative, which, he said, 'contracted the eyebrows and the bowels'. It was banned in some areas because of its 'aphrodisiac properties'. Dioscorides, a Greek physician who lived in the first half of the second century AD, implied that Pramnian was made from the juice oozing freely from very ripe grapes which pressed themselves. The wine represented only a 250th part of the juice of the grapes. It was rare and expensive and only the privileged tasted it undiluted, when 'like a drop of attar of roses it works magic'. Circe doped Odysseus' friends with an 'alcoholic porridge' of Pramnian wine, goat's cheese, barley meal and honey, making them so drunk they forgot who they were.

Bybline was light, fragrant and unusually fresh, although some vintages were allowed to develop a flor rendering them more like sherry. It either hailed from Byblos in Phoenicia, or was made from the Bibline grape grown on Thrace, the so-called cradle of the Wine God. Bybline enjoyed a great reputation. Archestratus, a contemporary of Aristotle in the fourth century BC and 'an early master of the art of good living', dismissed lovers of Bybline as 'conceited tasteless drivellers'. While grudgingly admitting it had a bouquet that lingered long, he said it was like drinking air. Archestratus preferred the wines of Lesbos: 'Your palate', he wrote, 'will tell you to prize Lesbian, not as a wine, but as a divine ambrosia. When you have drunk deep in the grace-cup of Zeus the Saviour you must drink an ancient wine, its once dark and lustrous locks thickly overgrown and grey with white flower.' Aristotle implied that Greek cellaring was inadequate.

Pindar (c.518-443 BC), who was descended from the nobility of Thebes, praised old wines but said mature Greek wines were rare. Theocritus in 285 BC boasted of drinking a wine that was four years old, probably from the island of Kos. Appollodorus, writing two centuries later, insisted good wine needed keeping six years. Pliny agreed. Euboan, another wine of repute, kept well and as it aged it turned sweet and dark. Hermippus gave it to the friends he loved best, while he palmed off young Peparethian, a wine he hated, on mere acquaintances. Thasian wine aged gracefully. Archestratus said that when mature it smelt of fresh-cut flowers. While listening to pretty young flautists he enjoyed a chalice of velvety, marmalade-coloured Lesbian that was 'generous to the taste, and old with the seasons of many years.' Eubulous (c.350 BC) said old wine was fine for old women. He preferred both fresh.

The poet Alexis drew a parallel between man's span and a jar of fine wine with the lid prised open. Old men were unpleasant and miserable, he says, while a mature Saprian, with its mellow scent of violets, bluebells and roses, put a soothing hand on a wrinkled brow and whispered endearments. William Younger says: 'To the ancient Greeks, luxury was an extravagance worthier of ridicule than admiration. Even the wealthier Greeks seldom displayed that lust for luxury which characterised so many of the richer and less intelligent Romans.'

In spite of the sex-mad cloven-hoofed gods, tantalising virgins, suggestive love poetry and 'wine-dark seas', the Greeks often drowned their wine in water. Traders sat by the roadsides with their amphorae, selling wine so diluted it was practically alcohol-free. To most Greeks wine was merely a light refreshment. Theophrastus (*c.*372–287 BC) pedantically approved of dilution as long as the wine was poured into the water and not *vice versa*. Respectable Greeks reviled drunkenness, and any man seen drunk in public was disgraced, although royalty were above rules. The Spartan king Cleomenes (*c.*235-220 BC) enjoyed his wine at full strength and was frequently inebriated. Leaking crocodile tears of guilt and self-loathing, he made his slaves drunk then forced them to parade about the streets in front of jeering crowds. He died of alcohol poisoning, after first going mad. Solon (*c.*638–*c.*558 BC), a founder of the Athenian constitution, saw the watering of wine as 'the way of moderation'. 'Holding an amphora by the ears', he wrote, 'and draining it is not wine drinking. It is base vulgarity. It is swimming in wine, nay, drowning in it.' Hesiod (*fl.* eighth century BC) was so ashamed of his drinking that he diluted his wine with three parts fresh spring water. The theory was that it quickly filled his bladder, leaving no room for more wine. In spite of this plea from the top for moderation, the average Greek enjoyed his wine to the full.

Philochorus, who died in 306 BC, referred to the legend of the 'Upright Dionysus' – not the swivel-eyed, soggy-bearded, cloven-hoofed hell-raiser of legend, but a civilised Rotarian who could walk tall after a skinful and not crawl on all fours mooing. Nevertheless, he did have the neat trick of transforming himself into a bunch of grapes to seduce Erigone. She later hanged herself on the tomb of her father Icarus, who had been murdered by drunken wine tasters after he introduced them to wine. In their stupefied state they thought he was poisoning them. We've all been to wine tastings like that. Xenophanes (540–480 BC), an Ionian philosopher and poet, enjoyed his wine neat and in quantity. ''Tis no sin' he said,' to drink as much as you can hold and still get home without an attendant, unless you be very old.'

Greek food was 'neither complicated or excessive', and helpings were so small that the Persians noted that 'the Greeks left the table hungry because they never had anything worth mentioning after the first course'. Even the best the celebrated chefs of the day could come up with was rustic fare featuring black puddings, stews, lentil soup, fish and above all congers. Even on Sappho's Lesbos, breakfast was a wad of dry bread dipped in a saucer of young wine. As a special treat there would be a handful of roasted chestnuts. Garlic and vinegar were the chief condiments. Aristophanes recalls a simple country lunch comprising 'a small goatskin of wine, two onions, three olives and a loaf'. For dessert there may be grapes in wine, figs and a cereal bar made from honey-soaked poppy seeds and pounded linseed.

The stuffed stomach of an ass was a delicacy. Thrushes, finches and hares all went into the pot, as they still do in Mediterranean countries. Surrounded by seas swarming with silver shoals, it is hardly surprising that fish, be it dried, salted, braised or boiled, was eaten daily. Eels made a cheap and nourishing meal and for Freudian reasons they were on the menu at many a Greek wedding. On a similar occasion Eubulous noted the following: 'Toasted Gallipoli cheese, boiled cabbage glistening in oil, fat lamb chops, plucked ring doves and as many songbirds as can be netted, limed or trapped, cuttle fish, sprats, wriggling polyps and as much good wine as the celebrants could lay their hands on.'

Symposiums and Sacrifices

The Symposium was a gathering of respectable Greek males, who, after having their feet washed, sat on couches, ate and shared wine with their most eloquent friends. After a general blessing with wine, the talk drifted from poetry to politics to world affairs. A series of libations to various gods followed. An amphora of wine was then hauled in by two muscular young men who poured some into a large, lavishly decorated *krater*. Water was added. The mixture was stirred and ladled into bowls by naked boys whose upwardly mobile parents considered it an honour for them to be invited. The bowls were placed around the room within easy reach of the company. Euripides (*c*.480–406 BC) as a boy served wine at such a function.

Invitees were expected to contribute a song, a poem or a piece of philosophy. As brains became addled, the seriousness of the evening gave way to childish games, riddles, raucous singing, discordant twanging and the odd gandery honk from a horn. Courtesans were invited to 'engage in spirited discussion' and accede to sexual demands in exchange for money or favours. This might involve realistically acting out a love scene from Ariadne and Dionysus, which once got so out of hand the actors had to be separated by an official. Eubulus, who considered huffily that too much drinking spoiled the entertainment, recommended a maximum of three diluted glasses, one for health, one for love and the third as a nightcap.

Plato (427–347 BC), another curmudgeon, had little time for pleasure and that most definitely included wine, especially for those under twenty-two years of age. Symposiums he said 'were for solemn and serious debate, talking and listening, but always decently. Wherever men of gentle breeding and culture are gathered together,' he said, 'you will see neither flute girls nor harp girls.' Drinking was wasted on the young, Plato concluded.

Maurice Healy, the Irish circuit judge and author of *Stay Me With Flagons*, would have been at home in the midst of philosophical wine tasters. 'Never bring up your better bottles if you are entertaining a man who cannot talk.' Healy wrote. 'Keep your treasures for a night when those few who are nearest to your heart can gather round your table, free from care, with latchkeys in their pockets and no last train to catch.' Hugh Johnson disagreed. Symposiums, he said, attracted 'the sort of pretentious gourmets we would describe today as "wine bores".'

The ancient game of *kottabos* was devised, according to Critias, a pupil of Socrates, in Sicily. Its popularity lasted three centuries. Warner Allen writes: 'After a delicate meal, sipping wine and water, the Greek gilded youth of both sexes, wreaths of flowers on their heads, entertained by pretty boys and girls, singing, dancing and tumbling, were in the mood for a little play, which called for grace and skill and demanded no violent muscular exertion.' Players tossed their watery dregs at a bronze saucer delicately balanced on a pole. A direct hit sent the saucer clanging onto a larger disc before hitting the marble floor with a resounding clatter, spraying wine in all directions. 'Style, the grace of the stance, the nice curving of the hand and wrist, the bending of the arm, as the wine was tossed high in the air, counted almost as much as accuracy of aim and the hitting of the target.'

Sophocles (*c*.496–406/5 BC), the great Athenian dramatist who gained many a garland himself in music and gymnastics, said 'kisses and love play were the victor's prizes'. Runners-up received five apples and nine kisses. Cratinus (*c*.519–422 BC), a comic poet who had partaken in many a game of *kottabos*, said that when a playful young lady, after imbibing 'a couple of great tankards' of wine and water, calls out her fancy's name and cocks her wrist to fling her wine, she is not aiming at the *plastinx*: her target is 'that part of her lover's anatomy of which she is most fond'.

The Greeks, though not as vulgar as the Romans, enjoyed the sickly waft of perfume. Though, in his review of Xenophon's play *Symposium*, Socrates said the pretty girls and a handsome youth who provided 'entertainment' did not require 'the additional pleasure of perfumes, to combine the delectable sights and sounds they had enjoyed'. This meant 'the finest Greek wines' reached discerning palates pure and undefiled.

Greek writers praised the health-giving properties of wine. Aristophanes (*c*.450– *c*.385 BC) said that wines like Pramnian, Chian or Thasian made men healthy, wealthy and ready for love. Hippocrates (*c*.460–357 BC), the celebrated physician who saved Athens from pestilence, recommended wine as both a preventative and a cure. Young wine, he said, which had been reduced by heating, was excellent for encouraging an appetite. But he sternly advised against the drinking of fermenting must. Aristophanes said new wine which was fruity and nourishing cured constipation. Dry white wine, which speedily passed to the bladder, kept the urinary tract open. Chilled wine led to convulsions and warmed wine to imbecility. Those of a nervous disposition, Aristophanes said, should drink no wine at all. Asclepiades, a Greek lyric poet and physician, begged leave to differ. Give mad people plenty of wine, he said.

Mnesitheos, another Greek physician, approved of occasional drunkenness, as long as the wine was of the finest quality. The drunken man was advised to vomit before bed. If a man had a cask of wine in his house he need never call a doctor. Men with erectile problems were advised to drink wine mixed with saffron. Eye infections were treated by laying a piece of bread that had been dipped in wine over the infected eye.

During the festival of Dionysus, the streets were crammed with enormous oxen drawing drays, piled with grapes, being trampled by sixty satyrs who sang songs and played flutes. Juice flowed through the dray, board floors and flooded the streets. At the festival of Attica, says William Younger, where Dionysus shared top billing with Demeter and Persephone, the rites were performed by women, who also prepared the banquet with meat, bread, a rainbow of fruit and flowers, bouquets and scents, and cakes shaped like the symbols of sex. Bands played, children sang and behind from every crumbling wall and portico came the sounds of surprise and delight as wild-eyed bearded men, their foreheads dripping sweat, took their pleasures.

At the Anthesteria, a festival of flowers, fertility and death, revellers drank to the dead in case the dearly departed returned. Every festival featured novel blind literally, tastings. The last man standing won. Dionysus was the lord of the vine cup. His aco-lytes included young virgins guarded by 'revelling satyrs, wild men who were sexually excitable' but surprisingly so gallant that the virgins did not have to 'indulge in unbri-dled orgies of sex' unless they wanted to. Mothers abandoned homes, husbands and children to revere Dionysus, the bestial god of intoxicated delirium. New wine was drunk in serious quantity by masked revellers, who thronged the streets singing and cavorting. Impromptu parties were arranged, at which infants were allowed to taste wine for the first time from a three-lipped jug. The celebrations went on for five days until snoring drunks, their masks askew, clogged the gutters.

The unsuitably named Pisistrates (546–527 BC) attempted to control the Wine God's followers by having a theatre built and staging *Bacchantes* by Euripides. It turned out to be another joyous excuse for more processions and more wine drinking. Groups sat around hoarsely chorusing toasts to the great God of Wine and anything else they could think of. Landowners held an exclusive festival, the Oschophoria, in which the processions were restricted to respectable youths carrying grape clusters and scattering vine leaves. The Apatouria, a wine-soaked rite of passage for young men, was held in September, followed swiftly by Epildon, the hangover festival, after which a goblet or two of honey, lemon and water cleared the head.

With the onset of winter, Greek men gathered on cliffs above the raging seas. Their beards tossed by the howling wind, they cast goblets of wine into the troubled waters as a libation to the seaweed-festooned gods lurking in the green depths. With spring came optimism. A rowdy celebration was held in Athens around 404 BC to honour Dionysus. A huge crowd gathered clutching animal skins leaking spicy wine. The unruly throng crawled up to the stone seats in the gods to drink and to hiss at the portly VIPs who claimed the cushioned thrones near the marble stage. While music blared, bulls were released and baited, semi-naked nymphs carrying bouquets of fen-nel and wearing ivy crowns fled from masked men, each one wearing an enormous strapped-on penis.

The hordes of roving Celts – 'an intemperate lot' – who greeted Greek wine ships docking near Marseille around 600 BC were not there to embrace Greek culture; they just liked wine. The Celts drank heartily, then, after robbing gold, jewels and pre-cious stones from their captives, instructed someone important to distribute the loot among their relatives. They then leaned over the nearest chair and politely asked their nearest neighbour if they wouldn't mind cutting their throats. It would be rude, and fatal, to refuse.

Scythians and Thracians, according to Plato, poured wine onto their clothes and walked around reeking and smiling. 'Wine,' Socrates (c.470–399 BC) said, 'is oil to the dying flames of life; it commits no rape upon our reason but leads to nothing more serious than agreeable mirth.' He was quite capable of sitting up all night with a few friends draining goblet after goblet before toddling off to work while his friends snored. He was sentenced to death in 399 BC for 'encouraging the young to criticise the existing order'. While awaiting execution Socrates sat in the sun, enjoying the Delian spring festival, swigging a few glasses 'to moisten the spirits and lull the cares of his mind'. For a chaser he drank hemlock and died, the great philosopher lying like a discarded smock in the setting sun while the vast throng of revellers laughed, drank and danced. Uninvited parasites (the word comes from *parasitos*, or one who sits at another's table) were considered fair game for mockery and ridicule. They paid for their food and drink by willingly soaking up insults.

At some banquets men and women battled to see who got plastered first. In his play *Dinner of the Seven Wise Men*, Plutarch (*c.* 46- after 120 AD) prizes were offered for the person who drank the most. Anacharsis drank so much he was disqualified. 'I would have won,' he groaned.

Greek women were not so easily controlled as their Egyptian counterparts. They were fond of wine and discerning when offered a blind tasting. They were the 'first connoisseuses', says Warner Allen, and they 'preferred old wine to old lovers'. Who wouldn't? They were so picky that they refused any dish featuring lentils, for it spoiled their sensitive palates. Callistion, according to Warner Allen, 'demanded and gained the memory of posterity for her inexhaustible swallow. She wandered through the length and breath of Hellas, swarms of lovers ever at her door.'

For the men the *taverna* was the place to go. It was sparse, out of bounds to scolding wives and it sold a variety of wines, from watered-down pap to vinegar. In the fourth century BC, wine from Corinth, described by Alexis as 'torture', was poured in the less salubrious dives. Corinth tarts were famous for the care and civility they brought to their work. William Younger grades them as follows: 'Some were common, some moderately common, and some whose capabilities were enlivened by a humour which, if not always intellectual, was at least appreciated for their "ripened charms".'

The quality of Greek wine was appreciated in Gaul, and wine merchants 'battled storm and tempest, throughout the year' to supply the Gauls with good wines. Even after the Greek colonisation of Enotria (southern Italy), Greek shippers continued to trawl among the islands on the lookout for tasty wines for the discerning Gauls. Pollis, King of Syracuse, was such an avid consumer of 'a sturdy mountain red', made from a blend of three grapes with Greek connections – Greco Nero, Gaglioppo and Malvasia – that the wine was named Pollino in his honour.

Hail the Romans

Around 750 BC the Greeks set foot in Sicily and founded Naxos near Taormina. Soldiers and sailors carrying pruning knives and sacks of vine cuttings, carpeted the conquered territory with a billowing sea of vines. Within three centuries Syracuse was an ant-hill of business, much of it to do with winemaking. Inexorably, the invaders moved north, an alien invasion of swarthy vine dressers, soldiers and entrepreneurs. Some became teachers and arbiters of taste.

Ambitious Romans learned to speak Greek and were keen to be seen at Greek plays. Unashamedly they recited Greek poetry, ordered Greek wine and food, adopted young boys for lovemaking and traded with the almond-eyed young girls who walked barefoot into the towns to sell their wares and themselves. The Romans were keenly interested in sex and used everything from bone marrow to oysters and cuttlefish that would (as John Davenport, the Victorian author wrote in 1859) 'strengthen the genital apparatus, exciting it to action'.

Wealthy Roman tourists went on long and uncomfortable treks to pay homage to Greek architecture. They relaxed with watered Greek wine and pretended to be as reflective and sensitive as their hosts. Cunning Greek peasants lurked at every dusty crossroads to sell to Roman tourists bowls of 'wayfarer's refresher, a spicy mixture sweetened with honey and laced with pepper'.

Nero (c. 37-68 AD), travelled with an enormous retinue of love boys servants, and a herd of 500 asses to provide milk for his wife's baths. He also took with him silver and gold cutlery and chalices fashioned from lapis lazuli. His wine had to be chilled with the purest snow scooped from the chilly heights of Mount Parnassus. Roman tourists sat for their portraits and paid itinerant artists with jars of Knidian or Cnidian, a wine so harsh it was 'returned to God at religious gatherings', or drunk through clenched teeth in a *kapeleiai*, one of the many lively tavernas that filled every back street with half-remembered songs and ribald laughter.

Mago (d. 203 BC), a Carthaginian soldier who studied the methods of phoenician and canaanite in Syria and Lebanon, was hugely influential in improving Roman viticulture. When the city was ravaged, Mago's twenty-six volumes were saved and spirited back to Rome to be translated into Greek and Latin. Sadly the classic work has since been lost. Varro (116–28 BC) rated Mago the finest and most knowledgeable writer on vinous matters. While the Romans made wines that were good enough to satisfy the ordinary man, the wealthy continued to fill their cellars with fresh young wines from the Greek islands.

SASSICAIA

1984

TENUTA SAN GUIDO

Imbottigliato all'origine dal produttore
Tenuta San Guido - Bolgheri (107 LI)

VINO DA TAVOLA DI SASSICAIA

750 ml e   ITALIA   12,5% vol.

An important finger post on the Italian road to quality. Raffia-entwined Chianti never tasted as good.

Herodotus (*c*.484–*c*.425 BC) noted that every hill was so covered with vines supported by stakes that southern Italy became known as the 'land of vine poles'. The Greeks had greatly improved vine growing and introduced the idea of storing and maturing wine in oil-sealed earthenware jars. In iron-rich volcanic soil in the shadow of Vesuvius they made strong dark wine. The Greeks, combining with the Syracusans, annihilated the Etruscans and annexed Campania. Within fifty years they were defeated by the Sabines, who acquired a thriving wine industry.

Cato despised the Greeks and tried to suppress their culture. Cato notoriously said that if a man caught his wife drinking he should kill her. Women who drank were deemed to lack virtue and restraint. Intoxication could lead to delirium and orgies. The Romans invented kissing to check if their wives had been drinking. Lucullus (*c*.110–57 BC), whose accomplishments included the introduction of the cherry to Italy, was so keen on Greek wines that, on his return from Asia, he donated 100,000 amphorae of Greek wine to the Romans. Julius Caesar celebrated his victories with both Falernian and the Greek Chian, and during his third consulship in 46 BC he served Greek and Roman wines at table. Chian, Lesbian, Mamertine from Sicily and the fabulous Falernian were poured. The Falernian silenced all debate, according to Virgil (70–19 BC).

Although the Romans were masters of the western Mediterranean, war left the countryside in ruins. Farms and property were destroyed, crops and animals erased from the landscape. The peasantry eventually began to reassert themselves. Vine shoots peeped through broken land, the reassuring stench of fermenting wine drifted over stricken villages. Fires were lit, and faces once grim, smiled. Civilised values quickly spread. As Hugh Johnson says: 'From 200 BC wine-growing began to interest [Rome's] increasingly worldly citizens; the security and wealth of empire brought a market for luxuries which would have shocked the founding fathers.'

Wine soon become an integral part of Roman daily life. They preferred the taste of white wine, or more accurately amber wine, for much of it darkened through oxidation. It was easier to drink sweet and without sharp tannins. If red wine was produced it was often bleached with sulphur fumes. Wines of both hues were reduced by boiling and flavouring with *nectaulis*, *elecampane* or *murtidanum*.

'Smoked' wine was also popular in Roman times. Full jars were stored above smoking fires. The wines were so pungent they brought tears to the eyes. Cato suggested women with colic or gynaecological disorders should drink smoked wine daily. Archeologists are still digging up broken wine jars inscribed 'smoked wine', 'dark wine', 'raisin wine', even 'vinegar'. Honey was shovelled into wine jars – 10 litres of honey to 13 litres of wine. Columella (first century AD), author of *De re rustica*, the fullest ancient treatise on practical agriculture, Pliny and Palladius (fourth century AD), who also published a work called *De re rustica* that owed a lot to Columella's earlier work, all mention honeyed wine in their writings. Tar was often added for flavour.

Roman Advances in Winemaking

AD 70. Rome was regarded as the most important wine-producing country in the world. Viticulture, as described by Virgil in his *Georgics*, has altered little. The Romans made a wide variety of wines, from weak and bland to rich and smooth, both reds and whites with a honeyed magnificence. The Basilica from Spain was also planted by the Romans, as was the Arcelaca, or Argitis, which made poor wine and was said to be related to the Riesling. The Cesar, with obvious Roman credentials, wheedled its way into the Yonne area of France where it still makes ordinary wine.

According to Virgil, at harvest time children 'played at balance-on-the-wine skins' while their fathers sang, rapped uproarious verse and wore outlandish masks made of bark. Their wives praised Bacchus with 'homely hymns and dishes of sacred cakes'. Virgil ordered his father to climb into a brimming tub, where 'the pressed juice already foamed. Pull off your boots,' he ordered, 'stain your legs with the must.' The old man disrobed and did his son's bidding, the warm wine bubbling above his gammy thighs.

The introduction of heavy presses meant cloudier, slower-working musts and longer-lived wines. After the initial fermentation, the wine was poured into jars, sealed and allowed to stand for forty days. Old tar-treated jars were best; they reduced absorption to one fifth. They were covered with muslin to keep out dirt and insects. The jars were then rolled out into the yard, covered with wooden lids and left to stand and simmer in the sun.

Small boys were paid to bathe the fat-bellied jars with water. In winter the maturing area was warmed by stoves or fires, imparting to the wine a smokey tang and a colour that gradually changed to brown.

The Romans also made fresh, lightly tinted wine by placing whole bunches of undamaged grapes in a *dolium*, or large jar, and bury it up to its neck in the ground. An enzyme fermentation split the grape skins, releasing the natural sugars, allowing them to mingle with the yeast cells on the skins. A similar method is used in Beaujolais today. The *dolia* were regularly inspected to skim off a scum which grew on the surface of the wine. After six months the wine was decanted into fresh amphorae and was ready for the table.

The Romans copied the Greek idea of using resin to seal porous jars. Columella said resin prevented wine turning to acid. Some wines, owing to their excessive weakness, would last for scarcely thirty days.'

A significant development in the future taste of wine was taking place in Gaul. The ingenious natives had begun to experiment with wild vines. A tribe called the

Allobroges discovered a frost-resistant black vine which may have been the Pinot Noir. The Roman growers were intensely interested and were prepared to trade Roman citizenship for information about the vine. Worries were expressed in the Senate in Rome about the upstarts in the provinces who were experimenting with unknown grapes and, worse still, making decent wines. The Allobroges were allowed to plant their new vine, and from its small glossy black grapes, looking as if they had been sculpted from jade, make their own wine. They made wooden casks in which to mature it. It was served neat and unblended. If oak-aged wine it was called *merum*. Occasionally pitch was added, but watering was forbidden. 'They are afraid of poisoning themselves by mixing spring water and wine', Cicero (*c.*102–43 BC) sneered.

The wine may have been an earlier form of Burgundy. The Bituriges and Viliscii tribes, inhabitants of what is now Bordeaux were also working on new vine crossings. The grape they are said to have discovered was Biturica, which the Romans also laid claim to. If the grape was the Cabernet, it would have been a sensational development, though Tacitus (*c.* 55–120 AD) was of the opinion that good wine was going to be very difficult to make in Bordeaux. It was a region, he said, which had a soil and a climate that were 'oppressive'.

Wine became an everyday drink in both bleak Burgundy and temperate Bordeaux. Bars and taverns sprang up to sell wine to passers-by. Huge barrels hewn from oak fitted snugly onto the chassis of chariots to deliver wine further afield. Casks were bound with chestnut saplings, as they still are in Burgundy.

Dioscorides and Cato revered wines from the Campanian vine, the Aminean. This Petrus of the day was full-bodied, deliciously smooth and priced accordingly. In 89 BC an amphora of Aminean fetched 400 sesterces, 100 times the daily wage of a labourer. Campania with its volcanic soil produced a succession of dark, fiery wines that were eagerly snapped up. Made on Greek principles, they had to compete with Greek imports which were delivered direct to Rome rather than via the Greek enclaves further south. In 89 BC a Campanian white wine was introduced and it was instantly popular. As prices rose a law was passed fixing a maximum for white Campanian, which Virgil asserts 'yielded the best-bodied vintages'. Though records began after the fall of Carthage and the sacking of Corinth in 146 BC, little information exists as to the quality and the taste of these ancient classics. Aminean might also have been a key ingredient in Falernian. Now called Greco di Tufo, it is still planted in Campania but lives quietly in reduced circumstances.

Pliny admired Psithian, an early *Trockenbeerenauslese* made from raisin juice, which he said could 'blur your speech and send you swimming home'. Psithian may have been an early form of the Muscatel, a grape known as the 'bee-vine'. The poet Anaxandrides recalls drinking, presumably with some assistance, an amphora of Psithian mixed with spring water, with little cakes made from the dried stalks and skins and goat cheese.

The Romans were unimpressed by Gaulish eating habits. Mealtimes were boisterous, with flying elbows, filthy grabbing hands, wild exclamations, greasy lip smacking, curses and flying wine. Blows were frequently exchanged, and grunting, eye gouging and testicle squeezing under the table were the norm. As most men were armed with crude swords and daggers, spiralling blood mixed with the bowls of wine and the roasted boar's head.

As Roman winemaking improved, the taste of Greek wine was forgotten. Vines quickly bound Italy's instep and inexorably crept north, twisting and turning themselves around her thick and knobbly leg. Weather played a part, becoming drier and sunnier, the skies bluer. The change in climate was recorded by the Greek astronomer Hipparchus (*c*.160–120 BC), who invented trigonometry. The surge in climate resulted in riper grapes and the golden harvest of 121 BC, is remembered for a brilliant Falernian harvested under the aegis of, and trodden by, the consul Opimius. An alleged sample of the famous wine, in a glass bottle, protected only by olive oil and sealed with gypsum, is on display in the Speyer Museum.

Like the Greeks and the Jews, the Romans mixed wine with water, partly because water was often impure. 'Get your water well out to sea,' Pliny warned. No Roman dinner table was correctly laid without an *oenophorus* filled with wine, the *calderium*, which often held warm water, and the *cratera*, or mixing bowl. For the successful Roman businessman, taste was not a consideration. It could hardly be when sprawling half-drunk guests were sipping wine in a fetid room reeking with the stench of candles, the swirling fumes of aromatic herbs, the vulgar pong of cut flowers which covered the mosaics like a soft carpet and with companions on either side with bodies and hair dripping gunge.

Workers had their daily allowance of wine heavily adulterated with water, which was understandable from the employer's point of view. After too much wine they lost the will to work. On 'one very melancholy occasion' all 400 tipsy slaves employed by a wealthy Roman were executed after lunch for not preventing their master's murder.

Wine was often poor, stale and vinegary. Honey was cheap, healthy and readily available, and it was used in massive quantities. Dufrutom, a reductive process, was used to concentrate musts and reduce the volume of wine. Dried peppers, fennel, mint, lime and orange juice and quantities of salt were also added to give ordinary wine a lift. Chalk was sprinkled in the jars to adjust acidity, as it is still in Spain. Goat's milk, dirt and egg whites were also used for clarification.

Spiced wine became so popular with Roman travellers that they carried their own leather bottles of mixed spices which they poured into any wine they might meet on the road. One such concoction was Piperatum, made with wine and ground peppers. In years when the wines were thin and acidic, abetted by Pliny and Columella, the Romans reduced musts by boiling them in lead-coated containers. The resultant wine killed thousands of drinkers. Death was slow and painful. Adding lead to wine continued for centuries. The French used it, as did the Germans; even English cidermakers added lead to their products.

The cure recommended for white lead poisoning was a mixture of sweet wine, opium and asses' milk. Juvenal (*c*.130–201) experimented with all manner of concoctions, including the blood of various creatures from bulls to ducks, mixed with every kind of seed and herb from juniper berries to hemlock, liquorice to garlic tops, all washed down with a glass of fine old Falernian. As the Emperor's physician and confidant, Galen (*c.*130-201 AD) was allowed to enter the imperial cellars and head for that roped-off corner where the best vintages were stored. Galen tasted the finest and rarest wines only, those with a minimum of twenty years' cellaring. From these he selected the wines his master should drink,' those without a trace of bitterness, for an ancient wine which has not lost its sweetness is the best of all.'

Columella had a trick for enlivening poor wines. He boiled unfermented grape juice with a layer of iris, fenugreek and sweet rush in the bottom of the boiler. He added the pungent mix to thin wine, then stirred in liquid pitch and turpentine resin. He then added spikenard, the Illyrian sword lily, costu, dates, angular rush, myrrh, sweet reed, cinnamon, balsam and a pinch of saffron. Then, with a straight face, he said: 'Care must be taken that the flavour of the preservative is not noticeable, for it drives away the purchaser.' Virgil had no time for all this mixing and blending or exotic roots and seeds: 'Just use honey to soften your wines', he sensibly wrote.

Falernian, an Enduring Legend

In AD 79, Vesuvius erupted and buried the city of Pompeii. A villa covered in ash that day belonged to one Florus, who had a bottle of Falernian in his cellar. This bottle was rediscovered nearly 2,000 years later, and was brought to Berry Bros in London by an avid collector, Dr Sambon, to be evaluated by the directors and a few friends. Dr Sambon windily spoke for the desiccated 'wine', which, he said, after the vicissitudes of time and the noisy passing of centuries, 'had retained its flavour and character unchanged'. Warming to the task, and unaware that Francis Berry, a firebrand with no time for fools, was drumming his fingers ominously on the polished oak table, his eyes narrow slits, the doctor droned on in the oak-panelled dining room. 'It indeed has the peculiar aroma of modern Campanian wines which I know so well,' he said with a self satisfied gesture, 'but though it most certainly is the residue of some choice wine of rare vintage, it is difficult to decide if it is oldest Falernian.' After the presentation Warner Allen reported: 'Francis, whose impatience with stupidity often found relief in explosions of wit and mordant humour, pronounced a characteristically caustic comment on the Doctor's imaginings.'

Falernian remains in the wine buff's psyche as one of the greatest wines of all time. Galen, who poured ordinary red wine on mutilated gladiators, most of whom survived, sipped exotic, expensive Falernian to settle his stomach. The finest Falernian was made with all the attention a rich Californian would bring to the task. Vines were planted wide apart in the places most likely to drain well and catch every sunbeam. Falernian was coaxed from Aminium grapes that had ripened on hilly vineyards on the Campania and Latium borders.

The best of it was made from grapes harvested on two hills, Mounts Falernus and Massicus. Martial (c. AD 40–c. 104) loved his Falernian dark and rich, and fantasised about kissing lips moistened with Falernian. While there were numerous wines claiming the noble name, the Falernian vineyards were clearly defined, although wines made from grapes grown in the Statan vineyards, close to the Falernian boundaries, though lighter and more elegant, were considered to be the equal of the legendary Falernian. The nearby Cales vineyards also traded on Falernian's fame.

During the reign of Sulla (138–78 BC), Falernian was faked and copied. To own part of the sacred site was to be very fortunate indeed. Sulla's son Faustus had a large tranche of Mount Falernus, in the middle of the slope – the choicest part. Too elevated meant cold winds and frost, too low and the soil was rich and damp. Faucine, a lesser wine from grapes harvested on the top slope, was also highly rated for its unusual crisp elegance. Galen called it 'a wine of breed'. As the pampered son of a dictator, Faustus had both the time and the money to make his wine with complete attention to every detail. His was considered the best of all. It was doled out sparingly. To be first in the queue one had to be a close relative or a powerful politician. Faustus's father's propensity to decapitate detractors meant negative tasting notes were unheard of.

Falernian came in various styles: rich, fresh and medium bodied, and elegant. The latter was considered the best, but if some ancient tasting notes are to be believed, very old Falernian was as bitter as gall. Some scribes described it as massive wine, as dark, strong, spicy and alcoholic as Barolo. Galen was of the opinion it was undrinkable until it was at least ten years old, and at its best between fifteen and twenty. Marcus Aurelius (121–180), a Stoic and wine enthusiast, kept a cache of finest Falernian securely binned in the imperial cellars. Martial called it 'immortal', and when a friend sent him an enormous wild boar, 'the victim of his spear', as a present, Martial quickly sent it back because he knew his cook would insist on serving the beast with a rich sauce flavoured with his finest Falernian.

Young men celebrated the finishing of an amphora of Falernian with bouts of temporary madness. Martial alludes to glasses being smashed. Even old drinkers were not averse to flinging their wine-stained crystal goblets against the nearest hard surface just for the sheer hell of it. Aper, a poor man with a chip on his shoulder and a hatred of fine wine, used to grab the goblets of fellow users of the baths and smash them, their precious Falernian tinting the bathwater.

Martial compared a kiss from a maiden's sweet lips, a breath of balm from Philas, the perfume of apples ripening in the winter chest, of amber warmed by a maiden's hand to the scent of a jar dark Falernian shattered but far off. Pliny said it was the only wine that caught fire when flame was applied to it and Horace asked 'What slave will swiftly temper the bowls of fiery Falernian with water from a passing stream?' Martial and Horace advocated the mixing of Attica honey with Falernian and said: 'It is meet that such a drink be mixed by Ganymede.'

Pliny implied that wines of the quality of Falernian were often adulterated. Wine merchants took an ordinary wine to which a sort of pigment was added to give the wine more body. 'So many poisons are employed to force wine to suit our taste – we are surprised it is not wholesome. Today not even our nobility enjoy wines that are genuine. So low has our commercial honesty sunk, that only the names of the vintages are sold, the wines being adulterated as soon as they are poured into the vats. The commonest wine is freer from impurities.' Martial compromised. While blending classic old Falernian with Vatican was akin to murder. 'Deadly poison', he snorted, stretching the noble Falernian with Attic honey was fine, because it 'thickens the nectar'.

In Petronius's *The Satyricon*, the wealthy and uncouth Trimalchio's 'stout mistress' Fortunata showed scant respect for the legendary wine. She sat 'gorged with food and wine, her tongue furred, her memory confused, her eyes bleared with drunkenness.' After stuffing herself with oysters she poured 'foaming unguents' into a fine unmixed Falernian, and to compound the felony, proceeded to guzzle the legendary wine out of perfumed bowls while the roof spun dizzily around. The band struck up an appropriate number during which men and women broke wind with gusto.

Burton Anderson, author of _Vino_, places the old Falernian vineyards 'on the hill behind the ancient ports of Terracina, Gaeta, and Formia'. Modern Falernian is, alas, a mere mortal. The vine is still grown on bits of the once-famous vineyards and a few wine makers are producing deeply coloured, robust reds with limited keeping potential. It is palatable enough but a long way from its heyday, and well behind the current great wines of Italy, let alone the great French classics. No blue plaque in memory of the ancient wine is fixed to a bent olive tree or a cellar door.

Surrentine wines, which gained a velvety smoothness after lengthy cellaring, were so sought after they were 'fattened' by unscrupulous merchants who poured dead yeast cells, pigments, tannins and other residues into the mix. Horace refers to the use of pigeons' eggs as a fining agent. Seawater, salt and animal blood were also used.

Horace loved Calenian, a near neighbour of Falernian, for its sprightly flavour and subtle nose, though it was ruined by his friend Vergilius, who poured into an amphora of Calenian a flask of neat spikenard, 'a perfume far stronger than that of the washes with which barbers will try to anoint one's head.' In Latium quality wines emerged among a swirling sea of honest everyday vino. The Caecuban grape flourished here on damp and boggy ground along the coast between Terracina and Formiae. Martial mentions vines showing an oasis of green among the reed beds and bulrushes.

Caecuban was fiercely dry and full-bodied when young. Galen implied it was rough and heavy. Warner Allen agreed, saying it was a wine 'to get drunk on, not to meditate on'. He compared it with the unfortified and unsweetened 'port' shipped to England in the eighteenth century. Caecuban needed time to slough off its dark tannins and shed pigment. Some thought it equal to the great Falernian in taste and character. Cooled with melting snow, it is said to have 'fuelled the fever' of the gluttonous Lentinus, who, when ill, tried to eat and drink himself well. Horace drank it after Chian and Lesbos to clean his palate, and when ill he drank it as a restorative. A few sips of Caecuban were enough to make Martial 'leer too lovingly at the pretty boy who poured it at a friend's house.'

Alban was revered by Martial, Pliny, Galen and Juvenal. At its best it was sweet, made from late-picked, low-grown grapes from the sunny hills around Emperor Domitian's estate south of Rome. A dry version was also made. The once famous wine now ekes out a living refreshing elderly pilgrims nosing around the Pope's country retreat at Castelgandolfo. Aleatico, a modern version of the ancient Lugliatico, is still cultivated in Tuscany, Emilia-Romagna and Latium, its spiritual home since Roman times. In Gradoli it thrives on volcanic soil and comes in several styles – fragrant, relatively low in alcohol or a blockbuster comfortable with a tarry espresso and a fat cigar.

Under Tiberius (42 BC–AD 37), drinking wine became vulgar and excessive. His orgies were lively and wine-saturated. He enjoyed other men's drunken antics and childishly screamed encouragement at exhibitionists like the Milanese Novellius Torquatus, who downed three gallons of wine in one giant, eye-popping, Adam's apple-juggling swig, 'leaving insufficient in the jug to dash against the pavement'.

8

A Shift Towards Elegance

From AD 169, after the admonitions of Galen, physician to Marcus Aurelius (121–180), whose personal taste in wine was for refreshing whites and elegant reds, there was a shift away from vein-clogging sweet wines. It signalled the birth of the appreciation of older wines. Galen organised vertical tastings, starting with the oldest. A group of serious tasters chewed, spat, nodded sagely and made notes. Thought-provoking wines of some complexity were steering wine lovers away from the monochrome thud of sickly sweetness. Pliny, one of the most accomplished tasters of his era, enjoyed the new sharp wines from the cool, hilly parts of northern Italy. Galen too enjoyed wines with a prickle of acidity because, he said, they were better for the liver. Gradually word spread that wine did not have to taste like maple syrup to be good. Barges ploughed the Tiber laden with sharp, dry wines of flavour and character. The search was on for light, dry wines. Galen discovered a brace in an unfashionable Rome suburb and Sabine and Tiburtine became popular.

Horace shared an amphora of Sabine with Maecenas (d. 8 BC), which he had made from his own vines and stored in a jar that once contained sweet Greek wine. This was not out of a sudden interest in low-strength wine. For a while Galen hailed the light Sabine wines and enjoyed their zesty acidity, and he appreciated their keeping ability. Some were said to retain their freshness after fifteen years in the jar. Horace wasn't convinced and he apologised to Maecenas for not being able to offer him a decent bottle of Falernian.

Another wine to flirt with fashion was Setine, grown in Setia on the Appian Way. Martial preferred the view, enjoying the wonderful panorama of vines healthily ripening on a hill above the 'fever-ridden reek' of a steaming marsh below. When the Emperor Augustus ordered Setine, because it 'never gave him indigestion', his acolytes fell over themselves to do likewise, even copying the master in his taste for snow in his wine. Martial was quick to agree. 'A really stiff, iced Setine,' he wrote, 'all the riches in the world could not compare with it.'

Drinking it never gave him indigestion either. Martial called it 'my lady Snow' and wondered when his doctor was going to allow him to drink it. Juvenal referred to old Setine, which he drank with friends. The wine jar was 'so covered in soot that name and vintage was obliterated. Silas Italicus unashamedly raved about the Setine wines, saying their proper place was gracing the table of the Wine God.'

Hadrianum from the Adriatic coast was another dry and acidic white which had its well-heeled devotees. Vatican wine was generally abused by the sages. When

Martial spotted Ammianus, a wine pseud – the type who carries a little cardboard box containing his own special tasting glasses – Martial said, 'You have a marvellous goblet, Ammianus, engraved with a viper worthy of the great Myron's hand. How appropriate! From it you are drinking Vatican poison!'

Virgil, who predicted the switch from sweet wines, frequently dropped unknown wines into his verse. His eventual writer's block may have something to do with the fact that the austere Rhaetic wine failed to trigger his dormant muse because, as he wistfully admitted himself, 'It cannot compete with Falernian.'

Pliny's tasting note on Surrentinum, a thin, fresh wine made from hard and not fully ripened Amineum grapes grown in Sorrento, on the breezy cliffs above Naples, drew rebukes. It was called 'full-bodied vinegar' by Tiberius, and 'ennobled gooseberry' by Caligula. It became known as a tonic wine, and when physicians recommended it as such, Tiberius accused them of having a vested interest. Galen liked it. 'Give it twenty-five years,' he said, 'and it will be as smooth and sleek as an athlete's skin after massage with olive oil.' Ovid wrote an ode 'to slopes made noble by Surrentine vines'. Its fame too has passed, but Burton Anderson says the modern version 'can prove to be of more than routine interest'.

Mamertine, a thin wine from Sicily, was plucked from obscurity by Julius Caesar, who used it at a prestigious banquet to celebrate a hat-trick of election results as Consul of Rome. Martial didn't care for it but Galen, while asserting that Sicily was not in Italy, thought it 'well strung'. Modern Mamertine is an alcoholic bruiser with a girth to match, but not without a certain redeeming fragrance.

Pliny listed an encyclopaedia of vintages from the chilly and unromantic north of Italy, like the famous Rhaeticum from Venice. Wealthy wine enthusiasts began to court their wine merchants, harrying them to deliver more esoteric wines. Wine tastings no longer required a man wearing a bull's head and a massive fake penis and festooned by naked nymphs to enjoy wine. Orgies were no longer *de rigueur*. Wines previously written off as salad dressing were now considered elegant. Wine snobbery was rife. Growers bought more land and planted vines high in the hills above Rome to satisfy the demand. Latium white wine, which even now, according to Burton Anderson, 'though popular, [cannot] lay claim to greatness', became immensely fashionable and ornately painted chariots delivered it to the most fashionable addresses.

9

Pompeii Burning

Pompeii, a town with a large population of Greeks, was a beehive of energy and activity. Pompeiians enjoyed life, drank wine – red, white and faked – in the 200 wine bars that were crammed in to the narrow streets. On Sundays parents took the children to the auditorium to watch screaming undesirables torn to pieces by lions, or to hiss and boo a pair of greased-up musclemen exchanging dinks and volleys with hatchets. Crystal ball-gazing wise women offered to read palms.

Huge *dolia* of wine, fizzy and cloudy, stood behind the counters of rustic inns with salted pigs, dried fish as stiff as cricket bats, round loaves shot through with poppy seed and jars of goat cheese mixed with herbs. Bar-owning prostitutes smiled in the shadows, ready to feed, feel and refresh the town's citizens. Old men sat on hard wooden forms, staining the plastered wall with their greasy thatches. They smoked, spat and played dice, x-raying every passing female. Occasionally they were led behind the bar by the landlady and paid for a quick hand job. Some bars were as tiny as telephone boxes, with a single fly-haunted amphora and a scattering of unrinsed beakers; from others came the sounds and smells of gentile dining. In the more salubrious places, fanned Pompeiian landowners dined on cured ham with green leaf salad and a goblet of crisp young wine.

Pompeii sprawled, brawled and reeked of garlic, vinegar and oil. Redundant centurions showed off their muscles, drunken tramps lay as if dead in the dust, cobblers, candle makers, jewellers, basket weavers and musicians hammered, banged, stitched, strummed and wove in the open air. In the baths, men, salmon pink and naked, lolled like skinned sea lions in the warm suds or lay drying on benches. Wine merchants' carts constantly rumbled by and boats stacked with wine skins cast off from the harbour.

The most famous wine merchant, Marcus Porcius, had his name engraved on the temple to Apollo and on the handles of his wine jars. Pliny took up residence in this balmy seaport at the age of fifty-five and spent the days sitting on his patio overlooking the city, writing and drinking wine imported from Spain. The ethnic mix of the place meant a wide choice of wines was available. The bigger wine merchants sponsored sports events or organised street tastings. They were important men, exporting wine to cities as far away as Bordeaux. Wine merchants were more important than lawyers and doctors, and when they died their tombs were adorned with images of Bacchus draped with the inevitable virgins.

Life was sweet until that day in AD 79 when the top of the mountain above the town flew off like a dustbin lid in the wind. Hot rocks rained down, followed by a shimmering curtain of ash. Pompeiians died when they stood, the choking ash crystallising them for eternity in whatever mundane or embarrassing thing they were doing. Men eating, vomiting or making love, the palm reader holding an unread hand, the centurion with his legs spread, his chest puffed out showing off, the men in the bathhouse cooked in their baths, the slave on the hill grilled where he stood, still in chains. The dog frozen as it gnawed a bone in the gutter, a grilled baby's smile fixed.

Pliny saw it all from his house across the bay. After an icy plunge and a light breakfast he had cleared his desk when he heard the roar and saw the red eruption shoot into the blue sky. A sooty nimbus hung over Pompeii. Pliny ordered up a boat and with slaves manning the oars, and his terrified secretary clutching a notepad, they set off and were soon directly under the fiery cloud.

Landing at Stabiae, near the town, Pliny had hardly set a sandalled foot on the scorched pavement when Vesuvius greeted him with a monstrous raspberry. The shattered mountain burned like a nightwatchman's kicked-over brazier. A smouldering river bubbled out of the mountain's fractured mouth and flowed and tumbled down to the town. Pliny stumbled upon a deserted hovel and pushed his terrified servants inside. Flames gnawed at the flimsy dwelling. Pliny curled up and slept as hot ashes fell on the narrow streets like dirty snow, and gathered glowing by cottage doors. Wood crackled, the thick warm air was filled with the stench of roasting human flesh, burning carpets and animals. Pliny's secretary gently shook the old man and suggested they return to the boat. He was dead. By the time Vesuvius had emptied her stomach, Pompeii and Pliny were buried under 3 metres of ashes and clinkers. Nearby Herculaneum was smothered under 30 metres of roasting rubble. Women and children ran into the sea only to find the water boiling.

Vineyards burned fiercely at night like a million small candles. Weeks later they were still smouldering, the stubs of vines burned close to the scorched ground. When the fire at last blinked and went out, the sloping vineyards were covered in a thick layer of iron-rich ash. Cautiously, workers were soon back on the bare brown hill, the air resounding to the welcome and familiar sound of mattocks hitting tarmac-hard ground. There was much clearing, burying and building to be done. Wine would soon return.

10

Roman Food

Roman chefs, Trimalchio said, 'will make you a fish out of a sow's belly, a wood pigeon out of bacon, a turtle-dove out of a ham, or a chicken out of a knuckle of pork.' Rome was a paradise for gourmands. There was 'fish from the gulfs and bays, game from the Laurentine and Ciminian forests, lamb from the hills about the city, cheese from Trebula and Vestini, oil from the Sabine country, pickles from Spain, pork from Gaul, spices from the East, figs and pears from Chios, lemons from Africa, dates from Damascus.' Montanus, a *bon viveur*, claimed he could 'tell at first bite whether an oyster had been bred at Circe or on the Lucrine rocks'. Even the older Pliny was not above boasting about the 'very fine thrushes' he'd eaten, while Pliny the Younger, his nephew, preferred simple fare, seasoned with philosophical conversation.

Roman dinners were pure theatre, lasting up to ten hours, the continual sweep of courses broken only by the introduction of a magician, a juggler 'accompanied by the gesticulations of a silver skeleton', an acrobat or a belly dancer. Food was heavily spiced and sweetened with wine. Meat was served with apricots and figs, the whole smothered in a spicy plum sauce. The wines were cut with spring water to postpone drunkards and vomiting. Prostitutes paraded around the tables, stroking the wine soaked beards of old men who had in their pockets nail parings from the baths, which they imagined were aphrodisiacal.

When Martial invited seven friends to a simple supper he offered them mature wine from Nomentan, his own estate north east of Rome. He had hoped for a pleasant and civilised dinner, 'where there shall be jests without gall, and no word you would wish unsaid.' Galen tasted Martial's wine and thought it mediocre. It was neither sweet nor light and it aged quickly. 'It will drink better if you like it,' Martial said, clearly unamused. Whatever his friends might say about his wine, Martial was happier with his 'parched little vineyard' than any of his wealthy friends with their fine estates and their worries.

Wealthy politicians vied to see who could put together the finest wine list. The famous Roman and Greek wines of the day were supplemented by Spanish Balearican, Lauronensian from Valencia, Tarraconensian from Tarragona and Baetican from Andalusia. All things Spanish were popular among sophisticated males, especially the sultry maidens who stamped, yelled and sexily pirouetted to the clatter of castanets.

At Trimalchio's infamous banquets, guests took hot baths after the first course. At this point the tablecloths were changed and scented sawdust mixed with saffron and talc was sprinkled on the floor. When the bathed and refreshed diners returned to newly laid tables, 'wine flowed in rivers; those weary of eating could finish the meal by getting drunk.' This was considered a 'a popular conclusion', after which belching and thunderous farting were encouraged. Trimalchio advised his guests to let rip and 'not to risk injury by self-restraint'. He also permitted those who could not be bothered to walk to the toilets to relieve themselves in the dining room. Martial tells of such a dinner when male diners simply clicked their fingers for a slave to bring 'a vase into which the diner measured with accuracy the wine he had drunk'.

Mulsum, a versatile drink made with wine and honey, was usually served just before the meal. The Greek version was called Melitites, a mixture of either unfermented must or dry wine blended with honey with a pinch of salt. Women drank Rosatum, a pink wine flavoured with rose petals and sweetened with honey. Voliatium was similar but flavoured with violets. Conditum, a spiced or aromatic wine, was also popular, but Pliny said it was ' like drinking neat perfume'. Myrrh was one of the ingredients. Piperatum was a sickly combination of wine and honey.

At certain gatherings 'drinking cups were solicitously filled' with a selection of wines, including some from Marseille and the Vatican – neither highly esteemed – up to the immortal Falernian. An amphora of the latter was carried in, and the vintage wine, 'blended with resin and pine pitch', was strained into a *cratera*. It was warmed with a hot plunged sword, depending on the season.

Juvenal (*c.*60–*c.*140) castigated low-born upstarts who ate 'huge lobsters garnished with asparagus, mullet from Corsica, the finest lampreys the Straits of Sicily can purvey, a goose's liver, a capon as big as a house, a boar piping hot, truffles and delicious mushrooms.' His guests made do with coarse wine of a humble vintage, bits of hard bread that had turned mouldy, sickly greens cooked in an oil that smelled of the lamp, an eel, first cousin to a water snake, a crab hemmed in by half an egg, toadstools of doubtful quality, and a rotten apple like those munched on the ramparts by a monkey trained by terror of the whip.

Wealthy Romans loved good food and fine wine and so keenly sought lively company that Apicius (*fl.* AD 14), a quadruple-chinned food writer, after guzzling his way through a fortune with the help of his many roly-poly friends, killed himself rather than live in penury. While we get a colourful picture of Roman excesses from Juvenal's *Satires* and Martial's *Epigrams*, which only too clearly impress upon us the sordid and depraved side of Roman life, there was a quiet dignity about the ordinary working man who enjoyed the comfort of friends whose health he drank in ordinary wine, some of it an early sherry type, oxidised and salty, from Ceret (Jerez) in Spain. Christians at the end of a hard working day blessed their frugal repast and 'did not recline to eat till they have offered a prayer to God with gladness and in singleness of heart', even though, according to Gibbon, 'the unfeeling candidate for heaven was instructed to resist the grosser allurements of taste or smell.'

The poor man with more children that bottles to his name turned up with his ragged friends for the New Year festival of Anna Parenna held every year by the freezing banks of the Tiber. Ovid said 'common folk come, and scattered here and there over the green grass, they drink.' Some prepared for a Glastonbury-type experience by building huts from branches they snapped off trees; 'others made shelters from cloths stretched on reeds.' All engaged in a massive 'piss-athon', reeling and kicking their dirty heels in the air. Mongrels barked and young men and their wenches 'made a spectacle for vulgar eyes'. Ovid watched them stagger home, singing and cursing, their tired children howling, and drunk old women lugging drunk old men.

After the first century BC and the advent of glass blowers, Roman wine enthusiasts could admire the colour, breathe in the bouquet and drink their fine wines from clear glasses as we do today. As glasses were delicate, they were expensive, and some were artistically monogrammed. Frontinus, who became famous for his glass, set up workshops in sandy areas. He invented a very commercial small glass barrel which was filled with wine and interred with wealthy corpses. Fancy glasses were beyond the reach of the labourer, who was happy to drink from jugs or wineskins, or if he could afford it, wood or metal.

The Romans were among the pioneers of using wood for ageing. The influence of oak was important and it had a positive effect on the quality and stability of Roman wines, as well as subtly altering their taste. Strabo recalled wine barrels in the north of Italy that were as big as houses. Horace was among the opinion-makers who liked wines that were aged in wood for at least seven years. Cork, used in Greece for stopping jars and bottles, was rarely used by the Romans, though Horace wrote a poem to an amphora stoppered for forty-six years with a 'cork sealed with pitch'. Winemaking had made great strides. Interest in wine was increasing all over Europe. Wine merchants all over the Roman Empire were locating new wines to satisfy the demand. Winemaking had leapt into modern times.

11

The Legions Plod North

It was envy of the opulent lifestyle of the Campanians that drove the Etruscans to invade their territory. They brought little with them except a few pottery jars and a brutal and dismissive treatment of women. If an Etruscan woman was caught drinking alone her husband could divorce her immediately or strike her down with his sword. In frescoes, dull-eyed women look detached and bored while their men guffaw heartily, drain their bronze beakers and belch.

When the Etruscans were evicted from Campania it is unlikely they returned to their wooded Tuscan hills with 'any compensation in the shape of skill in viticulture'. Martial refers dismissively to Tuscan wine. It was of the instant variety, dispatched as soon as possible after fermentation. Umbria made better wine than Tuscany. Galen refers to 'golden wine with an attractive taste'. Martial, privy to 'an old encrusted jar' of Spoletine, cantankerously preferred it to old Falernian. Modern Umbrians – an uneasy mix of Etruscan, Latin, Goth, Hun and Gaul – are proud of their ancient lineage but regard strangers with 'cool suspicion'. When sitting on a shady veranda sipping Orvieto, it is best not mention the 'T word'. Umbrians are not Tuscans and if you get the two confused 'they resent it and may politely but firmly tell you'.

As we have seen, wines made on the low hills of the Rhaetic Alps above Verona were highly regarded by the Romans. Made from Campanian grapes, Rhaetic, according to Suetonius (c.AD 75–160), was sharp and limpid. It quickly became a favourite of Augustus after his personal taster said privately: 'Its flavour is new to me, and while it is not that of a really fine wine, I am sure the Caesar will drink nothing else.' The imperial taster was right. Augustus, whose palate was as sensitive as the tongue of an old army boot, took to Rhaetic immediately, the wine displacing Setine in his affection. Rhaetic was fragrant and clean, and as such was considered sophisticated. It established a new wine region, marking 'a further stage in the Wine God's inexorable progress northwards.'

The imperial benediction bestowed on Rhaetic wine was brief. Galen was pleased – he considered it watery and overrated. What could one expect from fat table grapes, he wondered? Seneca (c.55 BC - 40 AD) wrote a poem in its favour with the caveat that it was not as fine as Falernian. Virgil, who thought it one of the great wines of the day, included among his favourites Hadrianum from Atri near Po Valley, Lunensan from near La Spezia, Genuan from Liguria, Praeturian from near Ancona and Cauline from Capua in Campania. Historians mention another Tuscan wine, the peculiar Veiian, said to be a turbid pink liquid, 'a plebian wine of the basest class'.

The Roman thirst for new wines was insatiable and vineyards sprang up where once only tangled brush grew. Mediocre wine flowed from nameless, highly productive grapes. It was cheaper than water and about as interesting. Dismissing the new commercial vineyards, Martial said it was better to own a well. The average Roman was content to drink lachrymose blends as long as they were teeth-rottingly sweet and strong. It looked as if the development of wine in Italy under the Romans had stalled. The legions carried on hacking their way into Gaul.

A vigorous wine trade was established in Marseille by the Greeks around 600 BC, 500 years before the Romans renamed it Massalia. The Greeks planted indiscriminately, made lakes of cheap, bland wines. Galen liked them; they were juicy and uncomplicated, like New World Merlot. Pliny said they were fine for blending. He thought the wines of Beziers were better but Narbonne was to be avoided. It suffered from 'systematic adulteration with objectionable drugs and bitter aloes'.

Warner Allen said no wine came out of France to challenge the ancient classics until the nineteenth century. Hugh Johnson dismissed the ancients *en bloc*. 'None of the first-growth regions of the ancient world would find a place in any such list in modern times.' With shades of today's head-in-the-sand chauvinism, the Gauls loved their dreary wine with a fierce, narrow-minded passion and would swop an energetic boot-licking slave for a brimming amphora any time. The invading Roman was not short of choice. He accessed his own Roman wines, the conquered Gaul's, Greek, as well as a garnetty river of strapping wine that wriggled its way from conquered Spain. This included a delicate early cousin of modern Rioja, and further south a dark stream from Tarraconensis (Tarragona). From Cadiz boats departed, loaded with sweet amber wines and fungi-scented whites – hoary ancestors of sherry, bone dry and nutty.

12

Cork and Glass

'Revolution,' says Hugh Johnson, 'came with the bottle, and a secure means of sealing it.' André Simon wrote that, before the eighteenth century, 'wine was almost entirely a long drink' – a draught beverage drunk straight from the cask almost as soon as it was rolled from the ship to the quay.

Archaeological evidence points to the Etruscans using cork as a stopper in 600 BC. By the fifth century AD, Greek wine was routinely sealed with cork, which had been known as 'an elastic, impervious material' for thousands of years. The Phoenicians used it, as did the Egyptians. The Romans sealed their amphorae with cork which they then smeared with pozzolana cement, some still do for Vin Santo.

When the Greek and Roman civilisations declined, cork was all but forgotten until the enlightened reign of Elizabeth I. English fishermen used the material for making floats for their nets. Enterprising cobblers found a use for cork in shoemaking. Shakespeare connected corks with wine bottles in *As You Like It*: 'I prithee, take the cork out of thy mouth, that may drink thy tidings.' (Act 3, Scene 2) The rediscovery of the cork led to the perfection of Champagne and permitted Claret and port to reach unforseen heights of elegance, balance and flavour.

Peeled from the bark of *Quercus Suber*, the cork replaced rags, hemp, leather, even pieces of soft wood which were previously hammered into the necks of squat, dark-hued bottles. Fine Claret and vintage port require the finest and longest corks – nearly 50mm – to improve in the cellar. However, cork is not cheap and, as many of the cheapest wines sold today are worth less than the cost of a cork, alternative closures like plastic and screw caps had to be found.

Corkmaking is still a fairly simple and even primitive business. Tiny Portuguese men shin up cork oaks with axes to remove the bark. It is thrown in among the weeds to dry and rot and develop diseases, while the tree's inner bark is exposed and bleeding. Certainly the cork has never been so unreliable. Twenty years ago a wine drinker might experience a corked wine once every blue moon. Now it is almost one per tasting session. Trichloranisole, which gives wine an unpleasant and unnatural staleness, is present in thousands of corks drawn daily in the United Kingdom, in homes, pubs and restaurants. It doesn't affect just the cheap wines. A sommelier at a London restaurant encrusted with Michelin stars poured into the sewers corked 1982 Château Margaux, 1985 Château Haut-Brion and 1990 Château Latour. 'It was a heart-breaking evening,' the sommelier said with a catch in his voice. Three great wines ruined. Someone should have been sued. Cork's three-century tenure as a wine stopper is threatened from all sides. Now only two bottles in every case are closed with a wad of tree bark. Tin and plastic are taking over. Jilly Goolden is not the only one who finds this distressing. She writes in the weekend *Telegraph*: 'Call me sentimental, call me a traditionalist, but corks have a romance to them.' Waitrose, that most winey of British supermarkets, is on her side and is encouraging its wine suppliers to ditch plastic corks. Simon Thorpe, Waitrose's wine buyer, says plastic corks cause leakage and oxidation and can be difficult to remove. They can also ruin your corkscrew. Tell me about it: I broke a beautiful old corkscrew trying, bug-eyed, to remove a synthetic 'cork'. Made from non-renewable, non-biodegradable material, they are not environmentally friendly and are consequently politically unfashionable.

Since the time Virgil counselled against drinking new wine and advised drinkers to wait until the first sunny days of spring, when 'the lambs are fat and wines are at their smoothest', a seal that afforded better protection than oil was sought. In his poem *Georgics*, Virgil mentions cork as an insulator of beehives. Horace on festive days often 'drew a well-pitched cork from the jar'. Cato also used cork to stopper his wines.

The first corks were conical. The pointed end was driven into the bottle, the large end protruding two or three inches out, 'thus giving a fair hold to the fingers for pulling out'. It was only after the invention of the 'bottle screw' or corkscrew that corks could be driven into slimmer, longer-necked bottles which could then be laid down to mature without leaking. The long spongey corks rammed into mid-eighteenth-century Clarets and port survived after lying in cold cellars swamped by acid and alcohol-rich wines for over a century.

When Michael Broadbent tasted a 1799 Château Lafitte [*sic*] in 1979, he professed it 'very much alive, a fabulous colour with a gently fragrant bouquet'. This imprisoned wine as it lay in the glass gradually unfurled all its dormant qualities. Light but meaty, ultimately fading but fascinating. The wine had been recorked in 1953 by a sensitive expert. So the cork must be the ultimate closure for wine, whether fine or modest. Broadbent's *Great Vintage Wine Book* is dotted with similar examples of how cork has triumphed over time.

The alternatives to cork are inadequate. Wodges of dull and antiseptic plastic are often impossible to separate from the bottle. In the event that you don't finish the wine, they are even more difficult to put back in – unless you use a jack hammer – and they leak. How annoying! As for the much-vaunted screw caps – well. Château Haut-Brion tried them as far back as 1969 and quickly rejected them. While it is common knowledge that red wines become soft, mahogany coloured and complex under a cork, Professor Emile Peynaud questioned the wierd theory that wine needed to breathe at all. He was supported by another Frenchman, Pascal Ribereau-Gayon, author of *The Chemistry of Wine*, published in 2000. Ribereau-Gayon was of the opinion that wine did not need a constant infusion of oxygen to change.

13

Modern Classics: the First Stirrings

From the Rhône Valley came Picata, named after a tarry wine brought into Marseille from Persepolis by a Greek immigrant or a Bible-punching Crusader. What is known for certain is that this dark, spicy wine from the Shiraz grape has been enjoyed for over 1,000 years. In 1677 it was one of the first ancient wines to be shipped to England in bottles.

Called Syrah in France, shamelessly they are changing it to the more commercial Shiraz, it prospered on the banks of the Rhône at Vienne and was exported back to Rome as Picatum. Like the numerous starry-eyed fans who inexplicably queue up for every last bottle of Cloudy Bay, Roman tasters, also heavily into new taste sensations, loved Picatum for its unusual smoky tang. Its success was transitory. Pliny and Martial both mention it; Pliny said it may have been highly thought of in Gaul, but didn't travel. Nevertheless growers in Campania were so alarmed at the success of this new foreign grape they made souvenir wine cups which they sent to the legions in France, stamped 'No more Picatum, give us Aminean'.

The brooding Syrah was reduced to the role of giving anaemic wines a blood transfusion, a bit part it would play up to the 1960s. At least its quality was recognised by Husenbeth, a Victorian wine merchant. 'Margaux, Lafite, Latour and Haut-Brion,' he said, all 'receive their fullness' from the wines of the Rhône.

Revisionists are now saying it wasn't the Romans or the Greeks who established the French wine trade, it was the Celts. They travelled widely, perfected the wine cask and made 2 metre-high, 1,200-litre bronze wine bowls, one of which is in on display in a French museum.

Among the itinerant entrepreneurs who rattled and jangled behind the marauding Romans begging for business were spear repairers, gravediggers, quacks, cobblers, prostitutes, wheelwrights, carpenters, flying wine makers, horse dealers and slave traders. Glass blowers quickly set up shops to make jugs, bowls, beakers and tatty miniature glass amphorae complete with handles. When the Roman Army macheted its way through the wild, forested hills of what is now northern Burgundy, the soldiers were made welcome by the powerful Aedui, one of sixty warring factions. Among them the aforementioned Allobroges, making a thin wine from a grape remarkably close to the Pinot Noir, long before golden Roman helmets were seen moving ominously through the undergrowth. Pliny and Columella attest to the

The humble Chenin is transformed here. Honey on the nose, limpid to the eye, sweet and sour combining on the tongue.

fact a vine similar to Pinot Noir was being used to make wine at the start of the Christian era.

Muddied legionnaires and their ragged followers drank to stay sane and appreciated the regular deliveries to the front line of wines from the sunny south. Wine sellers followed the advancing troops, pushing casks on wheels, ladling still-fermenting wine into proffered jars and battered mugs. When Caesar's army surged into the Champagne country, Hugh Johnson writes, 'he found two Roman wine merchants already started up business there.' The Emperor proved to be a benign dictator, encouraging the Gauls – who were envious of the Romans' opulence – to welcome the invader like a failing British car maker would a Toyota director.

The legions inched forward, chopping and civilising. They planted, according to Pliny, the Picata and the Biturica which, Columella warned, represented bulk rather than brilliance, but 'withstood cold better than damp, damp better than drought, and bore up cheerfully against heat'. It became Cabernet Sauvignon. Pliny tasted Bordeaux wines in AD 71. There were two kinds, he said: an austere red not unlike the wines of Campania, and a golden sweet white, like the wines the Greeks made on Lesbos. A shrewd summing up.

After his courtship of German wines, Ausonius, the most famous Biturican and a Christian poet, returned to Bordeaux. He was fêted and courted, became tutor to Emperor Valentinian's son Gratian 'and rose to the imperial purple'. Well-qualified as a vineyard owner, a sophisticate with a trained palate and influential wine-drinking friends, his muse should have been 'ready to sing the pleasures of the table'. Instead his poetry dried up and his writings veered towards oysters and how wonderfully plump, snow-white and tender they were. While Ausonius discussed at eyelid-dropping length the merits of the salty bivalve 'from the Hellespont to Caledonia', there was nothing about the new and exciting wines of his adopted Bordeaux that excited him. Warner Allen says Ausonius left behind 'not one true wine-lover's word on the character and quality of his own or any other wines'. He owned land in the Palus, an area noted for cheap, one-dimensional reds. There is no definite evidence he owned Château Ausone.

14

The Romans in Britain

Soon Roman boats were plying the Thames, the Severn and the Wye. This was cider and sour beer country. After the bloodletting, the ambushes and the reprisals, the Romans planted vines they had taken with them from Germany and Champagne. The first sour and watery vintage would have told them the dank climate was unsuitable. The river valleys in southern Britain were not steep enough, the land not canted to catch what sun filtered through the swirling mists that wreathed the dark forests.

The legionary put his sword in its scabbard and his secateur in his tunic pocket, mopped his brow and quenched his thirst with French, Greek, Spanish or German wine. The Romans prospered in Britain. The wealthy were cocooned in colonnaded mansions with their private armies and retinues of cooks, herbalists, ostlers and slaves. The soldiers intermarried with their local social equals.

'After a war of about forty years,' Gibbon relates, 'undertaken by the most stupid, maintained by the most dissolute, and terminated by the most timid of all the emperors [the incompetent trio, Claudius, Nero and Domitian], the greater part of the island submitted to the Roman yoke.' An exception were the Caledonians, whose subduing was more trouble than they were worth.

Gibbon conceded that Europe, Britain included, also benefited from the Roman invasion. 'Almost all the flowers, herbs and fruits that grow in European gardens are of foreign extraction,' he says. The apple – so English – is Italian, and when the Romans tasted exotic fruits from the far-flung reaches of their empire, they shipped them to Europe. Vines that had ripened in Sicily 'at the time of Homer' had yielded nothing but wizened berries before the Romans. It was the Romans who made them into wine and they could declare 1,000 years later that 'of the fourscore most generous and celebrated wines known to man, more than two thirds were produced on Italian soil. The storm of barbarian invasions blew away the brittle peace of the Roman sunset but the vineyards of France and Germany suffered no irreparable disaster.'

By the sixth century Gregory of Tours was proudly announcing that the Burgundy vineyards had not only survived but had produced record yields of excellent wine. It was so good it would knock that paltry stuff from Champagne sideways. Optimism and confidence restored, the forests around Burgundy were burned to release virgin land, which was ploughed and tilled for further planting.

By the seventh century the slopes of Franconia were covered with shiny green vines that may have been Riesling. Blossoming vines heralded 'the first glimmer of light in the darkness'. Cowled nuns swarmed on the schistose slopes. Bishops and monks were at the forefront of wine production, either in vaulted cellars or stone bothies in brooding valleys. They worked hard and drank heavily in their stygian loneliness. St Augustine defended Catholics against the charge that they drank too much. They, he said, preferred the juice of the apples, 'which was more delicious than all the wines in the world'. He confessed to personally being 'crop-sick through excess of wine'.

The French clergy enjoyed their wine. Pontus III, bishop at Châlons-sur-Saône, 'had a stomach as big as a cellar' into which he poured good Burgundy. On top of his daily dose he drank a bottle at bedtime, never used water except for boiling an egg and bathing in, and 'enjoyed a strong, robust, and vigorous health to the age of fourscore.'

St Benedict, in 529 AD, said a pint of wine a day was quite sufficient for any sick monk, or more if the doctor ordered. He advised healthy monks to 'drink sparingly'. One who didn't was Abbot Adam, who lived in ninth-century Angers. It was said of him that never a day went by but he was found 'wine soaked and wavering', dispensing blessing on all sides as he headed down to the cellar. 'His skin became dyed with wine and his body immune from corruption.' Three centuries later, the acidic Welsh holy man Giraldus Cambrensis boomed with displeasure when he saw how the monks of Canterbury laid their tables. There was 'wine, mead, mulberry juice, and other strong drink in such abundance,' he grumbled. The *Bible Guiot*, a kind of *Michelin Guide* for monasteries published in France in the twelfth century by a monk with a taste for fine wine and food, gave a five-star rating to the Augustines, who not only ate and drank well, but washed their habits at least once a year.

Wine flowed into England, principally from Bordeaux, but also from Burgundy, Anjou, Poitou and Normandy. In the fourteenth century up to 20,000 barrels of Gascon entered England. The King was entitled to take a couple of casks from each shipment as 'prisage'. He secreted the best in his numerous cellars and sold the poor stuff. In 1280, from London importers alone, the King's share was 238 casks. This was in addition to the 1,500 casks he bought, 1,000 of which were of the finest vintages, worth 37s each. He settled debts by allowing his creditor to help himself to his own wine as it entered port. The Archbishop of York was granted prisage on all wines shipped through Hull. Such backhanders were regulated in the sixteenth century, with the prisage set at a fixed and transparent rate for those who qualified for it.

Piments and Spices

Exotic spices and condiments played their part in the vulgar opulence of the Roman Empire. Piment was a blend of wine and spices; Hippocras, Clarry and Vernage were famous blends, the Dubonnet and dry Martini of their time. Piment rapidly became 'the drink of desire, a gustatory delight.' Poets never whispered of piments 'but with rapture and as a exquisite luxury'. To the ignorant and vulgar, they were dishonestly ascribed the gold-stitched mantle once worn by the legendary Pramnian. Like great wine, piments were reputed to be powerfully effective aphrodisiacs. No nerve-racked honeymoon could be successfully negotiated without the man gulping down a beaker of herb and spice-infused wine. Even Chaucer believed all he had heard about piments. In *The Canterbury Tales* he has 'wretched old January' sinking a few quick ones before tumbling into the sack with 'fresshe May'.

Consumers began to depend on crooked 'pigment specialists' and perfumers. Herbs and spices were used to disguise the pong of rotting meat, the sour tang of decaying fruit and vegetables. They were also used to 'enliven the mediocrity' of braket, an English copy of a French drink called bochet which had as its base ale sweetened with honey and perked up with pepper. It was cheap, easy to make and popular in the fifteenth century. Oxymel, hydromel and oinomel were often unstable marriages of honey, fruit juice and sometimes even vinegar and water.

To those of taste, piments became 'a voluptuous beverage' – even though housewives made it in their kitchens from cheap ale or wine and whatever wild thing sprouting by the back door. One such, Gariofilatum, was flavoured and preserved by adding cloves. Artistic types sipped them at the Royal Academy. Morat was a version coloured with mulberry juice. Hippocras and Clary were made with white or red wine, ginger, cinnamon, sugar (which was available but expensive), pepper, honey and 'paradise', the grains of a potent African ginger, a plant banned by brewers, who used it to thicken their beers. Vernage, a corruption of the Roman wine Vernaccia, which Dante once drank with eels, was spiked with herbs. If either Claret or Burgundy were the base wine they were called 'Bishop'. If Rhenish was used it was called 'Cardinal', and if the main ingredient was Tokay it was known as 'Pope'. The proliferation of piment was a low point in winemaking and bore 'pathetic evidence of the darkness of the age'.

Chaucer's List

Our knowledge of a medieval warm period between the ninth and fourteenth centuries seems to confirm the illustrations in ancient books of men in hose and women in flowing dresses picking large bunches of black grapes to make wine in England. 'It was a wonderful period for everyone,' says Dr Philip Scott, emeritus professor of biogeography at the University of London. There is ample evidence of home-grown wine with 139 possible vineyard sites in England. Fifty had religious connections and nine were designated royal. Most were in the South East, with Essex accounting for nineteen. Bishop Thomas de Cantilupe, born in Hambledon in 1220, owned vineyards in several parts of Herefordshire. Cantilupe, who wore hair shirts and an iron girdle, died in Orvieto in 1282. Richard de Swinfield, a close and irreverent friend, managed to steal one of Cantilupe's finger-bones. He used it to stir his wine.

At Christmas time in 1289, Richard de Swinfield, now Bishop of Hereford, moved to his manor at Prestbury in Gloucestershire. The bishop owned extensive vineyards and in 1289 his staff made seven pipes, each containing 126 gallons of white wine. It was valued at about half the price of French wine. The sale of wine was regulated, with wine retailers permitted to sell only one sort of wine to prevent the mixing of white and red. On Christmas Eve, the bishop and his friends ate nothing but fish – trout, herring and eel and a fine salmon fished from the Wye – at a cost of 5s 8d. Then on the following day, with fifteen friends, the bishop devoured a boar, two and three-quarters cattle, two calves, four doves, four pigs, sixty fowls, eight partridge and two geese. They drank ale and wine. In some abbeys wine was drunk every day and landowning visitors were fed and wined at long oak tables, while the ordinary monks in their grubby cowls served them.

In 1284 at Ramsey Abbey each monk was given four pints of wine on feast days and on the abbot's birthday. Though Verjus and sour wine was made from locally-grown grapes in England and drunk by a wincing populace, life was hard for the average monk in the Middle Ages. He was lucky to get 'penny-ale' and a fatty 'pece of bacun' between two hard slices of mouldering bread. In 1353 sweet wine had to be sold exclusively by sweet wine merchants, who were forbidden licences to sell any other kind. Very few citizens, except tavern keepers, were permitted to keep more than 10 gallons on their premises unless they were gentlemen with an income of £66 13s 4d and more and a house worth at least ten times that. New wine was all the rage. Old wine was considered passé, and was either dumped or given to the poor, who presumably lay in ditches dreamily developing a palate for mature Claret. Royal cellar clearances, to make room for new wines, were well attended, which suggests there was a fashion for older wines. English winemaking waned with the dissolution of the monasteries, but there were hundreds of English wines made from fruit and berries flavoured with herbs. Raspice or Respyse was seen in England in the thirteenth, fourteenth and fifteenth centuries. It was made, according to Boorde's *Dyetary of Helth*, from raspberries. By the seventeenth century it was forgotten except in the remoter parts of the country, where farmer's wives made it to drink on special occasions. Rappis, Raspis or Raspish was either coarse and astringent – as in 'Raspish wyne which biteth the tong and gette a certayn taste like wormwood' (Peter Morwyng, 1565) – or 'sweet as honey' (Thomas Heywood, writing in 1635).

A few wealthy eccentrics tried to keep winemaking in England going. When James Oglethorpe (1696–1785), founder of the State of Georgia and friend of Dr Samuel Johnson (1709–1784), Boswell, Goldsmith, Burke and Walpole, entertained his radical friends at his estate near Godalming, they sat on the veranda sipping English wine and eating snails, which Oglethorpe had shipped over from France and fed on vine leaves. Oglethorpe once released baskets of lizards which scampered among his terrified guests' legs before disappearing off into the Surrey countryside.

Historians owe a great deal to Geoffrey Chaucer (*c.*1343–1400) for his many, and usually jolly, references to wine. *The Canterbury Tales* introduced a Spanish white wine from Lepe and mentions Rochelle and Bordeaux. It has been described by one historian as a '*locus classicus* concerning the fourteenth-century wine trade'. One would not expect less from an intelligent and inquisitive scion of several generations of wine merchants. When Chaucer, to whom Richard II granted a yearly tun of wine in 1398 for services to the Crown, amusingly refers to the strong, oloroso-like wine which his father John shipped from what is now Niebla, lying between Moguer and Seville, he was advising against drinking too much of it. Lepe, one of the earliest fortified wines, was enjoyed in the boisterous taverns in the City of London which Chaucer frequented, leering at the wenches, swigging and surreptitiously scribbling. When a man 'hath drunken draughtes three', he was whisked from his dour London slum to bright and cheerful Spain where, in baggy English breeches, he waved his leather jug and yelled 'I'm Samson-Samson!' at the top of his voice. Lepe, which 'creepeth subtilly' and 'of which there riseth such fumositee', quickly scrambled the brain. Chaucer knew of piments too and he that 'drinketh ipocras, clarree, and vernage, Of spyces hote, t'increasen his corage'.

For his time, Chaucer was able and well-read; as well as finding time to write enough great poetry to 'have insured the immortality of half a dozen other poets', Chaucer held several positions of authority in the government and even led military campaigns, one of which resulted in him being captured and ransomed by the French for £16, which Edward III paid to have him released. He was incarcerated near Reims in Champagne, and one hopes he had an opportunity to taste the sharp, cloudy wines of the region. He visited Tuscany, where he was sure to have sampled the wines of Florence, and Milan, where he may have tasted the dry rusty wines of Piedmont.

Chaucer spoke Latin, French and Italian and had studied history, law, medicine, astrology and alchemy. He possessed a library of sixty books, more than most universities at the time. His references to wine include the Franklin, he of the ruddy complexion and daisy-white beard in the *General Prologue*, who ate wine-dunked bread for breakfast, and the rumbustious Sea Captain, who, while on duty in Bordeaux, stowed away casks of Claret for himself 'while the merchants were napping'. In the *Sea Captain's Tale*, Chaucer mentions a merchant who, when visiting his friend, the monk Brother John, brought with him a cask of Malmsey and another of sweet Italian wine. In the *Doctor of Medicine's Tale*, he writes of the beautiful young daughter of a knight, a lovely child 'who surpassed all others in the perfection of her beauty'. 'Drunken Bachus [*sic*] held no sway over her mouth, for wine and youth augment veneray like oil or fat thrown on the fire.'

Chaucer loved wine but advised temperance. Too much wine, he said, 'stirs up lust and drunkenness and is filled with quarrelling and wretchedness.' He who drinks too much becomes a miserable sot whose face is blotched, his breath is sour and he clumsily embraces disgust until he falls down in front of his guests 'like a stuck pig', his tongue gone and with it his self-respect: 'for drunkenness is the graveyard of a man's intelligence'. No drunken man can keep a secret.

It wasn't only wine that interested Chaucer. He loved ale, the men who drank it and the wenches who poured it for him, their breath warm and their breasts bubbling over their bodices. He wrote of the Miller, 'pallid with drink', so legless he could barely sit on his cob but yelling and twirling his arms like windmills trying to outdo the last tale with dozy incoherence. In another reference to wine, Absalon, the prattish parish clerk with his 'goose grey eyes and curly hair glistening like gold, scarlet stockings and shoes' as fantastically patterned as the rose-window in St Paul's, with a propensity for frisky barmaids, attempts his disastrous seduction of Fly Nicholas's wife, a tender ingenue 'with a body as lithe and supple as a weasel'. The besotted clerk tried every trick in his tawdry repertoire, including twanging on his lute and plying the object of his desire 'with wine mead, spiced ale and cakes piping hot from the oven.' In the event the only part of Fly's wife's anatomy Absalon kissed was her husband's hairy arse. Chaucer was a devout Christian and did not approve of men of the cloth unsteadily climbing the pulpit burping. Some priests were 'fat as a whale and waddling like a swan, as full of wine as bottles in a buttery!'

In the *Merchant's Tale* the newly-wed January drinks Hippocras, Clarry and Vernage, for he had a good store of strong aphrodisiacs. When the horde of well-wishers were shooed from the bedroom, January rubbed the bristles of his beard (which 'was like the skin of a dogfish and sharp as briars') against May's tender face. He 'laboured away until daybreak, when he took a sop of bread soaked in strong spiced wine, then, randy as a colt, jabbered like a magpie, sang and yodelled, creaking away like a corncrake, the slack skin around his neck ashake.'

When Cook's horse throws him, the Manciple sneers 'Pity he didn't stick to his ladle', as he helps the dazed chef to his feet and offers him a decent vintage from his gourd. Having 'played a tune' on the gourd the Cook hands it back half empty. He seemed remarkably pleased with the drink and even though dazed from the toss he recognises the quality of the wine and thanks the Manciple 'as best as he could manage'. The Manciple lectures the gathering that always carrying a supply of good wine 'turning grievances and rancour into love and harmony and appeases so many wrongs. O Bacchus, who canst thus turn earnest into jests, blessed be thy name! Honour and thanks to thy divinity.'

Another fourteenth-century poem further enhances our knowledge of the types of wine that were available in England then:

> 'Ye shall have Rumney and Malmesyne,
> Both Hippocrass and Vernage wine,
> Mount Rose and wines of Greke,
> Both Algrade and despice eke,
> Antioche and Bastarde,
> Pyment and garnarde;
> Wine of Greek and Muscadell,
> Both clare, pyment and rochell.'

Mount Rose was a sweet wine also known as Mountrosse, which may have come from Monterosi, north of Rome. It more probably emigrated from Monterosso al Mare, near La Spezia in northwest Italy. Historians say Algrade could have been from the sun-kissed paradise known as the Algarve. Antioche may have been Syrian, and the birthplace of 'Garnarde' it is believed was Granada in Spain.

Two of the oldest wines in the world are Malmsey and Commandaria St John. Malmsey was mentioned in a fourteenth-century poem that listed all the wines the author could remember. There weren't many. Malmesyne, from the Malvasia grape, may be the oldest wine known to civilised man. It was highly addictive. The Malvasia was grown 3,000 years ago and its sweet juice was enjoyed in Jordan at the 'fountain of the kid', the warm spring that gushed from the cliffs overlooking the western shore of the Dead Sea on the road to Bethlehem. Malmsey may have activated Solomon's muse when he wrote the *Song of Songs*.

It was introduced by the Venetians, who collected it from a host of countries, including Greece and Cyprus, blended it and exported it to England. Legend has it that the Duke of Clarence, when sentenced to death, refused the dagger in the throat and elected to dive head-first into a butt of Malmsey. If it happened, and the chances are slim, the terrified duke plunged into a barrel of Candye, the sweet wine of Crete, or Canary.

The Venetians upped the price until it forced the English to seek new sources for their wine. They found an alternative in mainland Spain and Portugal. Malmsey was much abused and the name stuck to any dark, sweet wines made in any dark sweet country warm enough to ripen the grape, which was also known as Malvoisie and Malevesyn. It was often shorthanded to Cret, Candy and Rotimo, and Edward III kept 500 gallons of it securely cellared under the Tower of London.

Commandaria St John was a favourite of the Plantagenet kings of England. When Peter I of Cyprus was entertained at the Vintner's Hall in 1362, his visit was

commemorated in a painting still hanging there unbeknownst to modern wine students as they quietly copy each other's answers. The popularity of rich, sweet wines
steadily increased up to the reign of Elizabeth I. It was she who gave a monopoly of
the sweet Cyprus wine trade to her favourite explorer, Sir Walter Raleigh. With the
profits Raleigh attempted to establish a colony in Virginia between 1584 and 1588.
Elizabeth Barrett Browning (1806–1861) wrote hymns of praise about it.

Commandaria, considered cheap wino fuel today, twenty-eight centuries ago this
unusual wine was famous. Hesiod, the Greek poet, wrote: 'When I rouse I feel either
to massacre or to put out my thirst by drinking Cyprus Wine. Leave the grapes ten
days to the sun,' he added, 'then ten nights and five days under shadow and eight
days in the pot.' Things have changed little. The unknown Mavron and Xynisteri
grapes, grown on what Hugh Johnson describes as 'ashy and sandy soils that must
have looked very much the same when the Venetians arrived [in the fifteenth cen-
tury]', are responsible for modern Commandaria St John. Growers now dry them on
plastic rather than hand-woven straw or grass mats.

17

The Importance of Sack

No one knows for sure the origin of the word 'Sack'. The Romans called it *ceretanum*, after Ceret, their name for Jerez. The first consignment of the oxidised white wine came to England in 1485, according to the Jerez archives. It was shipped from Puerto de Santa María to Plymouth. Sack was sufficiently important to travel in expensive oak barrels, made by a guild of skilled English coopers who set up a Spanish branch in 1482. The barrels had to be sound, made of the best oak available and stamped. When Ferdinand Magellan went off in search of his famous straits in 1519, he carried more sherry than guns. As he died in the attempt, killed in some local dispute, this may have been a miscalculation. The English were developing their unique and long-lasting love affair with sherry. A manuscript refers to 4,000 butts of wine from Jerez de la Frontera travelling to England in 1561. William Younger says: 'the praised and famous name appears to have been a creation of the Renaissance' and came properly into use in the early sixteenth century, when it was 'used for the provisioning of garrisons and castles'. The 'Maire of Bristowe's Kalendar' of 1577 reports in the delicious 'mummerset' language of the time: 'In this yeare came from Andoluzia suche sweete and pleasant secks in generall as by reporte the like was never knowen, as pleasant as Bastards.' Brown and white Bastard were in the cream sherry mould, popular rivals to Sack in the fifteenth century when J. Russell mentioned them in his *Boke of Nurture* in 1460.

In 1584 James VI of Scotland 'bestowed recognition on the wine'. Royal guests were 'upon their necessities by sickness or otherwise' given a 'bowle or glass of Sacke'. When he heard that Sack was being ill-used by his subjects as a 'common drinke' and was taken with meals by Army officers, who 'contrary to all order were using it rather for wantonnesse', he ordered the Sergeant of the Royal Cellar to restrict the Royal Household to 'twelve gallons of Sacke a day'. In 1589 sack was 2s 8d a gallon. A thin, embryonic Claret was 2s.

In Thomas Randolph's play *The Jovial Philosopher*, written in 1630, Aristippus says: 'Sacke is the life, soul and spirit of man, the fire Prometheus stole, not from Jove's kitchen, but his wine-cellar, to encrease the native peat and radicall moisture, without which we are but drousie dust or dead clay... Do you think Alexander had ever conquered the world if he had bin sober? He knew the force and value of Sacke; that it was the best armour, the best encouragement, and that none could be a Commander that was not double drunk with wine and ambition.' William Shakespeare (1564–1616), Ben Jonson (*c*.1573–1637), the poet Robert Herrick (1591–1674), Christopher Marlowe (1564–1593), Sir Walter Ralegh (the original spelling of his name) (1552–1618), Sir Francis Drake (*c*.1545–1596) and Edmund Spenser (*c*.1552–1599) were all willing publicists for Sack.

Shakespeare didn't just put Sack into the mouths of his characters; he drank it too in a galleried tavern, the George Inn at Southwark, the nearest pub to the Globe Theatre. And the Warwickshire-born bard knew how Sack was made too, although the idea of adding sulphate of lime to wine is an ancient one. One sniff and Sir John Falstaff in *Henry IV Part 1* could detect it. On being handed a glass of Sack, Falstaff, whom the Prince of Wales called 'fat-witted with drinking of old Sack', bellowed: 'You rogue, there's lime in this sack.' At the Boar's Head, Falstaff's tavern bar bill was inflated by the 5s 8d he paid for two gallons of Sack. Sack was a sweet comforting drink, quite alcoholic but smooth and easy to down, and such intemperance made Falstaff garrulous, and warmed 'the parts extreme'. He was often observed dishevelled, confused, and 'unbuttoned', snoring on park benches. The old man was unrepentant and said if he had a thousand sons, he would teach them one thing: 'to foreswear thin potations and to addict themselves to sack'. When asked by Bardolph in *The Merry Wives of Windsor* if he required eggs in his Sack, he boomed: 'I'll have no pullet-sperm in my brewage.' Sack is mentioned more than any other wine in Shakespeare's plays.

Poets less able than Shakespeare trotted out verse in support of Sack. One seventeenth-century versifier composed a twelve stanza paeon which included lines that could have been written by the marketing men at Williams & Humbert or Valdespino:

'It comforts aged persons,
And seemes their youth to render,
It warmes the braines, it fils the veynes,
And fresh bloud doth ingender.'

Sadly in these pathetically litigious days, they might have to prove it in court.

Apart from Shakespeare, Drake – variously a 'common pirate' or a 'great Christian hero' – did more for sherry than any other Englishman in history by destroying the Spanish fleet in 1587. Instead of piling his ships with gold, sleek Spanish horses and beautiful women, 'the most popular figure in England's naval annals' stole 2,900 pipes of sherry and sailed triumphantly for England. Sack posset was one of Sir Walter Raleigh's favourite pick-me-ups. It was made from Sack, ale and cream, sweetened and flavoured with nutmeg.

Robert Herrick was a pastoral poet and author of *Bid me Live*, *Gather Ye Rosebuds* and *Cherry Ripe*. Described as 'the most delightful of hedonist clerics', Herrick honed his writing skills in the Mermaid Tavern, a famous meeting place for writers in Cheapside, London. Ben Jonson, William Shakespeare, John Donne and Beaumont and Fletcher were regulars there, along with members of the Bread Street Club, who dazzled with their witty discourse and drank Canary wine. Herrick wrote:

'Welcome to Sack;
Thou mak'st me nimble
as the winged howers,
To dance and caper on the heads of flowers,
And ride the sunbeams.'

The *Collected Poems of Robert Herrick* were edited by another great sherry lover, George

Edward Bateman Saintsbury (1845–1933), author of *Notes in a Cellar Book*. Saintsbury was described by the socialist wine writer Raymond Postgate as 'an overfed hater of coalminers and conscientious objectors'.

Bristol, a bustling seaport since before the Norman Conquest, gave its name to Bristol Milk, the forerunner of the more famous Bristol Cream, imported direct from Jerez since 1634. It included Samuel Pepys among its devotees. In his diary for 13 June 1668, Pepys wrote: 'Good entertainment of strawberries, a whole venison-pastry, cold, and plenty of brave wine, and above all, Bristol Milk.' Pepys liked to pad down to his cellar at night in his sleeping bonnet to gloat. 'Claret, Canary, Sack, Tent and Malaga, all in my wine cellar together. I believe none of my friends now alive had his owne at one time.' Pepys was particularly fond of sherry and he even risked sailing to Cadiz in 1683 to collect a cask from a favourite *bodega*. He also liked mulled sherry and was not averse to stretching his sherry by tipping Mountain and strawberry juice into his barrels.

From the end of the seventeenth century, Sack gradually disappeared, to return rebranded as sherry. Sherry was advertised as early as 1731 and was mentioned in wine lists and City companies' accounts, but it was not until the late eighteenth century that it became well known. Its growing popularity owed something to medical men like Dr Wright, who wrote in 1795: 'Sherry, when pure, is one of the best of all our white wines.' Edward Spencer says: 'Sack, one of the most wholesome of wines, was first sold in England, in apothecaries' shops, as a medicine and was recommended by doctors for curing gout.' When Lord Chesterfield (1694–1773) was sent an inferior bottle as a panacea for his ailment, he dispatched a note by return: 'Sir, I have tried your sherry, and prefer the gout.'

The city of Bristol became synonymous with the wine. The cobbled streets were closed to carts and heavy horse-drawn drays in 1668 to ensure tranquility and protect the golden cargo nestling in butts and barrels below ground. To prevent vibration all goods were delivered on sledges or in light dog carts. Bewigged vicars and physicians tiptoed to their favourite taverns. London wasn't left out either. In the Customs records of 1697/98, two and a quarter pipes of sherry – a modest delivery – were checked into London from the East Indies, a warm journey believed by connoisseurs to improve the wine. The idea that warmth improved the wine persisted up to Victorian times. The healthy, sunburnt warmth found in sherry was hijacked by those merchants shipping insipid table wines. A mixture of Sack, honey, 'Liquorish, Long Almonds and various herbs boyled to a consumption' was used to disguise 'off' flavours in weak wines.

From 1704 to 1717 the Earl of Bristol was buying sherry in bulk for 4s a gallon. From 1720 to 1739, sherry was second only to Claret in his cellars. The Bristol Barber-Surgeons were equally enthusiastic, with sherry dominating and French wines nowhere to be found. Lord Mayor's Days in 1718, 1722 and 1724 were saturated with sticky fortified wines, including sherry and a tiny amount of Rhenish 'for the ladies'.

In a 'league table' of wines in the Christmas edition of the *Gentleman's Magazine* in December 1731, sherry was near the top and was still more expensive than the vastly improved and increasingly popular Claret. *Bell's Messenger* of 29 December 1799 gave the 'dealer's price' for a butt of sherry as £82, compared to Claret at £74. The overwhelming English preference was for wines from Spain and to a lesser extent Portugal, especially among the ordinary citizens; this was in spite of an increase in duty in 1782 to 4s a gallon on Spanish wines.

In 1790 John Hunter, His Majesty's consul for Seville and San Lucar, wrote to the Right Honourable Henry Dundas about purchasing sherry for the Navy. He required a 'wine of strong body and deep Colour; made from white grapes'. The cost to the Navy was to be 1s 8d per gallon. This would include the butt, a 'substantial cask made of American staves and bound with six iron hoops.' If the 'empties' were returned in good order a penny per cask was paid. In 1798 Harvey's, a Bristol leather importer, shipped eight butts of mature sherry. The quality was so good that by 1800 sales had leaped to 105 butts. Described in the firm's journal as 'Old' and 'Very Old', they were shipped from Cadiz to Guernsey before being brought into Bristol harbour.

Considered a serious 'intellectual and recreational' drink, sherry began to grace Oxford University dinners, which began with a ripe old Amontillado, 'giving forth a bouquet which was pure ambrosia'. Sherry 'was held in considerable esteem' at Oxford from the sixteenth century, when Thomas Warton was the Poet Laureate. William Turner (1775–1851), the landscape painter, loved sherry and on his deathbed he weakly accepted a last glass of sweet and silkily smooth old brown sherry.

After the eighteenth century War of the Spanish Succession, sherry shipments momentarily stalled. Orange trees were planted: marmalade rather than sherry was fashionable. The Catholic Church continued to be a good customer, with the Carthusians and Dominicans jealously guarding their full cellars of ancient sherry. Seville Cathedral, with its twenty-four altars and dozens of overworked priests saying 400 Masses each day, required an annual sherry tonnage of 2,500.

By the mid-1830s, imports of sherry climbed to 10,000 butts. By the late 1850s it was outselling port. By 1873, 68,000 barrels were annually rolled along the quays of Bristol, Liverpool and London. The British drank it with everything from soup and fish to roast pork and apple pie and cream, long before Professor Saintsbury's experimental sherry dinners. Paris cafés offered sherry cobblers. During Race Week at Goodwood in July 1845 the Duke of Richmond and his friends drank 176 bottles of sherry.

Jerez became a tourist destination. Richard Ford (1796–1858), author of *A Handbook for Travellers in Spain*, published in 1845, memorably described Jerez as a place with 'huge erections and a thousand *bodegas*'. He warned that pale old sherry was made by chemical means and at the expense of a delicate aroma.

Cyril Drummond writes: 'Sherry was laid down extensively in private cellars throughout the nineteenth century – pale, old browns and golden sherries. If at lunch the butler offered sherry, you drank it with seltzer. Old brown sherry was for after-lunch or midday consumption – and very good it was too.' In the cellars of Ashburnham House, old sweet sherry was a comfortable bedfellow to magnums of venerable Claret. Robert Surtees (1803–1864) did sherry sales no harm by making it a favourite of Jorricks, the 'lynx-eyed, fidgety, impatient glutton'.

Although drier wines were shipped from 1814, they never caught on and by 1815 there were signs the gentry were tiring of sherry. The Duke of Kent, in a two-day cellar clearance, sold his collection of London Particular and brown sherries. In June of the same year he disposed of all his Amontillado. In 1819 the ambassador from the Court of Spain, Duke de Frias, emptied his cellars in Portland Place, including his stock of fine sherries. The hedonistic Prince Regent bucked the trend and ordered a hogshead of sherry, stipulating a slightly drier version that was highly regarded, being 'light and delicate tasting'. William Younger quips: 'A luscious wine would perhaps have gone better with the décor of the Brighton Pavilion.'

When the novelist and essayist William Makepeace Thackeray (1811–1863) entertained friends at a public hanging, he served them chicken 'as hard as board' and sherry and soda which he said would 'clear their brains famously'. From the 1820s the English had developed such a taste for strong wines they demanded that ' weak, good pure wines' from France should be fortified with a shot of brandy before shipping to England.

In 1835 Prince Talleyrand, retiring French ambassador to the Court of St James, grimly descended to his cellar at Devonshire House to oversee its clearance. Macaulay noted: 'He sat deep in his chair making nasty noises in his throat whilst his ashy face looked out of the lank powdered hair that hung straight as a pound of candles to his padded shoulders.' The wines disposed of included 'delicious sweet Paxaretti', Montilla, and a dusty stack of old sherry.

When the Duke of Sussex died in 1843 his entire cellar was sold by order of his executors. It included thirty-eight cases of sherry, some of it 'very extraordinary, 100 years old from Her Majesty's Guildhall, given to his Royal Highness by Mr Lawson'. The cellars at Stowe House were auctioned by Christie and Manson on Tuesday 15 August 1848. Among the Cowslip and Canary, the Greek and Falernian, there were over 500 dozen bottles of sherry. They included Amontillado from a *solera* established in 1818. There were also wines from *soleras* from 1842, 1844 and 1845. A few country houses continued to drink sherry; on Christmas Eve in 1847, at Goodwood House decanters of Claret and Burgundy were eschewed and with the venison and roast beef sherry was drunk.

From the mid-nineteenth century, sherry was served cool – 'a civilised practice,' Golding says, 'that lasted into Edwardian times, when it was drunk slightly warmer than Champagne.' Fine wines were generally drunk at the end of the meal. Ale often accompanied the cheese course and Sauternes or Muscatel was offered with the desserts. William Younger says 'For practical purposes, "wine", to the majority of the English, meant port or sherry.' Mrs Beeton said in her book *Complete Etiquette for Gentlemen*, published in 1876: 'Sherry is the dinner wine.' In Spain sherry continued to be considered a quaint English invention among those who inhabited the finest houses in Seville. One glass, the *golpe medico*, was enough, at the end of the meal, to inhibit indigestion.

In 1970, when Michael Broadbent parted the curtain of cobwebs to delve into the Aladdin's cave belonging to the late Sir George Meyrick to inspect a stash of elderly Clarets, the first grubby bottle he held up to the naked bulb looked 'gone', until he opened it. A quick sniff indicated the wine was old sherry. There were rows of it with a sign that read '53 and a ½ dozen packed July 1885'. The normally diligent Broadbent was so excited he forgot to make a tasting note.

Queen Victoria, who despised sherry, must have been pleased when in 1901 Edward VII, on his accession, reduced his immense stock by 5,000 bottles. The *Daily*

Mail reported: 'Sherry is a neglected drink nowadays, quite fallen from the fashionable estate in which our forebears held it.' The *Sheffield Independent* said that sherry had become a matter of antiquarian demand, and attributed the ruin of the sherry market to the doctors. G.K. Chesterton, in a piece in the *New Age*, said the new King would have 'conferred a greater blessing upon his subjects if he had emptied his cellars into the Thames.' The *Newcastle Weekly Chronicle* said the royal sale 'will assuredly cause the yellow wine of Xres to fall even lower in public estimation'. Only a few old fogies, they said, would continue 'to take it with their fish'.

The *Northern Echo* questioned whether 'anyone living could remember by palate the difference between Madeira and sherry'. The *Gloucester Journal* regretted the demise of sherry, saying at one time only sherry was chiefly drunk at the festal board. Now, 'once a drug on the market', sherry was seldom offered. An article in *Queen* asked, 'Who is going to bid for the king's sherry? The *nouveaux riches* of course, whose guests will partake of it under the impression her late Majesty may have sipped it.' Among the bidders was Charles Walter Berry, determined to buy the last lot offered, Sandeman's Golden Sherry, Bin 7M, regardless of price. After a spirited battle, 'the ivory hammer fell at 570 shillings'. Berry purchased the wine 'to display loyalty to the innate virtues of sherry'. The sale was a great success, the Amontillado fetching the considerable sum of £18,457 15s, more than twice the purchase price of the old wine.

Saintsbury said 'medium sherries may be taken to the utmost satisfaction with food or without it, at any time of the day, except the first thing in the morning or the last thing at night.' He designed meals around sherry from old Amontillado with soup to Pedro Ximenez with dessert. F.H. Partington, who attempted a Saintsbury-style sherry dinner, said: 'As a curiosity it was interesting and indeed enjoyable, but rather a perversion of the true use of the wine.'

By the end of the 1890s merchants in Hamburg were doctoring cheap white wine and sending it to England to be sold as sherry. One observer commented: 'Sherry has lost most of its pride and much of its place in upper class English homes.' Sherry diminished in importance. The slump lasted until the 1920s. The advent of the 'sherry party', an attempt in the mid-1920s by Charles Williams, of the shippers Williams and Humbert, to arrest the slide in sales, did just that. Sherry was back in fashion and taken for its restorative properties. Desperate wine merchants advertised sherry as a wine to drink with food 'for those who find Claret too light and astringent'.

At the Berry Bros' dinners at No.3 St James's Street, London in the 1930s, regardless of how magnificent the wines were to follow, the first wine to the crease was invariably the house's choice Amontillado. Once it was sent in to bat before Dr Thanisch's 1921 Berncasteler Doctor, 1928 Chablis Fourchaume, 1904 Montrachet and still Champagne.

Regarding the keeping properties of sherry, in his *Great Vintage Wine Book* Michael Broadbent found the Harvey's Superior, bottled in 1937, 'too acidic and spirity'. Harry Waugh, another Harvey's man, who tasted his share of rare sherries, remembered a Palo Cortado he tasted in Jerez. It was from a Solera laid down in 1800. In the calm, non-hysterical terms of a wine trade elder, Waugh described it thus: 'Colour quite dark, bouquet revealed its age; no sugar at all, but quite rich. A wonderful complete wine.'

18

Champagne: Inimitable Fizz

For making the most famous and iconic wine in the world out of such unpromising raw materials as acidic wine produced on bleak northern terrain, one has to doff the top hat to the French. What a marketing coup! Champagne was a modest and cloudy *vin de pays* before Dom Perignon, the son of a judge's clerk, born on 5 January 1639, began as a gawky apprentice in the Abbey of Saint-Vannes at Verdun. He was a gauche nineteen-year-old with no history of landowning or winemaking in his genes. Within a decade he was managing Hautvillars, responsible for the production and the selling of the wine made there.

When he stoppered a bottle of murky pinkish dross with a wooden 'cork' tied with a length of olive oil-soaked hempen string and saw bubbles in the wine, he must have shouted with joy or at least clenched his fist silently. He had just invented Champagne and 'achieved one of the most worthwhile ambitions a man ever had – of manufacturing a bottle of truly sparkling champagne.' Perignon wasn't to know another Benedictine had beaten him to the bubbles. Working quietly in the freezing cellars of the Abbey of Saint-Hilaire in Limoux, an unknown monk poured his nervy local wine into a container of some kind and plugged it with a bit of Catalonian cork. Maybe Dom Perignon read of his brother monk's success in a beautifully scrolled book and copied him. History is littered with inventors whose ideas have been purloined. Limoux may be the first, but no one could claim the best of it is as good as good as half-decent Champagne. The same applies to Wagner's St Peray, Sparkling Saumur or Montlouis, both of which were and still are mildly popular in Britain, the real inventors according to one scribe of Champagne. What? I hear you utter. Well I am only going by something I read. Apparently, far from encouraging Champagne to bubble, Dom Perignon did his damnedest to curtail any suggestion of burping. But let us just sit back and buy that story for a moment. So, it was a staid seventeenth century Englishman called Christopher Merret, not a lonely and romantic monk called Dom Perignon who added sugar to sour old cloudy still wine and when he poured it a beverage with the effervescence of Fynnon's Salts erupted. In December 1662, when Perignon was still in short trousers, Merrett presented a paper, 'Some Observations Concerning the Ordering of Wines' to the Royal Society of London. The document was excavated from the dusty annals in 1998 by Tom Stevenson chronicler of fizz. Evidence suggests everyone who dabbled in wine Egyptian. Grrek and Roman were familiar with sparkling wine, because wine 'fermented under closed conditions' froths when poured.

1 Egyptian wall painting, *c.*1400 BC.

2 Ancient Greek wine jars at Knossos.

3 *Left: Perfect Happiness* by Boilly (*c.*1850).

4 *Below:* A medieval fresco from Florence.

5 Pol Roger advertisement.

6 Squire Mytton riding a bear during a drinking session.

7 Detail from *Lloyd's Coffee House* by George Woodward (1798).

8 *Right:* An advertisement for Julius Kayser & Co.

9 *Below:* Loading the boats with port barrels on the Douro (tiles from the railway station at Pinhão).

10 Perfecting a Champagne Cuvée.

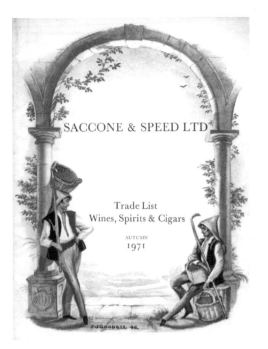

11 *Above left:* Cover of Saccone &
Speed's trade list.

12 *Above right:* Cover of the Army &
Navy Stores' list.

13 *Right:* Cover of Hay & Son's trade
list.

14 *Above:* Madeira vines.

15 *Left:* Bottles of Tokay.

16 Cover of Glendenning's
trade list.

17 Advertisement for Sauterne.

18 Moët & Chandon by Mucha.

This rare wine of excellent quality was obtained exclusively from a selection of the "Noble" grape "Bual" from the harvest of _1920_.

This wine was carefully matured in casks of the finest American oak for a period of _30_ years before being bottled in _1950_.

The seal of the Madeira Wine Company guarantees its quality and this document certifies its age and origin.

Sold and signed in Funchal, by the Madeira Wine Company S. A. on the _30 / 1 / 51_.

19 A Madeira certificate of authenticity.

20 Fifteenth-century woodcut of grapes being harvested.

Clockwise from above:

21 Mateus Rosé, an absolute icon. Its gentle fizz and soft sweetness triggered many a romance over the prawn cocktails in the barren '60s.

22 Alsace. I recall sitting in an orchard with a grower whose daughters, in native attire, fed us platefuls of bread smothered in goose dripping.

23 Once as risqué as a second Rum Baba, now a game '60s survivor.

24 Superbly crafted wines from a genial grower.

25 Legends once, they now make wine to lubricate tourists.

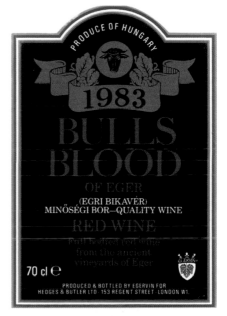

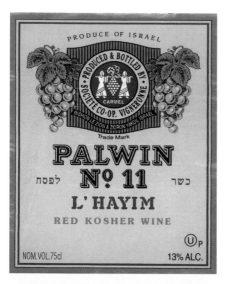

Anti-clockwise from above:

26 China has a long history of wine making (since 130 BC). This winery was established by Pernod Ricard in 1987. No need for Petrus to start quaking in its boots.

27 Sweet and bland but sure to kick-start the Bar Mitzvah. Moving away from the sweet and sleep-inducing to the French varietals, with mixed results.

28 Quality cabernet from a top producer. In spite of a glut the best Californians are elusive and dear.

29 Mateus Rosé's white sister. A fizzy, great thirst quencher.

30 Notable Napa Valley grower.

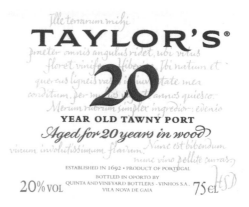

Clockwise from above:

31 Another bites the dust. The demise of the fragrant wine is sad, but predictable in an age of New World rocket-fuelled blockbusters.

32 Zinfadel is a modest grape but the great growers do magical stuff with it. Blind taste a twenty year from a top producer.

33 An Iconic brand with a link to Old Rhenish. An arthritic nun at eighty-four but still strutting her stuff.

34 Pioneering son of an established grower. After a sensational start in the 1970s, Torres has not attained Olympus.

35 Pommard with Volnay, Beaune and Nuits were once bottled and, blended in England, they were big, dark and fruity. Some even contained Pinot. Surviving bottles can be delicious.

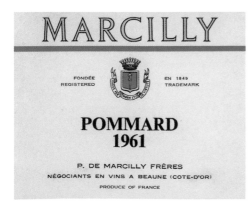

Anti-clockwise from above:
36 The Australians have cracked Pinot too. Only Riesling eludes them.

37 In the relaxed 1960s, this was the wine for steak, prawn cocktail and rainbow trout studded with almonds and served with thick chips.

38 The quietest, most modest and consistently best value red wine for the past fifty years.

39 Constantia, a noble name, was a famous eighteenth-century forerunner of great Cape Muscadels.

40 Who wants a thin acidic grape these days? Too much poor stuff from Burgundy but the finest are worth the mortgage required.

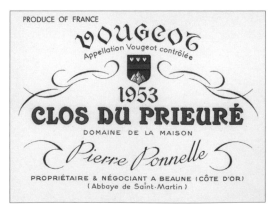

The bubbles were underpowered and were never pinned down to their source. But who knows? They might have been. Sufficed to say the world, a few flat earthers excepted, believe Dom Perignon invented Champagne.

The monk's full blooded sparkler made him the most sought-after wine maker of his day. While ordinary Champagne sold for 200 livres a barrel in 1694, the finest *cuvée* made by Dom Perignon at the Abbey of Hautvillers sold for 1,000 livres the cask. Aristocrats, idle seekers after the latest craze, hysterically embraced the fizzy wine from the start. It was 'so vivacious, darling', so unique, so expensive. On embossed, hand-made paper they dipped their flamingo quills into golden inkwells and wrote to 'Father Perignon', congratulating him on the magnificence of his wine. The modest monk became so closely associated with Champagne that many people thought Perignon was the name of a vineyard from which the finest wine came.

Patrick Forbes, author of the key book on the subject, says: 'By perfecting the grape growing, the winemaking and the art of judicious blending, Dom Perignon turned a fundamental weakness in the wine into a towering strength.' While some historians believe the original Champagne was made entirely from black grapes and that white grapes were introduced as late as the eighteenth century, a rare pamphlet written on vellum by Brother Pierre, Perignon's successor, confirms that Fromantins, Mauribards and Genests were used in Champagne-making in Dom Perignon's time to make a *blanc de blanc*. The person who decided to add wood chips to the infant wine to give it a spurious complexity is unknown. It was a practice not unknown at the time. In fact a wine called *vin de coipeau* was made this way. It was described as a 'new wine quickly made fit to be drunke by Beechen chips first boyled then dryed, and afterwards put into the vessell'.

Perignon's invention was at first dismissed by brooding growers, wine makers and customers. Bertin de Rocheret, an Epernay wine maker, voiced his unease in a letter to a friend. He didn't mince his words, calling the new sparkling wine 'that abomination', and implied that the gimmicky carbon dioxide in the wine had effectively eliminated the essential influence of the individual vineyard, the tang of the soul, the slant of the sun and the cant of the hill, the scent and flavour of the grapes in their own unique microclimate. 'Let beer, chocolate or cream fizz', de Rocheret thundered – just leave Champagne alone. But sparkling Champagne was soon firmly entrenched. It was gay, playful, the first great ice-breaker and party wine. Dealers and middlemen saw an opportunity and they seized it.

Gay young chauvinists, 'who sought refinement in everything' and who adored their own pompadoured company, adopted the turbid, slightly fizzy infant Champagne as their own. Over a dinner of the tenderest Normandy veal, the most succulent partridges that wandered the edges of the Auvergne forests and the plumpest rabbits that grazed the gentle slopes of the Roche-sur-Yon, the young gentlemen toasted each other in splendid high-ceilinged châteaux mirrored in the lakes that lapped their sturdy walls. The well-bred young idlers drank only the finest wines from the sunniest vineyards of Ay, Hautvillers and Avenay. Such was their constant extolling of the virtues of the wines of these prized slopes that three of the young men became known as the Trois Côteaux. Their dashing followers became known as the Ordre des Côteaux.

In 1662, one of the Ordre, the Marquis de Saint-Evremond, after committing some unknown misdemeanour, was banished to England, where he immediately began to promote 'the delights of Champagne wine'. Saint-Evremond's blue-blooded contacts included the likes of Charles II, and a nation obsessed with anything French, elegant and sophisticated ensured that Champagne was talked about in the right circles. The upwardly mobile aristocrats sycophantically followed the exciting new fashion. Soon Restoration writers could not lift a quill without mentioning flimsily clad beauties saucily dipping red nailed fingers or toes into Champagne. Wealthy roués were advised to top up their mistresses with Champaign (*sic*) because it achieved the desired result more efficiently than any amount of 'paint and love potions'. Young men acted idiotically under its influence. Princess Charlotte Elizabeth of Bavaria encouraged her pampered offspring to drink Champagne. 'When my son gets drunk', she boasted, 'it is not with strong drinks or spirituous liquors, but the pure wine of Champagne. The Count de Saillans 'one of the most accomplished horsemen of his day', was emboldened to challenge anyone to beat his horse's time from the gate of Versailles to the Hotel de Invalides. Bets were waged. The horses, like his owner, trained on Champagne and biscuits. On 9 May 1725, with a massive crowd shoving and cheering from all sides, the hung-over horse, reared ala the Lone Ranger and galloped off towards the distant front door of the Invalides. But the caped rider was not the quivering Count who had chickened out, but his loyal valet who came in two and a half minutes behind time. The count lost face and his Champagne sponsor, his horse went back to oats and water and his jockey returned to valeting.

The *Connoisseur* magazine of 6 June 1754 reported one overwrought 'blood' who drank Champagne from a lady's slipper. The besotted buck had a chef turn the girl's shoes into lunch. A ragout was made from the upper part; the sole was minced. Slices of the wooden heel were fried in batter and placed artistically in a garnish around the dish. Cheered on by his friends, the young man ate the lot. What the subject of this gallant act thought is not recorded.

Madamoiselle de Navarre, whose father owned several vineyards in the Champagne country in the eighteenth century, was so terrified of thunder and lightning she hid in her father's celler. 'Among fifty thousand bottles', he sighed, 'it was difficult for her not to lose her head.' Gluck, the composer of Orpheus and Iphegenia when his mind was in a ferment of creativity satin a flowery meadow with a magnum of Champagne. By the time it was emptied 'the air he was in search of was discovered and written down.'

The magic of fermentation was still misunderstood in the eighteenth century with growers compensating for poor weak, acidic must by shovelling in sugar and yeast. The results were catastrophic, witness this extract from the personal notes of a grower in 1770 who watched his bottles exploding, one shattered bottle setting off the next like firecrackers. 'In 1746' he recorded, 'I bottled 6000 bottles of very liquoreux wine; I had only 120 bottles of it left. In 1747 with less liqueur the breakages amounted to only one third. One producer announced a breakage of forty-five per cent in 1862. By reducing the sugar and yeast, in combination with better harvests made from clean, fully ripened grapes, and stouter bottles, damage was confined to a few minor explosions.

It was hardly surprising that Champagne became the most expensive wine in England. It was, said André Simon, 'a luxury in which one could not indulge without a long purse. It trapped pretty women like butterflies.' Simon should know. According to Pamela Vandyke Price he was 'delicately flirtatious with women, basking in their affectionate attention. Miaow! William Thackeray in *Barmecide Banquets* likened a stingy pourer of Champagne to the kind of phoney who wears 'screw-on spurs to his boots to make believe that he kept a horse'. He was nothing but 'a puny coward shivering on the brink of hospitality, without having the bottle to 'plunge into the generous stream!'

Michael Broadbent wrote 'The wine which fascinated me, because it is so rarely seen, was the old Sillery. It was highly desirable if a strange wine. It is hard to imagine what the 1874, the most famous and highest priced of all vintages, was like in its prime. At roughly a century old it was still a palish, straw colour, the bouquet strange, nutty – not unlike *vin de paille* from the Jura, and dry on the palate to the point of austerity.' Sillery, once the most famous of all Champagnes, took its name from a *catégorie hors-classe* village in the Mountain of Reims, a hilly strip of forest about 20km by 10km. Forbes writes. 'It's as if you are on the bridge of a ship, ploughing through a billowing brilliant sea.' Sillery, blended with the wine of adjacent Verzenay, was an attractive wine with the pink juice of the Pinot 'giving it the partridge-eye colour'. It was light, elegant – sharp, even. Just the thing after a bellyful of port and brown Bastard. Roger Brulart, fourth Marquis de Sillery, began exporting his deep pink wines to England. On 25 March 1667 the fifth Earl of Bedford took delivery of £12 10s-worth.

Through reputation and the right connections, Sillery found its way into many an illustrious cellar. It was not considered unseemly then for growers to write to friends in England asking them to introduce their wines to wealthy landowners and aristocrats. One Champagne grower wrote from Epernay to a client in England. In the letter, dated 4 March 1771, he pleaded: 'I beg of you to show this wine to as many friends as you can. First of all to Lord Hitchenbrooke, who has asked for it – I feel sure that Lord Sandwich, his father, will also appreciate it – to Lord Halifax, who has asked for it – and please let Mr de Rickaby taste it.' The grower was not above a little bribery. 'My wife,' he wrote, 'sends a cask of pears to Lady Egerton, and I am sending a hamper of "vin gris" to her husband,' he wrote.

Sillery reached its apogee under the waspish Maréchale d'Estrées, the first of many shrewd ladies to make an impact on Champagne. Nobody loved her but she refused to let that get in the way of her total dedication to improving the family wines and extending their fame. Three times a year she enriched the soil by making her peasants carry tons of black cinders down from the Mountain of Reims to spread on her vineyard. The Maréchale spent hours in the cold cellars supervising the making. She blended and blended until she found the secret. By mixing the wines of the Pinot Noir and the fragrant Fromenteau, an early version of Gewurztraminer, she discovered the superiority. The full-bodied Pinot leavened and perfumed by the spicy Fromenteau was a winning combination, and one wonders why it wasn't continued. Perhaps the blend explains Sillery's great success in England. Béquillet recorded in 1770 that it 'earmarks them for the king's mouth.' By 1766 Sillery Champagne was increasingly seen on English lists. In 1771 a consignment of 400 bottles, 'the finest ever', of Marquis de Paisieux Sillery fetched 4s 6d a bottle. Sillery was the 'in drink' in fashionable London. In 1775, a decade before her death, the indefatigable Maréchale had 61,650 bottles of Sillery in her cellars.

Then the Revolution came. A raggedy mob took revenge for past slights and insults. They gathered in cafés and on corners in Sillery and marched up the gravelled drive to the château, past the beautifully planted gardens, the stone lions and the quiet places. Shouting and cheering, armed with any sharp implement they could find, they attacked the château as if it were some great monster. Once inside and delirious at the prospect 'of settling accounts with the legatees of the detested old Maréchale', they tore down the curtains, smashed windows and vases and even crow-barred the floor and panelling because they featured the Maréchale's despised coat of arms. The Marquis was led away and ignominiously decapitated.

In 1779 Christie's announced a sale of Marquis de Almadovar red Sillery Champagne. Hysteria mounted, fingers prodded the air, heads bobbed and nodded, *The Times* was discreetly waved until the gavel fell at 91s a case, twice the price of a good Claret. By 1790 'almost everywhere', André Simon wrote, the English were asking for 'wine so vinous and strong' that nothing but Sillery would satisfy them. In 1794 a report of an auction revealed that while 'White Sillery' was selling at 75s a case, Châteaux Margaux and Lafite were struggling to reached 40s. When the Duke of Roxburghe put his cellar up for auction at Christie's in 1812 a dry Sillery described as 'Thackeray's Champagne' sold for 84s a dozen.

The first vintage Champagne sold by Christie's was Moët's 1815 Sillery, the famous Waterloo vintage. In 1829 Christie's knocked down a parcel of Moët's Sillery at 100s a dozen. Lafite went for 90s a case. The price gap was narrowing. Soon the famous Clarets would outstrip all but the rarest and most optimistically priced Champagnes.

The Great War churned up the vineyards and reduced the château to rubble. The vineyards recovered and they still yield wine but it is for blending. A name once famous is forgotten. As Forbes says: 'A lovely name, which once seemed immortal, is now hardly known even to wine lovers. If fate had been kinder, the Marquesses of Sillery would nowadays be not only the best-known champagne makers of all, but the most celebrated wine makers in the world, for none of the Champagne firms have a past in wine so ancient or so glittering as theirs would have been.'

In 1848, Burnes, a London wine merchant, tasted a glass of Perrier-Jouet 1846 and spat it out. He suggested the makers should reduce the dosage. The suggestion was madness. Burnes was persistent. A dry Champagne could be drunk as an aperitif, he suggested, even right through a meal. At the time, knowing the vulgar Russian tsars had the sweetest tooth in the world, the French sent them poor Champagne packed with up to 330g of sugar per litre. Perrier-Jouet sent Burnes a consignment of unsweetened Champagne. He launched it at a dinner given for Army officers whose palates were bound to be sufficiently sophisticated to savour the refreshing tang, the sour elegance. They rejected the dry wine. Burnes returned the unopened wines to Perrier-Jouet, who were incandescent. Burns should have listened to Henderson, a nineteenth century wine buff who said any man who says he really likes dry Champagne is simply lying. Henderson's own preference was Sillery 'which has always been in much request in England, probably on account of its superior strength and durable quality.' Having a penchant for syrupy wines he liked Ay even more. It was, he wrote, 'an exquisite liquor, lighter and sweeter than Sillery, and accompanied by a delicate flavour and aroma somewhat analogous to that of the pineapple'.

Broadbent tasted several large format bottles of 1857 Sillery with waxed corks from Lord Rosebery's cellars in 1967 and ten years later. His similar notes on this 'great curiosity' recall pale amber, nuts, smoke, old stables and oilcloth, assertive, yet delicate flavour, excellent acidity, slightly yeasty finish. Another opportunity presented itself in 1969. The vintage was 'believed to be 1870'. Broadbent's notes again invoke stables and nuts but this wine was not just still breathing, but thumping its chest like King Kong. Bone dry, fresh, firm and fine flavour 'it made a good aperitif'. A Sillery from 1874, another very fine year for Champagne, was tasted at Christie's in 1967. It was a Sillery too far. 'Cloudy, gnarled, twisted and beery' the poor old thing was dead on its feet. But the Sillery reputation kept the name alive and while the quality was still excellent in Edwardian times more Sillery was sold than could possibly be genuine. Thackeray had his creations guzzling endlessly but the taste for Sillery would soon become *passé*.

By the 1860 the English market was crowded with Champagnes labelled Dry or Very Dry. Ayala had their wine adopted by the Prince of Wales. Soon Bollinger, Clicquot and Pommery followed with dry wines. The enormous 1874, a creamy, five star wine converted the as yet unconverted. Char'es Walter Berry hailed it 'The most renowned vintage of the period. Excellent wines, fruity, full colour'. But it was the now almost forgotten Perrier–Jouet that garnered most of the rave write-ups. In a Christie's sale in 1887, Perrier–Jouet 1874 fetched an unbelievable 780s for a dozen magnums. A slough of poor vintages that followed the brilliant 1784 helped hike up the price.

Louis Roederer was founded in Reims by a father and son named Dubois in 1776. Louis Roederer inherited the company in 1833. By 1868 annual sales topped 2.5 million bottles. The Russians quickly developed a passion for Champagne which Talleyrand called 'le civilisateur par excellence'. Millions of bottles 'specially fortified to a pitch of strength and sweetness'. Cliquot were among the first Champagne houses to battle through the snow to flog their wares to vulgar Russians when drinking Champagne were wont to fling open their windows in order that 'the popping of the corks may announce the fact to their neighbours'. Vizatelly dryly commented that if Peter the Great 'only preferred Campagne to brandy Russia might have been Europeanised, [civilised] long ago'. It was a Russian who was responsible or the invention of Cristal, the first snob's Champagne. The Cuvee de Prestige beloved of footballers, luvvies and gangsta rappers. It was Tsar Alexander II who in 1876 demanded a special, dry, Chardonnay dominated wine from Louis Roederer, 'who's syrupy product ordinary Russians hitherto regarded as the beau ideal'. It is such a beautiful golden colour, the Csar trilled 'My friends must see it in the bottle. Do away with gloomy green. I want it see-through, puntless and with a gold label. Fake will do if you cannot supply the real thing'. Called Cristal Brut, the first 'Cuvee de Prestige' is a delicious and it is still consumed by oligarchs on their way to prison.

Moet et Chandon also have reason to remember the Russian's unquenchable thirt for bubbly. In 1814 a phalanx of 'self invited guests arrived in Reims. They were accompanied by equally playful Prussians. Both posessed 'unlimited powers of consumption', and 'insuperable objections' to paying for what they had consumed. After an hour or two of thirst-provoking arson, rape and pillage the invaders were ready for a glass or two of chilled fizz. They assembled all the wine they could and disposed of it in a manner' recalling the Bacchic exploits of Gargantua and Pantagruel'. The Mayor, Jean Remi Moet was so worried lest the party got out of hand and the Russians reduced the place to ashes just for fun, flung open the family firm's cellars doors and told them to help themselves. They did and the town was saved at least until the Prussians returned, twice, to finish the job.

Dry Champagne had definitely arrived. Patrick Forbes writes: 'It is not an exaggeration to state that dry Champagne is a British invention. Champagne-makers acknowledge the fact with gratitude, knowing that the innovation was largely responsible for the huge sales which Champagne has enjoyed in England ever since.'

Gladstone's reduction of duty on French wine in 1861 came at the right time for Champagne. By the 'Naughty Nineties', 9.5 million bottles were sold each year in Britain. Swinging young things with more money than grey matter guzzled it shamelessly. Champagne was the alcopop of its day. When the king went shooting he had a boy carrying a basket of chilled bottles. When he wanted a drink, his Highness yelled 'Boy!' In fashionable haunts, 'Boy' became the shorthand for Champagne. Sarah Bernhardt (1845–1923), the famous Jewish actress, who was one of fourteen children and from a somewhat deprived background, loved nothing better when she became an international star than to loll in a sudsy bath filled with Champagne. Perrier-Jouet was her bath water of choice.

Still Champagne outsold sparkling up to the early nineteenth century. Sir Walter Scott, (1771-1832), the Scottish novelist, historian and poet, who published a biography of Napoleon in 1827, asked Lord Bathurst and Sir Hudson Lowe to explain why the tiny, captive Frenchman was restricted to a mere bottle of fizz a day, thus depriving him of 'even the solace of intoxication'. But Scott, who was once a serious imbiber of Champagne, grew sick of London lionising and went back to his roots. 'I wish for a sheep's head and a whisky toddy against all the French cookery and Champaign in the world'.

A century later once-glittering names like Sillery and Ay had all but vanished. The Marquis de Sillery played a part in the decline. Observing how liberally Paris society were pouring sparkling Champagne at their outrageous parties, the Marquis used his influence to supply a fizzy Sillery at one of the fashionable Duc de Verdome's soirées. Patrick Forbes relates: 'Twelve luscious girls, scantily dressed as Bacchantes, each carrying a basket of flowers on her arm, suddenly made an appearance.' Men twiddled their moustaches in anticipation and exchanged expectant glances. 'At a signal from the Marquis de Sillery they plunged their hands into the baskets and presented each guest with a pear shaped bottle of Champagne, ten inches high, stamped with the Sillery arms and secured with sealing wax.' One old toper, the plump, be-ringed Abbé de Chaulieu, eyelashes aflicker, simpered, 'Hardly did it appear than from my mouth it passed into my heart.'

It is hard for us to gauge how good the famous still wines of Sillery, Aye and Verzenay were. Few contempory tasting notes survive. Broadbent's notes provide faded glimpses. 'Sweet Champagne d'Aye' from Lord Roxburghe's cellar was sold at Christie's in 1812 for 84s a case, an excellent price. The wine would probably have been in good condition. A Vin d'Aye from the moderate 1889 vintage, from Lord Rosebery's cellar, was tasted in 1967. The verdict was surprisingly upbeat. 'Yellow-amber, fair sparkle, honey bouquet, not showing age, dry, fullish, straightforward, remarkably sound and attractive. But not great.'

The rediscovery of the cork helped create the delicious drink we enjoy today. Many bottles retain their freshness after fifty years or more. In a tasting of 150 Champagnes held in Stockholm to find the best wines of the past 100 years, the winners were both grey hairs from the fine 1959 vintage. The tiny, gentlemanly firm of Billecart-Salmon, which owns no vineyards but teases much-loved neighbouring growers into leaving their grapes to ripen right up to the wire and risk devastating rain, won the main category of 'Champagne of the Millennium' with its Cuvée Nicolas François 1959. The *blanc de blanc* of the Millennium section was snaffled up by Pol Roger from the same vintage. Broadbent says: 'Top-quality Champagne of a big vintage needs time in bottle. It is such a waste to drink it too young before it has matured and developed its true character.' Blind tastings are not new a course They are too good a way for producers to humiliate their rivals, as long as the invited 'experts' make the 'right' decision. Over a century ago in London Pol Roger spanked several rivals in a blind tasting. The losers were Perrier-Jouet whose 'First Quality wine was classed below 'a cheaper wine of their neighbours, Messrs Pol Roger & Co. and very considerably below the Extra Sec of Messrs Perinet et fils, and inferior even to a wine of De Venoge's the great Epernay manufacturer of common-class Champagne'. Oops!

Krug 'wooed' the British market in the nineteenth century and sold its wine under some strange, unthinkable labels, like 'Extra Dry for Invalids' and 'Bonanza'. For export they labelled their wine First Quality and Second Quality. They did BOBs – buyer's own brands – as many a good but unheralded Champagne firm does for supermarkets and small independent wine shippers today. They even labelled their wine 'Specially selected for Murray and Co., Lucknow, India', 'A Scott and Co. Rangoon' and 'Joseph Travers and Co. Singapore and Penang.' By the mid-nineteenth century Krug also provided almost sickly sweet Champagne for the unsophisticated Russian market. The new English Champagne drinker was no more attuned to dry wines, and Krug loaded their wines with 15 per cent dosage for the British market, by now turning away from still Champagne and tuning in to sparkling and sexing it up with nips of brandy. By 1865 the British were sick of very sweet fizz, except for a few merchants like Barwells who sold sweet Champagne in their Norwich branch and continued to do so until well into the twentieth century. Krug and other houses reduced the dosage to around 5 per cent, except for the incorrigible Russians who demanded at least 10 per cent. When Gladstone famously pruned the tax payable on French wines in a vain attempt to wean the British worker off gin, Champagne sales soared – which suited Gladstone who, far from being a fine Claret fanatic, drank a quart of Champagne every day. John Arlott writes: 'So long as England remained prosperous, Champagne in general and the house of Krug in particular, also prospered. English wine merchants, a type virtually unknown in wine-producing countries, scoured the world, but especially France, Portugal, Germany and Spain for their wares.' Competition was keen, so prices had to be fair.

Krug was never the cheapest and when Joseph Krug, a shrewd businessman, died after blending the 1865, a wonderful year, under new management Krug began to reposition themselves in the Champagne market. His creed was simple. 'It is not possible to make a good wine except from good elements – wines from good growths,' he wrote. Krug's BOB days were well and truly over, but not a connection with the less dandified members of the Champagne-sipping fraternity. After the popular success Moët et Chandon enjoyed with Charles Leybourne, 'Champagne Charlie', whose theme song went 'Moët and Chandon's the wine for me', Krug hit upon the idea of labelling a *cuvée* 'North End' to try to cash in on Preston's winning of the league and cup double in 1888/89 without losing a match in either event. It was a remarkable feat, equalled only by Krug imagining such a gimmick would do their image any good, even though Krug at 3 guineas a case was cheaper than the quality market leaders Ruinart and Perrier Jouet at £3 12s a dozen, Mumm and Piper at £3 8s and Bollinger at £3 5s. M. Ernest lrroy who founded his firm in 1820, and whose wines were prepared with 'scrupulous care and a rare intelligence', and were laid down by such important clubs as White's, Arthurs and the old Carlton, are less feverishly sought after. How fortunes change, particularly with regard to Champagne.

The French, to their credit, find it easy to accept that a man or woman can be a socialist and a multi-millionaire. Count Robert-Jean de Vogue, who was both, was at one time head of Moët et Chandon. De Vogue greeted the Russian leader Khrushchev the same way Jean-Rémy Moët did Tsar Alexander II in 1815. He welcomed the Communist leader with 'the same magnificent salvo' of a hundred magnums of vintage Moët. A rose tinted, if politically dodgy Champagne harvest is painted by Vizetelly 'At vintage-time everywhere is bustle and excitement in these (normally) extraordinarily quite little villages nestling amidst vine clad hollows... there is a perpetual rattling and bumping of wheels over the roughly paved streets.

The majority of the inhabitants are afoot: the feeble feminine half, (in neat white caps or coalcuttle straw bonnets) with baskets on arm, thread their way through the rows of vines, planted halfway up the mountain, and all aglow with their autumnal glories of green and purple, crimson and yellow; while the sturdy masculine portion (in blue blouses or stripped to their shirt sleeves) are mostly passing to and fro between the press-houses and the wine shops.

Sir Winston Churchill's thirst for Champagne is well chronicled. He allegedly drank a bottle of Pol Roger a day in his later years. He was a walking advertising hoarding for the marque, one glass of which imparted a feeling of exhilaration. With 'the nerves braced, the imagination stirred, the wits more nimble', he wrote, painted and still found time to save the world. Britain hasn't lost its taste for Champagne; on the contrary, sales have rocketed, with 35 million bottles sold in 2003, an increase of 51 per cent since 1998, confirming Britain's status as the biggest drinkers of Champagne apart from the French, who pop and spray an indecent 175 million bottles annually. 'The lively pop of the cork is less esteemed in England than in certain circles in France, where many host would be sadly disappointed if the wine they put before their guests did not go off with a loud bang, causing the ladies to scream and the gentlemen to laugh.'

In an attempt to cash in on the sweet attraction of Sauternes, Messrs Normandin operating out of a town near Anguleme, recruited sparkling wine specialist from Epernay to convert Colombard grapes, which he thought were Semillon, into fizzy Sauternes. The wine was carefully made, going through 'the course similar to that pursued with regard to Champagne'. To preserve 'the delicate flavour the finest old Sauternes was administered with the most improved modern appliance, constructed of silver, and provided with crystal taps'. The oddball wine was entered at the Concours Regional d'Anguleme in 1877 and after passing all tests to prove it was not harmful to old ladies was awarded the Gold Medal in the Group of Alimentary Products. Encouraged by Normandin's success, Lermat-Robert and Co., a Bordeaux company launched their own Sparkling Barsac which they exhibited at the Paris Exhibition in 1878. Vizetelly refers to a sparkling version and 'a diabolical (and highly questionable) imitation' made not from New Jersey peaches, or Vermont apples but from a product of the oil-wells of Pennsylvania, the first, and last, 'petroleum Champagne'.

Mercifully neither product survives. Sparkling Burgundy, both white and red does. A magnum of a vintage white from Parigot and Richard of Savigny-Les-Beaune enjoyably lubricated a picnic during an outdoor production of Romeo and Juliet on the lawns of Kentchurch Court in Herefordshire in the summer of 2005.

Reserved old gentlemen like Professor Saintsbury used to rage about the appropriate time to pour Champagne. Not any more. Now that is as cheap as water and everyone from Essex Man and his glittery missus to tired schoolboys bathe in an shave in it, Champagne is no longer 'a treat'. It is a pick-you-up, and because of its carefully nurtured reputation one feels damn good just sipping a glass or two. 'Give Champagne,' droned the dyspeptic Mr Walker of 'The Original', 'at the beginning of dinner, as its exhilarating qualities serve to start the guests, after which they will seldom flag. When the Champagne goes right, nothing can go wrong.' Charles Dickens said Champagne 'takes its fitting rank and position among feathers, gauzes, lace, embroidery, ribbons, white-satin shoes and eau-de-Cologne for it is simply one of the elegant extras of life'. Vizetelly sums it up, 'The advantageous effect of sparkling wine at an ordinary British dinner-party, composed as it frequently is of people brought indiscriminately together in accordance with the exigencies of the hostess's visiting list, cannot be gainsaid. The hostess brightens, the host coruscates. The young lady on your right (who was previously preoccupied with her fan) suddenly develops into a charming girl, with a becoming appreciation of your pet topics and an astounding aptness for repartee.'

Krug's Clos du Mesnil is comfortably the most expensive Champagne made. Rarely seen and only released from its gilded cage after a dozen years of careful titivation, it starts with earnest selection of Chardonnay grown in an ancient walled four and a half vineyard in Le Mesnil-sur-Oger. Fermentation is in oak barrels. Long cellaring allows the wine to develop great flavour and length. The latest release is from a wet and windy 1992. Only 1,000 cases were made. It sells at £325 a bottle and there is no shortage of buyers. What is it best with? 'Oily, rich and fatty foods,' suggests Rémy Krug, 'like fish and chips, Maroilles cheese, which smells of sweaty socks – anything as long as you drink it.'

There is a growing fashion of sucking Champagne through a straw. At film premières and opening nights, quarter-bottles are doled out with straws. The idea is an old one. Chaucer had the Manciple berating the plastered Cook for imbibing through a straw. Sucking Champagne through a straw apparently 'allows air to mix with alcohol in the nasal cavity, and thus speeds the absorption of alcohol into the body.'

Perhaps the final word on this frothy subject should go to the Revd Dr Optimian on the marriage of his friend's niece. 'Let all the attendants stand by, each with a fresh bottle. Let all the corks be discharged simultaneously, and we will receive it as a peal of Baccic ordnance, in honour of the Power of Joyful Event.' There are many imitators, the same grapes, production, fancy bottles, and sometimes fancy prices – even England makes one – but there is only one Champagne.

19

Sweet Malaga

Nestling as we are in a cosy world of interesting wines from every grape and culture, sipping and savouring everything from mushroomy sherries to tangy bubblies, tart Sauvignons, chocolate-coated Merlots, nitro-glyceric Shirazes and genuflectable Clarets, it is hard for us to believe that our rude forefathers – and they were rude in every sense of the word – drank practically nothing but black treacly Mountain, as sweet as straight molasses, with cheese, shank of wild boar and upside-down puddings. 'Early in the sixteenth century,' says Warner Allen, 'the name sack was later extended to cover wines exported from other regions – the Canaries, Malaga and so on'.

The gorsely hills above the southern Spanish town of Malaga were first planted around 600 BC by the Greeks. It would be surprising if the Greeks did not use their own version of the Malvasia, a grape which Jancis Robinson describes as 'strongly scented with an almost musky perfume', and which Lorenzo de Medici, in his book *Symposium*, published in 1466, regarded as a panacea for all the ills of mankind. Once picked, the grapes lay in the sun in heaps to shrivel and leak. The teetotal Moors, for obvious reasons, called the sweet yellow wine 'syrup'. Once known for its fat, slug-like raisins, which were used in cooking, the first mention of a wine called Mountain occurs in the writings of George Byng, Lord Torrington (1663–1733), who got off his horse while clip-clopping around the English shires to picnic on 'bread, cheese and mountain wine'. A comfortingly sweet lubrication, Mountain soon attracted the attention of poets, playwrights and novelists, including Henry Fielding (1707–1754), who alludes to it in his novels.

Mountain became a cockle-warming treat on cold English nights with the snow falling and a gale lifting the thatch, and became immensely important to the Spanish Exchequer. By 1825 demand for Malaga was so strong every available scrap of scrub was removed to plant more vines. English ships were among the queue waiting to load up with barrels of the thick glyceric product. Other contributing grapes were the Garnache (or Grenache), the Pedro Ximenez and Moscatel de Alejandria. Professor George Saintsbury was among those who waxed enthusiastically about a Pedro Ximenez wine that was 'very old in 1860 and not a wine for babies'.

Dr Shaw, 'a stalwart champion of the grape', reported in 1724 that 'Mountain, excellent in the colick, also banishes fever, gout and all sorts of ailments.' Between 1731 and 1735 Mountain was advertised in the *Gentleman's Magazine* at up to '£30 per tun for old and £24 per tun for new.' At the time port was the most expensive wine imported, at up to £72 per tun. In the period 1700 to 1739, John Hervey, first

Earl of Bristol, who had one of the finest cellars in the country, took delivery of 'White and Red Mountain'. The accounts of the Barber-Surgeons of Bristol show that £56 7s 8d was spent on Mountain, compared to a mere £2 8s on Claret. They purchased Mountain every year from 1722 to 1726 at between 6s 8d and 7s a gallon. On the Lord Mayor's Day in 1724, '3 gallons of old Mountain' were reserved for 'the Barger going to Westminster'.

In a newspaper advertisement in 1752, James Royston, wine merchant of the Iron Gates near St Mary Axe in London, was offering 'Mountain wines dry and sweet ready for drinking at three years', at 5s 6d a gallon. Ten- to fifteen-year-old wines were 6s 8d a gallon, 'for ready money only'. In the Vauxhall Gardens Wine List of 1762, Mountain was sold for 2s 6d a bottle – the same price as 'Rhenish with sugar' and 6d dearer than port. In 1786, by the Act of 26 Geo. III, the duty on Spanish wine was reduced. This gave sales a smart kick upwards.

André Simon wrote: 'Mountain was more popular in England during the greater part of the eighteenth century than sack or sherry, due to the excellent quality of the wines and a very light export duty.' The English Chancellor could not leave well enough alone and a punitive piling of duty onto Spanish wines caused a reversal in the graph, with sales collapsing from 48,170 tuns in 1729 to a paltry 5,825 tuns by 1748. Another tweak saw sales rise again by 1786, but never again would they climb to their former peak. Fiddling with duty had all but killed off Mountain. There were few takers for the barrels of Mountain offered by Priddy's Foreign Warehouse for sale by auction in 1794. This was partly due to worrying reports suggesting that the wine offered was very poor. Total imports from Spain continued to drop, as did the quality.

In 1795 an essay by Dr Wright castigated the product being shipped, which masqueraded as Mountain. Which 'when genuine is admirable,' Dr Wright wrote, 'but now hath lost its reputation; the arts arising from sophistication have almost extinguished its name. I never saw any of it that was sold in this country that was tolerably good. The best I ever tasted was in a wine merchant's house in Malaga, 16 years old.'

Mountain made something of a comeback in the 1850s, with the hills around Malaga again green. As the quality of the wine had improved, English gentlemen were prepared to give their fathers' and grandfathers' favourite wine a try. Soon they were hanging inscribed silver neck 'tickets' around the necks of cut glass decanters. Mountain was back on the polished sideboard and challenging port as the Englishman's drink. Britain and America between them were hoovering up 36 million bottles annually. Then came powdery mildew, which made the vines sick and inefficient. On top of that Malaga became the first place in Europe to welcome phylloxera, a hitherto unknown aphid. The tiny insect that would soon nibble the continent's wine lands to destruction, causing French growers to leap off barn roofs and slash their wrists, also damned Mountain's sweet stream. Withered vines were abandoned, not least those that ripened on the Malaga hills. Some growers retired; others, the younger ones, shrewdly headed for Spanish-speaking Chile.

Malaga is still made in Spain's tiniest wine region, having tumbled from the second largest in the whole country. Some growers sell it laced with quinine, straight from the cask into lemonade bottles to holidaying Posh and Becks clones. The once mighty wine is now lying on its back in the gutter, dribbling, shaggy-bearded and covered in old newspapers. A town that once reeled from the Christmas pudding pong of over 100 *bodegas* now has just three operating from an industrial estate. The Pedro Ximenez and the Moscatel are the principal grapes bulked up by the mediocre Airen, the most widely planted grape in Spain, if not the world. Modern Malaga makes sixteen different types of wine in three different ways, as befits a wine that has lost its way. Strengths range from sleepy to unconscious.

Molino Real, a big name when Britons annually swallowed the contents of 36 million bottles, has returned to roost in England, at Adnam's in Suffolk. Biblically made from raisiny Muscatels, podged in stone troughs, then turned every day for a fortnight before being shovelled into an olive press, it spends time in blackened vats before bottling. Sweet, sensuous and thick enough to oil Santa's sledge, expensive enough too it is for Christmas.

20

Canary

Canary was Malvasia-based, a thick-skinned and heavily flavoured grape that migrated from Asia Minor via the Greek islands, especially Crete. One of its aliases was Malvasia Candia, an old name for the Cretan town of Heraklion. The Malvasia, with scant supervision, produced unspectacular juice that lent itself to ageing and fortification. Tobias Venner, in *Via Rector* in 1620, wrote: 'Canarie wine is of some termed a Sacke, with this adjunct – sweete: but yet very improperly for it is not so white in colour as sack, nor so thin in substance.' In an Anglo-Spanish dictionary of the eighteenth century, Sack is referred to as a *vino de Canarias*.

James Howel, Historiographer Royal of England, wrote in 1634: 'Good wine carrieth a Man to Heaven. If this be true, surely more English go to Heaven this way, than any other; for I think there's more Canary brought into England, than to all the world besides. I think also there is a hundred times more drunk under the name of Canary-Wine than there is brought in.' Howel considered genuine Canary to be 'the richest, best bodied and most lasting of wines'. This was proven when a leather bottle filled with Canary was dug up by labourers working on a country estate in East Grinstead, Sussex, in 1771. A waxed, crumbling cork sealed the filthy but still intact bottle. The leather was inscribed 'New Canary, put in to see how long it would keep good. April 1666.' The find was rushed to the owner of the estate, who after tasting with trepidation, pronounced it to be of good quality. Which was lucky: for when Canary was shipped young and gassy and bottled by unscrupulous merchants, it could be dangerous. One victim of exploding Canary reported that 'like cider it flew all around the cellar and broke the bottles'. Ben Jonson said of Canary: 'That which doth take my muse and me, is a pure cup of Canary wine.' Keats lisped: 'Have ye tippled drink more fine, than mine host's Canary wine?'

Samuel Pepys' physician, Dr Burnett, said: 'Old Canary or Malaga you may drincke to three or four glasses, but no new wine, and what wine you drincke, let it bee at Meales.' Pepys, always on the lookout for a new idea, had his bottles emblazoned with his modest family crest. 'My new bottles, 5 or 6 dozen with my crest on them,' he happily noted on 23 October 1663. One quack recommended Canary for 'removing obstructions in the lungs'. Philip Massinger in his comedy *The City Madame* scarily refers to 'all the conduits spouting Canary Sack'. All this sounds as if Canary was almost as unstable as those who drank it. But the best old Canary was considered to be 'remarkably fine, the equal to Tokay for richness'.

Writing in 1795, Dr Wright was cautious. 'The Canary wines of about half a century ago,' he said, 'were excellent. They were imported on the mother, or lees, and sold pure. They were fit for sick persons or valetudinarians; now they are like manners, mixed, mended, chopped, changed, and so altered from their salutary simplicity, that scarcely a trace of what they were, now remains.' Statistics prove how the wine quickly become unfashionable. Only 110 tuns were shipped to the United Kingdom between 1785 and 1799. The wine referred to as sack in fly-blown vestry books in dank village churches was probably Canary, often mixed with port. The combination made for uplifting communion wine.

Canary was also known as Palm, Palm Sack or Palme from the thirteenth century. It was probably named after the town of Las Palmas, but there was an even older wine called Palm made in the Far East from the fermented sap or the flower crowns of the date palm. Canary(or Palm) was popular during the first half of the eighteenth century and it was listed in the cellar books of both the Barber's Hall and the Earl of Bristol, who replenished his stocks in 1711, 1718, 1724 and 1734. In 1752 the Ironmonger's Company placed an advertisement in a London newspaper: 'A sale by candle, at Sam's Coffee House, at 6 o'clock in the afternoon, of 42 pipes of extraordinary good old Palm wine, clean rack'd, of a most delicate taste and curious flavour, fine and fit for bottling and in time for exportation.'

While most modern Canary wine is of moderate quality, on Tenerife an ageworthy sweet wine is still made in small quantities from the Malvasia. It is blended with imported wines and sold in carafes. Spanish wine specialist Jan Read says the Malvasia from Bodegas Mozaga is 'a wine of real character, halfway to a dessert wine.'

21

Rhenish

German wines, with which Britons have had a lengthy relationship, are now considered a weak joke with a petrolly flavour. They are manufactured to the extent that growers, unable to provide sufficient sunshine, have to ferment their wines dry, then fold in sweet, unfermented juice to disguise the searing acidity. In an age when sleekly oiled, muscle-bound, high-octane New World wines are all the rage, the Germans seem more adrift of the market than ever. This is unfortunate; for, at their finest, when made by some tweedy aristocrat, German wines – Riesling in particular – are just the mouth-watering antidote those who hate puréed Shiraz need, for contrast if nothing else. Shakespeare would probably agree. In *The Merchant of Venice* (Act 3, Scene 1), Salarino makes this racist jibe at Shylock: 'There is more difference between thy flesh and hers than between jet and ivory; more between your bloods than is between Red wine and Rhenish.'

Jokes about German wines are not new. Here's how to make hock from *The Art and Mystery of Vintners* of 1750: 'Take a handful of dried lemon peel, put them into ten or twelve gallons of white wine, add a pint of damask rose water. Roll up and down, lay it upright, then open the bung. Add a little branch of clarey and let it sleep for twenty-four hours. Then take it out. It will taste very well.'

In fact, fraudsters were harshly treated in Germany. In the late fourteenth century, swindlers had their cellars raided, stocks were destroyed and casks reduced to kindling. The accused were made to watch all this before being dragged kicking and squealing to the nearest river and chucked in, while enemies and business rivals gathered to cheer.

Rhenish, as it was called, was shipped to England before the Norman Conquest, when London markets heaved with Germans intent on flogging their watery wares. Shards of pottery from amphorae used for transporting Rhenish wines have been unearthed in London, Winchester and Canterbury. There is evidence they may also have been shipped in German casks made from the silver fir, a tree that grows on the banks of the Rhine.

In the twelfth and thirteenth centuries, Rhenish wine was also regularly arriving at Bristol docks. German wine was so cheap that a poor man could drown his sorrows by buying it from the cask at 6d a gallon, if he brought his own container. In the thirteenth century Rhenish was sold in the Steelyard in London. This ancient site of quiet gurgling and spitting now echoes to the hurried steps of commuters as they stampede into Cannon Street station.

Amid the welter of factory-made Liebfraumilchs and the cheap sparklers, wines made from the Riesling are one of the German wine industry's few saving graces. This magnificent yielder of ice-pure, elegant wines, at its indisputable finest when wrung from crushed slate soil by tweedy barons in cloud-wreathed, crow-haunted castles along the Rhine, may be related to an ancient vine that climbed trees along river gorges. It was identified as Riesling at Russelsheim near Frankfurt in 1435, on the Mosel about the same time and near Worms, the birthplace of Liebfraumilch, in 1551. By the mid-sixteenth century Rhenish was shipped to England in 'aums', containing 36 gallons. The small cask retained its popularity right through to the sixteenth century. As now, the bulk of German wine arriving in London was low-alcohol white. A little red was consumed by a few devoted wincers, just as it is today. A dubious consignment 'made near Bonn' arrived in 1542 and was sent to the taverns to be disposed of quickly. From 1520, German wines were shipped to England in stone-ware bellarmines, named after a total abstainer, Cardinal Bellarmino (1542–1621).

Aping the Romans, the Germans served wine and nibbles to semi-naked bathers in communal baths in the fifteenth century. A hundred years later, the better class of establishment employed a cheerful sot in lederhosen with a bunch of jokey cellar keys dangling from his waist. His job was to act the lout, drink as much as he could keep down, then belch like a donkey into the faces of perfumed guests who, it is said, found it most amusing.

Berry Bros have among the dusty artefacts in their cellars two empty German wine bottles. Both once contained Steinwein. One dates from 1540, the other 1731. Walter Berry averred that 'the 1540 could be sipped with satisfaction and the 1731 drunk with enjoyment'. The latter wine may have been Sylvaner, which was introduced to Franconia in 1665. Another interesting item in Berry's cellar is a bottle of Arrack from about 1770 which belonged to Lord Powis. It was said to be 'of exceptional quality' and had been distilled from the milk of a dead mare.

Dr Andrew Boorde, who in 1542 published *Compendyous Regyment or a Dyetary of Health*, wrote: 'Rhenish either white or red are good for all men. Your wyne must be fyne, fayre, and clene to the eye; it must be fragraunt and redolent, havynge a good odour and flavour in the nose; it must spryncle in the cup when it is drawn. [...] It must be colde and pleasaunt in the mouthe; and it must be strong and subtyll of substaunce. If it be moderately drunken, doth acuate and quicken a man's wits, comfort the heart, scour the liver; especially if it be whyte wine, it doth rejoice all the powers of man and nourish them; it doth engender good blood, comfort and nourish the brain and all the body, it resolveth flegm; it ingendereth heat, and is good against heaviness and is full of agility. Furthermore, the better the wine is, the better the humours it doth ingender.'

White Rhenish was a popular entry chalked on London taverns' blackboards. A little rusty red 'from near Bonn' occasionally turned up. Whatever the hue, Rhenish continued to reap bad reviews. Jack Wilton, the saucy page in Thomas Nash's story *The Unfortunate Traveller*, published in 1595, sneered: 'At the verie name of syder, I can but sigh, there is so much of it in Rhenish wine now a dayes.'

Ancient German wines, made in exceptional years, possessed extraordinary staying power. In 1977 Michael Broadbent tasted a 1653 Rudesheimer that had been
frequently topped up with good spatlesen wines. It boasted an astounding 15 per
cent alcohol and an engine block-dissolving 19.6g per litre of acidity. It was aromatic,
pungent, intense and powerful. Broadbent gave it ten stars, 'for a rare experience'.
The nineteenth-century wine writer Cyrus Redding agreed that old German wines
'endured beyond example' and 'possessed inextinguishable vitality'.

Samuel Pepys was an unfussy all-rounder who drank Rhenish with mushy peas
and Bristol Milk with strawberries, switched effortlessly from port to Sack, Madeira
to Claret. After dining 'very merrily on a dish of pease' in 1663, he went with his
friends to the 'Rhenish wine-house, where we called for a red Rhenish wine called
Bleahard, a pretty wine, and not mixed as they say.' The ladies in Pepys' party may have
sipped a German beverage called 'Rhenish in the Must', a forerunner of Süssreserve,
a mixture of unfermented juice and acidic wine of the same vintage. It was briefly
popular among 'women of taste' in the 1660s. We can brusquely dismiss the German
claim that they invented Sack, one of Pepys' favourite wines. They impishly claim it
derives its name from the Old High German *sacwin*, an ancient alcoholic beverage
made by 'steeping the lees of wine in water and then straining it through a bag'. They
did, however, invent Schillerwein, a white wine with an eyedropper of pale red which
briefly had a moment or two in the sun.

Sir Robert Walpole (1676–1745), Britain's first prime minister, who in 1710 survived a visit to the Tower after being accused of 'peculation', was fond of Rhenish. In
those days when German wines were not artificially sweetened, they were popular
as aperitifs. This sharpness did not, however, appeal to Boswell, who when entertaining his printer and bookseller at the Queen's Head in Holborn, wrote in his *London
Journal* that 'every man drank his bottle of Rhenish with sugar'. At the time, old,
unsweetened Rhenish of good quality was dearer than the thin, over-produced, over-
sweetened version.

André Simon writes: 'Between 1700 and 1800 scores of skilled tasters and bro-
kers travelled down the Rhine and Mosel seeking fine wines to ship on commission.
They had to be wines of sufficient quality to justify the high prices demanded of the
consumer in England.' By 1686/87 Rhenish wines entered Bristol in sufficient quantities to be noted separately in the customs accounts. Dublin-born George Farquhar's
(1678–1707) play *The Twin-rivals*, written in 1702, reflected the continuing fashion
for Rhenish, with Balderdash saying: 'I have brought you a whetting glass, the best old
Hock in Europe; I know 'tis your drink in a morning.'

The wine-loving Earl of Bristol always kept a space in his cellars for 'several sorts
of German wines'. He regularly imported Mosel and Rhenish in the early eighteenth
century and in 1740 took delivery of a prestigious parcel of Steinwein. The Barber-
Surgeons of Bristol shipped Rhenish at around 7s a gallon up to 1740. The auction
houses were showing an interest and when the newcomer James Christie began auc-
tioning wines in 1767, the first vintage wine he sold was Rhenish from the brilliant
1748 vintage.

Reaching a peak in the period 1724–1728, when 596 tuns of wine were shipped to the United Kingdom, German wines were barely getting a look by the end of the century. Only 178 tuns were shipped between 1784 and 1788. Portuguese wines were taking over in some style and in the same period they shipped to England 12,642 tuns. The nation's taste had swung away from weak, northern whites to strong southern reds. Harvey's of Bristol, a newly established wine importer, aided by a 'strong following wind of public favour', packed their list with Iberian wines. While port and sherry sales were now measured in hundreds of butts and hogsheads, German sales were gauged in bottles. From 1794 to 1800 Harvey's shipped fourteen bottles of Hock and the equivalent of 231,000 bottles of port. The swarthy pot-bellied Iberian was climbing all over the the the blonde German *Mädchen*.

The Germans fought back, determined to prove to the doubting English that their light, white wines could be both honestly made and delicious. They are still trying. They abolished solera-type blending and tightened the rules on the recipe for vintage wine. The year on the label would no longer be a vague guestimate. The *mea culpa* offensive worked. More accurately labelled wines of better quality were selling at home and abroad. Growers felt confident again and planted 40 per cent more vines, particularly along the Mosel where every shaly sod hanging above the river was hand-dug, hand-planted, hand-hoed and the grapes hand-picked. The work was laborious and time consuming, but the sight of lime-green leaves fluttering above the Mosel drew poets like bumblebees. Tourists followed to taste the gentle new wine in lop-sided Hansel and Gretel taverns in Hobbit-like villages.

Lord Byron was there to admire the colourful peasants toiling on handkerchiefs of land. The sun burst through Blakeian clouds to toast the pendulous fruit. Sweet sharp wine flowed and refreshed. God was in his heaven and to prove it, in 1811 he sent a comet across the sky, blessing the vines in Bordeaux, Burgundy, Tokay and up the Douro. The skys were blue and bees swarmed above the vines. Wealthy growers separated overripe bunches from the merely ripe. Smiling girls in bonnets gathered shrivelled raisins in hand-woven baskets. When gently squeezed, each raisin shed a tear of nectar. Complex wines were made. Johnson says: 'The first-growths of the Rheingau had mastered the making of superlative sweet wines.'

It was a godsend for growers and consumers struggling with nomenclature when German wine became Hock in the eighteenth century. Harry Huggett, in an essay on Rhenish wines for the *Sette of Odd Volumes*, said they were originally called 'hockamores'. But in his book *Travels through Germany*, Riesbeck talks about 'the little village called Hochheim, from whence the English give all kinds of Rhenish the name of hock.' There is another theory. When Queen Victoria visited Hochheim in the nineteenth century she referred to the wine she was tasting as hock.

By 1825 German growers were keeping their best wines for up to a decade in wooden fuders. In spite of the extra oxidation and colour, the growers considered their best wines too delicate to drink with food, even the sturdier, fuller-bodied wines from German-controlled Alsace. George Meredith (1828–1909), the poet and novelist who was educated in the Moravian School at Neuwied, near Koblenz, knew his German wines and called them 'brooks of many voices'.

The improvement, when German began to taste 'very well', was due to the Riesling. Jancis Robinson says 'the ultimate compliment' was paid to Riesling when it was planted in the elevated and eminent Schloss Johannisberg vineyards in the Rheingau. Rhenish became again the most expensive wine in England. A dozen bottles cost 50s in London, compared with its nearest rival, the sweet 'Frontenial' (*sic*) at 31s 6d. Hugh Johnson, another huge fan of the maligned Riesling, says the Romans planted the Mosel banks and although the wine was low in alcohol 'they soon learned that the new "austere" taste, being safer than water, was treated as an all-purpose drink'.

Auctioneers continued to do good business with a rash of cellar clearances. German wines were among those disposed of when Mr Phillips cleared out the last few crates of the Prince de Talleyrand's vast collection on Tuesday 31 March 1835 – he flogged 144 bottles of 'excellent' Mosel and eighteen bottles of Eau de Cologne. The dismantling of Queen Caroline's fine German wine stock, which was at Brendenburg House, took place in July 1818. Items on offer included: '48 dozen of 1748 Old Hock, 18 dozen Louisberg, 23 dozen 1761 fine, old Joanisberg [*sic*], 3 dozen very fine old Hock, supposed to be 180 years old, and 14 bottles of Stein Hock.' André Simon writes: 'Most of these wines were sold at very high prices, from 12s 6d to 20s per bottle, some being described as in English bottles, others in French bottles, some in dwarf Dutch bottles and even in dwarf German bottles.'

The sale drew a coterie of unusually fragrant bidders, including the Duke of Sussex, 'one of the galaxy of royal brothers', who purchased 'a truly astounding quantity' of '1718 old Ransacker' (*sic*). Randersacker, an attractive dry wine from Franconia, was highly prized. Sadly its day has gone and most of what they produce now is consumed on the spot by natives and tourists alike.

German growers began to look for a new grape, something more prolific and less picky than the Riesling, one that was impervious to disease and would ripen in rain. They planted Müller-Thurgau, the bastard offspring of the noble, low-yielding, late-ripening, temperamental Riesling and the common Sylvaner. It was a designer grape to combat the frostiest of frost, thigh-deep snow and rain falling like poisoned arrows. Imagine the consternation when in 1979 a minus 20-degree frost clasped the German vineyards in a deathlike embrace. The Müller-Thurgau wilted immediately, lying like broken piano wire on every hill. The noble Riesling though puffed out its medal-festooned chest like an old spike-helmeted Prussian; it not only survived, but offered honeyed bunches the following autumn.

Prince von Otto Eduard Leopold Bismark (1815–1898), the German statesman, was a stout supporter of German wines and sausages. He also smoked cigars, ate twelve dozen oysters at a sitting and devoured whole lobsters – shell, claws, popping eyes, the lot. When given presents, it was not cufflinks he rushed to unwrap; it was the large package containing up to 80 metres of sausages. His consumption of German wine was equally impressive. Two bottles at lunch, still only 'feeling comfortable' after his sixth bottle.

At the beginning of the twentieth century wine merchants carried at least a dozen Hocks and Mosels, from 'Liebfraumilch, a fine Riesling Hock', to Berncasteler Doctor. The more adventurous listed German reds from Ingelheimer and Assmannshausen at 3s and 4s a bottle respectively. Harrod's 1906 list named thirty-three still German wines and ten sparkling, sacrilegiously including a fizzy Berncastler Doctor, which at 64s a case was 1s 1d dearer than the still version from 1893, one of the top three German vintages of the nineteenth century. 'Doctor' had a reputation for curing gout, for which it was recommended by German doctors.

The most expensive Hock at Harrods in 1906 was 'Steinberger Cabinett' 1884, a moderate vintage. In 1867 Harvey's were selling the 1862 Steinberger Cabinet Auslese at 180s a dozen at a time when a case of Pale Old Cognac could be had for as little as 60s. At 140s a case Scharzhofberger Auslese 1893 was the most expensive German wine on Harrods' list. On cold, frosty mornings above the heaving Mosel, vineyard workers heated up a smoke-blackened billycan of Mosel on their bonfires and drank it as a City worker would his early morning latté. The German pruner still parboils his wine on windy hills. Johnson says; 'With a spoonful of sugar in a plastic cup, it has much to be said for it.' We'll take his word for it.

After the First World War what small interest there was in German wine disappeared. Professor Saintsbury wrote: 'German wine has of late shared the unpopularity of German everything.' He went on sizing up the loss to the English table. 'Not that Hock has ever ranked with me among the first three, or even the first five or six greatest wines. After the first two glasses it would be no sacrifice to leave the rest.' Saintsbury felt that German wines were best as 'beverage drinks, very fresh and pleasant quenchers', to be sipped when the dinner guests have just arrived and hung up their coats. Saintsbury found the intense flavours of the fine, late-picked wines to be too much of a good thing, in his words 'overpowering and almost barbaric'. He could, he said, easily drink a bottle of Hock at dinner 'and a bottle of Claret after it', but 'for finer purposes' he regarded German wines 'as chiefly curiosities, and accordingly they never figured largely in my wine lists'. He said some of the highly scented wines were 'the most abominably faked of all real or pretended juices of the grape' and he once attributed 'a persistent attack of an unpleasant kind' to an 'unduly prolonged sampling' of a sparkling Mosel, which had 'a horrible suspicion of the laboratory'. In spite of his protestations, Saintsbury was fond of 'a small tumbler of red hock', as 'when sleep was not easy to obtain it did the trick admirably, and without deferred discomfort.'

At the Dowager Swaythling's Wine and Food Society dinner in 1935 Saintsbury would have been suitably aghast to know that with the second course, a plate of beautiful speckled trout netted from the tranquil banks of the River Itchen, the Dowager poured Liebfraumilch. Mind you, it was a Spätlese from the sensational 1921 vintage. Remember, the now derided and filthily abused German pap was once, it is hard to believe, priced well above the Leovilles, Pichons and Margaux, as well as fine Volnay and Pommard on Berry Bros' 1896 list.

Wars have done no favours for German wines and the patriotic bank clerk was not going to drink German when he could drink a pint in the snug of his homely local.

Hardly surprising that Deinhard's, an English shipper associated with all ends of the German market, shipped nothing German from the beginning of the Second World War to 1948, when entente was warily resumed. German-domiciled Coke-swigging GIs are blamed for kicking off the new-style German sweet and mediocre wines which began the recovery in the UK and elsewhere.

Maurice Healy, whom Pamela Vandyke Price said was, like Saintsbury, 'superficially genial', was characteristically pompous about German wines. 'I always find in them a vulgarity I discern everywhere in the German character,' he said. 'They seek to conquer you with violence.' As for Mosel wine, Healy waffled, 'It was like a simple maiden, unsure of herself, conscious of her inferior rank. She will jest with you, and dance the polka or barn-dance, and will not be too proud to pocket a few marks for the favour.' Cyril Ray, who memorably included Muscadet, Soave and Asti Spumante in his Desert Island case, wanted his last bottle of wine to be a Mosel. 'I shall drink it to Mozart's last concerto,' he said.

22

Tokay

The history of Tokay is unclear. One account is that vineyard workers noticed how on a sunny, volcanic hill the Furmint grape and extinct Porcin were attacked by bees. A local monk, Mate Szepsi Laczko, from the village of Erdobenye, pressed the rotten fruit and from juice as sweet as runny honey he made wine that took months to ferment. The wine was sensational. It was head-shakingly weird but lovely. The simple monk was stumped to describe it, but it was certainly richer and there was more to it than any wine he'd ever tasted. Accidentally, like the Egyptians, Greeks and Romans before him, Laczko had stumbled on *Botrytis Cinerea*, the grape-shrivelling fungus known as noble rot. The Tokay monks kept their secret for a century before the Germans found out and told the French. Soon everyone in Tokay wanted to make the perfumed wine. Those who claimed residency needn't pay tithes. There was mass immigration from the surrounding twenty-eight villages. Peasants made the wine and copied the monks by gouging holes in the black rock to house the small barrels lapping with frothy young wine. Under a carpet of black mould, Tokay grew a cottony beard. Like sherry it mellowed as it aged.

A Hungarian wine merchant, Gergeley Kalmar, got wind of the furore and bought up as much Tokay as he could to sell to eager clients far from the insignificant slope where the Furmint dozily ripened. The Poles, thriving at the time, were keen on luxury goods. Kalmar was quick to introduce them to Tokay. German and Scottish émigré merchants were quick to move to the wine business.

By the seventeenth century the Polish aristocracy gorged themselves on the sensuous nectar, expunging all other wines from their cellars. In the period from 1519 to 1754, Hungarian and Polish entrepreneurs joined the Scots and Germans in exporting Tokay to Poland. The transplanted Scots, 'agile merchants of ready wit', proved particularly adept at wheeling and dealing. Some made fortunes out of the bronze wine. The fame of Tokay spread to Russia. Peter the Great installed a wine buyer in Tokay to select the finest new wines. Covered wagons, escorted by fur-hatted sabre-dangling soldiery, delivered the precious wine to the Imperial cellars in St Petersburg.

Catherine the Great was so taken by the wonderful Hungarian wine she gamely decided to have a Tokay vineyard planted in Russia. On 30 January 1785, 19,000 Furmint vine shoots were taken to Moscow, accompanied by several of the best vine dressers and three experienced wine makers, Mihály Nagy, Janos Kormos and Mihály Szilagyi. The Tsarina's agent, Ensign Bimbolazar, oversaw the new and soon thriving 'Tokay' plantations. 'The offspring of these vine shoots,' writes Zoltan Halasz, 'still yield good wine, though of a different taste and flavour than Tokay, in the sunny hills of the Crimea.'

From the latter part of the seventeenth century, Tokay trickled into the Low Countries and Scandinavia before finding its way to England via Vecelli, an Italian trader who set up a wine importer's business in England. He sold Tokay to 'the most prominent people', including George IV. Vecelli's selling point for Tokay was as 'a remedy for convalescents'. The golden wine had from the outset established a reputation for bringing dying tyrants back to life. According to Ben Howkins, 'the Princes of Transylvania insisted that these rich, fragrant vintages be nurtured to almost magical potency.' Italian humanists believed that the Tokay hills contained tiny fissures of pure gold which somehow leaked into the grape juice. Philippus Aureolus Theophrastus Bombastus von Hohenheim (1493–1541), a nutty Swiss alchemist, boiled and dissected bunches of Furmint grapes in a futile attempt to extract the 'gold'.

Frederick the Great, and his house guest Voltaire (1694–1778), shared many a bottle until they fell out. By the eighteenth century, Tokay was so desirable it was offered only to very important people. Pope Benedict XIV sycophantically wrote to Maria Theresa, Queen of Hungary, to thank her for a delivery of the finest Tokay. 'Happy is the country which grows them. Happy is the Queen who sends them. Happier still am I who drink them.' Tokay idolatry had became fashionable in the Vatican, and bottles of the finest and oldest wine kept cruets of holy water company in many a Papal bedside cabinet. When Carlo de Brosses, future president of the Parliament of Burgundy, visited the Duke of Burgundy, he was impressed by 'the incredible luxury of menswear and the diamonds of the ladies', but especially the Tokay from the cellars of the Grand Duchy.

'Tokay,' André Simon wrote; 'was the best, and the best-known, Hungarian wine in England during the eighteenth century.' He refers to an entry dated 4 June 1701 in the *Treasury Papers* (Vol.LXXIV, No.36), which concerns a parcel of Tokay seized by Customs when it landed in England. The Customs officer accused the Emperor's agent of shipping rare and valuable Tokay into the country disguised as Rhenish. Fashionable wines soon leaked into plays and in *The Miser* (Act 3, Scene 2) by Henry Fielding, Fred says: 'I have taken the liberty to order some sweet-meats, sir, and Tokay in the next room.'

Jonathan Swift (1667–1745) tried Tokay for the first time on the insistence of a banker friend with whom he was having lunch. The Dean was disappointed. 'Admirable, yet not to the degree I expected,' he said. He tried it again as a digestif after a very large lunch, at which liberal quantities of Burgundy and Hermitage were drunk. 'Tockay' (*sic*) did nothing for Swift – more his fault than the wine's, he conceded. Robert Browning (1812–1889), in his poem *Nationality in Drinks*, apportioned Claret to France, Tokay to Hungary and to the English he ascribed beer. Most great English country houses had a few bottles of old Tokay in their cellars. An inventory at Ashburnham in 1845 recorded 'Tokay, dry and sweet'.

In 1819, Prince de Tallyrand, French ambassador to the court of King James, cellared Tokay 'from Sobieski, the King of Poland's cellar, 60 years old'. When auctioned later it sold for 15s per bottle. Without the royal connection it would have been half that.

At international competitions Tokay came away wearing more gongs and gold braid than Elton John. An 1863 vintage Tokay won the gold medal at Breslau in 1869. At the Vienna exhibition, Hungarian wines won 116 medals. At the Paris Exhibition in 1896 Tokay won the gold medal, the first time a French wine was pipped for the prize. At the same event in 1900 Hungarian wines took three Grand Prix and seventeen golds. The Poles, after two centuries of dedicated imbibing, remain among the staunchest supporters of Tokay, as are the Belgians, Swedes, Norwegians and Finns, with the British and Americans bringing up the rear.

Gregor, a Hungarian wine merchant who settled in London in the 1860s, dealt in the very best Tokays, obtaining favourable recommendations from influential London medics on the restorative qualities of the great wine. He even managed to persuade the 'faculties of several British Universities' to state officially that Tokay was especially good for sickly, and wealthy, patients during their convalescence. Warner Allen concurred. 'I have proved by experience that Tokay Essence is an unequalled restorative', he wrote. 'Its effects are instantaneous and magical, as remarkable in their beneficent way as Circe's black magic, and worthy of Nestor's Pramnian for its startling powers of recuperation.' Warner Allen's eighty-nine-year-old aunt was dying of bronchitis. The doctors had all but given up hope when he remembered the bottle of 1811 Tokay Essence in his cellar. A few spoonfuls ladled down the old lady's throat had her, if not exactly doing handstands, at least out of danger. She went on to miss her centenary by six weeks. Warner Allen admitted later perhaps he saw the legendary wine 'through rose-coloured spectacles tinted by reverence for antiquity'. He felt a 'more mature palate and nose' might have spotted that the old wine actually had little or no bouquet and 'a taste rather like brown bread and butter'.

In 1933 Berry Bros published a booklet in which they listed a number of miracle cures wrought by thimbles of Tokay administered to those without hope. The 1811 vintage was again wheeled out, dusty and skeletal. The bouquet was 'overwhelming in its intensity and silky in its richness. The first sip bewildered the palate with a harmonious multiplicity of exquisite sensations.' Tokay's reputation for removing the screws from coffin lids meant that Berry Bros had to ration it. When Broadbent tasted the same wine forty years later, he found it 'somewhat murky' but with an exquisite bouquet, sweet and luscious on the palate and with a 'fabulous finish'. Broadbent, who tasted more old Tokay than anyone alive, uses the word 'acidity' a lot in his notes. It's hardly surprising, then, that the fabled wine kept so well.

André Simon drank a Comet Tokay Essence from Berry Bros. Consumed with the contents of the fruit bowl in 1939, it was, Simon said, 'a wine of supreme perfection, luscious and fresh; with a magnificent bouquet, as sweet and discreet as the perfume of a vineyard in June when the vines are in full bloom.' Entirely free of all traces of the medicinal, the 1811 was 'a miracle of a wine'.

When the great rusting steel door of the famous Fukier cellar in Warsaw was jemmied open before the Second World War, found among the dead birds and the dried leaves were 382 bottles of Tokay 1606. The wines had stood to attention for three centuries, their corks pulled every six years like rotten teeth. When the liquid was poured it 'tasted of cocoa, strawberry and vanilla'. George Saintsbury said Tokay was not a wine at all. It was a liqueur, but 'a Prince of liqueurs'.

In the nineteenth century the Massandra winery was built in the Crimea to supply the Tsar's court with monstrous syrupy versions of the delicate Tokays and Sauternes the Russian royals swigged at the parties at Livadia, their palace near Yalta. Coal miners were recruited from Georgia to dig the cellars by hand, chipping away at solid rock to make three caves big enough to house a massive range of red, white and golden wines. Prince Goltzin was installed as wine maker. Massandrian wines survived the fascist onslaughts on Russia during the Second World War, thanks to the locals who ghosted them away at night in wheelbarrows and handcarts and hid them in the hills. Huge vats of maturing wine which couldn't be shifted in time were hacked to matchwood with axes and the wine poured down the drains. The sewers were scented for a while and the Black Sea turned red.

Before the war a few barrels of the 1909 Crimean 'Tokay' were shipped to England to be sold cheaply to the 'port 'n' lemon' brigade. It is unlikely the tourniqueted, fag-dangling factory girls who swigged it for a tanner a glass held the wine aloft in the Woodbine-infused light and waffled about its colour and bouquet. A Russian Royal Estate wine which Michael Broadbent tasted in 1972 'had an incredible crust like old port, and a lovely warm amber colour and a rich, deep, old Muscat bouquet'.

Hugh Johnson, with others responsible for the exciting comeback of this brilliant wine, tickles the fancy with his stories of 'inert noblemen and enormously senior men of religion springing from their beds, or alternatively into them, as a drop of Tokay touched their lips.' George V was the last English king to put the resurrection theory to the test when he fell ill in 1931. The King had been under intense pressure, with an economic crisis looming, unemployment out of control and Britain's finances about to crumble. If ever there was a Tokay moment this was it. A court servant was sent out to find the golden tonic. Joseph Vecchi, who ran a Hungarian restaurant in London, dispatched two bottles of the 1899 vintage, a brilliant five-star year, to the royal bed-chamber. His Majesty leaned on a royal elbow and sipped the famed elixir. He lived another five years, dying on 20 January 1936 at the age of seventy.

Rich bastards drinking Tokay did not appeal to the Bolsheviks. They bopped the roy-als, shot up the cellars, swung from the chandeliers, made a mess on the carpet and set up grisly factories to make a 'people's wine'. The wine was a joke but the poorest peasant didn't get it. A wine like oxidised Muscadet was shipped to England shamelessly wearing the Hungarian tricolour. Few bought it. Tokay was a legend but only a memory.

British enthusiasts had an opportunity to try wine from the Tsar's cellars when royal relics were auctioned at Sotheby's in 2004. To the surprise of some, the wines fetched dizzy prices. A 1913 Massandra 'Madeira' for example, fetched over £5,000 a bottle. An 'Ai Danil red port' was knocked down for around £3,000 a bottle. A Russian 'Tokay' went for £3,000, and Seventh Heaven from 1880, made by Prince Lev Sergervich Golitzen, topped £1,000.

Returning to the genuine article, a Hungarian once said of Tokay: 'Think of the most beautiful picture you have ever seen, the most wonderful symphony you have ever heard, the most beautiful sunset on earth, the fragrance of the most exquisite perfume, in the company of the person you love most in the world. Add a touch of original sin – and you have Tokay.'

23

Port, the Englishman's Wine

Two dusty young Liverpudlians, the sons of a wine merchant, swatted flies with their hats as they trekked up the Douro in 1678 with orders to buy up as much wine as they could. They were under orders to ship it home as quickly as possible. There was a shortage of Claret and English wine merchants were attempting to fill the void. The brothers bought barely fermented rough red wine, pressed by the brown-footed natives, who mixed it with elderberries to deepen the colour. The Liverpool duo hit on the idea of strengthening and fortifying the ruby wine with a liver-dissolving brandy to kill off the still-working yeasts and anaesthetise the wine for its long boat journey to England. For the very first shipment, in 1678, a large black-bottomed boat shook off its moorings, sat deep in the water and crawled off, piled several layers high with 408 pipes of this new kind of wine. It was an enormous gamble. The Liverpool lads had invented port. At least that is their story.

However, Claret drinkers were doubtful and they sipped it without enthusiasm. Many spurned the new mixture and turned to the lighter table wines of northern Spain. Eyeing fat port casks still pregnant with wine in their cellars, worried innkeepers mixed it with Alicante to tame its coarseness. Claret drinkers were still unconvinced, but when they tasted this stronger, sweeter red wine they smacked their lips and took another sip, and another. Within five years port sales in England had risen to over 13,000 pipes. Potential port shippers sped to Portugal to cash in. Among them were some whose names would become household among the cognoscenti: Croft, Warre and Taylor. They all toiled up the Douro, dossing down in foetid tavernas, flopping on sacks among the bugs and the rats. Next morning, after decanting a hatful of water from the well over their heads, they mounted their mules and hat-rack ponies and trotted up brown lanes and down cobbled streets to be the first to snap up the best of the rich, red wine.

One young Englishman, Thomas Woodmass, an apprentice wine buyer, was quite surprised when his hired mule died between his legs. He legged it the rest of the way, surviving a mugging en route. He gained Oporto and was embraced by the British contingent already ensconced there with their cockfighting, cards and boozing, with the doleful moustachioed faces of jealous Portuguese filling every pane-free window.

British merchants soon became so powerful they were above Portuguese law and exempt from taxes, and when they died any debts they had died with them. As Protestant invaders in a superstitious, statue-kissing Catholic country, the British had their own thrifty God who beamed benignly on them as they grew portly and rich.

The Factory House was their club. Theirs was a blessed existence. The smooth, superior, public school-educated men who refused to speak 'dago' kept a 'pat on the head and a kick in the arse' relationship with the Portuguese. The natives flashed their teeth and their eyes and forbade the holding of Protestant services and the burying of 'heretic' Englishmen in Catholic graveyards. They even stole fair-haired English children to bring them up as Catholics. Religious fervour reached boil-over point and the countryside 'swarmed with priests, monks and mendicant friars'. Masses were high, churches and cathedrals glittered and reeked of tallow. Women queued to plant kisses on lipstick-stained icons. The British dug in, unwanted, unfashionable and snooty, but making vatfuls of money.

The British were no newcomers. The connection went back centuries. Staff-swinging, dagger-thrusting Crusaders were among the first Britons to set foot on Portuguese soil. Portuguese fishermen were allowed to catch cod off the coast of England in 1353 after Alfonso IV and Edward III concluded a deal that involved swapping fish for Minho wines.

But the English established vineyard holdings in the Minho before vines were planted in the bleak sun-browned Douro. The Claret-deprived English preferred the light, easy-drinking red wines of the Minho to the often poorly made reds from the Douro. One reason advanced by André Simon was that the excessive sweetness in the Douro grapes meant that the heavy rich juice fermented so violently in the fly-ridden heat that it boiled until the sugar was exhausted and the resultant infant wine was troubled and unstable. Anthony Hogg, author of Traveller's Portugal, says, 'The red wines known as "Red Portugal" were weak and nasty by the time they reached the London taverns, which explains how Samuel Johnson's contemporaries could drink three bottles and remain sober.'

When the English and the Scots located which of the balmy hills and snug valleys yielded the ripest and tastiest fruit, they ring-fenced them with regulations. Port was shipped in bulk first. The invention of the bottle allowed the young wine, brandy and unfermented sugars to merge and mellow. The edifice that is vintage port was nearing completion.

In spite of the strong British presence in Oporto, the first port shipper was a German, C.N. Kopke, who began trading in 1638 and sold his wine under a specific estate name, Quinta Roriz. The first English firm to appear on the scene was Warre, in 1670. Competition bred quality. Painstakingly made, port got smoother and better. The new full-bodied, sweet drink laced with brandy was perfect wine for an English winter. Claret was no match for a jug of port heated with a red-hot poker and served with a bowl of walnuts in front of a fire as wide as a cinema screen. The London Coffee House clientele enjoyed port so much they put it in their coffee. John Croft advocated port after dinner. 'An Englishman of any decent condition cannot dispense with it after a good dinner', he snootily waffled.

As ships bearing port regularly sailed for England, the French were jealous and unhappy. The English were happy with port and they drank it at every opportunity. Exports in 1728 almost doubled to 18,200 pipes, which inevitably encouraged certain shippers to take short cuts. Greed as usual was punished by a dramatic fall in sales. In 1794 John Maddox, a Bristol wine merchant, sold port for £1 a dozen. Claret fans continued to drink lighter red wines. A fly-stained invoice dated 24 September 1713 belonging to Sir Walter Gilbey shows that while port was selling at £24 a pipe, Old Lisbon, another Claret substitute, was fetching up to £32 10s a pipe.

By the early eighteenth century, Portuguese farmers were ploughing out their wheat to plant vines. The 1734 crop was an astounding success. Newly flush Portuguese farmers, accompanied by their wives, rode into town to shop for fancy waistcoats; their wives bought curtain-rail earrings and had their hair washed and styled. The English sneered from behind their Venetian blinds. John Croft noted the 'meanest Labradores, vying with each other in the gaudiness of their apparel'. Shrugging off English derision, the Douro farmer continued to make port which was accepted as very fine in London. A rare enamel bottle 'ticket', made in Battersea between 1750 and 1777, once hung around the neck of bottles of Companhía Geral's 1756 port. Paper labels were introduced soon after, with the 1755 vintage being the first wine of any kind to have a paper label.

The first vintage Port listed by Christie's was the 1765. It was not a great vintage. The 1767, also of ordinary quality, was offered at £4 13s for sixty bottles. Educated men boasted about their consumption of Port. Dr Johnson, whose tedious work on *A Dictionary of the English Language* exhausted him, drank port at mealtimes for the effect it had on him.

Portuguese Jesuits made port on their considerable holdings. It was shipped to England, where it was known as priest's port. The popularity of port grew. Land was cleared, new vineyards were created in less than ideal areas. Egged on by dishonest British merchants who had orders to fill, the Portuguese dunked baskets of elder-berries in the juice of young and barely ripened grapes to darken the wine. They stirred in liquid sugar and brandy fit only to run a dragster on. Like some English shippers the Portuguese farmers topped up their pipes with Spanish wines, sweet or dry, red, white or pink. The juice of imported Greek raisins was used and the unhappy mixture was fortified with crude 'whisky'.

The result was predictable. One sniff and the English stopped buying. Prices dropped. A pipe of port found no takers even at a couple of pounds. Grapes rotted on the vine. The Portuguese lowered their asking prices to rock bottom. The British held their noses. Rumours abounded that certain unscrupulous British shippers took advantage of the farmers' plight by demanding the pick of their daughters to seal a bargain.

English traders were known as factors, hence the odd name of the Port Factory, the headquarters of the English with its typically arcane laws of form and manners, with women tolerated to scrub toilets and polish knobs. The dark-skinned Portuguese were not welcome. They responded by creating a Companhía dos Vinhos do Alto Douro in the mid-eighteenth century, a body intended to curb 'the unbounded greediness of the English Merchants'. The Douro would be strictly demarcated, separating qual-ity vineyards which would produce only the finest wines for the English market. Elderberry trees were uprooted to remove the temptation.

The vintage of 1775 was a large one, a five-star. The 1797 vintage was even better, according to the shipper George Sandeman, who, after passing a decanter of it to and fro with the Duke of Wellington at Torres Vedras in 1809, declared it 'the best vintage ever known'.

The Companhía of which so much was expected turned out to be corrupt and self-serving. Bribery was rife. Officials with sandpaper palates and fag ends protruding through greasy moustaches were responsible for handing out export licences. With legs dangling they rode their mules up to the Douro, knocked back the samples, burped, signed the export documents and pocketed the bribe. The Marquis de Pombal too was in on the act, encouraging his henchmen to write out phony licences which enabled the prime minister to ship Carcavelos, produced on the river Tagus, a considerable distance outside the demarcated port region. Nevertheless, in spite of its faults, and they were legion, the Companhía helped restore the Englishman's confidence in port.

Grapes were still foot trodden and the juice fermented in the Douro. Transporting the infant wine down to Oporto for maturing was laboriously done by horse-drawn drays on narrow, winding dirt roads. An obvious alternative was by the river Douro. The Companhía tackled the considerable and dangerous task of removing massive stone slabs from the river bed to make it navigable. The work took a dozen years and the results pleased the English, who could now gain access to the banks where their finest wines were made. The roads were upgraded in 1788, and the British had to pay a levy on every pipe shipped to pay for them. Oak forests were planted for wood to make 115-gallon casks as the taste in England had gradually switched from dark, fresh and moustache staining to lighter, fragrant and more mature wines. The port business had fully recovered and many a poor Portuguese family benefited. The British were topping up the country's coffers with their taxes. The Portuguese began to like the British.

Port was now the most popular wine in England. Great vintages oozed from the bleakly romantic Douro, which became a sticky flypaper for poets, novelists and travel writers. Among the first was William Beckford (1760–1844), who studied architecture and music under Mozart, and wrote *Vathek*, a best-selling novel. He was followed by George Borrow (1803–1881), who wanted to sell English Protestantism to fundamental Roman Catholics. One day while wobbling across a rickety bridge over the Tagus, his mule's panniers stuffed with bibles, Borrow was set upon by a pack of razor-toothed mongrels. He quelled the dogs' desire to tear him to pieces by resorting to 'the calm approving glance of reason'.

Robert Southey (1774–1843), an unpopular ranter against the Church and its 'diabolical belief in eternal punishment', was sent to Portugal to rid himself of his radical ideas. He found the poverty and ignorance hard to bear. The squalor, packs of dogs licking their testicles in the sun, and the gap-toothed beggars disgusted him, as did the narrowly missed contents of chamber pots as they unexpectedly cascaded from above. The only thing Southey liked was the ebony wine that came from the mysterious Douro. Southey eventually fell in love with Portugal. In a misty-eyed letter to his brother-in-law Samuel Taylor Coleridge (1772–1834), Southey wrote: 'I would gladly live and die here.' He began to write a history of the country but never got round to finishing it.

The twenty-one-year-old Lord Byron (1788–1824) visited Lisbon with a valet, a butler and two friends. Unamused by dogs, barefoot children and filth, it was hate at first sight. However the charm and untamed beauty led him to write *Childe Harolde's Pilgrimage*, in which Byron immortalised Portugal, but not the people, wondering why nature should 'waste her wonders on such an undeserving race'.

When James Boswell (1740–1795), a young Scot 'with a very good conceit of himself, of spirit and fashion, heir to a good fortune', met Samuel Johnson (1709–1784), he was disgusted by this man 'of most dreadful appearance'. The meeting was to make both Boswell and Johnson famous. It didn't do port any harm either. The men's regular meetings were lubricated with port, although Boswell's constitution was a less able than his corpulent friend's to handle it. 'A bottle of thick English port is a very heavy and inflammatory dose', Boswell whimpered. 'I felt last time that I drank it for several days, and this morning it was boiling in my veins.' While his biographer lay sick, the ox-like Johnson was whistling merrily as he banged about his disordered kitchen preparing his nightcap, large draughts of sweet port laced with Capillare, an ancient hair restorer said to 'cause the hair to grow thick, fair and well coloured'. Warner Allen wrote: 'Johnson's company and an indulgence in port were inseparable but the crude blackstrap of the eighteenth century, a cheap wine coloured with elderberries, was a cheap price to pay for the unique privilege which immortalised two names.' Johnson is best remembered by non-literary types for spitting out the Claret he was handed by Sir Joshua Reynolds and declaiming: 'A man would be drowned by it before it made him drunk.' He was persuaded to try another glass before he made that remark. 'Poor stuff! No Sir, Claret is the liquor for boys; port for men; but he who aspires to be a hero must drink brandy.'

Glass blowers had been experimenting for centuries with various kinds of miniature amphorae, designed to take the wine from cask to table and pour it. The switch to bottles by port manufacturers was important for the development of the drink. The 1775 vintage was the first to be laid down in bottles. The experiment took time to bear results, but in the end was an astounding success. Port was magically transformed.

John Croft, in 1788, advocated six years maturing for port; four in wood and two in bottle. Others said fifteen years. William J. Todd wrote: 'Port was secure in its position as the after-dinner wine of the hard-drinking English country noblemen, gentlemen of fashion and country squires, and perhaps we should add the better-paid clergy.' In 1801 the British drank between 60,000 and 70,000 pipes. Port was even finding its way into the premier universities. A cartoon in *The Times* in 1798 reflected this. 'To which University,' a lady asked Dr Warren, 'shall I send my son?' 'Madam,' the old man answered gravely, 'they drink, I believe, the same quantity of port in each.'

By 1852 imports reached 80,000 pipes. This peak was followed by a numbing trough, with port sales tumbling to 15,000 pipes by 1858. Gladstone's 'Single Bottle

Act', which enabled grocers and chemists to deal in wine was blamed. Todd writes: 'By flooding the market with inferior wine, it brought port into relative disfavour with the more discerning classes.'

When Marshal Soult took Oporto in 1809, the port dynasties temporarily bolted back to England, returning after the Duke of Wellington (1769–1852) kicked Soult out of Portugal and even ate the splendid dinner the French chefs had carefully prepared for the Marshal, at the Palace of Carrancas. The British celebrated with Wellington at the Factory House, fawning while decanting their best vintages for the Dublin-born hero. Many years later, the Iron Duke, ancient and suffering mental fatigue, sat amid old friends in the officers' mess of a regiment of which he was an honorary colonel. As the decanter endlessly circled the table, the old soldier's stories grew taller and taller. 'Why,' the Duke slurred, 'I remember when in the lines of Torres Vedras they brought me a bottle of port one night, which, on being opened, was found to contain a dead rat.' 'It must have been a very small rat,' a subaltern interjected. Wellington fixed him with an electric glare. 'It was a damned big rat, Sir!' 'Perhaps it was a very large bottle, then,' the subaltern squeaked. 'Damn! I tell you it was a damned small bottle!' The subaltern sunk deeper into his chair, fiddling nervously with his gold buttons.

Edward Spencer writes: 'The man who had Comet port [the legendary 1811] in his cellar was a man to be cultivated and dined with. I have heard my father speak, almost with bated breath, of how, after the retirement of the ladies to discuss tea and scandal by themselves, the dining-room door would be locked by the host himself, who would pocket the key thereof. Many of the guests slept where they fell.'

In 1831, James Forrester, an eager, charming and unfashionably liberal twenty-two-year-old Yorkshireman, arrived in Oporto to take up a position in his father's firm Offley Forrester and Company. Forrester was a refreshing change from the conservative Englishmen and Scots who ran the Port business. He learned to speak Portuguese and mixed easily with landowners, politicians and the poor men who trod the grapes. Forrester got to know the Douro well. In Alec Waugh's memorable imagery, he 'inhaled the smoke that curled through the tiled roofs of the biscuity cottages, scenting the air with the smell of brushwood that burns under old iron pots.'

Forrester hosted a dinner in Regua for the major players in the port trade. At the end of the meal he briskly handed round a pamphlet entitled *A Word or Two on Port Wine*. His guests read the leaflet out of politeness. It contents were passed around the room by elbows and grimaces. This newcomer was accusing them of dishonesty by colouring their wines with the juice of the elderberry, stretching it with sickly sweet *geropiga* that was cooked up across the river in Gaia. Men who moments earlier were genially sipping and reminiscing on Waterloo, suddenly narrowed their eyes and sternly filled their waistcoats. The pamphlets fluttered towards the table as his guests hurriedly left.

Sarah Bradford writes: 'Forrester, clever and influential though he was, was a Don Quixote tilting at the windmill of commercial interest, and in this respect it is fortunate for the subsequent history of port that he lost.' Forrester was advocating a return to the organic port of a century earlier: short-lived wines to which man made no

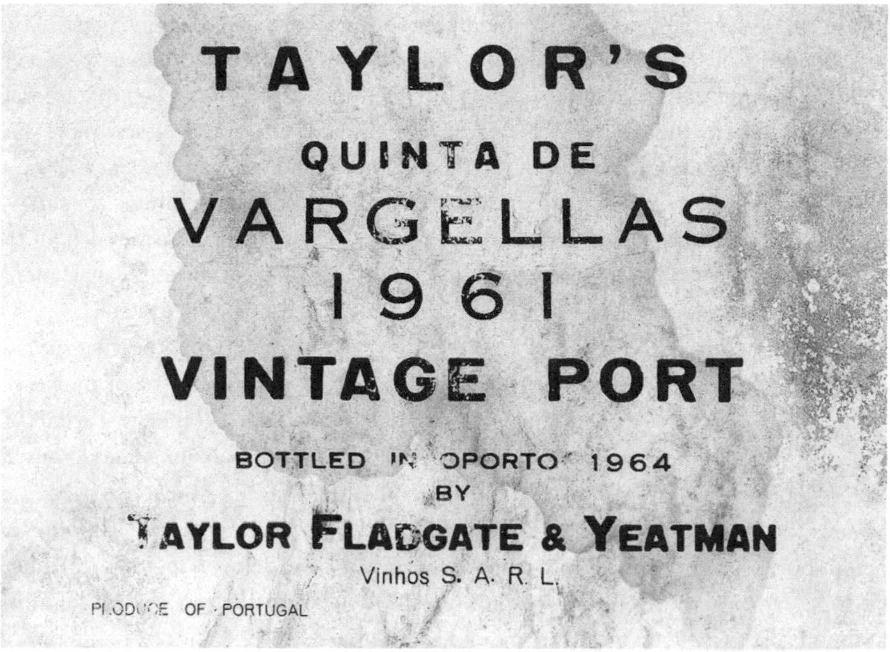

TAYLOR'S

QUINTA DE

VARGELLAS

1961

VINTAGE PORT

BOTTLED IN OPORTO 1964
BY

TAYLOR FLADGATE & YEATMAN

Vinhos S. A. R. L.

PRODUCE OF PORTUGAL

An exquisite blend of brandy and rich red wine. The French drink more port but the British sip the finest vintages.

contribution other than growing and pressing the grapes. His 'port' would have been more like the iron-rich table wines that are now being made up the Douro, not the wonderful, sweet dark wines with a touch of fire in their bellies that can outlive their maker by a hundred years and startle his great-grandchildren with their power and majesty. By the mid-nineteenth century, the port trade was concentrating on making first-class wines. Forrester was embraced once more as a friend, his influence for good acknowledged.

His unexpected death at fifty-three was dramatic, sinister and has never been satis-factorily explained. After lunch at what is now known as Taylor's Quinta de Vargellas in the Douro, Forrester was returning by river with two ladies 'well known in port society'. For whatever reason the boat capsized. The ladies were saved but Forrester, weighed down with a heavy money belt stuffed with gold sovereigns, went to the bottom. His body was later recovered but not the money. The mystery still lingers in the Douro.

Cockburn (1814) and Grahams (1820) joined the pantheon of port shippers. New people, whether wine trade or rag trade, were not automatically allowed to set foot in the Factory House. The snobbish old guard, many of whom made their money in cod, were determined to keep it as a private club. Even John Graham, still a big name in port, had a little difficulty but made it eventually. All other trades were permanently excluded. Alec Waugh describes the quintessentially English scene in 1952. After 'an excellent, straightforward dinner' accompanied by white Graves and 1929 Pontet

Canet, 'guests were invited to leave the dining room, taking their napkins with them, and move into an adjoining room where a second table waited, set with forty places and two vintage ports, the light but elegant 1917, declared by fifteen shippers, and the extraordinarily toothsome 1927, which raised huzzahs from twice as many. It was a lovely sight, a gleaming stretch of mahogany under a cluster of chandeliers, bowls of red roses, high piled fruit; a Doulton dessert service, cut-glass decanters, a cherry-coloured carpet to match the china; a delight to the eye but an even greater delight to the senses, of touch and smell. [...] Coming into that cool, fresh room, its air scented with fruit and flowers, I had the sense of being transported to another planet.'

The English way of life, where not getting their hand-ironed Times or their supply of Earl Grey were the biggest irritations, was severely at odds with that of the peasant families who eked out a miserable existence. Vizetelly paints a mucky portrait of Celleiros, 'perhaps the dirtiest village throughout the Alto Douro.' The squalid houses, rudely built, are too frequently grimy on the outside and foul within. The roads are often filthy in the extreme, indefinable smells assail one's nostrils as much from the open doorways as from the refuse-littered street. The pigs, who are legion, live either in the street, or in the common room of the family to whom they belong – a dimly-lit foetid apartment where vermin abound, where the atmosphere is close and smoky and the walls charred and blackened from the absence of chimneys. The eye lights on dirty children, yelping curs, emaciated poultry, and, above all, long-legged pigs, basking at full length in the middle of the road, disdaining to move out of your horse's way, and who, after indulging in a refreshing mud bath, will considerately retire, dripping with slush, to the single room where their owners live, eat and sleep.'

In London, port was again joyously drunk in pubs with a full pipe and a full belly in front of a glowing coal fire. Not long before, it had been served with meat and veg as a table wine because of its 'roughness' – so rough that a London wine merchant was heard to remark in 1834 that 'until port was at last rid of its astringent harshness, it could only be offered medicinally and could never be taken with pleasure'. Thomas Southam, a nineteenth-century wine merchant, had this advice on handling vintage port. 'Though apparently firm-crusted, they will sometimes slip their crust through the vibration of transit by railway or otherwise. The bottle, when required for use, may remain upright a short time, and great care should always be given to decanting.'

Phylloxera invaded Portugal in 1871. The Douro was devastated: 32,000 hectares out of a possible 50,000 decimated. This 'caused alarm in Great Britain'. But by the end of the nineteenth century around twenty companies were back in business, shipping port to London and Bristol. Port continued to be drunk with pleasure by all classes. The poor drowned it with lemonade; clerks in Wimbledon kept a few cases in their cellars with the coal. Gentleman of substance had pipes of it delivered by horse and wagon to their country seats to be bottled or drunk straight from the cask. Good vintages survived their owners by several decades.

Sarah Bradford writes: 'The days of the charlady's "port and lemon" were fast approaching. The trade was buoyant and optimistic, encouraging the British to buy land and houses in the Douro, to move into production and to lavishly entertain the sycophantic writers who eagerly shuffled up to the dusty Douro to genuflect and sing for their suppers.'

The twentieth century began with three great vintages. Twenty-one shippers declared 1900. Even unknown Port, humbly bottled by a W. Smith of Bishop Stortford, gavotted on Broadbent's tonsils. 'Rich, stylish, elegant. Quite a tang. Perfect drink.' Although twenty-five shippers plumped for 1904, it was a lighter year. Broadbent found Taylor's at seventy years old to be 'gentle and attractive'. The 1908 was declared by twenty-six shippers. The 1912, hailed by many as the 'port of the century', was the last good vintage before mustard gas wafted around the First World War trenches. The Factory House closed its doors, dust sheets were thrown over the antique furniture. The lid was closed on the grand piano.

With the clouds of war at last lifted, the Douro celebrated with a very good 1920, followed by a fabulous 1927, which was celebrated by thirty ecstatic shippers. Port sales in Britain reached a zenith in the 1920s. It was still made exactly the way it had been for centuries. Sombre-eyed, half-naked men, their black moustaches beaded with sweat, carried every glistening grape from the steep, terraced vineyards on their backs to the granite *lagares* for pressing, 'jog trotting as Africans do'. Dumping their cargoes into the coffin-like *lagares*, they climbed in when it was full and danced up and down like children playing on the springs of an old bed. Full of ferments and passion, the men danced wild-eyed, their knees pumping to the discordant caterwauling of primitive instruments and the insistent beat of a Portuguese drum.

Alec Waugh paints a colourful picture of brown women arriving after their chores were completed and the children were kissed and tucked up in bed, to lift their skirts to the increasingly wild music. Screeching with ecstasy they climbed into the purple suds to writhe with the men, their juice-stained legs flying like young mares in heat. Waugh comments: 'The joke about "June babies" may not be founded on too strong a basis of fact, but many marriages can trace their origin to the evenings in the *lagares*.'

The Factory House, which had been closed since the start of the First World War, reopened in 1934. The carpets were hoovered, the damask cushions were fluffed, stern paintings were feather-dusted and the decanters were washed, drained and replenished. English ladies rushed to Knightsbridge to be measured up for new ball gowns. The reason? The Prince of Wales was paying a visit to cheer up the ex-pats. Their skill at arranging great parties had not been lost. The organisers drew up a list of names. They were restricted to 'persons of their own class' and 'Portuguese of consequence'. What jockeying there must have been for that gilt-edged invitation! What floods of tears were shed! What spectacular tantrums were thrown and what locks pulled out by the roots by the disappointed! It was the social event of the century. The port families were not forgotten after all. There was great shame in not being there. Wrists would be slit. Suicide notes would be scrawled on gilt mirrors in blue blood.

The royal visit was a great success. Faith in port was restored. The Americans, after Prohibition, had begun to drink port. The French were taking delivery of thousands of pipes – 9,000 in 1936. The British were back in charge. Vintages were promising, and there were still a few pipes of the brilliant 1927 for very special customers. Sales were brisk. A battered icon was slowly recovering. Then the wings fell off.

The Second World War effectively ended the English love affair with port. Many a poor man or woman still savoured it in shuttered pubs. Keeping their voices down, they stretched the scarce red stuff with lemonade, listening with goggle eyes for the dying of the doodlebug's engine. Before the war 'thousands of gallons of port were sold over the counter, rubies in the pubs, tawnies in city wine bars'. Sarah Bradford records the reaction of one pub landlady she interviewed. 'A working man or woman could put down a large glass of good port for ninepence,' the woman said. 'One pub in the East End used to sell 100 pipes a year'.

Frank Yeatman, a game veteran of many a good Factory House luncheon, was asked by his doctor how much port he drank. 'The normal amount, a pipe a year,' the eighty-year-old chirped. Evelyn Waugh recalled the halcyon times when gentlemen laid down pipes of port for their sons, wrote: 'all too often there was not much left of that pipe by the time the boy reached his twenty-first birthday, most of it having already gone down his father's throat!'

The Englishman's drink was elbowed into a dark corner by cheap imitations from the Dominions. Consumers showed a renewed interest in sweet sherry. Unused to a battle for market share, shippers caved in. By the 1960s twenty firms had vanished. Life had been so much fun living in Portugal with a friendly dictator in charge, attending pig-sticking parties, playing the odd game of cricket with one's peers in Oporto. A few shippers came out fighting. Their names can be seen today on supermarket shelves. As Bradford observes: 'Selling port today is no longer a business of gentlemanly agreements between old friends over lunch.'

Port does not need an immaculate provenance to be good. Michael Broadbent's favourite was an 1851 from a long-forgotten shipper or bottler called Stibbart. Broadbent, who tasted it twice in the 1970s, called it 'the most magnificent old port I have ever drunk.' William Todd drank ordinary port with 'new walnuts and a self sacrificing daughter or niece to remove the skins, or with fruit cake after the cheese, avoiding citrus fruits.' Raymond Postgate wrote in 1951 that drinking a full, round port fulfilled 'the simple and innocent greed of a child let loose in a sweet shop'. On one thing the British working class, middle class and upper class agree: that there is nothing like a good glass of port.

France assumed top spot in port consumption with Britain second. However, the British are drinking quality: most vintage port is still consumed in the United Kingdom. Even though Evelyn Waugh said 'intelligent women are the sworn enemies of good Port', the drink is increasingly enjoyed by modern women under the age of 35. While the tawny of a couple of decades old can be a very fine wine, the British, after several brief flings with white port, have kicked it into the long grass. It is not very good, being thick, sweet and blowsy and never has been. 'White port was not highly regarded,' says John Delaforce. 'It was restricted to a shelf above the kitchen stove where it could be easily reached by the maid who made the popular wine jelly.' Yet, in the first ever sale of port organised by Christie's in 1768, for 'an Innkeeper and Farmer at the White Hart and Post Office, Petersfield', red port fetched 15s 6d a dozen while white port reached 17s 6d a dozen. 'White Port is not only the cheapest but the best Wine about Town,' Sir Richard Steel said on March 1710. Ballantyne, an Oporto-domiciled English wine merchant, took an order for 80 pipes of white port in one week in 1780. It was clearly popular in England then but eventually lost out to sherry and has never recovered.

For those who have not tasted white port, one of the best places to try it is on the banks of the Douro at Vila Nova de Gaia. Make it a balmy evening on a noisy and fervent saint's day. Have unruly rockets shredding the clouds. Chuck in a folk band down from the hills made up of singing harpies with staring eyes and dental problems and the cast of *Deliverance* playing garden tools and hand saws.

Port is a wonderful drink, especially when it is good and fully mature. No other wine has the eye-closing, grinning potential of very fine old vintage port. Nowadays not many drink it to destruction as John Mytton and his like did a century and a half ago. These were rich, idle men with nothing better to do than commit slow and sleepy suicides drinking Port. The fatal dose is about half a crate a day in case anyone Swedish is looking for a new form of euthanasia.

Evelyn Waugh agreed. 'Port,' he said, 'should be drunk at the table; only in the masculine calm which follows the retirement of the women, when the decanter travels from hand to hand round the bare mahogany.' Waugh described 'an excessively rare eighteenth-century piece made in the shape of a semi-circular arc which fits across the fireplace: some of them have brass tramlines and a little wheeled carriage to carry the decanters. He is a fortunate host who possesses such a piece of furniture; he must, however, confine himself strictly to male company, for no body of men once established there can be persuaded to leave for the chintz and chatter of the drawing room.'

Taylor's, arguably the greatest port house, is not just alive and well, but about to clamber onto the millionaire's band wagon alongside Le Pin and Petrus. Taylor's have just made a Super Port. It is exclusive and obviously expensive. This Julio Iglesias of a wine is made from seventy-year-old Nacional vines, Portugal's answer to Cabernet Sauvignon, Pinot and Syrah. Grown on the Quinta de Vargellas estate, which Taylor's have owned for over a century the grapes are individually bathed in unicorn's milk every morning, injected with botox and have their tiny legs waxed. Only four pipes of this port have been made. The first vintage 1995 was not a great year. Cosseted and fed on gold dust in its eighteen-month sojourn in cask, the dusky giant is now bottled and stashed away in Portugal. Will this blue-cheeked baby grow up to be fine, fragrant and elegant, in the style that made Taylor's famous? Few will ever know. I fear at the price it will command for its exclusivity the new Super Port will be purchased by cheesy collectors who will put it on display in glass domes.

24

The Mystery of Maturing

The activities of a few noble entrepreneurs, huge investment, improvements in grape selection, careful vinification and the introduction of cask, cork and glass led to the mystery of maturing and the emergence of fine wines. Old wines, beautiful to smell and to look at, that were once drunk young and bubbly out of pewter pots, were now poured into decanters and served in ringing glassware. André Simon observed that great vintages 'were sipped and savoured, discussed at length over the mahogany, with dessert, whilst reminiscences flowed and candles burnt brightly into the night.' The wine snob was already unravelling himself from his bandages, ready to stalk the earth, write for wine magazines and ruin dinner parties the length and breadth of the land.

'A wider choice of wines of interest and quality became available,' André Simon wrote. 'Meals altered accordingly. There was more variety and refinement in the choice of dishes, and table manners improved.' French wines, in spite of their continued popularity among men of taste, continued to suffer and were almost unobtainable. Even higher rates of duty slapped on them in 1745 meant they were all but banished from English wine lists, much to the delight of shippers of inferior wines from elsewhere.

In the early eighteenth century, the Earl of Bristol bought 'Obrian', 'Margoose Clarett' and 'Château Margou' to add to his eclectic assemblage of Navarre, Rhenish, Florence and the rest. The relatively modest intervention of a few wealthy enthusiasts, however, made little impact on shipments from France and imports continued to plummet. 'At the dawn of the eighteenth century,' Simon wrote, 'the total recorded imports of wine from France into all English ports amounted to less than 1,000 tuns per annum, practically the same quantity as was imported from the Rhine and Mosel.' Ninety per cent of wine imported into England from 1699 to 1703 was sweet Spanish and Portuguese.

Old wine was considered 'past it' and was unpopular. Port was faked and Madeira 'was universally consumed in much greater quantities than the island produced'. Hock often went bad. Sir Edward Barry, author of *Observations Historical, Critical and Medical on the Wines of the Ancients*, published in 1775, growled like a stern headmaster: 'A prejudice in favour of old wines prevails too much amongst us. No hock could be worth drinking after six years.'

Duties heaped by the British onto French wines had the desired effect: they all but destroyed exports to the United Kingdom. By 1708 the trade with France collapsed to a humiliating 1 per cent. The government's policy of foisting inferior Portuguese wine onto the public instead of the French they enjoyed resulted in a falling off in wine consumption generally. Smuggling French wines into Britain was tempting and profitable. The aristocracy, who had 'an exhaustive table of wines' tucked away under their magnificent houses, hardly noticed. They had the means to obtain the finest French wines in new 'cylindrical bottles', bulbous, long in the neck, attractive to the eye and blown by craftsmen 'who were not only skilled, but lovers of beauty'.

There were cries for the 'unfair' duty on French wines to be lowered. Not everyone agreed. Sir Richard Steele (1672–1729) had a letter published in the *Spectator* of 19 April 1711: 'Verily, Mr. Spectator, we are much offended at an Act for importing French wines. A bottle or two of good solid edifying Port at honest George's made a night cheerful and threw off reserve. But this plaguey French Claret will not only cost us more money, but do us less good.' Much of what Steele describes as 'solid Port' was in fact little more than a rough table wine to which shippers added a vicious young brandy to palliate the coarseness. At 7s a gallon, a man could, and frequently did, pleasantly drink himself to death on it.

Country people made their own wines. Even wealthy landowners sent their servants out to scour hedgerows for blackberries, elderberries and wild damsons. Kitchens were noisy and redolent with the smell of boiling and fermenting and topping and tailing of black and redcurrants. Christmas presents included corkscrews, 'related tools' and 'coat-hanger creamware bin labels', and indicated how respectable home-made wines had become. Currant, elder and ginger wine, perry, milk punch and old beer bin labels happily hung with Claret, Chablis, Nuits, Johannisberg, Champagne, port, Marsala and gold sherry.

Spanish and Portuguese table wines shipped to England

Vineyards were flourishing in Alicante in the twelfth century. Red, white and brown wine has flowed from there ever since. The English were well acquainted with the name, whether it be Aligaunte, Alicant or Alycaunt. They were all chalked on blackboards in English taverns in the sixteenth and seventeenth centuries. Such was the yearning for something cheerful made from grapes grown in the sunny Levante, it was even mixed with English beer – 'Buttered beer coloured with Allicant', according to a play by Francis Beaumont (1584–1616) and his co-author John Fletcher (1579–1625). The odd fresh egg or two were beaten into Alicante to provide a healthy and satisfying breakfast or a belly settler last thing at night.

In the mid-eighteenth century, a time of great uncertainty as far as the supply of French wine was concerned, it was useful to have a plentiful supply of Alicaunt to stretch the French names. For modern Alicante the magic of earlier times has long evaporated. The region still makes a variety of wines, from the basic brews, earthy and powerful – Monastrell-driven reds which happy tourists use to accompany their chicken and chips – to Fondillon, a solera-made, intensely sweet dessert wine.

In a north-east corner of Spain, ancient, overgrown terraced vineyards bear witness to serious wine production, including Garnatxa, a rancid behemoth that was wiped out by phylloxera in the 1900s. Professor Saintsbury called it Ampurdam and thought it came from the Channel Islands. He called it 'fiery and disagreeable but at fifty or sixty years old it became by no means despicable.'

When in 1363 the kings of England, Scotland, Denmark, France and Cyprus sat down at the Vintner's Hall in London to feast on twenty-one kinds of fish and thirteen kinds of bird, they dipped their royal noses into beakers of the popular sweet wines of the day, which included Muscadel, Malmsey, Vernage, Osey, Crete and Bastard.

Bastard, white or brown, which takes its name from the mainly Portuguese grape, the Bastardo, was mentioned in 1460 in J. Russell's *Boke of Nurture*. It also merits several mentions in plays by William Shakespeare (1564–1616). It seems the Bard had little time for coarse Spanish wine. In *Measure for Measure*, Elbow says: 'Nay, if there be no remedy for it, but that you will needs buy and sell men and women like beasts, we shall have all the world drink brown and white bastard.' Shakespeare refers to Bastard again when he has Prince Hal sneering: 'Your brown bastard is your only drink.' It is mentioned again in *Henry IV, Part 1*.

In *The English Housewife, Containing the Inward and Outward Vertues which Ought to be a Complete Woman*, published by Nicholas Okes in 1631, there is a novel recipe for white Bastard. 'Draw out of a pipe of bastard ten gallans, and put to it five gallans of new milke, and skim it as before, and all to beat it with a parill of eight whites of egges, and a hand-full of Baysalt and a pint of conduit-water, and it will be white and fine in the morning.' There were several recipes featuring Bastard, some sweetened with honey.

From the beginning it was considered inferior to Sack. In 1638 Luke Hutton, in *The Blacke Dogg of New-gate*, wrote 'brown, beloved Bastard'. *The Art and Mystery of Vintners*, published in 1682, refers to 'wines commonly compounded: Ipocris, Brown Bastard, White Bastard.' William Golding writes: 'Whether always compounded or not, Bastard in the seventeenth century was usually a rich, sweet wine, the brown variety being the sweeter of the pair, and most of it came from the Iberian penin-sula. It was often a workhorse blending wine, sometimes with honey added, a *vin miellé*.' Broadbent reckoned an 1870 Blandy's Bastardo he sampled at a Saintsbury Club dinner in 1977 was 'one of the most magnificent Madeiras ever tasted'. The Bastardo clings on in Australia and California, where a dysfunctional relative of the once famous grape is bewilderingly known as Cabernet Gros, Touriga or Trousseau.

Benecarlo or Benecarlos was made in Valencia and was popular before the advent of Tarragona, 'the poor man's port'. A modest beverage, it was among the many used to give anaemic French wines a lift. James Denman wrote in *The Vine and Its Fruits*, published in 1875: 'The town of Beni Carlos in Valencia supplies in considerable quantity a strong and full-flavoured wine which is exported to France, expressly to mingle with Claret for England.' It was also transported to Oporto to be used in the manufacture of 'a thin, pale Port'.

Garnarde, Gernarde or Granad were fashionable in the fourteenth century in England, when Chaucer referred to them in the *Canterbury Tales*. All are likely to have been crude anagrams of Granada. Some say they were paying homage to the Garnacha grape, which thrives on aridity and quickly followed the sun from Aragon to France.

While the English taste was mainly for soothing, full-strength wines, Galicia introduced sharp, low-strength, dry wines to England in the fourteenth century. William Younger unearthed a rollocking and rustic gem called Hollocke or Holloc. Noisy London taverners called it Hallacker. Another sweet Spanish wine was sold as Corrunna. It might have been better known but for Spanish Custom officials insisting on shippers travelling long distances inland to obtain permits from the governor for every shipment. Lucina or Lucena was shipped in the early eighteenth century and caught the eye of the Earl of Bristol, who purchased £15 16s-worth of white Lucina between 1720 and 1739. Lepe, known to Chaucer, was white and strong and often used to give French wine a boot. It is hardly surprising this sun-kissed wine with its fiery nose and warming alcohol became such a favourite.

In February 1668 Pepys took dinner with the Spanish ambassador, who introduced the loveable diarist to 'some new sort of wine lately found out, called Navarre, which I tasted, and is, I think, good wine'. The Kingdom of Navarre was once important and extensive with vineyards in Bordeaux. In the Middle Ages famished pilgrims tramping to Santiago de Compostela halted to drink this light and refreshing wine. Navarre was cellared by the celebrated connoisseur the Earl of Bedford in the 1660s and it was enjoyed by Catherine the Great of Russia. When phylloxera ravished France, wine growers in Navarre filled the gap by effectively making wines the French could sell as their own produce. Plenty of it came to England to be sold as Claret.

Urdiales, or Ordiales as it was better known in England, came from the Castro Urdiales in the Spanish province of Santander. It was shipped to England for King Henry III in 1237. Spanish wines that were dark, sweet and cheap and variously labelled Osey, Ossey, Oseye, Osoyo, Ossoy, Aussay or Ausoye were exported to the Low Countries, Scandinavia and England from 1200. They continued to be drunk by the pewter mugful under one or more of those names by plain-talking men watching bare-knuckle boxers and cock, bear and dog fights in seedy taverns up to the nineteenth century. The wine undoubtedly came from a number of sources and was blended in London. Known to Shakespeare, much of the base ingredient was Spanish but the waters are muddied by an *Oxford English Dictionary* definition which connects Aussay with Alsace via the Latin word *alisatius*, namely a wine from that region. It is a fact that Alsatian wine was shipped to England from about the thirteenth century.

Paxarete or Pajarette, a dark sweet, *vino de color*, is still made from the concentrated juice of, among others, the Pedro Ximenez grape 'and finished by mixing the wine with essences'. Throughout history it was used to add colour and sweetness to thin wines. The Greeks used Hepsema for the same purpose. The Romans named something similar Sapa and Defructum. A host of ancient wine historians, including Pliny, Columella, Virgil, Varro and Martial all mention it. The Spanish version was expensive and in fashion as a high calorie dessert wine in eighteenth-century England when Messrs Edward and William Cox, the Derby wine merchants, took delivery of a hogshead of Rota Tent on 11 February 1791. It was shipped from Jerez with a consignment of six butts of 'Most Superior' sherry and a hogshead of Paxarete. Sherry was £4 a butt, Rota Tent £9 and the Paxarete £14.

The fact that the Prince Regent took delivery of a hogshead of a wine known for its 'light, delicate taste and fragrancy' meant there was more than one kind. It helped to popularise a cheaper version which was eagerly lapped up by the royal subjects. Fine, mature Paxarete was esteemed enough to have a 'ticket' engraved 'Paxarotta' to go around decanters filled with the dusky snooze inducer. The best of the modern kind is called 'color de macetilla', or the wine of the little mallet – because it fetched such high prices at auction. It is not as nauseating as it sounds, says Jeffs, but 'has a remarkable and complex flavour, on first impact appearing to be sweet, but having a stringent aftertaste'.

In 1391 Riptage was chalked on the walls of London taverns. It was often sold as Spanish but came from somewhere in the valley of the River Minho, between Portugal and Spanish Galicia. The precise definition of Ribadavia, Rivere or Ryvere is similarly befuddled by the passage of time but seems to refer to any wine shipped along the River Ebro. Confusingly, wines shipped from Aragon or Catalonia were also called 'river wine' or 'Wyn ryvers'. It may also have been the first infant Rioja, which has been drunk with pleasure in England for at least 500 years, or a light red from the banks of the River Minho between Galicia and north Portugal. Ribadavia was said to be light and fragrant. The playwright Thomas Haywood liked to make a song of the name, singing over and over again, 'Vino deriba davia'. How swiftly those cold dark nights must have passed.

Decayed artifacts, excavated old wine tanks and press houses prove winemaking in Rioja goes back at least 900 years. Documents in the Municipal Regulations refer to winemaking in 1102. Gonzala de Barceo, the first poet of the Castillian language, sang the praises of the beautiful chestnut-coloured wines of the Rioja, which in the Middle Ages played no small part in the economy of the region. In 1650 a law was passed protecting the quality and guaranteeing the provenance of Riojan wines. In 1787 a consortium of growers was set up under the label La Real Sociedad Económica de Cosecheros de la Rioja Castellana to encourage vine growing, oversee winemaking and promote sales and distribution.

England played a small part in the improvement of Riojan wines. While Luciano de Murrietta, a Spanish-domiciled, right-wing Peruvian, lived in London in the mid-nineteenth century, he tasted so much good dry and elegant Claret he decided to visit Bordeaux to find out how it was made. He spent some time in the town, and by the time he returned to Rioja in 1850 his notebooks were full of new ideas which he immediately put into practice. The stone troughs, clay jars, the olive oil and the untrained vines had to go. With them went the quaint habit of mixing building mortar with white Rioja because it was cheaper than water. Wooden vats, disciplined pruning, a more thorough grape selection and small oak casks were introduced. Arming his barefoot workers with fly swatters and soap also helped. Rather than send his first new-style Rioja to London to have his optimism crushed, Murrietta dispatched his creation to friendly Cuba and Mexico for evaluation. Amid cries of 'Olé!', the Cubans gave it a thumbs-up. The cask destined for Mexico, meanwhile, bobbed about in the sea, the ship having sunk en route. The emboldened Murrietta copied a rival Claret lover, the Marquess de Riscal, in building himself an impressive *bodega*. Owned by the Creixell family, Marques de Murrietta Y gay recently celebrated 150 years among the leaders of Riojan wine. Dalmau, made from the fruit of fifty year old vines grown, mainly, in the lofty Canajas vineyard, which is allowed to slowly macerate then lengthily aged in new French oak barriques. Fairly exclusive, the owners describe it as 'thought provoking'.

In 1902 a Royal Order was passed which defined the name of Rioja and its remit and in 1926 a decree established the Consejo Regulador, which defined the limits of the region and controlled the issuing of labels. In 1991 a ministerial order granted the wines of Rioja the Calificado, a label of quality; it was the first Spanish wine to be so honoured. Britain is now the most significant market for the wines of Rioja.

Rota Tent, Tynt or Tente was a dark, sweet, reddish-brown, unfortified, low-alcohol dessert wine from southern Spain. It was originally made from grapes grown around Rota, near Cadiz. Samuel Pepys liked it straight from the little cask he kept in his cellar, but Tent was popular in England long before that. It was celebrated in Elizabethan literature and was humorously referred to as 'a rich wine, drank generally as a stomachic'. Later it became the wine of choice in the Church of England 'for Communion purposes'. On 6 January 1902 Berry Bros delivered twelve cases of Rota Tent to King Edward VII.

Sitges, or Seges, came unsurprisingly from Sitges, a small coastal town eighteen miles south-west of Barcelona. It was yet another sweet wine from the Malvasia which enjoyed modest sales in London. A few bottles were included in the dispersal sale by Messrs Christie and Manson of the contents of the Stowe House cellars in 1848.

Torrentyne was a sharp little wine, possibly from the Torrontes grape, grown in the cooler, and hillier, north of Spain. It was a popular antidote to the massive, heart-stopping sweet wines so copiously drunk in London taverns. Tarragona takes its name from Tarraconensis, a huge area in Roman times which made a vast amount of wine, much of it for export. Modern Tarragona is a thick, sweet, heart-warming brown wine sold in flagons. It kept many a weary grey head out of the gas oven in smog-smothered Britain in the 1950s. It was also poured into chipped mugs by young seducers working on unpublishable novels in attics from London to Edinburgh. It now does its penance by supplying swathes of pious Christians with their Communion wine.

Vidonia was yet another Spanish wine popular in England in the eighteenth century. Witness this advertisement for 'Vidonia of the Madeira flavour' placed in a London newspaper on 14 January 1795: 'Parker and Wilson respectfully inform gentlemen who may be desirous of purchasing pipes and hogsheads that a vessel shortly sails from Tenerife. This is an opportunity to purchase a wine of flavour and quality equal to many Madeiras at 17 shillings per dozen.' Vidonia was made from the Chasselas Dore grape, of 'insipid' Swiss wine fame. Jancis Robinson reckons the Chasselas 'may well be the oldest known vine variety cultivated by man'. Who could possibly disagree with the fragrant one? Vizetelly for one who claims it was made from the Vidueno, 'a juicy round white grape'. There was also apparently, a rarer black variety.

Apparently the red Chasselas bears a striking resemblance to those painted on the walls of Egyptian tombs. Vidonia also masqueraded as Canary – William Younger says it was one of the finest brands. It was dryish on the palate, which may have been why the dons of the Senior Common Room at Christ Church, Oxford purchased it between 1770 and 1870. It cost 4s 3d a bottle, expensive for the times. The dons 'kept on buying it until the mid-1820s when sherry became the dominant white wine in the Common Room'. In *Bell's Weekly Messenger* of 29 December 1799, a pipe of Vidonia could be had for as little as £53. 'The suddenness and completeness with which these wines have disappeared from the Englishman's table is surprising', wrote a saddened Tommy Layton.

25

Portuguese Table Wines

Bucelas, Bucellas, or 'Blucellas', as R.S. Surtees' (1803–1864) vulgar creation Jorrocks called it, is Lisbon wine. It was a nondescript little dump in the late-nineteenth century according to Henry Vizetelly whose book *Facts about Port and Madeira* appeared in 1882. It had 'stragged from the valley half-way up the adjacent hills. There was a shabby public square, bordered by a few trees. In front of its stands a plain stone cross, olives and poplars seem to gird it round'. The odd dozy bullock hauled a cart with wheels 'of the ancient Roman type'. The grower Vizetelly visited was a 'stalwart, handsome man with well-chiselled features, jet black hair and beard, and a complexion the colour of mahogany. He wore blue trousers elaborately patched, undressed leather boots, a crimson sash, and a clean white shirt, evidently put on for the occasion.' Bucellas sprang from Arinto grape which Vizetelly wrote 'is commonly believed to be the same as the Riesling, the prevalent grape on the banks of the Rhine'. The importance of a bountiful crop in this poor, God forsaken backwater is shown by the fact that from the 20 July the growers placed ragged, gap-toothed guards 'armed with rusty firelocks' to protect their grape-laden vines. The plucked grapes were carried on the backs of tough, gaunt and grim-visaged men to the press houses which had a black cross daubed on the doors to keep out 'the evil one'. The grapes were trodden by mix parties of men and women the latter at 9*d* being 4*d* cheaper to employ. Vizatelly visited Sandeman's, who were the principal shipper of Bucellas to England, to taste various vintages of the wine. Starting with a year-old wine which the Englishman recalled 'was remarkably fresh in flavour, with a slight greenish tinge, and in many respects the counterpart of a youthful hock. The older wines were 'rounder and more aromatic; their flavour more pronounced, with a soft, almondy after-taste, they retained all that pleasant freshness which only a wine without adventitious spirit is likely to display'. Formerly, Bucellas was fortified but the new style, lighter wines Sandeman's shipped, 'being the best of their class', were labelled 'El Rey-Royal Bulock Hock'. Vizetelly also tasted a mellow oxidised Arinto that resembled an elegant Manzanilla Sherry and was sometimes fobbed off on unsuspecting taverners in England.

Unusually refreshing, but often thickened with Calcavella, it was once the most popular and one of the most expensive white Portuguese table wines in England. At £72 10s a pipe, it was more expensive than any port shipped by Harvey's of Bristol. Made predominantly from the Arinto grape, with a little gentle persuasion from the Esagna Cão, otherwise known as the 'dog strangler', Bucelas was mis-sold as Portuguese Hock in Victorian England. The Duke of Wellington enjoyed it and told his friends what a wonderful little number it was. It was ever-present on posh side-boards and drinking it was the height of 'chic'. In the Victoria Wine Company's list of 1880 Bucellas was described as 'not cheap, a pale wine made from the German grape' – that is, the Riesling with which it was often confused, probably by port drinkers. Modern Bucelas struggles on in intenstive care with one or two growers wringing their hands by its bedside.

Caparica, Caprick, Capricke, Caprycke, or Caperrikis was, according to William Younger, 'a rich wine from near Lisbon, recognisable among the Tudors. Likely origins are Portugal or Spain, slightly less probable are mainland Italy and Capri; least probably of all Cyprus.' Holinshed's *Chronicles* decribes Caprike as a wine associated with the Elizabethans and he claims it came from either Capri or Cyprus.

Carcavelos, Carcarvelos or Carcarvella, 'a white wine of an agreeable sweetness with a pungent taste', and formerly held in great repute' was created by the indomitable Marquis de Pombal at Oeras in the eighteenth century from grapes ripened on the banks of the Tagus near Lisbon. When Pombal lost interest he had the vines ripped up and wheat planted. Vizatelly, who was introduced to Carcavellos on his visit to Sanderman's wrote 'fine flavour with an expensive bouquet. A much older wine had developed into a luscious, mellow dessert wine. Often mixed with port, which was against the rules, it was briefly popular in the nineteenth century and lifted the unhappy Napoleon's spirits on Elba. It was shipped to England in hogsheads and was often served at important dinners. In 1794 it sold for 30s a case at a time when a dozen bottles of the finest port cost only 27s. The price rose to 38s a dozen for a 'fine, old' version in 1799. Perhaps because of the price, Carcavelos was rejected by trenchermen but remained a novelty. Harvey's of Bristol never shipped it direct, preferring to take their modest supplies from a British agent. One of Portugal's DOC wines, Carcavelos is still made in small quantities from the juice of up to nine black and white grapes, which is then fortified with brandy. After an injection of *vinho abefado*, a mixture of grape juice and grape spirit, the wine is laid to rest in casks for up to five years, where it develops a vague similarity to tawny port.

Charnico was the 'quick-spirited liquor' enjoyed by Horner the Armourer's drunken friends in *Henry VI Part 2*, Act 3. It was named after one of the villages near where it was made. Charnico was launched as a rival to Sack. It failed, but the Portuguese finally got their one great wine when they invented port a century later.

Colares, or Collares, a stringy red from the charmless little Ramisco vine, has all be disappeared, its sandy vineyards gnawed by JCBs making golf courses. It was once highly regarded in England. In 1877 Collares was described by Vizatelly as 'a pleasant red wine, possessing somewhat the character of a full-bodied Beaujolais. It was listed as one on one of the two Portuguese table wines in the Factory House cellars amid Champagne, Sherry, Hock, Sauternes, Ch. Margaux and Ch. Lafite. Growers did their best to infuse the light coloured Collares with a dash of colour, 'always a great consideration with Portuguese wines' says Vizatelly. And it still is. Growers tended to rack their wines rather than filter or fine them to preserve what colour their was. The best of it fetched £16 a pipe. Lesser wines, blended with juice from outside the region were sold cheaply. Vizetelly tasted a white Collares made from 'the Arinto, Castello and Dona Branca'. He described it as 'pale in colour, soft, fresh-tasting, pleasantly dry, and altogether not unlike a Grave'. Only sixty or so barrels were made. If it came to England there is little evidence of it.

Red, white and sweet wines, several labelled 'Lisbon', appeared in many a well-thumbed mid-eighteenth-century cellar book. They included Bucellas, Carcavellos, Colares, Malmsey, Bastard, Moscatel, Muscatel or Muscadel, Caparica and Charnico. Very fine 'antique' Malmseys were also made in the Upper Douro. Considered by Vizatelly to be 'archaic curiosities' they were either blended or privately cellared for the delectation of the Port barons and their friends. Lisbon white fetched £56 per tun in London in the 1730s, almost twice the price of Mountain, Canary and sherry. Only port at £60 a tun was more expensive. John Gay mentions 'Lisbon new or old' in his poem *Wine*, written in 1708, and the Earl of Bristol cellared 'White Lisbon'. At the Lord Mayor's Installation Banquet in London in 1762, 220 bottles of Lisbon were consumed. Lisbon was second only to port on that occasion, easily outperforming Claret and Champagne. Lisbon was also served at a banquet held at the Stationer's Hall on 23 April 1778, when the wine list was packed with the most famous wines of the day. Sir Robert Walpole (1676–1745), under his 'little Gothic castle' in Strawberry Hill, Twickenham, kept 'numerous' casks of sweet Lisbon, which he had doled out to his less fussy visitors, keeping his finest Clarets, Burgundies and Champagnes for his special friends.

Messrs Wynn and Custance shipped Lisbon to London from their spacious adega with its 'long vista of arches, occasionally in solid masonry of immense thickness' in which 'some couple of thousand pipes' were stored.. 'Here were,' Vizatelly wrote, 'deep tinted Sacavem red wines, some dry and clean tasting, others extremely sweet, and a rich and poten Arinto from the same vineyard where the soil is darker and richer than in the Bucellas district, and soft, sweet, ladies' wine going chiefly to Russia and the Baltic. 'White Lisbon, once 'universally drunk by City men at luncheon' faded in the nineteenth century. The red version suffered the indignity of being mixed with cheap southern French and palmed off as Claret in taverns. Vizatelly was of the opinion it was better for the British importer to buy Lisbon wines direct from the grower rather than 'receive them through France, after they have been emasculated by mixture with the undrinkable vins verts of our enterprising French neighbours.

Setubal is a voluptuous sweet wine made from Moscatel grapes done to a turn on the Arrabida hills south of Lisbon, which were demarcated in 1907 for Moscatel de Setubal. Unfortunately the robots in the European Union got wind of the fact that it was only 70 per cent Moscatel – the famous scented vine that drove the Greeks and Romans batty – and the name has had to be omitted from the label since 1986. Setubal, or Moscatel de Setubal if you can find an old, highly illegal bottle at auction – is frequently, and surprisingly, bypassed by those searching for uncomplicated dessert wines at a reasonable price. Assisted by the ludicrous price of even moderate Sauternes, this age-worthy, honeyed, muscatty mouthful is great value for money. Old Setubal, while never reaching the classical pitch of Château d'Yquem or the finest German Trockenbeerenauslese Rieslings, helped unlock the tongues of young poets, like Thomas Gray (1716–1771), who flocked to Strawberry Hill to dip their strawberries in bowls of thick cream, knock back their Setubal and sing like a canary. Setubal is one of the most reliable and long-lasting of sweet wines. It gains a toffee-like sweetness, and from the less warm vintages, a tasty acidity, but never loses that wonderfully heady Moscatel flavour that reminds one small boy of his mother making the Christmas pudding cake in Ireland long, long ago. Cue wistful fiddle playing. For bottles that have survived a century or more, the words that most frequently pop up in tasting notes are 'pungent', 'meaty' and 'Madeira-like'.

Lucebon and Algarbe were cheap blends shipped from the Algarve and sold in London taverns. Both were served 'loose', in jugs straight out of casks.

26

Madeira

Madeira, like port and Champagne, was discovered by accident when Zarco, the one-eyed sea captain Juan Gonçalves, landed on the heavily wooded island of Madeira in 1418 and planted the Portuguese flag on its summit. Portuguese settlers set fire to the thick woodland to make room for houses and tillable land. When the ash cooled, sugar cane and black grapes were planted.

Tiny canals, *levadas*, to carry water from the island's highest point were built by *guanches*, slaves from Tenerife. Nowhere is free of the delightfully soothing murmour of trickling water. Africans were shipped in to work the cane plantations. Vegetable and vine growers were elbowed aside to make sugar, the magic new sweetener that was about to replace honey. The Genoese brought with them grape cuttings – the Cretan, or Malvasia – which ended up being the main ingredient in Malmsey. A 'Malvoisie of the Isle of Madeer' was shipped to London as early as 1537.

England took to the burnt wine. Sweet Malmsey was particularly popular among young married couples for, according to a poem by William Vaughan in 1600, a few gasses stoked up the sex drive and 'strengthened the back'. Shakespeare knew of Madeira and alludes to it his plays. In the period 1720 to 1739 the Earl of Bristol bought £44 6s 6d-worth of Madeira. At the Lord Mayor's Installation Banquet in 1762, ninety bottles of Madeira were consumed.

Vineyards were increased to accommodate the new business and, before a harbour was built, casks of Madeira bobbed in the sea, guided to the waiting boats by swimmers with otter-like skill. The equivalent of 600,000 bottles of Madeira were exported to England and America via Africa and Asia. When the botanist Sir Joseph Banks first saw Madeira up close on Captain Cook's *Endeavour* in 1768, he was impressed by 'the sides of the hills being entirely covered with vineyards almost as high as the eye can distinguish'.

Cook hoisted 3,000 gallons on board and pumped in brandy and *vinho de surdo* before setting sail on a voyage of exploration. The British rushed to Madeira and set themselves up as middle men. As the natives were 'idle' and more interested in sleeping off the effects of their rough table wines, the wines of Madeira were soon in British hands. Many of the early sales were concentrated on keeping Her Majesty's messes sozzled in India. Wine barrels sweated on Funchal dock before being loaded onto ships to wallow about in zephyr-less seas for weeks. Loving the intense heat, the wines improved en route, their colour edging from gold to amber. When tasted they were smoky, bitter, unique. The new method caught on. Known as *vinho da roda*, it soon replaced *vinho canteiro*, wine matured for years 'in cask in the old-fashioned way, as the islanders' favourite wine. England was a willing market for the new burnt-tasting 'sherry'. Madeira that had voyaged to either the East or West Indies were according to Vizatelly as 'not particularly deep in colour, but remarkably powerful, and with that indefinable flavour which Madeira acquires after being subjected to the combined heat and motion of a voyage to the tropics in a ship's hold'. Adam Smith, in his *Wealth of Nations* (Book IV, chapter 4, page 204), says: 'A general taste for Madeira, which our officers found established in all our colonies at the commencement of the war in 1755, was brought back with them to the mother country, where that wine had not been much in fashion before.' But Dr Wright was gloomily reporting in the same year: 'Madeira wine, about forty years ago, was very common in Britain and is one of the most useful and best for elderly persons in gouty habits. When the functions of life have begun to fail, it make the most pleasant whey or negus of all wines.' By 1775 Madeira was well known all over England.

By the beginning of the eighteenth century, thirty shippers operated out of centrally heated cellars in the back streets of Funchal. They grew the grapes, made the casks, blew the bottles, printed the labels and even chopped down trees to feed the big stoves which were introduced in 1794 to obviate the need to take every consignment on a world cruise. By the mid-eighteenth century the Madeirans copied port by adding spirit. Noble varieties – Sercial, Bual, Verdelho – were planted to compliment the Malvasia. English toffs favourably compared Madeira with port. Taking a leaf out of the Prince Regent's cellar book, some were already secreting caches of the exciting new drink in cobwebby corners. Colonists were doing the same in Africa, America and even Russia.

In 1764 and 1765 Isaac Martin Rebow sent to his customer B. Kennett 216 bottles of Madeira at £1 16s a dozen. By 1794 it was whipping port, with Priddy's Foreign Warehouse in London offloading 1788 vintage port at 21s a dozen. From the earliest journal (1794–1800) in the archives of Messrs John Harvey and Sons of Bristol, the company in 1795 paid £65 a pipe for Old London Peculiar, rising to £84 a pipe in January 1799. By the end of the year a pipe of Madeira had risen to £101 18s. By 1800 it had shot up to £105 a pipe. Some liked it so much they drank it throughout the meal.

At one of Professor Saintsbury's candle-lit 'dinners', guests drank nothing but Madeira with terrapin and canvasback wild duck. Saintsbury drank Madeira in his old age. 'I am sorry to say,' he wrote, 'I have myself put into a glass of modern Madeira, from the most unimpeachable of providers, a little spoonful of carbonate of soda.' It was only after recommendations from Army officers returning to England from duty in America that the English forswore Canary and Mountain and switched to the new wine. The seldom seen Terrantez is an even better wine, and a glass from an ancient vintage is a sublime treat. After tasting an 1840 Bual 'with tremendous smoothness', William Golding wrote: 'The increasing refusal of the modern world to leave fine wines to age makes it probable, and sad, that our grandchildren will never drink a superb Madeira.'

Then the infant Madeira had to take a fierce dig to the solar plexus. In August 1860 oidium, which had devastated the vineyards of Europe, arrived. Warner Allen says: 'Nine tenths of the vines had been destroyed by it or rooted up and the remainder were very sickly.' From a high of 30,000 pipes of Madeira made in 1851, for the next decade not a drop of wine was made that was fit for export.

The Americans continued their touching love affair with Madeira. In the 1839 wine list of Astor House in New York, Madeira took pride of place with thirty-nine entries, including a 'Wedding Wine' at $8 a bottle, and 'Caroline, an Old Family wine' at $6. Wine lovers in Savannah disposed of legendary vintages, and silver-ticketed cut-glass decanters abounded in Georgia. Rainwater, a light type of Madeira made from the Canica or Cunningham, was cherished by the Americans. The grape still lives, making diabolical wine in Canada.

In the nineteenth century the French adopted the barbaric habit of drinking sweet Madeira before dinner, as they do now with Sauternes and port. The French attach-ment to Madeira goes back to 1752 when Louis XVI had the wine in his cellars. The French tried making a French 'Madeira' but, to much chortling from the English, the experiment flopped spectacularly. Cambridge dons enjoyed Madeira and some, unfor-givably, preferred it to port. In country mansions, including Ashburnham, Madeiras from the nineteenth century were well represented. At Race Week at Goodwood, Madeira was eagerly, but daintily, quaffed.

In 1901, on his accession to the throne, Edward VII put his collection of old forti-fied wines up for sale. André Simon, who had an opportunity to taste some royal rejects, eulogises shamefully: 'There never had been – and certainly never again will be – seen such Madeiras as those sold by order of the king.' The wines cellared in the equivalent of the Ritz were 'concentrated essence of vinous perfection'.

Warner Allen joined Simon as guests of Messrs Cossart Gordon for a tasting of nineteen venerable Madeiras, which 'showed how the Wine God persists in his beneficence over old wine even against the curses of Nature'. The first wines tasted were from Soleras. One of them was laid down in 1808, a famous vintage regularly topped up with younger but still excellent wine. The wines of that great year that faded quickly were made from the French version of the Malvasia, the Malvoisie, according to Noel Cossart. A Verdelho 1910 had Warner Allen deliriously spouting Virgil's 'redeunt Saturnia regna' – 'the Golden Age returns'. The next flight began with a Sercial, which Simon regarded as the classic among classics because of 'its distinction and the austerity of its farewell'. Warner Allen particularly enjoyed a brace from the Terrantez which showed 'a fine full body with a celestial bouquet completed by an ozone-like finish so clean and dry as to be almost bitter, the perfect almond taste.' Noel Cossart gave six of the wines a first. Warner Allen's favourite was Reserve Visconde Valle Paraiso-Bual 1844.

The seven best wines on view had an average age of 120 years. The youngest was seventy-nine, the oldest a majestic pensioner of 170 years old. Some had been kept in glass demijohns for over thirty years. The Terrantez 1862 spent forty-three years in wood and thirty-one in a demijohn. However, the undoubted megastar was the oldest – a wrinkly, face-lifted, fake-tonsured legend known as the 'Methuselah of wines'. It was the 1789 Cama de Lobos, Churchill's favourite al fresco studio, again from the amazing Terrantez. This extraordinary wine was in the wood for 111 years, fifty years in demijohn, and nine years in bottle. The spectre was applauded by the assembled romantics, who for a moment suspended all critical faculties. It was, said Warner Allen, 'embalmed history, glory on the palate and the nose'.

At one of his 'memorable meals' in 1939, André Simon drank 1792 Madeira that had been bottled by Blandy's in 1840 for Napoleon. It was sent to St Helena but was returned on the advice of the miniature Emperor's physician. The wine had not been paid for, so when 'someone had been so indiscreet as to ask for payment' the wine was promptly returned. 'It was,' said Simon, 'a perfect wine, no trace of decay, a wonderful concentrated bouquet and quite a remarkably dry finish.'

When the world stopped drinking Madeira growers panicked and planted Tinta Negra Mole, a Pinot Noir and Grenache cross guaranteed to yield juice that was high in sugars but low on quality. It did nothing to reclaim the halcyon days of Madeira. Instead it made wine for the casual tourist and the kitchen. The trade is now compressed to about eight companies, the main player being the Madeira Wine Company. From their prehistoric premises in Funchal, Madeira is delivered to the world under twenty different labels. Like port, the better wines still find their way to England. America retains an interest. The Japanese, ever keen to copy their baseballing idols, take a small amount.

Nowadays you can drive from the bottom of the island to the top without seeing a single vine. You will see oranges, little green bananas, cabbages, sweet potatoes and espada ripening in the sun on a fisherman's slab, and rooting pigs. From a lofty café you can drink *vinho verde*, red or white, with plain food and observe in the distance the tanned back of a young woman, straight out of a deodorant advertisement, hacking at the ground with her mattock, the sound softly echoing. She is working on her vegetable patch, not planting vines. In fact there is a shortage of grapes on the island. Souvenir wine is mainly dross but fine old bottles with a personalised certificate can still be purchased in Funchal. Madeira is better than it has been for a long time but few seem to care.

27

The Birth of Red Burgundy

By the sixth century, Gregory of Tours was boasting that the wines of Burgundy were better than those of Champagne. By the thirteenth century, Church, State and invader all made wine and established communities in Burgundy. The Church had the pick of the donations and its holdings grew due to the generosity of the King and dukes, who, in order to reserve a soft spot in heaven, gave their lands to God. Landowners in Gevrey, Vosne, Beaune, Aloxe, Fixin, Santenay, Auxey, Chassagne, Pommard and Meursault all made substantial gifts of land and vines, buildings, materials and tools for working the vineyards and making wine. Tapestries depict vines trained and neatly tied to stakes. The religious houses had teams of dedicated and captive workmen, who could hoe and sweat and gaze at the sky and mumble prayers or baths to their maker all day. It was back-breaking, they ate sparingly and drank sour beer.

The first Burgundy, shipped to England in the twelfth century, was bland, blended and not clearly defined. It was called Auxerre, after the port it sailed from. It was a 'wine of vintage', made from a mish-mash of grapes both white and red, and it sold between October and Christmas. It would be another century before the Pinot Noir, the heart and soul of Burgundy, would appear. Rather like old-fashioned tea, the new unracked wine had to be strained through the teeth. 'Wine of rack', kept in wood into the late spring, was a more expensive wine with some cellaring potential. The distinction was not lost on Henry I's wine buyer, who ordered one sextuary (up to 6 gallons) of 'clear wine' and the same quantity of unracked wine for the King's staff, whose number included the Chamberlain of the Candles.

If too much wine was bought it soon went bad. On learning his wine buyer had seriously overestimated the royal thirst by as much as fifty tuns in 1342, Reymund Seguyn, the King's butler, was commanded to 'distribute certain feeble wines among the poor brethren of York and Notyngham and to give the putrefied wine to other poor who wish to have it.' It's the thought that counts. Henry IV had an even better ruse. He granted a licence to John Banham and John Walters to ship thirty tuns of old, undrinkable wine to Ireland and swop it for freshly caught salmon.

A complaint was made in 1307 that vintners and merchants brought 'mixed, putrid and corrupt wines' which were sold in the market towns to naïve customers. While the vintners of Bordeaux were the biggest sinners, wines from Burgundy were also poured into the mix and stirred.

English merchants traveled the French regions buying up unwanted wine from past vintages to take back to England for mixing with something less nasty prior to distribution. Burgundy still had a reputation for leanness and being over-acid. Such insipid potions were not unknown to Shakespeare, who has the King of France spouting in *King Lear*: 'Not all the Dukes of waterish Burgundy shall take this unprized, precious maid from me.'

In 1512 Louis XII of France sent a present of thirty-six puncheons of *vins de Beaune* to his cousin James IV of Scotland. Generic Beaune remained synonymous with reliable Burgundy until into the seventeenth century, when the fine wines of the Côtes de Nuits, which helped bolster the blend, claimed back their birthright and sold under their own *village* or *domaine* names. 'In Burgundy,' Stephen Gwynn wrote in the late 1920s, 'all is held in small plots, worked either by the owner and his family, or else leased to a *metayer* who pays as rent a fixed proportion of the yield. The result is a stalwart breed of men who for the most part call no man master; who live a laborious life which needs a stout back and arms for the constant hoeing and clearing of the soil, ands also a skill like that of the highly trained gardener.' He goes on to say: 'Young men are deserting the trade, drawn away by higher earnings into the towns; many vineyards are going back to wastelands – a loss to the world.'

Henry VIII showed a keen interest in Borgoyn, on offer in Paris as Bourgogne since 1421 and sold at 1d a gallon. A better wine labelled Beaune, a blend of good wine from all over Burgundy, was twice the price. In 1538, the keeper of His Majesty's cellars tracked the wine down to a merchant in Brussels, the Belgians being traditional lovers of Burgundy.

By the seventeenth century St Evremond was declaiming that the wines of Burgundy, once so wonderful and popular, had 'lost their old Reputation with the Citizens'. The main complaint against the Burgundians was that the new wine was 'of a great and horrible bitterness'. The problem was the Gamay, the thin, scented, over-produced Beaujolais grape which flourished in the great *communes* of the Côte d'Or, issuing forth a fireman's hose of vinegar. This was in spite of the fact there were isolated fields of 200-year-old ungrafted Pinots yielding purple nectar. Realising the Gamay gave fine Burgundy a bad name, an edict was issued ordering its removal. Not many growers took notice. The already thin wine was diluted with hot water prior to sale which gave it a spurious softness. But after a long and bumpy journey on sinuous, potholed roads to its final destination, the wine had cooled and it was 'stinking'. A primitive form of chaptalisation was tried in the Middle Ages to boost the sharp dry wines. Honey or boiled must was added to the vats, the way the Greeks and Romans had done. Sugar beet, an animal feed, does the job today, even though the wines may be expensive and considered rare and fine.

Red Champagne tied itself to Burgundy's coat-tails, much to the annoyance of the Burgundian growers, who accused the Champenois even of using branded Burgundy casks to pass off their wines and deceive the public. John Gay, a poet and wine enthusiast, mentioned Burgundy and Champagne in the same breath, as did wine merchants in London.

By the end of the eighteenth century names like Chambertin were topping any price a mere Beaune could fetch. Nuits followed and by the mid-nineteenth

century a panoply of Burgundy names were established in English cellars as gentlemen pitched one against the other in tastings. The less confident stuck to wines from
the Côtes de Beaune. 'Volnay' tripped off the English tongue more easily than 'Grands
Echezeaux'.

Though Burgundy was enjoyed in England during the Renaissance it was never as
popular as the more reliable and accessible Claret, with its established connection with
England. While the British generally disliked the French, the Bordelais were almost
family. Claret was plentiful, more reliable and easier to buy with London full of agents
representing the various châteaux. With their better climate and their careful and
complementary selection of grape types, hundreds of good growers made wines with
style and flavour which arrived on English shores fresh after a bracing boat journey.
Selling Burgundy was difficult enough without all the transporting problems. The
wines were often made from mouldy grapes plucked in vineyards scattered by insane
laws of inheritance. Burgundy was perceived as a wet tangle of weeds and untamed
vines in gaps in the forests. Gloomy monks hoed behind stone walls; women, their
mouths full of pegs, hung tattered washing outside leaning hovels as their sour-faced
husbands trudged to work in bleak, muddy fields.

'Although Burgundy was known to connoisseurs in England,' writes André Simon,
'this excellent wine suffered from the fact that it had to be carted to the banks of the
River Yonne, loaded onto barges and sent off on a slow, rustic journey to Paris, then
on to Rouen when it was trans-shipped to London. The bargees were seldom honest
and always thirsty. They either filled their blackened billy cans with wine and topped
the casks with rat invested canal water or left them with ullage so by the time the
wine reached London or Bristol the wines were sour and oxidised.' The snail's pace
of the lolling bargees meant 'a great loss of time, money and wine'. A consignment of
430 hogsheads of Burgundy sent to Paris from Macon in 1789 arrived fifty hogsheads
light. The fifty barrels of wine 'were used for filling or otherwise disposed of' at inns
like the Rose, 'where the Beaus and the Sparks with their Mistresses went to Feast' in
1691 on exotic food joyously dispatched with expensive Burgundies.

The French, who liked wine that was young and cheap, liked Burgundy so not
much of it made it to eighteenth-century London. What did was immediately
embraced as new and exciting. Burgundy became 'the wine for men of taste and
fashion'. They not only stocked it in their cellars but expected to find it when they
went out to frolic. Burgundy also had more of a reputation as a wine for invalids
than Clarets did. The better vintages were 'full-bodied, refined, delicate and alcoholic
without being heady. Drunk in moderation, they give internal tone and facilitate
digestion. They give strength to the body, warmth to the heart, and vivacity of mind
in the highest degree.'

In 1725, Monsieur Arnoux, a homesick French teacher in London, burned oil
in his attic writing a paean to the wines of his native Burgundy. He put Burgundy
into three classes. The lowest were *vins de primeur* – young, volatile, scented wines, at
their best when the whiff smell of yeast was on them. The better wines of the Côte
de Beaune, and their plumper cousins from further north Arnoux called *vin de garde*,

wines needing cellaring to achieved harmony and balance. He placed Chambertin at the very top, with Clos de Vougeot, whose wine maker in medieval times was Dom Goblet, not far behind. Chambertin of the 1724 vintage (too old even for a Broadbent tasting note), fetched as much as £42 a cask at the cellar door. Two full casks of Volnay cost the same.

The big names of the Côte de Nuits were clearly meant to be kept for at least two years, but the best could stagger into their fifth. Sir Edward Berry called them 'Wines de Garde' in 1775. Predictably they were led by Chambertin which was even then considered to be the best red Burgundy of all. In the Vauxhall Gardens wine list of 1762, only Champagne was more expensive than Burgundy. At 6s a bottle it was a bob dearer than Claret, three times the cost of port and eighteen times dearer than 'a great Mug of Table Beer'.

In 1789 Baron d'Archenholz, 'a shrewd observer', travelled through England assiduously recording criticisms, as travel writers are wont to do. Having ascertained that 'common people enjoyed themselves during the winter with warm beer mixed with bitter essences, and with ale in which gin, sugar and eggs have been boiled together', he also noted how terribly expensive Burgundy and Champagne were. 'Notwithstanding this,' the Baron wrote, 'the consumption of these wines is very great in London, where they like everything that is powerful and heavy.'

Wines from the Côte de Beaune were for early consumption. Sir Berry included 'Volnet', which had to be dispatched within a year, 'Pomard' and 'Chassagne' among the early quaffers. Arthur Young, writing in 1792 with even quirkier spelling, claimed red 'Clos de Veaujeau' to be the epiphany, with the white version not far behind. 'La Tashe', 'de Vaume Romane' and 'Richbourg' he rated highly, with the wines of 'Beaume' making delicious wines at 'Volny', 'Pomar', 'Aloes', 'Beaume' and 'Savigne'. Of the whites he placed 'Maureache' on the loftiest pedestal.

By the end of the eighteenth century Chambertin was the dearest, Nuits followed. The Emperor Napoleon, while languishing in exile at Longwood on St Helena, enjoyed Chambertin. He drank half a bottle with lunch or dinner, 'usually with water'. It was 'tossed down without paying any attention to flavour and savour'.

By the mid-nineteenth century Burgundy *domaine* and *village* names were becoming established in English cellars. Gentlemen organised tastings. The public stuck to wines from the Côtes de Beaune; few could afford to follow Napoleon.

Burgundy's single-minded, single grape's tart savouriness and a bouquet of cow dung and wet collie was hard to grasp. There were great wines, maybe the greatest of all, but they were few: the wine had to be made in a great year by a master craftsman. The stubborn Pinot had to yield to the spur and the whip to produce fine wine. Too many unambitious peasants used diseased and unripened fruit from their scattered plantings. If only they could afford to make small parcels from the best grapes on the best slopes. If only the weather had been better and the natives not quite so allergic to outsiders, those Parisian entrepreneurs who followed the sun to Bordeaux might have been tempted to take a stagecoach to Dijon or Beaune and plant roots there. The risk was too great though.

The delicate taste of good Burgundy appealed to women and in the eighteenth century the Earl of Bristol, a committed 'Claretophile', had a dozen flasks laid by 'for my dear wife'. At 6s a flask it was the most expensive wine in his cellar. His cellar book recalls 'St George Wine' (Nuits Saint-Georges) and white Muljo (Meursault) Burgundy. Feeble attempts at the classification of Burgundy are revealed in the entries, however eccentric the spelling. Then as now, white Burgundy, with the exception of Le Montrachet, was considerably cheaper than red.

In the eighteenth century, Burgundy was well enough known to be plugged in contemporary plays like Dr Hoadley's *Suspicious Husbands* and in Bickerstaffe's *Lionel and Clarisse*, when Colonel Old Boy says to Harmand: 'Come Harmand, I'll bet you a buck and six dozen of Burgundy that you wont have spirit enough to bring the affair to a crisis.' When the dark wines of the Côtes de Nuits were shipped to London in the eighteenth century they were poured from cut-glass decanters garlanded with enamelled 'bottle tickets'. For some, fine Burgundy had arrived.

The first 'Gladstonian' wine list produced by the Foreign Vineyards Association of Regent's Street, London in August 1860 listed among a heavy stock of familiar sweeties such esoteric items as 'Amber' or 'Pink' white Burgundy, 'first quality' Chablis boasting 'very high flavours', 'Grand ordinaire de Nuits, table', and 'Celebrated Clos de Vogeot' ('from the Clos'). It also offered 'Superb Richbourg, rare', Corton-Greves and Chambertin-Musinée.

Oidium wilted vines and rotted grapes all over Burgundy, but it was the arrival of swirling clouds of a miniscule, winged, root-eating sex machine called phylloxera that changed the face of the crowded Burgundy vineyards forever. Unruly vine bushes were torn out of the ground. To enable new tractors and sprayers to do their job effectively the vines were spaced out in neat rows, the tendrils anchored to wires. Peasants without the means to buy new vines, wire, stakes and shiny machinery gave up. In the seventy-five years that followed the plague of phylloxera, the Burgundy vineyards shrank from 131,500 hectares to a hardly visible 10,000 just after the Second World War. An ancient way of growing grapes, and of French rural life, had vanished.

'I pity the poor high street buyer who is sent to Burgundy to try to do the impossible, find drinkable Pinot to match the opposition from California, Australia, New Zealand, Chile, and God help us, even Romania. The situation has hardy changed over 500 years. Even the most enthusiastic Burgundy connoisseurs admit that the wines of Burgundy are too expensive, too variable in quality, too quick to fall apart, and too difficult and trouble-some to find'. What ancient chronicler wrote that? Robert Parker, in 1993.

Auberon Waugh says: 'The evil influence of wine investors, who treat fine wine like rare postage stamps, allows famous producers to put any rubbish into their bottles as long as it has a famous label and an "approved" year.' He's right, of course. There are too many 'front room wine merchants' who buy the bad years of famous names and badger gullible 'trophy wine' collectors to buy them.

Burgundy is often served cool, but in Colette's time it was quite a comfort to drink it hot on a frosty night when she was out on the stumps with her father at election time. 'At the nearest tavern,' she wrote, 'the hot wine would be steaming on the embers, with the flotsam and jetsam of lemon peel and cinnamon bubbling on its purple swell.' Plenty of the emaciated and justifiably 'undiscovered artisanal' red Burgundies, still beloved by small country wine merchants, could benefit from this treatment.

While the lighter red Burgundies from the Côte de Beaune gave enormous pleasure to our forefathers, the best of them were capable of great longevity. A bottle of the five-star 1885 from Lord Rosebery's cellar tasted in 1967 with its original cork was 'a revelation'. So much for plastic corks and screw caps! A 150-year-old Chassagne Rouge 1832, from a village principally known for its whites, was the oldest red Burgundy Broadbent tasted. Though 'pale and watery', its faded charms still delighted him. Parker would have reached for the Luger. A 1921 Beaune 'Cardinal', bottled in Scotland and stored for a half century in the Glamis cellars, was 'very pretty, sweet and fading but charming'.

At 32 acres, the legendary Chambertin is a large vineyard by Burgundy standards. Twenty-three people own a slice of it, all making wine of varying quality, not much of it worth the requested £100-plus a bottle. Parker is typically blunt: 'Most of them are a complete rip-off.'

Aubert de Villaine, co-proprietor of Domaine de la Romanée-Conti, presided over a tasting of his new wines, which he poured in thimblefuls. The atmosphere was tense. M. de Villaine stood as a high priest above the assembled traders, wine hacks and gatecrashers. DRC is iconic. He spoke of his *terroir*. The implication was that the Californians, New Zealanders and the rest can steal his precious Pinot but they cannot nick his soil. We all nodded like Cortina dogs. A member of the wine community who makes a negative comment about DRC wines is begging for disembowelling. One esteemed specialist almost had his tongue removed at the Domaine for casting aspersions on the 1975s (a dreadful year). Michael Broadbent said the 1927 DRC was 'pretty feeble for the greatest name in Burgundy', while their 1975 La Tache had 'a touch of rotten grapes on the nose and does no credit to its name'. One can hear the hiss and rattle of the guillotine. In his defence, Broadbent did rather like the exquisitely flavoured 1929 Romanée-Conti he tasted when the wine was fifty-nine years old. An eminent Mistress of Wine who got the wrong side of the powerful Domaine a few years ago was banned from entering its portals until she recanted. Her most recent outpourings on the estate's wine reveal a pleasing contriteness.

28

White Burgundy

Michael Broadbent says, 'For the purist, for the dedicated connoisseur, white bur-gundy, the perfect union of grape variety, soil and climate, at its best is the summit of the wine maker's art, but as the world demand for white Burgundy so far exceeds its production, the prices asked, and paid, are exorbitant.'

Montrachet, was renowned in the fourteenth century when Jean de Crux tended his vines with the monkish application. Chardonnay has been the dominant grape since the sixteenth century, helped at times by a few buckets of the bastard children of the promiscuous Pinot Noir, the Pinot Gris and the Pinot Blanc.

In the eighteenth century, the Beaune-born priest and teacher Father Claude Arnoux (1695–1770) believed Burgundy ought to be red. In his unofficial classifi-cation he put the finest white Burgundies well behind the reds of the Côte d'Or. Although he placed Montrachet first among the white wines, he said they were 'the most curious as well as the most delicious white wines in France'. Made in tiny quantities, customers bought the wine before the grapes were picked. Meursault, 'well-known throughout France, the Low Countries and Germany', was popular in England as a reliable, though admittedly inferior, alternative to Montrachet.

Meursault, Charmes and Perrières regularly featured in English trade and private tastings but often drew mixed notices. Arnoux said Meursault would 'do honour to and give pleasure to those who drink them'. But they were warned buyers not to keep them longer than eighteen months, as it was liable to oxidise. Montrachet first appeared in Christie's catalogue in 1775. Meursault, often spelt 'Mulsaux', took its first bow at the same time. They came from the cellar of the departing French Ambassador to London, the Marquis de Noailles. Both were upstaged by Chablis, then called Chablet, which was the first white Burgundy to be offered by Christie's, in 1770.

An 1818 Montrachet sold by Christie's catalogue in 1828 fetched only 42s a dozen. The 1832, sold by the estate of James Watt, made 84s a dozen at seventeen years old. A small cache of very elderly half bottles of the 1804 went for 47s, probably to a drinker of Sack. Old white Burgundies with their reputation for nutty longevity appealed to vinous necrophiliacs.

Father Arnoux said Puligny, which 'made wines similar to Meursault, was a name hardly known at all'. Puligny and Chassage, which both handcuff themselves to the far more lustrous Montrachet, made little impact on the English wine scene until the 1950s. Now even moderate bottles easily top prices paid for good Meursault.

Arnoux wrote it is essential that all wines should be bottled at source and delivered by a respectable carrier. An order for at least 1,000 bottles would have to be made. 'If a noble lord thinks that it may be more than he shall require, he had better arrange for some other noble lord to order some of the same wine at the same time.' In 1728 it was unlawful to ship wine from France in bottles. 'Good Burgundy' was, according to Arnoux, a bargain. A 'queue' of wine, equal to 500 bottles of fine white or red Burgundy, could be purchased in London, duty free, for as little as 1s 3d a bottle.

A eighty-five-year-old 'smoky' Clos de Charlemagne from a forgotten vintage in the 1890s was the oldest white Burgundy Broadbent ever tasted. The colour was 'pure amber. It had a fudge-like nose and a very long, firm finish.' Broadbent does not believe in cosseting old wines. Once the wine is exhumed and the death shroud of cobwebs and sloughed-off spider skins removed, it should be poured into a decanter and consumed without too much ceremony. A 1919 Clos Blanc de Vougeot squirted into a decanter at 5 p.m. and glugged with friends at 9 p.m. was a big, firm wine with a great depth of bouquet, and with a ' lightly honeyed overtone on nose and palate'.

Dr Macbride wrote in 1793: 'Vin de Chauble' – also known as Chablis – 'is a pleasant wine and not unwholesome to be used at table instead of beer.' Chablis was hugely copiously and enjoyed drunk in Paris. In England, though, it was mildly popular among the upper classes. From the middle of the seventeenth century that noble anorak, the Earl of Bedford, had Chablis in his cellars. After hosting a dinner for some literary types, Sir William Hardman wrote: 'I flatter myself they never sat down to a better selected meal in their lives.' His guests, who included George Meredith and Dante Gabriel Rossetti, enjoyed Chablis with 'oysters bearded, brown bread and butter'. The wine selection went a little awry after that, with Amontillado served with the *filets de boeuf grillés*, and sparkling hock with the *fricassé de poulet*.

In the nineteenth century Robert Browning (1812-1889) wrote:

> Then I went indoor, brought out a loaf,
> Half a cheese and a bottle of Chablis,
> Lay on the grass and forgot the oaf,
> Over a jolly chapter of Rabelais.

A sparkling Chablis appeared in London in the nineteenth century. Where it came from is a mystery; it may have been concocted by one of the many underground London wine merchants. Its success, if indeed it enjoyed any, was fleeting. When English chefs introduced the *hors d'oeuvre* from France, they recommended it be accompanied by either Chablis or Montrachet. Soon tiring of the combination, the upper classes switched to Sauternes .

Pebble-dry, lime-green and translucent, genuine Chablis is a finely honed dry wine of character, and attempting to buy a satisfying bottle should not be a gamble but out of 100 vintages analysed by Rosemary George only a quarter rated the epithet 'fine'. Although sharp and thin in poor years, give it a bit of sun and a dry autumn and Chablis can live up to its famous name. Faced with the fuller-bodied Chardonnays from everywhere, Chablis is a tricky product to sell. Even the wine shops and super-markets in Auxerre, fifteen miles as the damp crow flies from the sodden vineyards, rarely stock the region's best-known export. Those merchants who made a career out of cooking up phony Chablis over the years did the genuine article no favours. In the 1920s the situation became so embarrassing that Chablis growers had to put '*authentique*' on their labels. Nowadays many small Chablis growers are happy to sell their hard-worked wines at the cellar door to friends and tourists.

29

Claret, the Connoisseur's Wine

'Air Claret well before using, but never heat it before a fire, and never place the decanter of wine in hot water' – instructions from the 1905 wine list of Thomas Southam and Son of Shrewsbury. Pale and weak red Bordeaux had been the house wine in taverns, drawn by wenches with cleavages and ringlets who fetched it foaming from the cask, since the thirteenth century.

Sensing there was money to be made out of the light, fresh-tasting wines of Gascony and Guyenne, in 1384 the English sailed from Kingston-upon-Hull, Lynn, Great Yarmouth, Scarborough, Sandwich, Newcastle and Southampton to southwest France, risking pirates who trawled the seas looking for easy pickings. The popular Graves wines, from near the city of Bordeaux, were quickly sold out. New supplies, mixed with inferior wines from outlying vineyards, were palmed off on the less savvy English, as were mixtures from Perigord and even Armagnac. The knowing ones sweated it out on the river nibbling dog biscuits, waiting for the better wines to be brought down from the Côtes de Blaye and the Côtes Bourg.

By the middle of the fourteenth century 20,000 tuns of French wine were unloaded on English docks. A single ship could carry up to 300 *tonneaux*. Claret accounted for 31 per cent of all English imports, compared to less than 1 per cent today. Ferrying wine across the channel in all weathers built up 'a tradition of sea-manship', Edmund Penning-Rowsell writes, that was to stand England in good stead and pay dividends in the coming wars against the Spanish, Dutch and, inevitably, the French.

'Wines of the vintage' were shipped from Gascony in September or early October while still hiccupping with yeasts. Older wines that had been racked at least once – 'wine of rack' – were more expensive, deeper in colour (a highly prized element in the fourteenth century) and generally smoother. There was also a demand for freshly pressed grape juice. Working biliously, it was shipped to England for Henry III and for Bishop Beckington, who drank it in 1442 while discussing the marriage between Henry VI and the daughter of the Count of Armagnac.

Bordeaux estates began as cross-patched fields, worked by share croppers. Women toiled like bonneted gleaners in a Constable painting, harvesting fruit from which wine only suitable for blending was made. Growers experimented with vines and methods of cultivation. Dozens of different grapes were tried. Eighteen black varieties and twenty white were identified in the Graves region alone. Growers finally dis-covered the three types that made the best wines: Cabernet Sauvignon, Petite Verdot and Malbec. The plummy Merlot and the thin but aromatic Cabernet Franc would eventually complete the classic blend.

If physicians could get around to recommending the health-giving properties of any wine it did its prospects no harm, particulary if they advised spooning it into sick children at every opportunity. 'Riders', a tiny leather-bound book published in 1669 by Scardanus Riders of London, 'Bedeckt with many delightful varieties and useful verities'. Forbearing to sleep after meat and red wine and Claret are excellent remedies, especially for children, against the worms.'

Henry VIII loved roasted blackcock, with young, fruity, blended red newly arrived from France or Spain. Records from 1717 indicate that Britain, in spite of her interest in Claret, was a small player, shipping only 6,000 tuns, while Holland imported 34,075 tuns. An invoice belonging to Messrs Oldfield of York shows that Claret was selling at up to 5s a bottle outside London. Dr Robert Druitt, a London physician and author of *Report on the Cheap Wines*, wrote: 'At and above eighteen pence a bottle, Bordeaux wine can be had retail fit for any gentleman.' Below that figure was courting bellyache unless one was judicious in selection.

Wine from the Médoc was first listed by Christie's in their March 1776 catalogue, when they offered 'an excellent fine-flavoured' wine from the 1771 vintage. In 1787 a consignment of nineteen hogsheads of 'high flavoured Claret of the First Growth' was sold for £34 per barrel. A pipe of port fetched a mere £1 more the same day. Sweet, beefy, brandy-infused wine had been put in its place by light, elegant, low-strength table wine. The first named Clarets, Canon and Pontac, were sold in hogsheads a year later.

Although the pot-bellied barrel known as the *barrique* was well established by 1789, Bordeaux shippers learned from their colleagues in Oporto the importance of delivering wine in bottles after the success of the first bottled port vintage, the 1775. The idea of bottling all Claret at source was encouraged by London tasters, who described a mature 1798 Lafite as 'marvellous'. London bottling still enjoyed a sound reputation. In 1811, a London-bottled Château Margaux 1802, described in Christie's catalogue as 'a celebrated Margot', sold for a high price in 1811, the famous Comet year whose wines were still lively 115 years later.

Rain-spoiled dross followed until 1815, the Waterloo year, when the vines issued forth wines that for all I know are still being drunk in military clubs by white-whiskered warriors weighed down with medals. It was to be a brief respite as more bad wine followed. Cyrus Redding recorded the state of depression that hung over the unpicked vineyards and 'the gripe of poverty' that clutched 'its toil-worn victims'.

From 1830 to 1880 the Médoc flourished until the arrival of that multi-talented aphid, phylloxera. A cure was slow in coming. This tardiness resulted in a devastated countryside. When William Golding drank a pre-phylloxera Château Lafite 1875, he described it as 'a big, healthy, robust wine' and doubted if the best Clarets today could be made any better.

In the eighteenth century the trade with England expanded to such an extent that Claret enjoyed 'the greatest acclaim and popularity' of all table wines sold in

No. 363 FRANCE

18 — EIC W LTD — 74.

Château Montrose (St Estèphe)

1, Woodville Gardens,

Ealing, W.5

(Vintage 1934)

A front-room wine merchant in the 1930s, bottling Claret in his coal hole perhaps.

the country. Claret became *the* wine, so fashionable and revered that Burgundy and Champagne toddled anonymously in its wake. According to the Gironde Archives, between 1735 and 1740 four wines, described as *premiers crus*, fetched the best prices on the Bordeaux market. They were in the hands of powerful and wealthy Parlement families who could lavish money on their estates.

A study of Christie's catalogues for 1781, 1831, 1881 and 1931 by Edmund Penning-Rowsell revealed that the great Clarets rarely appeared at auction. Of the 207 sales Christie's held in a three-year period from 1779, most of the sales were to do with house clearances, with sideboards, clocks, ricks of hay and garden rollers taking precedence over wine. As Penning-Rowsell observes, 'in those days there seemed little occasion or desire to make money out of wine, unless it was the stock of a bankrupt wine merchant; besides, wines were not subject to inflation. Nor was there much interest in old wines, partly due to the lack of a decent bottle shape that would facilitate laying down.'

30

The Great Châteaux

An advertisement in the *Tatler* on 6 June 1710 declared: '46 hogsheads and a half of Extraordinary French Claret will be put up for sale at £20 per Hogshead at Garaway's Coffee House in Exchange Alley on Thursday, the 8th inst. at 3 in the Afternoon, and to be tested in a Vault under Messrs Lane and Harrison, Sweeting's Lane, Lombard Street. Catalogues may be had at the publick Sale Warehouse on the Stairs of the Royal Exchange'. Wine was sold in Lloyd's Coffee House, 'by the candle'. When the wick guttered, the last bid stood.

Claret was Jonathan Swift's favourite wine. When he succeeded John Stearne as dean of St Patrick's in Dublin, Swift emulated his friends by having his Claret profes-sionally bottled. On the thick, blackish green flagons he had a medallion welded, a glass 'button' which was inscribed 'J. Swift, Dean, 1727'. He kept some of his best bot-tles for Stella, who loved Margaux, 'the *cru* of most repute in Ireland'. Swift thought Irish-bottled Claret was infinitely superior to the English version. 'I am resolved' he said, 'to have half a hogshead when I go to Ireland if it be as good and as cheap as it used to be.' Although poorly paid in his draughty Irish deanery, and miserly in many ways, Swift loved entertaining, and with the help of his many friends got through six hogsheads of Claret a year. His own personal consumption, the dean estimated, was an annual hogshead.

When broke, Swift was reduced to drinking sickly Spanish Benecarlos, Thomas Sheridan, Richard Brinsley Sheridan's grandfather, goaded him in a letter from his country estate, Castle Hamilton: 'You drink Benecarlos,' he sneered, 'while I drink Margaux.' Swift's Dublin cellar, 'which once was seldom without eight or nine hogs-heads', was subsequently used to provide coal holes for several small houses above, their inhabitants never knowing, nor caring about the love and attention the old dean bestowed on the barrels below.

Sir Robert Walpole began importing modest Claret in bottles. Twenty-five years later he was shipping great wine by the cask. In 1732/33 he took delivery of four hogsheads of Margaux and a hogshead of Lafite every three months, as well as the odd cask of Haut-Brion. Dinners held at Walpole's country seat, Houghton Hall, harked back to the excesses of the Romans and mirrored the efforts of Russian oligarchs or old knuckle-dustered Greek shipping magnates. Walpole was not above using Admiralty contacts to evade taxes and freight charges by using asking Royal Navy to hide some of his wine in the holds of their ships. Houghton Hall was a visited by 'Lords, spiritual and temporal, commoners, parsons and freeholders innumerable. We drank loyal healths, talked of the times, cultivated popularity and in private drew plans and cultivated the country.'

In 1793 four great châteaux came to dominate the London scene. They were Margaux (or Margoo, Margoose, Margou or even Margon), Haut-Brion (often called Obrian or Houbrion), Lafite (or La Fitte, Laffitte), and Latour. The latter only was 42s a dozen, a mere 6s dearer than a case of tavern Claret. Château Haut-Brion and Château Lafite made the best prices. A second category of fine wines included Rauzan, Lascombe, Léoville and 'Gruau ou la Rose'. They sold for about half the price of a First Growth.

Irishmen exerted quite an influence on the development of Claret. Nathaniel Johnston from Ulster, Abraham Lawton from County Cork and Thomas Barton from Tipperary. Johnston was the most influential and was partly responsible for introducing mature Claret to the ordinary wine drinker. He started by bottling unnamed Claret, unmixed with Hermitage, as was the fashion then. After a year in cellar the results were suficiently impressive for Johnston to specialise in mature Claret in bottles. With no unreliable shippers, unwieldy leaking casks or rented cellaring to worry about, Johnston's smooth Clarets also appealed to wealthy connoisseurs. Among his clients was an Irish archdeacon who placed an order for 'sixty dozen of the best Claret in bottles of the first growth of Lafitte [*sic*] and twenty dozen Château Margaux'.

Small collectors emerged, buying a bottle at a time. There was no need to invest in a cask and there were hundreds of small estates from which to choose. Claret's reputation as a reliable, affordable and mature wine was established. There was also a stability of ownership in Bordeaux which guaranteed supplies, unlike the factions in Burgundy, who disputed everything from ownership to production and wine-making methods. Claret was made by gentlemen, for gentlemen, or at least that was the message. Bordeaux prospered. Moneybags from Paris erected vast châteaux which were effectively weekend retreats. Fortified and ugly as the banks they owned, these imposing edifices glowered above the small grey villages, bellowing new money and power.

The wines of the Graves region had a ready market in England since the thirteenth century when three-quarters of the wine drunk in the royal household was red Graves. The French oiled the wheels and greased the axles by lavishly entertaining English wine buyers, flaunting their best wines and unleashing their finest chefs.

Graves region was keenly sought after and expensive, until a series of problems threw a pair rusty secateurs into the works. Rotten vintages, English interference and incompetence all hindered the development of finer Graves, especially Haut-Brion, from making the headway it deserved. Soon this famous name was outsold and overtaken by the bland Palus wines, which sold at a fraction of the price. It was even beaten into third in 1647 by a 'red Barsac', in a 'rough classification.'

The Pontacs were shrewd farmers. lawyers, politicos and wine growers. Under Arnaud de Pontac they became bulk wine shippers in 1505. A century and a half later, now sophisticated and wealthy The Pontacs concentrated on fine wine; they planted vines around their country retreat, Château Haut-Brion, perched on a hillock of sand

and gravel, a combination that was useless for growing potatoes. The new wine was hard, like the soil, with a delicious fragrance. The Pontacs decided it was too good to blend it with anything else. They named it after their farmhouse and sold Pontac as a second label. The launch was in London with the wine hacks of the day – playwrights, poets and pamphleteers – present in fancy trews and feathered berets. It was a spectacular success. Chateau Haut-Brion was exactly what the English gentlemen lacked. The wine was snapped up and the price shot up.

On 16 July 1683 John Evelyn referred to Château Haut-Brion, 'whence the best Bordeaux wine comes'. More than twenty years earlier, on 16 April 1663, Samuel Pepys sat in a London pub, the Royall Oak, enjoying a new and unique experience for a rough diamond of his class and salary. Next morning, feeling bright and energetic, Pepys penned a positive tasting note about 'Ho Bryan'. Shutting out his companions' gabbling, Pepys had gazed into the deep-coloured wine and sniffed the heavy bouquet. It smelt expensive, had an unusual tang about it, and the purest taste he had ever encountered. Pepys wasn't the only one to recognise the 'particular' appeal of Graves, but he was one of the first in England. Its savoury hardness, derived in part from the gravelly soil, allied to a high iron content made it a tonic wine.

Château Haut-Brion's popularity is shown in this advertisement in the *Tatler* of 24 September 1710: 'Sixty hogsheads and 12 tierces of new excellent French O'Brien Clarets, the very best vintage.'

'Aubryan' features prominently in the diary and expenses of John Hervey, the Earl of Bristol, one of the most important buyers of fine wine in England. On 10 July 1705, he paid Nath Torriano for three hogsheads of wine: two of Obrian (Haut-Brion) and one of white Langoon (Langan). Between 1703 and 1725 the Earl bought twelve and a half hogsheads and 2,126 bottles if Claret, much of it Haut-Brion.

Château Haut-Brion has had over twenty-five owners in the past 500 years but it was when M. Pontac became synonymous with the estate. Arnaud de Pontac was a shrewd perfectionist and a brilliant lawyer. By exposing his creation to the palates of the fussy English he did what the Germans, the Spanish, the Portuguese, Italians, Californians and later the Australians still do. He waited for word-of-mouth approval and watched the orders flood in. Thomas Jefferson's positive comments did the same thing for Haut-Brion in America when he sent six dozen 'Obrien' 1784 to a relative with the comment that it was the very best Bordeaux wine since 1779. The provincial wine merchants William Cox of Derby in 1790 sold fourteen dozen of 'fine old Haut-Brion Clarett' for the sum of £25 18s. In 1793, when ordinary Vins de Graves were offered by a London wine merchant for 2s a bottle, Haut-Brion was 3s 6d; at the same time, a cask of Château Giscours could be bought for as little as £12. Viscount Gage preferred to complement his turkey with three cases of young Vins de Graves he bought in December 1800.

Michael Broadbent says he has had 'more unalloyed pleasure from Haut-Brion than almost any other Claret; down-to-earth, suave, somehow fewer mannerisms and criticisable facets than most other great Châteaux.' However, his tasting notes on old bottles of Château Haut-Brion are generally not as enthusiastic as his comments on

A succulent beefy
wine from this
luscious vintage,
Californian in
richness and in
depth.

other famous relics. While he found the 1904, a moderate vintage to be, 'a lovely drink' in 1976, a 1906, also a nondescript year, tasted in 1969 was 'a beauty despite greasy cork and very slight ullage'. The 1909, poured from an eight-bottle Imperiale, was 'impressive but curious' in 1969; the 1910, an awful year tasted in 1971, was 'faded but holding on'; the 1923, tasted in 1976, had a ' sickly nose and a touch of acidity'; the 1928, a wonderful year, tasted in 1979 was 'perversely impressive'; the 1929 tasted in 1979 was 'mountainous and perverse'; the 1931, a lousy vintage tasted in 1980, had a 'curious, meaty/varnishy nose'. A bottle from the 1937, another modest year, tasted in 1979, was a 'fairly stringent specimen', while a 1943 modest vintage tasted in 1978 had a 'touch of sourness'. The 1945, however, had Michael falling to his knees, trilby in hand. 'Absolute perfection,' he murmured.

Incidentally, it was the brilliant 1929 Château Haut-Brion that almost brought Broadbent's hitherto charmed and blessed existence to a bloody and untimely close. The elegant Broadbent against the rugged Aussie Len Evans was a match Don King would have slavered over. It was all down to a difference of opinion when the '29 was poured at Evans' bash in Sydney in 1977. The burly Aussie took a swig and thought the Haut-Brion was the dingo's bollocks and said so with a finality that would brook no argument. Broadbent stuck his vastly more experienced nose into the glass and said 'overblown'. Enraged that a poncy Pom should challenge him in his lair, Evans reached over a hairy mitt to tear out Broadbent's giblets. He might have done, but for 'the large-framed Mr Fraser, the Australian prime minister, sitting between us, who kept us apart', an amused Broadbent said afterwards.

In 1730 a report detailed the prices and and different qualities of Bordeaux wines. The first quality included Pontac, Lafite and Château de Margaux. The latter made only 300 tuns of wine a year. 'This is, however,' the report concluded, 'the wine that is the most highly esteemed of the province. It sells at 1,200 livres to 1,500 livres a tun and it is the English who buy the greater part of this wine.' In 1793 Château Margaux was £24 a tun in London, the same price as Lafite and Latour.

Château Margaux was introduced to the masses in London coffee houses at the dawn of the eighteenth century. In a long and distinguished history, Margaux, originally called either La Motte or Lamothe, has had many owners, including Edward II. It was pillaged by English soldiers in the fourteenth century when it was in French hands. M. de Fumel, who also owned Château Haut-Brion, bought Margaux and extended the vineyard, planting it with the best vines in 1750.

Margaux was the first estate to use the Château prefix. A M. Berlon, an eccentric manager of the château in the early eighteenth century, leavened the famous red wine by mixing it with a crisp white wine made from Sauvignon Blanc grapes picked before sunrise. M. Berlon poured the white wine into vats containing up to twenty-eight *barriques* of strong red made from late-ripened Cabernet Sauvignon. Fermentation was encouraged by shovelling ultra-ripe grapes into the mix. The best wine was sold as Château Margaux. The poorest was given to the workers. In 1836 the Aguados, a Franco-Spanish family, purchased Château Margaux. The estate prospered and the wine became especially sought after.

Thomas Jefferson purchased 1784 'Château Margau', which he described as 'one of the best vintages which has happened in nine years'. In 1788 'Margau' made its debut in Christie's catalogue alongside another nervous debutante, 'Lafete'. Both came from the cellar of a French ambassador with spelling difficulties. A 1798, 'Château Margot's celebrated vintage', bottled in London four years later, fetched £9 2s 6d a case, or 15s 2 ½d a bottle. This was a swingeing increase at a time when the going rate for Château Margaux was £2 9s a case. The oldest Margaux in tip-top condition was the 1893, a brilliant vintage, tasted by Michael Broadbent in 1979. When helped from her bath chair, and with ear trumpet in place, this frisky octogenarian was soft, sweet, smelling of violets, with no decay and amazingly rich.

Château Margaux was first bottled in the Château's cellars in 1923. They recanted in 1930 and shipped in cask until 1949. No-one seems to have told the English firm Skinner and Rook of Nottingham, who submitted a consignment of their own bottling of Château Margaux 1952 to Christie's in 1968. The US president Richard Nixon, an avid admirer of Château Margaux, instructed his White House staff to pour a less stellar wine for his guests but to fill his glass with the 'real McCoy' wrapped in a napkin.

Château Margaux is an elegant wine. Even with 70 per cent Cabernet Sauvignon it can be drunk straight from the cask on a cold morning before breakfast and still taste wonderful. For centuries, English, Scottish and Irish wine buyers have strode into Margaux's scrubbed and silent cellars, gazed at the big oak vats with the polish brass fittings and removed their hats and flung themselves on the wet floor. After tasting the wines they were invited to a good lunch with old bottles. White wine has been made at Château Margaux for centuries. Pavillon Blanc du Château Margaux is made from Sauvignon Blanc grapes grown on 30 acres of the estate. This light and delicate wine is fermented in oak vats and aged for six or seven months in *barriques*. Only 40,000 bottles are made, meaning it is often found overpriced.

When Thomas Jefferson visited Bordeaux in 1787 he noted: 'There are four vineyards of first quality: Château Margau, La Tour de Segur, Hautbrion and Château de la Fite.' The first three were 'not in perfection till 4 years old'. He found those of 'de la Fite' lighter and easy to drink at three years of age.

By 1824, three decades before the Official Classification, Henderson, in his *History of Ancient and Modern Wines*, wrote: 'Lafitte, Latour, Château Margaux and Haut-Brion are so greatly esteemed that they always sell from 20 to 25 per cent higher than any other of the province of Bordeaux.' Fearing the use of cork was spoiling their wines, the owners of Lafite introduced hand-crafted glass stoppers for the vintages of 1820 and 1825. The stoppers jammed in the necks and bottles were smashed and valuable wine was spilt by frustrated butlers, waiters and gasping old gentlemen. When the bankers Rothschild purchased Lafite in 1868 they needed little persuasion to switch to cork.

The reputation of Lafite was now worldwide. In 1839 Astor House in New York listed Château Lafite 1834 from an excellent but rain-reduced vintage. At $3 a bottle it shared top price with Cos Destournel 1827, a fine wine from an abundant year. Château Brane Mouton, also from 1834 and later to become Château Mouton-Rothschild, was available at $2.50.

When Anthony Berry opened a bottle of 1864 Lafite for Harry Waugh and Edmund Penning-Rowsell in 1968, the latter was amazed. 'Perfectly round, gentle and soft with a sweet nose', he remembered. A rare triple magnum of 1865 Lafite was bought by the first Earl of Rosebery from Cockburn's of Leith and in 1869 was placed in its own bin in the Earl's cellar. It stayed there untouched except for a change of cork by Berry Bros in 1930. The large bottle snoozed for a further thirty-seven years until it was awoken by a racket in the cellars as the doors were flung open and brown-coated men from Christie's came to take it to London to sell it to three American doctors. They took it to California. With only cork between it and disaster, the level of 'the august and aristocratic' old Lafite hadn't fallen an iota. It was siphoned, sniffed and sipped. 'Staggering,' Harry Waugh said. 'Such a beautiful deep colour. The bouquet was a delight. The flavour miraculous, so much fruit, such a lovely finish.' The elderly Lafite flattened the other contenders at a dinner described as a Lucullan fantasy. 'There is something about these great pre-phylloxera Clarets that no modern successor can equal, certainly not for longevity anyway', Waugh said, raising his glasses to dab an eye.

Maurice Healy, author of *Stay me With Flagons*, said: 'Lafite has filled my glass with wine and my heart with gratitude probably more often than any other wine.' Morton Shand said Lafite's flavour and bouquet 'are considered so grand and sublime as to afford a symposium of the virtues of all other wines'. Warner Allen commented on the 'perfect balance which merges all virtues in a transcendental unity'. T. Earle Welby thought the 1864 Lafite was 'the best Claret of the nineteenth century'. When Broadbent tasted it in 1979 it still had enough left to send the veteran connoisseur into raptures. 'No decay, no oxidation, no over-acidity or tiredness,' he wrote, 'just perfection.'

Lafite was often stretched by Spanish red wine or Hermitage. In the 1830s a wine merchant in Leith advertised 'Lafite Hermitaged'. The British could argue they were merely keeping up a French tradition. Letters ascribed to M. Goudal, a *régisseur* of Château Lafite in the 1850s, confirm that poor years were made more flavoursome by the judicious addition of Hermitage. Lafite was bought in 1868 by 'outsiders', the Rothschilds, through the financial clout of Baron James de Rothschild. He died before setting foot in the vineyard. James's three sons, Alphonse, Gustave and Edmond, inherited the property.

A clearance sale at the property followed, with seven bottles of the mediocre 1797 fetching the equivalent of 10s a bottle. Sixty bottles of the finer, and rarer, 1802 went for even less. Sixty-nine cruddy bottles of the excellent 1803, which Michael Broadbent called 'amazingly clean' and 'very much alive with a firm acidity' when he tasted it in 1979, went for 13 francs a bottle. The real interest in the clearance sale was in the 1811, the 'mythical' Comet year. Several publicity-seeking hoteliers gesticulated, waved their newspapers and tapped their strawberry noses until the price climbed to 121 francs a bottle. At around the same time the 1858 vintage was knocked down at the far more civilised Christie's sale for a mere 9s a bottle.

When Maurice Healy, Walter Berry, Warner Allen and André Simon tasted Lafite 1864, Simon wrote: 'It was the most glorious wine I'd ever tasted. Quite outstanding, outliving all the great wine of that fabulous vintage.' When he sampled the 1869 in 1954, it was 'astounding, lively, ruby red, sweet, smooth, gentle and charming, its bouquet discreet but intensely clean'. Broadbent was fortunate to taste a magnum of the same year from Glamis Castle, where it had lain with thirty-nine magnums for 100 years. After a little exposure to fresh air, like an old man with stiff joints, it coughed, spluttered and recovered. The world's most respected palate tasted 1949 Lafite on at least thirteen occasions. It evoked 'the rarest of orchids and Mozart piano concertos'.

In 1877, when the seventy-three-year-old Disraeli was stricken with a host of ailments from Bright's disease to bronchitis and asthma, Dr Kidd, a homeopath – at the time a scorned member of the medical profession – examined Disraeli's diet and 'wisely forbade port'. Instead he prescribed 'the finest Château Lafite'. The change in the old man's health was amazing. His vitality improved to such an extent he was later called 'a lion of the Congress' at Berlin, encouraging Bismarck to drop his monocle in surprise and exclaim: 'Der alte Jude, das ist der Mann!' The newly invigorated Disraeli swanned from one hectic Berlin party to the next, an activity that was 'enough to exhaust most men' says Robert Blake, one of his biographers. When asked the best way to drink Château Lafite, the owner Baron Elie replied: 'Claret is a pleasure, not a dreadful duty. Just pull out the cork and lap it up.'

Vines have flourished at Latour since the fourteenth century, but its appearance at London wine auctions, while not as well catalogued as Lafite's, go back to 1792, when Christie's sold a lot of fifty quarts of the 1785. In 1803 the Restaurant Beauvilliers in Paris was selling Latour at 6 francs a bottle.

Michael Broadbent's first tasting note refers to the 1863. He noted the trademark deep blackish colour. The wine, he says, was 'virtually opaque with incredible depth and life for its age'. He called it 'a perfect drink' when he tasted it at the Château in 1970. The 1874, another superb vintage, came from Lord Rosebery's cellar. Tasted in 1967, the usual reference was made to 'quite deep colour'. Even the odd bottle from a very rainy 1881, which emanated from Sir George Meyrick's cellar at Hinton Admiral, 'had an impressively deep colour' and, more importantly, was 'very good for its age'.

At a meeting of the council of the Wine and Food Society, André Simon lined up Château Latour 1920 to follow old sherry and a *Spatlese* Hock. Simon sipped a glass of cold water and mentally loosened his bow tie. He wrote afterwards: 'The Latour smiled its way upon the scene quite unafraid and absolutely charming.' Michael Broadbent tasted the same wine in May 1979. By this time surely it was arthritically limping towards the grave. Not a bit of it. It had 'a very fine deep colour; excellent bouquet, mature but still peppery, rich and cedary, fairly full bodied; a magnificent flavour, soft velvety and well balanced.'

On the subject of poor vintages, when Charles Walter Berry and his friend Reg sat down at the Hotel d'Orsay in Bordeaux in the 1930s they ate 'a modest repast' with a bottle of 1923 Cos d'Estournel, which Berry quaintly said 'was too old for its age'. On the table stood a bottle of Château Latour from diabolical, rain-rotted 1930 with a card that read 'For propaganda – 12 Frs'. It so infuriated Berry he lost complete control of his exclamation marks! Fancy offering a gentleman wine merchant a dismal wine from a great Château pretending they were doing him a favour. 'Run through your mind the two together,' Berry said. 'Latour, 1930 … and then imagine what the public will think.'

Latour was bought by the English Pearson family in 1963, with a quarter of the shares owned by Harvey's of Bristol. The introduction of stainless steel for fermentation on the advice of Harry Waugh in 1964 caused much shrugging in cafés and bars. The vintages that followed were excellent. The 1966 boasted 'magnificent colour and was enormously rich'. The 1970 was a great keeper. Latour made the best of a ghastly 1968. The estate returned to French ownership in 1993, but this, the most reliable of the great Clarets, will always have a grip on English hearts.

'I arrived in Mouton one morning in November 1922,' Baron Philippe de Rothschild remembered. 'I was twenty years old, and my father had given me full administrative rights. Mouton had no running water, electricity nor telephone, only candlelight, water pitchers, oil lamps, hand pumps, and carriages – 1922 was still exasperatingly nineteenth-century. I walked out into the courtyard. A pig squealed, hens cackled, a cow looked at me sideways. Through the linen hung up to dry, I could see the steam rising from the manure-heap. Was it really in these anomalous buildings that one of the best wines in the world was produced?'

Château Mouton-Rothschild is a comparative newcomer to the Olympian band of great Clarets. Originally called Brane Mouton, and restricted to selling to Ireland, Scotland, Hamburg and Holland, it was driven by what Penning-Rowsell called 'an urge for promotion and change'. No stone was left unturned until Mouton achieved Premier Grand status. The Rothschilds invested massively, beginning with the English, fox-hunting Nathaniel, who, when crippled by an accident in the field, moved to

France and in 1853 bought Château Brane Mouton. Work commenced immediately. Architects, builders, painters, plasterers, engineers, septic tank specialists – everyone from botanists to bottle washers – were recruited to tear down, renovate, replant and repair.

By the late nineteenth century Mouton vintages were occasionally seen in the cellars of important English collectors. The first Mouton-Rothschild mentioned in Broadbent's fascinating *The Great Vintage Wine Book* is the five-star 1864, tasted in 1979. When the original cork was eased out, the first of two bottles tasted was spoiled by 'sourness and an acid finish'. The second, despite the level being mid-shoulder, was 'surprisingly sound and delightful'.

When a 'Jefferson' bottle of Branne (*sic*) 1787 – i.e. Mouton-Rothschild – was tasted at the Château in 1986 in the presence of junior members of the Rothschild family and what Jancis Robinson describes as 'many shiny-suited Germans who looked too big for the furniture', Jancis and Michael Broadbent represented the Brits, two of our finest professionals, at an eclectic bash of mainly curious amateurs. The venerable old wine was a sturdy 'treacle-brown' colour, surprisingly lively, exuding a classy nose that filled the room. The French chorused 'Extraordinaire!' The large Germans thundered 'Wunderbar!' Broadbent muttered 'Dunked ginger nuts'.

When Penning-Rowsell first visited the Château in the late 1950s he was unimpressed by a large and open visitors' book 'covered with the large-scale signatures and gushing praise of American visitors'. What with the sycophancy and 'the indirectly illuminated Mouton arms at the end of the chai', visiting Lafite afterwards, he said, was like entering a monastery.

In 2004 the Queen and President Chirac celebrated 100 years of tetchy Entente Cordiale at the Elysée Palace. To break the ice, 1995 Dom Perignon was sipped before the guests sat down to stuffed quails with which they drank Mouton-Rothschild 1988. This was an elderly wine by French standards. When Khrushchev dined with de Gaulle in 1955 the oldest of the Grands Crus consumed was, I think, only seven years old. With the Chambord gâteau of minted chocolate, the 1990 Château d'Yquem was poured. Chirac has a thing about Mouton and it's not surprising he was the minister of agriculture who signed the crucial and unique decree which permitted Mouton-Rothschild to become a *Premier* Grands Crus in 1973. Up to then the Baron's lead capsules defiantly growled: 'Premier ne puis, Second ne daigne, Mouton suis'.

On the occasion of Tony Blair's fiftieth birthday, President Chirac gave the prime minister half a case of Mouton-Rothschild 1989. Only half a case? The stench of their disagreement over Iraq hung heavily over both.

Château Mouton has enjoyed a celebrated existence since its inception and regularly outperforms most other collectable wines in the nail-biting atmosphere of auction houses around the world. Is it worth buying as an investment? Is any wine? The 1986 vintage, which Parker has twice hung with the laurel wreath of maximum points and offered a 'drinking window' of between 50 and 100 years, rose to well over £300 a bottle in 1997, but like most ageing liquid assets it has since halved.

31

Saint-Emilion and Pomerol

'At the beginning of the nineteenth century,' Penning-Rowsell wrote, 'there were no notable estates in Saint-Emilion or Pomerol.' A fine Médoc often retains for some years a marked austerity and even astringency, calling for a certain experience to appreciate fully, while a fine Cheval-Blanc, say, with its fruity, welcoming aroma, and a big, rich, almost sweet flavour, makes the wine a very easy Claret to drink. Maurice Healy visited Saint-Emilion with an ear cocked 'for the tread of its tragic ghosts' – a reference to the young Girondins who holed up here in June 1794 and were guillotined. One of them, Guadet, rushed home to hide in the cellars. He and his father, a wine grower, were decapitated. Gaudet is remembered on a street sign.

Saint-Emilion was accorded the rights of a *commune* as long ago as 1199, long before the Médoc was cleared and planted. The soft, easy wines, often stiffened with reds from surrounding villages, were enjoyed in England from the time of Henry VIII. White grapes had once flourished in the clay soil and made fine Saint-Emilion blanc but they were grubbed up to satisfy a demand for red wine.

The Merlot made an appearance in England in an unspecified Saint-Emilion from the fine 1841 vintage. The unusually supple wines were 'much liked in England with prices moderate until the quality became known, and then they went very high'. Saint-Emilion scarcely surfaced in tastings for the next fifty years until Château Canon, from the poor 1892 vintage, was mentioned. In 1979, it was 'very perfumed', with an attractive old nose, 'charming, delightful and holding well but with a singed ivy leaf taste'. Another anonymous Saint-Emilion, Château des Laurets 1893, was rich but acidic.

A glance at the wines consumed during André Simon's memorable meals reveals the Frenchman as a thorough-going Médocain. One such meal, hosted by Lord Rendelsham in 1913, was described by Simon as 'far from perfect', but the wines were exceptional. After an excellent Ausone 1900 came Margaux 1899, Lafite 1874 and a brilliant Latour 1875. With dessert, Château d'Yquem 1869 was served. It was magnificent then and still magnificent 100 years later. Barry Neame, another *bon viveur* of yesteryear, who like Simon got a kick out of entertaining wine-loving toffs, often presented dinners featuring Cheval Blanc. On 16 May 1934, he served Cheval Blanc 1920, the best year since 1900, with roast Surrey fowl, bread sauce, sausage, bacon, Worthing beans and potatoes.

Simon was among Neame's guests on 22 November 1939, when the fare was giblet soup, grilled fillets of beef, spinach and French beans, roast partridge, fried mushrooms, crisp potatoes and cheese soufflé. Two vintages of Cheval Blanc, 1921 and

1906 – both moderate – were followed by Château Latour 1899 and Château Haut-Brion 1900, 'one of the most perfect vintages ever'. The Haut-Brion spanked the Latour. The 1906 Cheval was wrinkled and emaciated but the 1921 was such a sensation it had the distinguished tasters in a tangle. It was so ridiculously luscious some of the tasters called it 'a freak wine and not a true representative of modern Claret'.

Alec Waugh also called the 1921 Cheval Blanc a freak when he tasted it in very hot summer, 'when the Australian fast bowlers Gregory and McDonald terrified the English batsmen on sun-baked pitches'. It tasted like Burgundy, Waugh said, and 'fetched fantastic prices'; it was at its peak in the years 1932 to 1938, 'when English winemanship was in its fullest flower.' The gigantic 1921 hailed a return to form for Cheval Blanc and led to its acceptance as a great Claret, almost on the same level as the *Premier* Grands Crus from the left bank.

Warner Allen recalled a magnum from the middling 1924 vintage with 'a saddle of lamb that melted in the mouth'. It was a dinner that he and his friends guiltily enjoyed during the grim days of the Second World War, when 'the Food Ministry Gestapo were watchful for evidence of the lightest rationing peccadillo'. While admitting the Cheval Blanc 'was well provided with the virtues of its clan and was quite seductive', Warner Allen, who never found a fine Saint-Emilion that would beat a fine Médoc, remarked: 'I can never remember so well the beauties of Saint-Emilion when they have found themselves side by side with the subtleties and delicacies of Médoc.'

When Broadbent first tasted the 1926 Cheval Blanc as a stripling at Berry Bros, he thought it 'the plumpest, ripest, and most velvety Burgundy'. Laid down from birth in the Berry cellars, the wine was decanted four hours in advance. It was nigh perfect. Subsequent bottles tasted at half a century old all proved to be thrillingly five-star. A 1928 was poor, but, said Broadbent, 'storage and the state of cork are critical factors'.

From 1945 onwards Saint-Emilion and Pomerol regularly appear in English tasting notes. The 1947 vintage, when Cheval Blanc, Ausone and Petrus all made a massive impact with the quality of their wines, proved the pliable Merlot was not just a dozy old ewe in woollen drawers but big and butch and itching to take on Cabernet Sauvignon, the number one red wine grape since the eighteenth century. A few collectors and investors began to take seriously the softer, sooner drinkable, Merlot-based Clarets.

Château Ausone had a direct link with Roman times, being supposedly built on ground above the villa once inhabited by the Bordeaux-born Ausonious (AD 310–c.390), a lawyer, colonial administrator and 'graceful poet of the silver age', who paid tribute in verse to the local wines even though his writings were said to be 'marred by licentiousness'. Ausone dates from 1781 and was listed in the 1868 edition of Cocks and Feret's doorstopper, *Vins de Bordeaux*.

Ausone is often rated as the leading château in Saint-Emilion, with Cheval Blanc some distance behind. Both were rejected by the 1855 classification and the influential new capitalists who turned the scrubby wasteland of the Médoc into the wine equivalent of Las Vegas. The first edition of the Claret drinker's bible, published in 1850, dismissed the wines of Saint-Emilion, merely listing the well-known Saint-Emilion names without affording them the detailed comment reserved for the wines of Médoc. Smarting, the Saint-Emilionnais made sure that at the International Exhibition in Paris in 1867 that they were well represented. They entered most of the best wines of the region, including Ausone, but minus Cheval Blanc, who snubbed the junket. In spite of this demonstration of velvet power, the big guns from the Médoc took most of the gold medals. The wines of Saint-Emilion would continue to fetch derisive prices and be held in low esteem even though the 1868 Cocks and Feret listed forty-four First Growth Saint-Emilion wines. Cheval Blanc had been knocked off its self-appointed pedestal by Bel Air, while Ausone was dragged up by the braces from the netherworld. Although Ausone, Bel-Air, Cheval Blanc and Figeac all sold for good prices, they were the tip of a soft iceberg with gasometers of flat ordinary wine underneath.

It is said that had Château Ausone not been such a tiny producer – it made only twenty-four *barriques* of wine in 1893 – it might have been included in the 1855 classification. This is improbable. Even though Saint-Emilion is one of the larger vignobles in Bordeaux, the holdings are small and the Merlot, notwithstanding its current popularity, was never considered a serious grape by devotees of the longer-lasting Cabernet Sauvignon. Nevertheless, when Edmund Penning-Rowsell sniffed a frail old Château Ausone 1880, a dismal year, his lined face cracked and his moustache vibrated with unexpected joy. 'The nose was fruity,' he wrote, 'the body had a fulness.' It had, he suspected, been laced with Hermitage.

Charles Lorbac, author of *Les Richesses Gastronomiques de la France*, published in 1867, hardly mentions the wines of Saint-Emilion. They were too popular for their own good and growers resorted to mixing Saint-Emilion with other wines to supply demand. Maurice Healy wondered why Château Ausone was considered the principal wine of Saint-Emilion. He couldn't remember drinking anything older than 1899, a vintage he described as 'a model of silky finesse which kept on revealing new charms as long as the glass was refilled'.

To some extent it is a situation that still exists. Penning-Rowsell comments: 'Few of the better growths alone had much of an international reputation until after the First World War.' Then, in 1955, the often rejected and humiliated Saint-Emilionnais 'sprouted first growths like generals in a military dictatorship'. Judging by the large number of ordinary wines masquerading as Grands Crus, it is hardly surprising the attitude still applies.

Broadbent is lukewarm about Ausone vintages between 1945 and 1970. He described the 1949, an exceptional year, as having 'burnt flavours, full of character but not very attractive'. The Cheval 1952 he said was 'eccentric but sane and healthy'. He liked the very good 1959 but found it as 'as idiosyncratic as ever'. At a tasting at Calvet's in Bordeaux in the 1930s, Charles Walter Berry sampled 1877 Margaux, 1871 Latour and an 1899 Cheval Blanc. There was blood on the mahogany, with the off-form Right Bank wines well and truly vanquished. It was lucky the Cheval came after the others, Berry said, as 'it would have killed them'.

When Berry and his sidekick Reg arrived at Château Pavie in Saint-Emilion they were invited to a lunch of home-grown mushrooms with which, to their collective horror, they were offered a semi-sweet and very sulphuric 1928 white Graves. The wines improved, as did their tempers, with a series of interesting bottles, the repast terminating in a smooth tidal wave of 1895 Cheval Blanc poured from Magnums. Under the influence of the Cheval Blanc – bless the wine – Berry chatted up the owner's daughter. With the meal and the whispered conversation over, the smitten Berry stood up. 'Now Madeleine, I thank you for your charming company. I only wish I could speak your language as happily as you do mine – au revoir, thank you so much.' What old man hasn't made a fool of himself after a three-hour French lunch?

Old tasting notes do Pomerol few favours. A half-bottle of 1907 Petrus tried its hardest. Like an abandoned swab it grimly clung on to life, but with a puff of reviving oxygen it tasted 'rich, elegant and fine'. A Château Nenin 1924 was oxidised and falling apart. An ullaged Château La Pointe, also 1924, however, retained its fruit and had 'some of that silky Pomerol texture'.

Though neither Petrus nor its Saint-Emilion rivals, Cheval-Blanc and Ausone, were included in the 1855 Classification, Petrus was at least awarded a Gold Medal at the Paris Exhibition of 1878. Harry Waugh's old employers, Block, Grey and Block, never stocked Petrus even though they were 'top flight' Claret specialists. Chalie-Richards, another fine old wine merchant, later to be absorbed into Justerini and Brooks, offered the finest Clarets from 1917 to 1937 but omitted Petrus. Uniquely among the snooty old traditional merchants, Berry Bros sold 1925 Petrus at 4s a bottle and the far better 1923 at 6s 6d. There is no mention of Petrus in André Simon's *Vintagewise* published in 1945, nor in *Stay me with Flagons*, although Maurice Healy plugs Cheval Blanc several times.

Petrus was owned by the Arnaux family in the eighteenth century but it was not until the blue-rinsed, frenetically active and ambitious Madame Laubat took over the estate from her husband Edmond in 1925 that Petrus shook its head, knuckled its eyes and stood up. Madame Laubat never doubted the quality of her wine and called it 'un empéreur'. She welcomed well-connected wine merchants and a few civilised old gents who wrote about wine as a hobby. When they took their leave after a fine lunch she gave each male a pansy. Nothing sinister there. On her death in 1961 the estate passed to her immediate family, who made the most significant decision in the estate's history: they sold part of it to Jean-Pierre Moueix, who helped make it the star it undoubtedly is today. Pomerol wines, though virtually unknown in England, were popular in Holland and Belgium, 'leaving the traditional Bordeaux trade to provide the British market with the sharp, savoury wines of the Médoc and Graves.'

Petrus's 'lack of acceptance in the nineteenth century', writes Harry Waugh – who with Ronald Avery 'discovered' the wine in the 1960s – 'was caused by the virtual obscurity of the place' and its wines. Waugh, who 'unashamedly confessed to a weakness for Pomerol', said while pundits penned reams about the elegance, distinction and the 'race' of the Médocs, 'they missed golden opportunities' in Pomerol and Saint-Emilion.

Château Petrus, with its deliciously soft, early-drinking accessibility, is now one of the most expensive Clarets of all: a distinct, and fairly recent, uplift in the estate's fortunes. The once-dismissed Merlot from the lowest yields, picked from old, gnarled bushes by experienced staff in the morning, is now pampered, the secret with Merlot, and treated like a wrinkled diva. It is no coincidence that the great warm years of 1945 and 1947, under the stewardship of the redoubtable Madame Laubat and with up to 30 per cent Cabernet Franc in the mix, made soft, dark, perfumed wines. Now that the Cabernet Franc has been reduced to just 5 per cent, vintages can be wiped out by bad weather.

But when it is good it is 'awesome', as Robert Parker found out with the 1990: 'dense, rich, concentrated. With tons of tannin, gobs of glycerine, and an exotic coffee, tobacco–herb, super-ripe berry-scented nose and flavours.' He gave it a straight 100 and could not bring himself to spit it out. 'Another legend!' the Marylander said. The Moueixes though, thought the 1989 was the finest Petrus since 1947. How far the little Merlot has come since it was dismissed as the peasant's grape, covering every Pomerol hovel with bland bunches of dessert grapes a few centuries ago! David Peppercorn says: 'Every wine-lover should find a way of experiencing Petrus.' Nowadays, winning the lottery is as good as any.

32

The Rise of Sauternes

In London in 1733/34, 'Small White Wines' from Bordeaux were selling at £20 a hogshead, half the price of Claret. Picking the ripest grapes was the norm then and *pourriture noble* had already been noted on shrivelled Semillon in the Graves area by the inquisitive priest, the Abbé Bellet. When Thomas Jefferson, the wine-obsessed future president of the United States, tasted his way around Bordeaux, he noted that while dry white Graves was appreciated in London, Paris had, and still has, a sweeter tooth.

Nosing around the lesser villages of Sauternes, Jefferson noted that the samples offered by a certain 'M. Diquem' were smooth and powerful and worthy of an asterisk in his notebook. The wine was made, according to an ancient version of Cocks and Feret, from 'two-fifths Semillon, two-fifths Sauvignon, and the remainder Metternich and Muscat'. The Metternich referred to is Riesling, a grape still sparingly used at Château Doisy-Daene, a Second Growth Barsac. Later, when enjoying a chilled bottled of 'Diquem's' in the company of his friend George Washington, the president was so impressed by Jefferson's eulogising that he immediately ordered three cases of the attractive, gold-tinted, full-bodied dry wine. By the end of the eighteenth century, Château d'Yquem had gradually evolved into a natural, unfortified and unsugared sweet wine, with cellaring the most sublime sweet wine on earth.

From 1794 to 1800 Harvey's of Bristol sold mainly Portuguese and Spanish wines. No French white wine was listed. But the Duke de Frias, the Spanish ambassador to London, didn't care for his own country's wine. When his London cellar was dispersed in 1819, it contained 108 bottles of Sauternes.

When the Duke of Sussex's eclectic collection of wines was sold in 1843, among the bottles of Catawba, Lachrymae Christi, Cyprus and the Val de Penas were six bottles of Barsac and three of Sauternes. The Stowe House sale in 1848 revealed little of interest to Sauternes lovers – just fourteen unnamed bottles sold in a job lot under 'Other Wines'. The Gladstonian list in August 1860 included 'Sauternes of Barsac at 36s the dozen and Haut Sautern [*sic*] Fine, 1847 first growth, 42s to 50s a dozen.' 'Château Yquem' 1846 was offered at 50s a case and the magnificent 1847, which was described as 'curious and very rare', was a bargain at 120s a case. Ordinary wines from the south of France such as Masdew, 'grown between Perpignan and Collioure', found their way into quality cellars like the one at Ashburnham.

Raymond Postgate said: 'Sauternes must be drunk in the right company – which is a plump, pretty and slightly greedy young woman.' Professor Saintsbury on the other hand, drank 1870 d'Yquem with red mullet. Not surprisingly he then wrote: 'Sweet wine has a tendency to sicken.' Loftily, he found 'many good drinkers' who agreed with him. Thackeray drank Sauternes after dinner – 'the only blot,' Saintsbury harrumphed, 'on his wine record'.

The idea of selecting only the sweetest, juiciest, most shrivelled grapes for the white wines of Sauternes dates back to 4 October 1666, when a contract was drawn up by the notary of Barsac for the Squire François Sauvage. It states: 'In order not to harm the reputation of the said wine [Château d'Yquem] harvesting shall be done only when the grapes are fully ripe.' Another former owner of Yquem, the Marquis Bertrand de Lur Saluces, revealed in a conversation with Edmund Penning-Rowsell that the use of nobly rotted grapes began in 1860. On the other hand Jean Bureau, an old and experienced *maître de chais* at d'Yquem, recalled tasting the burnished nectar in 1845.

The 'Comet Year' of 1811 lies embedded in the consciences of wine historians. It was a genuine five-star vintage for everything – port, Claret, Burgundy and Sauternes. Château d'Yquem made a stunning wine which last sold at Christies as 'very fine Sauternes' in 1837. No-one living has tasted it, including the man himself, Broadbent. The next famous year was the aforementioned 1847, the year the Tsar paid a king's ransom for a cask from the vaulted side chapel they call a cellar at Château d'Yquem. Christie's sold the same wine for £6 a case of twenty bottles in May 1867.

An inventory of the d'Yquem cellars drawn up in 1822 revealed three casks of vintage 1753. Russian archdukes were the chief customers. Constantine paid £800 for a cask of the 1847 vintage. A later tsar insisted on his 1869 d'Yquem being delivered to Moscow in inscribed cut-glass decanters while his subjects ate swill and slept with pigs. Michael Broadbent enjoyed the wine a century later, noting its 'crème brûlée bouquet and lovely acidity'.

Wine lovers have long and uselessly speculated on which is finer: Trockenbeerenauslese or the finest Sauternes. For what it's worth, Château Rayne-Vigneau, or Vigneau-Pontac as it was labelled then, and classified as a Premier Cru in 1855, was matched against an array of late-picked German wines in a fringe event at the 1867 Paris International Exhibition. The judges, a democratic mix of French and Germans, gave the thumbs-up to the Sauternes. To Maurice Healy, the jowly and dewy-eyed old Irish judge, that first sip of Château d'Yquem was 'paradisal. The room was filled with a perfume that recalled the Arabian Nights. It embalmed the air. It is the most beautiful wine God ever allowed man to make; it ought never to be drunk profanely.'

At the Astor House Hotel in New York, guests bought 'Y. Chem' (*sic*) for $2 a bottle in 1839. The French were just as dyslexic, for around the same time the Restaurant Beauvilliers in Paris was listing 'vin de Soterne'. Bernard Ginestet in his book *Sauternes* writes: 'For me the undeniable glory of Sauternes is to be found with Rocquefort cheese, mould against mould. Spread the cheese in the hollow of celery stalks and savour it with the divine nectar.'

When and with what to drink Château d'Yquem has occupied the minds of wine-loving plutocrats for generations. When Brillat-Saverin (1755–1826) cooked lunch

APPELLATION BORDEAUX SUPÉRIEUR CONTROLÉE

"Y"

Lur-Saluces

• 1979 •

BORDEAUX SUPÉRIEUR

750ml   MIS EN BOUTEILLE A LA PROPRIETE

L.S. PROPRIETAIRE A SAUTERNES (GDE) FRANCE

A rarely made dry wine from Château D'Yquem. A throwback to the days before noble Rot.

for a group of friends, he poured small glasses of Sauternes with two dozen oysters each, kidneys á la brochette, a terrine of truffled *foie gras* and a fondue. Baron Philippe Rothschild from Mouton and his cousin Baron Elie of Lafite were both *foie gras* men. At Baron Philippe's daughter Philippine's pre-wedding luncheons, after a marathon of great Clarets from both estates, guests were poured Château d'Yquem 1934, 1945 and 1921 with *pâté de foie gras*, as is the custom in Bordeaux.

The late Marquis de Lur-Saluces, owner of the estate, agreed but insisted Château d'Yquem should be served very cold, 'but never completely iced' and never with dessert. Lumpen Muscats and Frontignans were the proper partners for the sweet courses because their high degree of alcohol and 'a pronounced taste of cooked grapes which dominates any other flavours.' D'Yquem, the Marquis said, was best with 'a delicate fish – turbot, sauce mousseline, or salmon, lobster, fillets of sole and *foie gras*. And of course it goes well with fruit. But towards midnight, when one has just come home, it is perfect served very cold with a dry biscuit.'

Vivyan Holland bizarrely believed sardines in olive oil and fine Sauternes were inextricably linked through their respective vintages. He was so convinced of some celestial connection between the entombed little fish and Sauternes that he arranged blind tastings of sardines and Sauternes from the years 1919 to 1930. The tasting panel, selected for their strong stomachs, included André Simon. When the results were announced the tastiest sardine vintages directly mirrored the better years for Sauternes: 1921, 1926, 1928 and 1929. Holland believed the sardines were best after at least twenty years of cellaring. A rusting tin from the 1908 vintage was hugely enjoyed by the Committee of the Saintsbury Club in 1940. What was the best wine to drink with tinned sardines? A fine and mature Château d'Yquem, of course.

When the wonderfully haughty G.B. Stern was researching her book *Bouquet* in the 1920s, she visited a Sauternes grower who boasted that his grandfather had invented the nectarious confection. Stern became irritated by the man's assumption that because she was female she should like sweet wine. 'It was the old idiot fallacy,' Stern elegantly fumed, 'that ladies preferred sweet wine. Why should we? Has not a woman eyes, organs, dimensions, senses, affections, passions, even as a man has? Have we not palates, intelligence, taste, subtlety, and a fastidious discrimination – even as a man has? Must we be indulged, given compliments, lies, and sweetmeats, relegated to the drawing-room to gossip or to fuss, to read pretty novels or to show off to an envious rival our frocks?'

'So,' Stern hissed as she rammed her red sports Fiat into gear, 'M. Garosse's grand-father is responsible for producing this clinging, highly-perfumed, luscious and full blooded horror known as the great wine of Sauternes, is he?' With a screeching of tyres she roared away in a mini-tornado of dust, yelling that she would never again drink that ghastly sickly wine. 'Only dry wine from now on,' she screamed. '*Vin sec*! Not bloody *demi-sec*, but *sec, sec, sec*!'

In the Victoria Wine Company's 1897 wine list there were only two wines with vineyard names on the labels. One was Château d'Yquem; the other Moulin à Vent, a Beaujolais. On the company's 1980 list there were many more wines with vineyard names, but easily the most expensive was Château d'Yquem 1975, a moderate vintage, at £29 a bottle. How can the owners have the neck to sell sub-standard d'Yquem? It's like flogging a Rolls Royce with four flat tyres.

When Cyril Ray was being entertained to lunch 'at one of the great first-growth Châteaux of Barsac', Sauternes was served with every course. Ray gagged. At last the meat course arrived, a beautiful, fragrant roast gigot of lamb. Now for a decent glass of Claret, Cyril thought. The wine chosen was 'that honey-sweet and scented mira-cle', Château d'Yquem, 1921. Noting a stunned and ever so slightly miffed silence emanating from Ray's side of the board, the host ventured: 'Don't you think our white wines here are very pretty?' 'Oh yes, indeed I do,' Ray said, wondering where the nearest aspidistra was parked. 'I knew you would agree with me,' his host said. 'By the way,' the Frenchman laughed, 'what do you think of those fellows in the Médoc drinking those sour red wines of theirs?' Ray's jaw tightened and he may have muttered 'Jaysus Christ!'

One of the oldest d'Yquems tasted was in a very rare bluey-green flower-inscribed bottle from the era of the Sauvage family, who sold the estate to the Lur-Saluces in 1787. The frail old wine was 'a reddish brown colour' but still rich. Alas, when hit by the fresh air it staggered, clutching its chest before dying on the spot. In 1900 the estate made another brilliant wine with grapes that had shrivelled but not rotted nobly. In spite of a lack of acidity, the wine lasted and was suave and sweet at seventy-five.

A torrid summer in 1921 brought the grapes to a honey-dripping ripeness. The already buttercup-yellow juice quickly turned bronze in the barrel but the intensity of the sweetness left an indelible mark on lucky palates throughout the century. It is still available, the way new Lamborghinis are. Don't expect a great wine experience: André Simon was advising us to 'drink it up now' in the 1950s as 'it is not likely to get better'. The next great year was 1929. Picked on 23 September, it was flexing an impressive six-pack well into middle age. The 1945 vintage had enough acidity to preserve it for a very long time. The 1950s produced two great Yquem vintages – 1955 and 1959 – which Broadbent called 'probably the last of the heavyweight classics'. The advice as to what age one should drink d'Yquem is nearer twenty-five years than fifty – just don't drink it young.

33

Hermitage

Hermitage and Côte Rotie were among 'the Wines upon the fruitful Rhône' referred to in Thomas Shadwell's (*c.*1642–1692) play, *The Woman-Captain*. But in their *Wines of the Rhône*, the authors Livingstone-Learmonth and Masters claim that after 2,000 years of winemaking the Rhône remains 'an unknown quantity'. Even the 'magnificent' Côte Rotie, the source of the Roman import *vinum picatum*, and Hermitage 'have never become widely known'.

The British ambassador to the Hague purchased twenty bottles of Hermitage in 1710 and the eager Earl of Bristol took delivery of Hermitage in 1714, 1716 and 1738 and Côte Rotie in 1737 and 1738. His cellar also included a 1704 'Avignon', Châteauneuf du Pape's great, great, great grandfather.

Dean Jonathan Swift's dabbling in Hermitage brought him nothing but misery and loss of face. After receiving glowing reports of the Rhône wine from his friend Mr Arbuthnot, who lived in Rouen, Swift not only ordered 150 bottles for his own cellar but advised his Dublin friends to fill their boots. It was an embarrassing disaster. Most of the wine sickened before turning to vinegar. Swift complained loud and long, blaming everyone from the hapless Arbuthnot to the contemptible shipper. Swift should have bought his Rhônes in Dublin, because, as he said after the tragic event, 'Good wine is ninety per cent living in Ireland.'

To Alexander Pope, who was practically a teetotaller, Swift wrote, 'As to my Hermitage misfortune, it is a very afflicting circumstance whereof your abstemious ship is no judge.' But wait. A few bottles of the accursed Hermitage which Swift abandoned to moulder in shame and disgrace turned out to be magnificent when tasted seven years later. A foolish man with money and his choice of friends, Swift blew most of the royalties he received for *Gulliver's Travels* on wine. He pleaded to John Gay, who was recruited to mind the money for him, 'A hundred guineas will buy me six hogsheads of wine, which will support me a year.'

That unusually well-travelled American Thomas Jefferson was among those who appreciated Hermitage, more so than an English 'expert', who dismissed the lovely black velvet as 'port without the brandy'. The freezing Scots enjoyed a robust wine and in 1780 the Forster Brothers, who were based in Bordeaux, sent a Scottish client an invoice covering the cost of 'keeping over 5 and a ½ tuns of Hermitage 1st. Class from the 3rd of June, 1780 until the 1st of January, 1783.'

John Wright, in his *Essays on Wines* of 1796, recognised the health-sustaining properties of good strong wine when he referred to 'some very pleasant wines from near Orange, labelled Hermitage and Côte Rotie'. They were, Wright said, 'stimulating, as a restorative, a natural delicacy, because they are untainted with bad brandy, or any other noxious spirits'. A gentleman, 'even a delicate *bon vivant*', could drink Rhône wines well into the early hours without suffering from 'mawkishness, headaches and fever'.

'Old Hermitage' was sold by Priddy's Foreign Warehouse in 1794, even though it was a rare sight in London near the end of the eighteenth century. When the London cellars of the ambassador of the Court of Spain, the Duke de Frias, were decanted into the salesrooms in 1819, the collection included 486 bottles of red Hermitage and 180 bottles of the white – Hermitage was a trendy wine in ambassadorial circles in the early nineteenth century. When the Prince de Talleyrand sold twenty-six bottles of 1825 White Hermitage, a wine Cyrus Redding said would 'keep for a hundred years without deterioration', he received 65s per dozen. 'Lot 6, 21 bottles of Red Ditto', was bought by a Mr Cooper at 70s per dozen. Six dozen bottles of unremarkable 1822 Tavel red, which had spent a year in wood, fetched 48s a dozen. The Talleyrand cellar also housed a monstrosity called 'French port'.

The mid-eighteenth century, when dozens of cellars were broken up, was an opportune time to purchase mature red wine. Some were doctored with Hermitage but they were none the worse for that. The well-attended sale after the death of the Duke of Sussex in 1843 was a microcosm of wine in England at the time. The Duke's enthusiasm for wine from every available quarter is illustrated in the crates of dusty

Delicately fragrant and bone dry from miniscule Château Grillet. Sun-kissed and pampered, the once-tricky viognier can be fat and wobbly.

bottles, magnums and flasks that turned up in the auction rooms of Messrs Christie and Manson in 1844. Among them were fifteen bottles of red Hermitage and six bottles of 'very fine' old white Hermitage.

Professor Saintsbury wondered which was the better wine – 1846 Hermitage or Romanée-Conti 1858. He opened the Hermitage in 1886 and pronounced it 'the manliest French wine I ever drank'. At the Stowe House clearance in 1848 auctioneers speedily shifted gallons of fine port, sherry, Madeira Claret and Constantia. Among the 'Other Wines' nestling with the Canary and the Cowslip were sixty-six bottles of Côte Rotie.

Côte Rotie and Hermitage are now secure in the pantheon of fine French wines. Once modest and unknown, the Guigals and Chaves, growers since 1481 and among the oldest wine makers in the whole of France, and the Jasmins and Clapes, whose forefathers sweated over their ox-blood reds in modest hovels, only to see them taken to Bordeaux and Burgundy for blending, are now canonised by recent converts to their powerful, fragrant and now fashionably expensive wines.

34

Other French Wines

In 1714 the Earl of Bristol imported 'a white Coindrieux' from the ancient Viognier grape, which was taken, it is said, from the Dalmatian coast by Emperor Probus in AD 281. Jancis Robinson knows of a grape currently grown on the Dalmatian island of Vis, called Vugava, which shows similar characteristics.

In the late eighteenth century, Château Grillet was appreciated for its clean, fruity style. Among its admirers was Thomas Jefferson. The Court of St James purchased twelve dozen bottles of Château Grillet from the Wine House in St Peray for King George IV in 1829. James Christie, the Lord Steward, wrote to the suppliers: 'In selecting this wine I trust you will be careful that it is of the very first vintage and such as may be fit for immediate use.' The King liked it young and fresh; some say it is better that way. Jancis Robinson would gently point out that she has tasted fifty-year-old Grillets that were as fresh as a young colt on a frosty morning. I remember a 1971 Grillet that at twenty-five years old was crisply magnificent.

When he died, the Duke of Sussex left behind six bottles of a little-known white wine called St Peray. Made principally from the Marsanne, the same grape that sires hard-wearing white Hermitage, St Peray is now better known for a pleasant sparkling wine. Apart from its attraction to English aristos, Napoleon lost his wine virginity to a bottle of St Peray when as a young soldier he was based at Valence. Eminent writers like Lamertine, Daudet and de Maupassant all had their heroes and heroines spraying St Peray. Most famously, perhaps, it was the wine that inspired the dying Richard Wagner to finish his last great work, *Parsifal*, in 1882. To oil his pen Wagner had it delivered by the crate with the morning milk.

The Muscat of Frontignan, also known as Frontignac and Frontiniac, an uncomplicated sweet wine, goes back at least to the eighth century. It was sent to England in the fourteenth century labelled 'Provence'. 'Frontiniac' was mentioned in Thomas Heywood's *Philcothonista*, published in 1635. Canary, Malaga and sweet Sack were more fashionable, so wines sold as Frontiniac in London taverns were frequently a mixture of all three, bulked up with a bucket or two of Lunel. A nineteenth-century pig-skinned book of kitchen lore, collected and carefully penned by the cooks in an ancient Herefordshire house, gives this recipe for 'Frontinack': 'Take 6 gallons of water. Put in it when cold 12 pounds of sugar and 6 pounds of raisins, stoned and chopped. Put in the white of two eggs to clarify it then set it over ye fire and let it boyl a full hour, taking off ye scum as it rises. Then take the flower of elder, full ripe and ready to drop. Rub off slightly the white flowers to ye quantity of a peck and put them into ye liquor. When it is half cold put in 6 spoonfuls of lemmon juice and a spoonful of ale yeast that is not bitter. Work it 3 to 6 days, stirring it every day then let it stand 2 or 3 days to settle. Then draw it off, fine through flannel and bottle it.' And it was only a penny a pint.

The South African Simon van der Stel, governor of the Cape of Good Hope in 1685, made a wine from the Hanepot grape, stole the name 'Frontignac' and fooled the English with his honeyed beauty. James I liked it too, and when it was shipped to London in 1711, via Bordeaux, it glistened in its cut-glass decanter with silver 'ticket' – alongside Haut Pregnac and Bommes Sauternes on patina'd sideboards.

John Locke (1632–1704), the philosopher, after an enforced stay in Montpellier, developed a passion for 'Frontiniac' and recommended it to his friends. As the impression of vine leaves have been found in the tufa rock near Montpellier, there is a distinct likelihood wine was made there long before the Romans arrived. Thomas Jefferson, the most celebrated wine lover among US presidents, enjoyed a glass of Frontignan.

Priddy's Foreign Wine Warehouse offered 'Frontignac' at 42s a dozen in 1794, which made it the same price as First Growth Claret, dearer than Old Madeira and twice the price of both 1788 vintage port and Old Lisbon. It also featured in the Vauxhall Gardens' 1762 London list priced at 6s a bottle, the same as Burgundy and a shilling dearer than Claret. Now fortified with a nip of rough brandy, and enjoying a little burp of success after years in the doldrums, Frontignan is still not considered worth a mention in some wine tomes. From Victoria to Elizabeth, the British loved its finger-licking stickiness. In the 1960s the sadly defunct Peter Dominic sold the cheap, southern French dessert wine as Castle Cream. Unlike Pliny's sleepy bees who dogged the ripening Muscatel, Castle Cream failed to take off.

Even when Claret was the most sought-after wine in England, the dark and accessible wine of Cahor appeared in London under its own label. Hugh Johnson is of the opinion that Cahor was better and stronger than most local Bordeaux, which made the touchy Bordelais a little jealous of a swarthy rival. The Dutch liked the dark, iron-rich wines of the lot and shipped it by the boatload. Not so dark and more commercial now, Cahor is being challenged by sultry Malbecs from Argentina. Laura Catena, a fourth-generation scion of one of the principal Argentine winemakers, recently launched Alto, a finely tuned Malbec with Bordeaux pretensions. The asking price is £26 a bottle, the same as a fourth or fifth-growth Bordeaux. Fifty-year-old Malbec, toasted and mollycoddled, is said to make a wine that 'rivals the great wines of the world.' We'll see.

The seaside town of Sète was one clearing centre for wines in Roman times. From it's hot, productive vineyards bulk wine continues to pour. However, the wines of the Midi were once hailed. On an 1711 invoice Languedoc proudly nestles among the Vins de Graves and the sweet wines of Sauternes. They had 'a freshness and beautiful deep colour' and were a perfect ingredient in 'artificial Claret or Burgundy Wines'. Sometimes they were actually labelled Claret. But there were problems when he ordered a supply of Languedoc masquerading as 'french Clarett', James Soleirol in

1722 wrote: 'at ye same time taking back and allowing for 26 flasks of bad wine sent to me in ye Country.'

In the eighteenth century Languedoc was dispatched to Tuscany to spruce up anaemic Chiantis and to bolster geriatric Barolos. When aphids, diseases, wars and a succession of dismal vintages struck Bordeaux, Midi growers, hosed their outhouses, scraped their shovels and collected their mules from the creek. Barrels of young wine lashed to barges moved sedately north to mingle their common blood with regal Bordeaux. Between emergencies. When Claret orders were filled, the growers went back to rubbing their grizzled chins like Lee van Cleef in *A Fistful of Dollars*, drawing in the dust with a stick.

The battery-acid sharp, low-yielding, disease-sensitive Picpoul or Piquepool, otherwise known as the 'lip stinger', was a minor hit in the seventeenth century and latterly as an ingredient in vermouth. It came in three colours – white, grey and red. The grey version seems to have disappeared, but the white and red cling on in tiny oases. Demand for Picpoul Blanc, a pleasant little white wine, is currently on the increase. Hope springs eternal in the hearts of Southern growers.

Old enamelled bottle tickets occasionally turn up in junk shops bearing the legend Chambéry. It enjoyed a limited appeal as an aperitif. Half a century ago Maurice Healy said: 'If you are a wise man you will not have taken anything except a glass of sherry or Chambéry before the soup.' He called it 'an agreeable aperitif, which is not as widely known as it might be'.

Legend has it the baby son of King Henri IV had his lips brushed by a clove of garlic dipped in sweet Jurancon at Pau in 1553. This delicious sweet wine from the Gros and Petit Manseng ages well and is well worth finding. Colette claims to have been a virgin when she found her liquid prince. He was 'aroused and imperious'.

Ratafia was popular in London in the eighteenth century. Talleyrand, the French ambassador to London, was among those who liked this unusual drink. Described as 'a cordial or liquor' dating back to the sixteenth century, it was flavoured especially 'from the almond, cherry and peach'. Several claim to have invented Ratafia including Justerini, a young Italian, who arrived in London in 1749 clutching a secret recipe for something the locals drank in bars back home in Bologna. Combining with an Englishman called Johnson, Justerini manufactured the drink in London out of unfermented grape juice dosed with brandy. The two young men later opened a wine, spirits and beer shop which swelled to Justerini and Brooks.

Ratafia de Champagne was made for the family and key clients of Veuve Clicquot in 1823. They released it for general consumption in the 1920s. It is an enjoyable peach-coloured aperitif not totally unlike Pineau des Charentes, 'the aperitif of the Cognac winefield'. Patrick Forbes advised: 'Cut a canteloupe melon in half and pour a little ratafia in the centre. It is delectable.'

35

Italian, Austrian and Romanian Wines

Venetian traders included England among their customers after the Crusades, which had given the invading Christians a taste for wine. The Frescobaldis, still an aristocratic name in Tuscany, collected taxes in England to finance the religious wars, swapping Florentine wine for wool. Traders shipped Trubidiane, the ubquitous Trebbiano popular in the fourteenth century, and 'Greek' from Tuscany, an early Vin Santo which is still made from two Greek grapes, the Malvasia and the Grechetto. England also took delivery of sweet wines from Apulia and Calabria. The lucious Rybole, also known as Riboldi from Rivoglio, appeared in London in 1365. Sir Richard Steele, editor of *Tatler*, shared with Congreve and Estcourt, the actor, a liking for Florentine wine, even if it occasionally 'went sour'.

In medieval Florence poor Tuscan farmers who needed to stretch the daily jug copied the ancients' idea of mixing wine and water. At the tables of the wealthy, and in the better kind of tavern, wine was consumed 'pretto', undiluted. White wine was more popular than the light 'vermiglio', which was shipped from Sardinia and Greece. Full bodied wines were imported from Tunis, Cyprus, Rhodes, France and Bordeaux. Schiavo, Trebbiano, Vernaccia, Malvasia and Moscadello were consumed by the nobility from silver goblets decorated with leonine heads, and embellished with enamels.

The poet Redi wrote;

'O, happy am I!
As from the darkest clusters
Of a mature Canaiulo,
I squeeze a juice so pure,
That in the glass splashes,
Jumps, bubbles and sparkles!'

The Tuscans drank their best wines and are said to have shipped the poor stuff to England, although some of the criticisms levelled against Italian imports were as harsh as the wines.

Sir Edward Barry, whose *Observations* appeared in London in 1775, wrote: 'We seldom meet any good (Italian) Wines. Chianti formerly much esteemed in England, has entirely lost its character; large quantities of the red Florence are still imported in flasks; but from the disagreeable roughness seldom drank. They have freshness and a beautiful colour and are probably chiefly consumed in making artificial Claret or Burgundy Wines, or in giving lightness and spirit to vapid port.' The English physician Dr John Wright wrote in his *Essay on Wines*, published in 1795: 'Most of the Italian Wines we saw sunk below mediocrity.'

André Simon disagreed; 'Italian wines,' he wrote, 'appear to have received at all times special consideration. From 1728, when the importation of wine in bottles and small casks was prohibited, Acts of Parliament, of the first year of the reign of George II [1728] were specifically drafted so they did not prohibit the importation of Tuscan in Flasks.'

John Gay in 1708 mentions 'Florence pure', although Samuel Johnson said: 'Florence wine I think the worst; It neither pleases the taste nor exhilarates the spirits.' In 1711 Jonathan Swift, after 'a scurvy dinner', drank Florence in a London tavern at 'four and sixpence a flask'. His tasting note was succinct: Florence was a 'damned wine'. Swift was also given bad Florence by Sir John Bolingbroke. He later recalled the time he and Sir Andrew Fountaine, 'a virtuoso of repute', repaired to a tavern where they drank a bottle of Florence and another of Portuguese for 16s, a considerable sum. Swift wished he had spent £16 and bought something better. 'I was very uneasy last night with ugly filth that turned sour in my stomach,' he groaned. An advertisement in *The Gentleman's Magazine* around 1731 reduced the price of Florence from £40 to £30 'a chest'.

Lord Chandos, a great connoisseur of Italian wine, had access to some of the best available Italian through his friendship with the British consul at Livorno. He once employed an impoverished Handel as his *Kapellmeister* and was rewarded with *Chandos's Anthems* in 1719. He cellared Montelpulciano, Verdea, Florence and 'Moscatos from Montalcino, Montefiasconi, Calabria, and Syracuse'.

Francesco di Marco Datini, a fourteenth-century Tuscan wine merchant who opened his thick ledger every morning and uttered the prayer 'In the name of God and profit', shipped his wines in large containers of 114 English gallons and in the *barile*, which held 45.5 litres. A Venetian butt holding 48 gallons was used for shipping Candy wines. Wines from Naples and Sicily came across in *bottes*, a cask capable of holding 100 English gallons.

Charles Longland, an English wine merchant who had gone to Italy in 1653 looking for wines, wrote from Livorno on the seventeenth of January: 'Owing to the sea voyage some types of Florence were not successful in Britain. They were not up to the journey, unless they could be shipped in cask in the cold months between January and March.' Longland railed against unfair rates of duty that helped Spanish and French wines. Tuscan diplomats in London found their native wines so expensive they drank 'foreign wines'.

Williamson, an English wine merchant who shipped Florence to England succeeded in getting a friendly physician called Salmon to say that both red and white Florence were good for the stomach. By 1691 the ubiquitous *fiaschi* were on tavern tables in London. Lamberto Parranetto says that Tuscany became the favourite place

for the English aristocracy to find agreeable wines. Queen Anne was happy to accept
gifts of Tuscan wine from her friend Cosimo III, the Grand Duke. Filippo Mazzei,
'an unusual and enterprising person', raised his shutters in Bond Street in the eighteenth century to specialise in Italian wines. Nevertheless, there are documents in
the Castle Brolio archives which confirm that Chianti was shipped to London from
1715 to 1735.

When Florence died as a brand Chianti flourished. The poet Fulvio Testi (1593–
1646) helped with the copywriting:

> 'If you come I shall pour for you
> Etruscan Chianti, similar to Ruby, that
> kisses you, and bites you and makes
> you shed sweet tears.'

The 'robust, pleasant and harmonious' Tuscan wines became popular. Soon the in
fame of this wine overran Tuscan borders and was known as far afield as England.
Exports of Chianti became so substantial by the end of the sixteenth century that
Cosimo I, the Grand Duke, banned the export of Tuscan to maintain a supply of wine
for the people of the Grand Duchy. Counterfeiting soon followed, but in 1579 all
wines exported in large flasks containing 2,280 litres of wine were fitted with lead
seals. Innkeepers and tavernkeepers were warned not to buy unsealed flasks as no
Tuscan wine could be sold if a seal was broken. Tampering was so widespread that
persistent miscreants were 'given to lashes and forced to carry a board around their
necks saying "I am a forger of flasks".' The fashion was to drink Chianti cold. The philosopher Peccana wrote: 'Ice and snow are the fifth element of good drinking because
a cold drink is natural according to history and only the thirst is warm for passion.'
Flasks were designed with pockets to hold snow or ice.

Baron Bettino Ricasoli played a major part in defining modern Chianti. By selecting the Sangiovese as the key element, with the sweeter, darker Canaiolo and the
white Malvasia, Ricasoli's vision was to see Chianti established as the new Florence,
respected in England, where it had once been laughed at. On the day before he died,
on 23 October 1880, Ricasoli sat up in bed in the cold, rough-stoned Castle Brolio
and wrote 'a five-page letter to a "famous exporter" offering to sell him his magnificent collection of fine old Chianti on the condition that the exporter would make his
wines widely known in Great Britain.'

At a tasting in Vienna in 1873, 'at which the best wines in the world were gathered',
Henry Vizetelly (1820–1894) wrote: 'Chianti was a wine of great finesse and a pleasant
acidity, not dissimilar to the wines of Beaujolais but with more colour and strength.' The
composer Giuseppe Verdi (1813–1901) enjoyed Chianti and was a jogger long before it
became obligatory. His wife wrote: 'He sleeps and drinks Chianti, nothing but Chianti,
and more Chianti. Long live Chianti and He who has provided such a good one.'

Adolfo Mellini purchased fine wine from the Nippozzano estate owned by the
Marquis Albizi and shipped it to England in flasks 'sealed' with olive oil. It was not

a shrewd move. Those who bought the odd-looking wine drank it with the oil. Melini dispensed with the olive oil and the straw-entwined flask and put the Chianti into a Claret-style bottle. No-one bought that either. When foreign dignitaries visited Florence, then the capital of Italy, they were served fine Claret and Château d'Yquem.

Aliatico, a dark port-like red wine often containing up to 16 per cent alcohol, appeared on Priddy's wine list in London in 1793. Made from the ancient Lugliatico grape, Aliatico is made in Tuscany, Latium and the isle of Elba, Napoleon's favourite.

Campelyte, Campletes, and Campolet were all variations of the same wine shipped to England from Tuscany in the fifteenth century. By 1650 it may have been made exclusively from the Campolet grape. A wine labeled 'Greek' came from anywhere but Greece. The main sources were Tuscany, Apulia and Calabria. It could be sweet and yellow as honey, or as green and sour as a inripe Granny Smith. An 'Italian' wine labelled Grenache was probably Greek. Dr John Wright who put a gaitered boot into Italian wines in general, said of Lachrymae Christi: 'On account of its name it hath been much talked of but it rarely comes to England.' However, when the executors of the Duke of Sussex disposed of his wines in 1844, they discovered eight dozen Lachrymae Christi in one of the estate cottages.

When Heine, the poet, visited Baron James Rothschild before the latter purchased Château Lafite, the poet was unusually morose. To cheer him up, the Baron offered his guest a choice of the finest vintages in his cellar. The tasting concluded with Lachrymae Christi. Heine studied the golden colour, sniffed and slurped and chewed for a moment. 'Do you know why this wine is called Lachrymae Christi?' Heine asked mischievously. 'No, but I hope you will tell me,' the Baron said. 'These are Christ's tears,' Heine said. 'He weeps at the sight of two wicked Jews like us drinking such a precious wine where there are thousands of poor Christians in Paris without a crust of bread!'

Melfi, sometimes labelled Rapolla, was occasionally drunk in London by the more adventurous taverner. It came from Melfi in central Italy. Montelpulciano was advertised in *The Times* on the sixteenth of April 1793. The 'noble' wine was a favourite of the poet Francesco Redi, who, in the seventeenth century, described it as the 'King of Wines'. Lord Chandos preferred it to a red wine he shipped from Syracuse which, though rich, strong-bodied and fine, 'did not fill the mouth as Montepulciano'.

Marsala, often misspelt Marsella on old enamelled bottle tickets, was offered on the first Gladstonian Wine List as 'thoroughly racked and shipped by Ingham's at 25s a dozen'. Marsala has been drunk in England for at least 250 years, thanks to the arrival in Sicily in 1763 of John Woodhouse, a Liverpool-born entrepreneur with a taste for port. Sales for the sweet brown wine were given a leg-up when Admiral Nelson arrived in Sicily in 1798 and proceeded to stock his ships with the new drink, not for its flavour, but as insurance against scurvy. Nelson liked the island so much he bought a vineyard there. In his book *The Pleasures of the Table*, published in 1931, Sir Francis Colchester Wemyss remembers how he and his fellow officers at Sandhurst toasted Queen Victoria every night in Marsala at 2d a glass.

Colli del Trasimeno

DENOMINAZIONE DI ORIGINE CONTROLLATA

BIANCO

ITALIA

Imbottigliato all'origine

Azienda Vitivinicola "la Fiorita" srl.

Panicarola Perugia

Lamborghini

Lambo chucked the dregs of coffee on the floor and poured me an inch of red wine. Good eh? No wooden cask, candles, or cobwebs here. I sell my wine.

Marsala warrants a footnote in the histories of great houses, but it was chiefly used in their kitchens. The Asburnham Records of 1836 to 1840 mention Marsala and 'Sicilian', which may have been the same. William Younger says: 'A not uncommon sequence of wines at a dinner in the 1850s was sherry or Marsala after the soup and with the fish.' Maurice Healy called it 'the Cinderella of fortified wines' which 'grade for grade compared very favourably with other fortified wines.'

The Duke of Sussex was among wealthy wine enthusiasts who purchased Orvieto from Count d'Acetto in the nineteenth century. He also listed ten bottles of 'Ravenzara'. Details of the latter are smothered in cellar dust but the Romans made wine in Ravenna from the vanished Spionian vine.

Picolit, or sometimes Piccolit, from the tiny 'piccolo' grape, is nowadays a light, sweet, fractious wine once titteringly hailed as 'the Château d'Yquem of Italy'. Picolit may be a serious non-achiever today, but it was famous and expensive in the eighteenth century, when Count Fabio Asquini presided over an estate that exported 100,000 bottles, much of it to English royals and their European cousins. Monsignor de Rinaldis confirmed in 1765 that even the Pope was not averse to a glass. In 1767 Antonio Zanon said Picolit 'was delighting the tables of Europe'. The Contessa Giuseppina Perusini Antonini, a legendary Picolit producer, used to sit in her basket chair at over 100 years of age sipping a glass of her wine while keeping a keen eye on proceedings in vineyard and cellar.

Mario Soldati, 'an irrepressible dilettante', described Picolit as 'the colour of topaz', with a nose that exuded 'the scent of among other things, gardenias, and dates, and the flavour of pears, peaches, plums walnuts, almonds and honey'. It tasted 'antique, intense, robust, soft and delicious. Deep down it was bitter, serious and Gothic.' Vernage, or Verunge, was 'a kind of Malmsie', a popular luxury among the English moneyed classes as far back as the fourteenth century. It was so rare and collectable that, according to Hugh Johnson, 'only three taverns out of nearly 400 were licenced to sell it retail.' At 2s a gallon it was the most expensive wine sold in London in 1419. Malmsey was next highest at 1s 4d. Claret was a mere penny a bottle. The Romans enjoyed a light wine called Varnaccia which may be related to the wine drunk with eels in Dante's (1265–1321) *Divine Comedy*.

Varnaccia di Oristano, still made in Sardinia, would have appealed to the early English palate. It came sweet or dry but it was of the rich brown style that was fashionable in the fifteenth century. Effectively an Italian 'sherry', its method of manufacture uncannily resembles the Spanish classic. It is cultivated on flat, loamy vineyards near rivers. It is bush trained, low to the ground to absorb maximum heat. The ripe grapes are collected in earthenware jars and the wine is fermented above ground. Flor is the result, a creamy fungus which drops its tentacles into the wine, metabolising the ethyl alcohol, acetic acid, sugars and glycerol and leaving this unusual wine dry and golden with a mushroomy tang and a healthy 15 per cent of natural alcohol. Soft old *riserve*, which must retain 16 per cent alcohol and be at least four years old before being released from it's cage, is as tough as old boots and can live for ages. Sardinians until fairly recently drank it throughout the meal. Burton Anderson swears it goes well with *bottarga originaria*, mullet or tuna eggs dried in the sun. Sadly the wine is now too expensive for the locals to quaff at mealtimes. Instead they lap up venerable old bottles at first communion, weddings, funerals.

Vernaccia di San Gimignano is quite different. Devotees seem to enjoy its understated blandness. It is certainly a survivor, with papers going back to the thirteenth century. When Italy introduced the *Denominazione di Origine Controllata* in 1963, this wine was among the first to be protected. Burton Anderson says it 'is unique among Tuscan white wines in that it theoretically contains no Trebbiano or Malvasia. Traditionally it was a wine to age, its bronze tones largely the result of contact with air. Vernaccia was noted for its somewhat woody flavour with a lightly bitter vein.'

Verdea, or Verde, and occasionally Muscadine, was once a crisp, slightly fizzy Tuscan wine. It briefly found favour in the mid-seventeenth century, and in 1670 no less a connoisseur than Lord Salisbury kept some in his cellars alongside the £17 hogsheads of Burgundy and the £6 casks of white Graves. Rybole, said to have come from Istria, once part of Italy, was sold in three sweet-wine taverns in London in 1365.

Sweet Muscatels from Syracuse were popular in England in the eighteenth century. James Brydges, later Lord Chandos, was paymaster for the Duke of Marlborough – a task which enabled him to stock his cellar by tweaking the books. A keen and knowledgeable collector, Chandos kept a few crates of Syracuse in his cellar alongside everything that was considered fine or merely interesting in those days. The nineteenth-century Stow House cellar clearance included ten dozen of Sicilian white wine.

Austrian and Romanian wines

Austrian wines have made but a minor impact on the English wine trade. Gumpoldskirchen – 'one of the great gastronomic attractions in Vienna' – was still selling in Britian up to the 1960s and maybe after. In their 1867 list, Harvey's of Bristol advertised Voslauer, an Austrian Claret, at 24s a dozen bottles. Voslau in lower Austria still makes light wines in the Thermen region, but they remain elusive. Beset by wine scandals, including mislabelling and adding an antifreeze chemical to the wine, Austrian wines have recovered elsewhere but not here. This doesn't bother the Austrians, as we were never very keen; but it is a shame, as in the north of the country they make some of the finest Rieslings in the world.

In 1937 a party of 'distinguished English gourmands, including several titled persons', traveled to Romania to sample the country's food and wines. The cuisine was 'excellent and original', said Richard Wyndham. It was accompanied by native liquor, Tuica, 'a gratifying discovery', and Braghina-Dragasani 1921, a white wine 'long past its prime'. The reds were avoided, 'owing a view held throughout Romania that their red wines are vastly inferior to their whites'. But Romania once made wine that made even the English wine snob sit up. Cotnari was the one wine that made sensitive Romanians proud. An excellent sweet wine made from the Grasa, Frincusa, Tamiaosa and Feteasca Alba grapes, the best of it was made by peasants inhabiting hilly terrain in Moldavia. In the nineteenth century its reputation touched both Paris and London where it was said, probably by Romanians, to rival Tokay. An oak-aged version of moderate strength and ambition is still made today.

Rumneys owes its fame, such as it was, to Prince Mihály Apafi of Transylvania, who was a weak statesman but a strong drinker. A pail was his favourite goblet and when he raised it to his lips, if a guest abstained he, the guest, lost his head – literally. But the Prince had a problem. No matter how much he drank he stayed sober. Irish punters during the Cheltenham Festival are familiar with this distressing problem. As the Prince vainly soaked his beard and vest glugging Rumneys, he repeatedly doffed his velvet hat to allow the alcohol to evaporate via his brow. Rumneys was known as 'bad sherry' in England. It was said to be of Greek origin, Romania being the Latin name for Morea, the southern mainland of Greece. Though Muscatel grapes were used in its production, and some Rumneys were well made and luscious, they never really threatened proper sherry. The poor Romanian version was shipped to England by shifty dealers attempting to spear a slice of the lucrative English market. Encouraged by English rogues, the Romanians mixed any sort of tired and ropey wine with a few buckets of firewater, labelled it 'sherry' and dispatched it to England. To their shame and embarrassment, a few Spanish shippers felt so threatened by this illegal trade they made a wine called Rumney in Chipiona near Jerez. Some just stamped the magic word 'Rumney' on casks of ordinary sherry destined for back-street British taverns.

41 *Right:* Arnald of
Villanova, author of
the first book on wine,
published in 1478.

42 *Below:* The Tabard Inn,
Southwark.

43 The earliest port wine label.

44 A nineteenth-century London wine merchant's advertisement.

May our pleasures be boundless while we have time to enjoy them

Pub. by Wm Holland Nº 50. Oxford St.

45 *Right:* A gentleman enjoying his wine in the 1790s.

46 *Below:* Port advertisement from the 1940s.

For very fine wines

OLD CUSTOMERS are informed that limited supplies will shortly be available of HAWKER'S "PEDRO DA FONTE" & "HUNTING" PORT at 180/- and 210/- a dozen, and HAWKER'S "FINO" sherry at 204/- a dozen.

HAWKER'S HUNTING PORT
JAMES HAWKER & Cº Lᵈ
PLYMOUTH

HAWKER'S
OF PLYMOUTH

SOLE MAKERS OF THE FAMOUS PEDLAR BRAND SLOE GIN

SPARKLING SAUTERNE,

"SEC" OR "EXTRA SEC." 1875 VINTAGE.

Sparkling Sauterne is brought out in competition with more heady Sparkling Wines.—"*The Times.*"

Sparkling Sauterne is a pleasant, fairly dry, and perfectly natural Sparkling Wine.—"*Pall Mall Gazette.*"

NORMANDIN, MAIGNEN, & CO.,

CHATEAUNEUF,

And 22 & 23, GREAT TOWER STREET, LONDON.

47 Sauterne advertisement from 1880.

PRICE LIST.

Port. (FROM THE WOOD.)

	Per Gall.	Per Doz.
6—Full-flavoured, nourishing Wine	11/6	26/
8—Older and smoother	13/6	30/
9—Dry, old, highly recommended	—	36/
10—Very old, dry, tawny	—	42/
CRUSTED, IN BOTTLE—According to age	—	42/ 48/ 51/ 60/

Sherry.

12—Sound dinner Wine	8/6	20/
13— Ditto more delicate	9/6	22/
15—Good light Wine, pale	10/6	24/
16— Ditto gold	10/6	24/
18—Delicate, soft, pale, no heel	13/6	30/
19—Full flavoured, gold	13/6	30/
20—Pale, very delicate and soft	15/	33/
21—Fine high flavoured, pale, dry	—	36/
21a.—High flavoured soft, light gold	—	36/
22—Very full flavoured, deep gold	—	36/
23—Very fine, old, light gold	—	48/
24—Pale, very soft, rich old nutty flavoured	—	48/
25—Amontillado, very delicate and old	—	54/
26—Dry, old, light, Amontillado character	—	42/
26a.—Full flavoured, gold, not sweet	—	42/
27—Very old, high flavoured, pale, dry, with great flavour	—	51/ 60/
MANZANILLA, very old	—	42/
VINO DE PASTO, very old, and *of the greatest delicacy*	—	63/
ROTA TENT, the finest imported	—	36/
28—Very dry, pale	—	38/

Madeira.

| 1 Very old, pale, dry, with great bouquet and flavour | — | 60/ |
| 2—Light gold, rich nutty flavoured | — | 48/ |

Marsala.

| Best imported | 8/6 | 20/ |

Val de Peñas.

A very dry red Spanish Wine, with Burgundy flavour ... — 24/

Valencia.

Good sound dryish red Spanish Wine ... 6/ 16/

Roussillon.

First growth of vintage 1863 ... 8/6 20/

Catalan.

Pure, full flavoured, fruity, red Wine of Port character, strongly recommended for the use of Invalids ... 8/6 20/
The same Wine, drier and older ... 8/6 20/
The demand for our CATALAN has become so great that, in order to protect the Public from Branded and blended imitations, we have found it necessary to send it out capsuled, with a Registered Trade Mark, and our genuine Catalan will always be so distinguished.

Masdeu.

A very full-bodied red Wine, from the French side of the Pyrenees. It resembles dry Port ... 24/

Red French Wines.

VIN ORDINAIRE, good light Wine, without acidity	14/
BON BOURGEOIS, very good light Wine	16/
MEDOC, full bodied dinner Wine	20/
ST. EMILION, light, with flavour, recommended	24/
ST. JULIEN, a delicate after dinner Wine	30/
KIRWAN, full flavoured, with delicacy	36/
LE GRAND PUY, high flavour, with rich bouquet	40/
LA-TOUR, and other very choice growths	60/ 72/
BURGUNDY, St. George	24/
Ditto, Chassagne	26/

White French Wines.

WHITE BURGUNDY, pleasant light Wine	14/
Ditto ditto with much flavour	20/ 24/
Ditto ditto CHATEAU GRILLET, of extreme delicacy	30/
SAUTERNE, strongly recommended	20/
HAUT SAUTERNE	36/ 56/
CHABLIS	28/

German Wines.

STILL—RUDESHEIM, rich full flavoured Wine, which we strongly recommend	28/
Ditto HOCHHEIM, very high flavour	48/
Ditto RÜDESHEIM BERG ORLEANS, extraordinary quality	62/
SPARKLING MOSELLE MUSCATELLE, (2 doz. Pints 4s extra)	36/ 46/
Ditto Ditto extra quality	66/
Ditto Mock Ditto	66/

Champagne.

AŸ, good light dry Wine	22/
Ditto, dry with flavour, much recommended	30/
IRROY'S, MOET'S, RUINART'S, ROEDERER'S, &c.	60/ 76/

Spirits.

	Per Gall.	Per Doz.
BRANDY, good ordinary, pale or brown	17/	36/
COGNAC BRANDY, pale or brown	20/	42/
Ditto finest imported, in wood	24/	48/
Ditto MARTELL'S, his own bottling	—	56/
Ditto very old	—	70/
GIN, good ordinary	12/	26/
HOLLANDS, Dutch, in original square Bottles	14/	30/
Ditto finest imported	—	36/
WHISKY, Scotch, good ordinary	16/6	38/
Ditto ditto fine old, highly recommended	18/	38/
Ditto ditto very fine, 10 years old	21/	44/
Ditto Irish, fine old	18/	38/
Ditto ditto very soft old	21/	44/
Old JAMAICA RUM	14/	30/
Ditto extra quality	17/	36/

TERMS—NET CASH.

WINES PER DOZEN.—Our prices include Bottles, but not Cases. Two Shillings per Dozen allowed for Bottles returned.

WINES PER GALLON.—The prices quoted do not include the cost of Jars, or Casks. These must be paid for in the first instance; but if they are returned, their full cost will be refunded. The prices are—

1 Gallon Jar	1/6	6 Gallon Cask	8/6	½ Doz. Case	1/6
2 "	2/6	10 "	9/	1 "	2/
3 "	3/6	14 "	10/	1½ "	2/6
4 "	4/6	20 "	10/	2 "	3/
5 "	6/6	28 "	10/		

One dozen, or two Gallons and upwards, delivered by our own cart, or carriage paid, within the Metropolitan district.

Six Dozen, or Twelve Gallons and upwards, delivered Carriage paid to any Railway Station in England.

Bankers:—LONDON AND WESTMINSTER BANK.

Post Office Orders to be made payable at the General Post Office

CHARLES KINLOCH & Co.

14, BARGE YARD CHAMBERS, BUCKLERSBURY, E.C.,
London, October, 1865.

48 Kinloch wine list from 1866.

49 Krug for Preston North End.

50 Tavern scene from *The Rake's Progress*.

51 Vauxhall Gardens, once a respectable pit stop in London.

52 *Right:* Moselle advertisement, 1906.

53 *Below:* Nefarious-looking Australian tasters, 1882.

54 Loading pipes of infant port on the banks of the Douro.

55 Eighteenth-century coopers at work.

56 Oporto, *c.*1890.

APRIL
1940.

Dear Sir,

Pour the Afona GRAND OLD GOLDEN South African
Sherry into and serve from a decanter, forget its
origin and neither you nor your friends would know
it from a 72/- Spanish wine.

Because of the preferential duty it costs
only 62/- per dozen, carriage paid on six bottles
and upwards, thus 12/- saved is 12/- earned.

The high quality of the wine has put paid to
prejudice, then bits engendered by the War may have
helped.

The Afona Sherries are real aristocrats, you
don't know what you are missing, why not fill in
the enclosed card, try a sample six bottles.

We are, Dear Sir,
Yours faithfully,

JACKSON & GUTTRIDGE.

CFC/EdR.

57 Promotional letter, April 1940.

58 *Right:* Tasting Burgundy in Tanner's bottom cellar, 1962.

59 *Below:* Memorandum showing the deception inherent in the 1960s.

M E M O R A N D U M   ███████████ **LIMITED**   ███████

     From   ███████████   Date   4th June, 1969

     To   ███████

     Subject   <u>PULIGNY MONTRACHET 1964.</u>   REF.   ███████

███4666

         Stocks of the above wine are running low. When exhausted please draw Chassagne Montrachet 1964 from ███████████ and relabel as Puligny.

     cc.

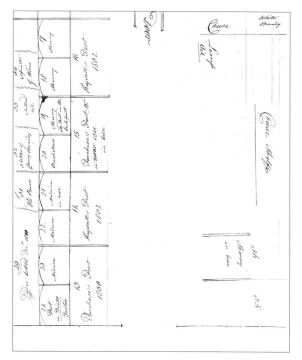

60 Cellar plan of a well-stocked country house in the nineteenth century.

61 An eclectic country house wine list from 1851.

EUROPEAN WINE COMPANY,
LONDON, E.C. Established 1858,
SOLE AGENT FOR ROSS,
C. H. LEWIS,
FAMILY GROCER, WINE & SPIRIT MERCHANT,
8, HIGH-STREET.

	Per Bottle.		Per Dozen.	
SHERRY.	s.	d.	s.	d.
Prussian Sherry	1	3	15	0
1 Dinner ditto	1	8	20	0
2 Superior ditto	2	0	24	0
7 Fine Pale	2	9	33	0
9 Very Old	3	0	36	0
12 Fine Golden	3	6	42	0
ROYAL VICTORIA	2	3	27	0
PORT.				
Spanish Port	1	3	15	0
Tarragona Port	1	6	18	0
1 Old Port (5 years old)	2	0	24	0
3 Superior (9 years old)	2	6	30	0
6 Old Crusted	3	6	42	0
4 SPLENDID OLD (11 years)	3	1	37	0
CLARET.				
Vin Ordinaire	1	0	12	0
Medoc	1	6	18	0
Bordeaux	1	8	20	0
St. Julien	2	0	24	0
CHAMPAGNE.				
Fine Sparkling (Carte Blene)	2	3	27	0
Epernay	2	10	34	0
Verzenay	3	0	36	0
Chansarel's (First Quality)	4	0	48	0
SPARKLING SAUMER.				
Silver Foil	2	0	24	0
Gold Foil (Dry)	2	5	29	0

SPIRITS.

Every Six Bottles contain an Imperial Gallon.

	Per Bottle.		Per Dozen.	
	s.	d.	s.	d.
Colonial Brandy (33 u. p.)	2	3	27	0
Ditto (Finest)	3	0	36	0
Hungarian Brandy	3	0	36	0
Cognac Brandy	3	6	42	0
Ditto (8 u. p.)	4	1	49	0
Ditto (Older)	4	6	54	0
Ditto (Very Old)	5	4	64	0
London Gin (33 u. p.)	2	0	24	0
Old London Gin (Full Strength)	2	5	29	0
Old Tom Gin ditto	2	7	31	0
Scotch Whiskey (33 u. p.)	2	3	27	0
Ditto (17 u. p.)	2	8	32	0
Ditto (Very Old Proof)	3	4	40	0
Old Highland Whiskey (10 u. p.)	3	4	40	0
Irish Whiskey (33 u. p.)	2	3	27	0
Ditto (17 u. p.)	2	8	32	0
Ditto (Very Old Proof)	3	4	40	0
Brenan's (V.S.O. 10 u. p.)	3	6	42	0
Schiedam Hollands	2	5	29	0
Ditto (in Green Cases)	2	8	32	0
Jamaica Rum (33 u. p.)	2	3	27	0
Ditto (17 u. p.)	2	8	32	0
Ditto (Proof)	3	1	37	0
Old Pine Apple (Proof)	3	6	42	0

The wines and Spirits will all bear the Trade Mark and Patent Capsule of the "European Wine Company," and can be obtained of the their Agents at the same price and quality as sent direct from the Company's Stores. Single Bottles are supplied.

62 The European Wine Company's stocklist, 1880.

63 Tonic wine, an advertisement from the 1850s.

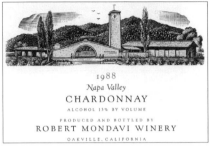

Anti-clockwise from above:
64 A classic reborn, thanks to Hugh
Johnson and a few other visionaries.
Essencia is arguably, the most
wonderfully complex sweet wine of all.

65 The Greeks forgot how to make until
Carras, with imported French expertise,
showed them.

66 Robert Mondavi, Napa's passionate
innovator. A charming pensioner, he's
still a man.

67 Lebanon's Chateauneuf du Pape.
Sipping is believing.

68 Nice wine, once embarrasssingly
called 'the Lafite of the south' by an
hysterical hack.

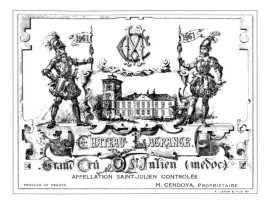

Clockwise from above:

69 Old Lags weep at the perfection of the '61s. Anniversary bottles are still good value.

70 Superb vintage, reliable grower, bliss in a bottle. Sip slowly, smiling.

71 Fine, crisp Riesling from an excellent grower in Liederhosen. For putting in tall, knobbly stemmed green glasses not radiators.

72 Dante drank a forefather of this with eels. A minor Italian white with Roman connections.

73 Fine white Burgundy is the best Chardonnay on the planet. Period, as they say.

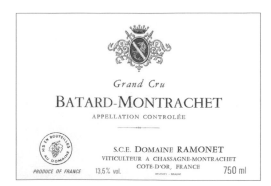

Clockwise from above to below:
74 Graves is an ancient wine that has been supplanted by Chardonnay. Delicious with a little bottle age.

75 A tiny acorn near the equator, the leading Kenyan wine.

76 Full bosomed muscatel. A sticky fingered treat and cheaper than Sauternes.

77 English bottling carries a health warning but don't be put off, examples are fast disappearing.

78 Cellar-cool, this tasty lightweight was a memorable aperitif.

36

Cape Wines

South Africa is the grandfather of New World wines. The Boers painfully sipped sour wine from green grapes until Jan van Riebeeck of the Dutch East India Company arrived in 1652. He experimented with grapes, pruning, manuring, irrigation, pressing, fermentation and the wood in his barrels. Vines were imported from Spain, France and Germany, countries which were already supplying wines to London, South Africa's target market. Simon van der Stel in 1679 imported a French wine grower and the Muscat of Alexandria grape, and built immaculate wineries. He marked out a tract of good grape-growing land near Table Mountain and called it Constantia. The Muscat took to the sun and soil of South Africa. The swollen, juice-dripping grapes were unctuous. The bees came in swarms at harvest time, just as they did in Greece and Rome. The grape was nicknamed the 'honey pot'.

By June 1719 South African growers were ready for an onslaught on the lucrative European markets. Six small casks were filled with table wine and sent to Amsterdam. When opened they were full of vinegar. Bigger barrels were tried to no avail. The wine was then shipped in bottles; thousand of bottles merrily rattled to Holland, the spiritual home of the Boers. They fizzed when opened and tasted like iron filings. The next consignment was the dark sweet wine made near Table Mountain. It had been a well-kept secret among the winemakers. It was highly prized and cost 20s a pint was 20s. It was a delicious, and so alcoholically preserved, that no squirmy yeast could survive for long in it. The Dutch loved it, and although other wine farmers could not give away their ordinary wines, the whole of Europe couldn't get enough Constantia. The unsold ordinary wines were turned into fiery brandy. Warehouse walls were blackened with the stuff. The Boers drank it and soon were Olympic champions at destroying their livers.

The British appeared in 1795, unfurling an old contract that meant growers had to sell their precious Constantia to the invader and to send the rest to England. One English visitor said Constantia was 'exquisite and richly flavoured', qualities he attributed to careful grape harvesting and obsessive winemaking when only the ripest and healthiest grapes were pressed by nimble-footed slaves. One delicate English lady visitor stifled a tiny cry of horror when she was handed a glass of wine pressed by black feet. She was only slightly mollified when told the fermentation process 'would carry off every polluted article'.

South African wines were first auctioned at Christie's on 4 May 1770 under the heading 'Cape wine from the cellars of General Armiger'. Constantia, excavated from the cellar of 'an ambassador on the way home', starred a year later. It fetched 15s to

21s a dozen – not a glittering debut. In 1718 the bold Earl of Kerry sent his cellar to Christie's. Among the bin ends and the oxidised Rhenish was a consignment of 'White Cape', which brought the house down, such was the eagerness of the bidders. It finally went for 52s a case, with good Burgundy languishing in its wake. Constantia, which was among the 'most choice wines' prised from the hands of a 'Gentleman Deseas'd on a sunny June day in 1784', topped the 'White Cape'. The gavel descended with a crack at 52s 6d a dozen.

As rave notices for the unctuous nectar continued, prices began to rocket skyward and by March 1800 they went into orbit at 140s a case. To get things in perspective, that was twice the price fetched by great Claret. But by 1806 prices were fluctuating downward, with Constantia selling at a mere 60s, still considerably higher than 'Margot' and 'La Fitte'. The next consignment of bottled Constantia at Christie's had been plundered by Sir Dennis Pack in the capture of the Cape in 1807. Even with Sir Walter Scott among the bidders it barely reached 70s a dozen.

In spite of slipping sales, Constantia continued to garner rave reviews, even from the French. In 1816 André Julien was so impressed by Constantia that he placed it 'among the finest liqueurs in the world'. Only Tokay was better, in his opinion. André Simon confirmed it was 'the only wine from the African Continent that was ever acknowledged in France as well as England, the peer of the best French and Peninsular dessert wines.' Unfortunately the South Africans were unable to cash in on the success of their one ace. Their table wines were inferior to most European opposition and they found few buyers. The English, who were more inclined towards the Portuguese than the Dutch, raised the tariffs on all Cape wines even when diseases were threatening European vineyards. Constantia remained 'eagerly sought after by plump, white napkin'd European connoisseurs'. Jean-Anthelme Brillat-Savarin (1755–1825), the author of *The Physiology of Taste*, nominated Constantia as 'the contribution of Africa to a gourmet's dinner'.

Riding in on the back of the delectable Constantia, other South African wines furiously tried to gain a foothold in England. Cape Burgundy, 'from the French grapes transplanted and sure to be enjoyed by those families who have been upon the Continent', was offered by the Commercial Hall Wine Company (established 1806) of 340 Oxford Street in London at 30s per dozen or £65 per pipe. Cape port was similarly proving difficult to sell to English consumers accustomed to the dark blood of the Douro. Dr Robert Druitt didn't help sales when he wrote in 1865: 'A bottle of Cape port sent to me by a patient, being undrinkable, shall be given to the poor,' even Constantia hit rock bottom.

At the disposal of Prince de Talleyrand's London cellar in the early nineteenth century, a case of Constantia went for 8s a bottle, compared with 9s per bottle for Malaga and 15s for sixty-year-old Tokay from the King of Poland's cellar. Professor Saintsbury wondered if there existed anywhere a bottle of the original old Constantia he remembered from his youth; he was 'happy to say I once drank it'. He recalled an outstanding wine 'of the sort to last' and felt 'sorry for anyone who had not, at least once, drunk real Constantia'.

At the Duke of Sussex's Kensington Palace cellar sale in 1843, the largest stock of any wine was Constantia, eighty-five dozen of Red Seal and Black Seal. The Stowe House cellar sale in 1848 sold off forty-three dozen Red Constantia in pints and ten dozen in quarts. In the 1860s Constantia Red and White Seal appears on wine lists at 42s and 6s a dozen respectively. The Duke of Richmond and Gordon's cellar in 1845 also contained a good percentage of Cape wines, including Constantia. The proverbial writing was on the wall for the once venerated Cape nectar. In December 1860 Constantia fetched just 15s a dozen compared to fine Claret at 100s. Collectors no longer clamoured for the last case the way their modern counterparts eagerly pursue that last case of off-vintage Le Pin.

Maurice Healy, pompous and antisemitic as ever, was on a boat going down the Danube when he first tasted Constantia. He was in the unwanted company of two friendly Jews, father and son, who tagged onto him while sheltering from a squall that lashed the deck. Healy bought the Constantia from the boat's wine list and unwillingly shared it with the 'offensively friendly' companions, whom he wrote 'smirked in a most self-satisfied way' and 'whose table manners were not calculated to improve my appetite. I poured out a glass; it fell like treacle from the bottle, looking like blackberry-juice. I tasted it, for I will never condemn any man or thing untried. It was horrible; horrible. I leaned forward, and with a gesture of great courtesy, I filled the glasses of the two Hebrews. With profound obeisance I lifted my glass and pledged them; I then affected to see somebody calling me on deck and I fled.'

Hugh Johnson, holding a glass of 1830 Constantia in 1970, described it as pale and soft, with 'odours of balsam and a trace of orange'. It was sweet, mouth-filling and exceptionally harmonious. He compared it with a Malaga from the Duke of Wellington's estate in Molin de Rey. While brilliant, neither, Johnson said, had retained the taste and flavour of the Muscatel grape.

In the nineteenth century Cape sherry was shipped to England to stretch the product from Jerez and Madeira. Thick and dark, the phony sherry was called Kimberley Club after the diamond mine. Around 90 per cent of it was controlled by the oldest producer of sherries in the country, the Co-operative Wine Growers' Association of South Africa. As a result of tariff preferences granted to wines produced in the British Empire during the Napoleonic wars, the Cape wine industry succeeded in developing a flourishing export trade to Great Britain.

South African growers attempted to make a lighter, more elegant wine, similar to those made in Jerez. A deputation was sent to Spain to investigate Flor, the fungus that mysteriously grows on the surface of certain casks of wine. In the 1930s chemists at Stellenbosch University succeeded in isolating 'flor' yeast from samples of local wine. Extractive matter was excluded from the blends to achieve the greeny gold clarity admired by drinkers of Spanish Finos and Manzanillas. The South Africans even adopted the Spanish trick of 'plastering' the must to stabilise acidity. Bodegas were built on the Spanish model, and the Solera system of blending and ageing young wine was introduced. Cape estates targeted the lucrative sherry market in the United Kingdom. With preferential duties dating from 1919 and a long association with Britain, together with the difficulty of obtaining the Spanish product due to wartime blockades, South African sherries gained a foothold. The quality of the product and the South Africans' smooth organisation meant they were difficult to shift from their new position once the war was over.

37

Australia: Belligerent Innovators

On 28 September 1788, Captain Arthur Phillips stood in his sunny vineyard with a group of sullen convicts and predicted that wine milked from the virgin hills and dales of New South Wales would one day 'become an indispensable part of European tables.' No-one believed him. They should have, for in 1791 the first two bunches of grapes were cut in the Governor's garden in Sydney. The holy ground is now a hotel parking lot. Captain Phillips, with the drive and vigour of the immigrant, would soon be joined by a host of energetic and imaginative men like William MacArthur, a noted oenologist who went on to establish an estate of 60,000 acres. Both men played their parts in the development of the infant wine industry. Hugh Johnson, who tasted a bottle of MacArthur's wine over a century and a half old in 1988, said it was 'sumptuous' and 'of enormous richness'. Spectacular sales drives in England were still some way off. A fresh attempt to jump-start an interest in far-off Australia occurred in 1824, when cuttings from the promising Muscat of Alexandria grape were sent to Sir Thomas Brisbane in New South Wales from his fellow aristocrat Lord Charles Somerset in South Africa. Emboldered by this, in 1825 the Australian Agricultural Company ordered a consignment of vine cuttings from a nursery in Chiswick, London. They were lost in the post. It seemed as if the Mother Country was trying to screw up a brawling infant's efforts to cut the apron strings. The Agricultural Company persisted and eventually took delivery of the disease-resistant if unspectacular Verdelho, or Verdelet, as it was also called.

It was James Busby (1801–1871), nicknamed the Father and the Prophet, who would play the most pivotal role in the way the new business would organise itself. The Edinburgh-born Busby first took an interest in growing things by following his estate manager father around in Ireland. The experience inflamed in him a passion for wine. The Ascendancy cellars were well stocked and the owners spent a lot of time away. Busby honed his palate and chose Australia as the place to make career in wine. It had the weather, the rich, virgin soil and plenty of cheap labour – although the shackles and handcuffs might be a problem.

Busby was determined to make better wine than the South Africans and was not averse to knocking the opposition. 'Cape wines,' he said 'had a peculiarly nauseous and earthy taste' and yet they were 'consumed in abundance'. Busby's attention to grape growing, pruning, pressing, winemaking and cellaring are classic. On cellaring he said: 'A very necessary precaution is that the cellar should not be near any stable or dunghill, or in the neighbourhood of any bad smell whatever.'

Busby could barely wait to visit England and show the wine experts there what Australia could do. In 1823, another pioneer, Bartholomew Broughton, stationed on the convicts' paradise island of Tasmania, sent over samples of his 'port'. The English liked it. It was cheap, and that was quite a consideration.

He brought with him a 10-gallon cask of his own wine, which he was invited to taste at a lunch which included 'a very eminent Oporto wine merchant, and a respectable Bourdeaux [*sic*] wine merchant'. The confident Busby was entering a lion's den but there was no way he was prepared to extend his sunburned neck for the chop. Confidently he tapped his little barrel and filled a jug. The wine was black, thick and unfiltered. Both wine traders 'sipped suspiciously'. They exchanged glances and smacked their lips before pronouncing it 'a very promising wine'. Busby mentally hollered 'YESSS!' The Bordeaux shipper thought it resembled port without the brandy. Like many a modern Australian wine grower when confronted with negative comparisons with European wines, Busby bridled. He insisted it was more like Burgundy than port. 'They agreed with me that it was so,' Busby triumphantly recorded.

In February 1831, Busby set off on a fact-finding mission to France and southern Spain, 'in the hope that his observations might be useful to the Colonists'. He was a guest at a sherry bodega. 'The twilight was far advanced as we entered the wine district – at one place we could distinguish a man with a musket, who had been posted to watch the grapes, it being the very middle of the vintage.' He was impressed by the town of Jerez, 'which is reckoned one of the richest, if not the very richest in Spain, in proportion to its population, and which owes its wealth entirely to the valuable wines produced in its vicinity.'

Like a schoolboy at his first biology lesson, Busby eagerly observed every aspect of winemaking in Jerez de la Frontera, from the Palomino growing on the chalky 'white-out' vineyards to the drying of the grapes on circular asperto grass mats, to the fermentation, blending and maturing. Having tasted a wide range of sherries, Busby commented that some destined for the English market were not what they seemed. 'Malaga is delivered to Jerez, then transhipped for England under the name of sherry,' he said, 'after having been mixed with other wines to give them the qualities in which they are deficient. All low-priced wines are largely mixed with brandy, being intended for consumption by a class of people who are unable to judge of any quality in wine but its strength.'

Busby watched the men take handfuls of gypsum, sprinkle it on the grapes then slither into the sticky troughs and begin their grotesque dance. Wearing peculiar nailed shoes, they 'jumped with great violence'. While they leapt and sweated Busby sipped a jet-black Pedro Ximenez and marvelled at its sweetness. Surely there never was a nectar as sweet, not even in the Iliad? 'Call that sweet?' the cellar master might have said as he poured something even thicker and blacker than runny tar.

His head crammed with unanswered questions, Busby headed for Malaga. He stopped by an inn at a crossroads to slake his thirst and satisfy a craving for meat. 'My companions seemed to consider themselves fortunate when the bill of fare included a stewed rabbit or hare, and this in a country rich enough to support ten times its population in the greatest abundance,' he wrote. 'Almost every hill was covered with vines, the produce of which is all converted into raisins.' 18,617cwt of Muscatel raisins, paying the highest duty, were annually sent to England from Malaga alone. There were literally tons of inferior raisins looking for buyers for as little as £1 a hundredweight. The fastidious English buyer preferred to pay £2 12s 6d a hundredweight for top quality fruit from the Muscatel vine.

Don Salvador, whose farm Busby visited, paid his men 8 ¾ pence a day. They breakfasted on lentil soup, lunched on pork and for supper had cold soup, bread and as many grapes as they could eat. The wines were stored in massive *tinajas* which held the equivalent of three butts and were sold as soon as possible to farmers and labourers, who rolled up for their weekly wine in ass–drawn carts, filled their goat skins and departed.

In Perpignan Busby was introduced to a M. Durand, who cultivated three different grape types. One of them, the Grenache, is now Australia's most widely planted red grape; another, the Mataro or Mourvedre, is Australia's fifth most important red grape; and the Carignan, while largely ignored by the Aussies, is the most widely planted red grape on earth. Busby was sent on his way with a huge bundle of vine cuttings, the Grenache and Mourvedre among them.

He visited Rivesaltes to study the making of the famous sweet wine there and found the vineyards a dazzling display. They were 'so thickly covered with stones of various coloured quartz as to make it difficult to tread upon.' In places where vines grew with great vigour and to an old age, 'the soil is of such a nature Australians would consider it absolutely sterile'. Rich stable dung was used in the winter to give the washed-out soil some strength. The Muscatel was picked at optimum ripeness and left lying under the vines for eight to ten days before pressing. The juice was poured into casks which were left unbunged for up to a month. After this, the wine was pumped into a new cask which had been fumigated not by sulphur sticks but a piece of rolled brown paper that had been soaked in brandy.

On arrival at Hermitage the first thing Busby learned was: 'The greatest part of the finest growth is sent to Bordeaux to mix with their First Growths of Claret. Four-fifths of the quantity are thus employed.' The importance of Hermitage to the London merchants was exemplified in one of the vintner's sons speaking English 'very correctly' after a year spent in England. After climbing the Hill of Hermitage to genuflect at the altar of the progenitor of most great Australian red wine, Busby slyly pocketed a handful of the dun soil to take back to his hotel room. That night he poured vinegar on the dirt. Obligingly it fizzed. 'The degree of effervescence', Busby solemnly wrote by the yellow light of a guttering candle, 'indicated the presence of a considerable portion of lime'.

Busby wrote: 'The best red wines of Hermitage are made exclusively from one variety, the Ciras [Shiraz].' As far as the future of Australian wine was concerned it was 'a Kodak moment' if ever there was one. This grape, Busby said, 'was originally brought from Shiraz in Persia and... yields a dry and spirituous wine, which easily affects the head.' He wondered why the sacred hill of Hermitage had to be annually defiled with great dollops of dung when he thought it only helped produce more vine and leaves and less of everything else. His host, a M. Machon, shook his finger. 'If you use the dung of the horse or the sheep a bad smell will not pervade the wine. But the dung of the pig or the cow? Never!'

For red wine the best and the worst bunches of 'Ciras' grapes were chucked into a cavernous wooden vat capable of holding 16,000 gallons. Juice-soaked men trod away like carthorses in the fumes and darkness until a red tide of wine threatened to engulf then. They were dragged out to sit on a plank placed across the vat and recover, their legs indolently pumping to keep the rising cap below the surface of the boiling wine. The richest and finest juice was allowed to ferment for just five days and was worth 300 francs a cask, the equivalent of 210 bottles. White Hermitage, Busby was told, was made from two white grapes, the bland but prolific Marsan (*sic*) and the fragrant, shy yielding Rousette. Busby indicated that when the two grapes were pressed, the juice of the Marsanne tended towards sweetness, while the Rousette made bone-dry wine with a cold sliver of acid. When the resultant wines were blended the result was a slightly sparkling wine which 'was said to be without question the finest white wine of France, and it will keep for 100 years, improving as it gets older.'

Busby said his farewells and headed for Burgundy. The vine's 'extreme closeness and feebleness' surprised him. 'The infamous Game [Gamay] is holding a considerable place.' The grower explained that the Gamay 'was undoubtedly the best kind of vine for the poor man'. Having 'engaged a cabriolet from the *maître d'hotel*', Busby left for Gévrey and Clos Vougeot, where at first hand Busby saw the French devotion to *terroir*. He recognised the importance of the different layers of soils, which although they might only be a few yards apart, could make the difference between a Grand Cru and a village wine.

At Clos de Vougeot Busby watched men wearing huge wooden clown's shoes treading the grapes in troughs. He wrote: 'The best wine is always produced from the most rapid fermentation.' In poor years the wine was little better than *ordinaire* no matter what method was used. In some years, like 1824, the wine was so bad the rugged vineyard labourers were toasting their wives and washing down their rabbit stews with pure Clos Vougeot. While the red Clos Vougeot was Pineau (Pinot Noir), the white wine was made from two grapes, White Pineau (Pinot Blanc) and Chaudenay (Chardonnay), 'which resembles it so much, that the two kinds are confounded'. Busby noted the casks designated for the white wine were purified by a light rinsing with grape spirit.

Carrying yet more vine grafts, Busby must have been jumping up and down on his suitcases by this time, as he set off in the direction of Champagne. He was quietly impressed by the 'immense stocks' in the cellars of Ruinart and 'the most perfect cleanliness', the organisation and the attention to detail, and the intriguing methods of making Champagne. Ruinart shipped their wine, after three or four years' maturation, to England. 'What is sent to England is more spirituous and froths more strongly than what is sold for domestic consumption,' Busby wrote. On his last night in France, he noted: 'The excellence of French wines should be imputed to a peculiarity in the soil, rather than to a system of management which others might imitate.' These words have a even greater resonance today. Busby returned to Australia with nearly 600 different vine species.

Geoffrey Blaxland a retired explorer, who had planted a small vineyard at Brush Farm in the Paramatta Valley, also sent wine to London. The Royal Society of Arts awarded him a silver medal. Blaxland sent another sample in 1828 and won gold. In 1828, George Wyndham, a migrant from Wiltshire, a father of twelve sons and two daughters and owner of a fine house built from stone quarried by convicts, planted vines on his farm at Dalwood, in the Pokobin area.

Those great, iron-shod Australian wines of yesteryear had immense keeping qualities. An 1867 Tintara Claret went AWOL for 100 years before resurfacing at a Christie's sale in 1977 where it sold for £1,000, then disappeared again only to reappear to be bought by B.R.L. Hardy for a 'five-figure sum'. The 136-year-old wine is said to be one of the oldest Australian wines still unpoured. The colour, balance and flavour of the wine will never be tested. Instead the ancient wine, made from grapes grown in the McLaren Vale in South Australia, will stand in a padlocked, CCTV-guarded, bullet-proof glass case in the foyer of Hardy's HQ. Berry Bros' online newsletter reports: '[The] fifth-generation family member and wine maker Bill Hardy says the bottle's true intrinsic worth is its unique place in the history of Australian wine and as a reminder of the vision and commitment to quality of our great Australian viticultural pioneers.'

In 1893 Londoners were buying Australian Carbinet (*sic*). In their 1905 wine list Thomas Southam and Sons of Shrewsbury, since absorbed by Tanner's, offered their own bottling of 'Carbinet' as well as 'Hermitage' and Harvest 'Burgundy' (6d allowed on returned flagons). Burgoyne and Co's Highercombe Amber was recommended by the *Lancet*, as a tonic wine. Southams exhorted their customers to buy 'Colonial Wines which had improved steadily in quality … Valuable characteristics will be found in them which render many a service to invalids.' They added patriotically: 'One result of the Fiscal Question may be that if preferential treatment is given to the Colonies these Wines will have more chance of increased consumption in England.' Thomas Southam had a great belief in curative properties, wherever wine came from. Mosel was 'much recommended by German doctors to their gouty patients', but beware the 'trashy wines of the poorest quality, furnished with attractive labels' and sold to the unsuspecting buyer by 'traveling hawkers'.

In 1895 the *Wine and Spirit Gazette* printed a letter from a disgruntled Australian living in London, who complained that the Australian government was subsidising 'trash, injurious to the good reputation of genuine Australian wine'. The subsidised wine, 'carrying a testimonial from a Government expert', was knocked down for 3d a gallon at a public auction in Mincing Lane. The enraged Aussie would gladly have paid that 'for the satisfaction of seeing the stuff turned down the Thames Street sewers'.

Harrod's 138-page green-covered wine list for 1906, which contained vintage ports going back to 1847, Grand Cru Clarets since 1878 and no fewer than eight pages of bottled water, listed over forty Australian wines. They were mainly brands like Koala, which made liberal use of French names, including Sauvignon and Cabernet advertised separately, a Hock ('very fine wine, Rudesheimer character') and Emu ('Specially Selected, Shipped and bottled by Harrods Limited'). These included a 'Malbec in Imperial Quarts'. Every bottle of Orion Brand 'Generous Burgundy', or 'Medium Light Claret' was 'Guaranteed Pure by a Government Certificate on every label'. Burgoyne's 'The Finest imported' listed Fruity Kangaroo port, Branxton and Oomoo Burgundy and Chasselas White. The Army and Navy Stores' Christmas 1934 wine list which was crammed with beautiful wine (Château Latour 1929 at 8s a bottle and Château d'Yquem 1921 – 'surely the greatest', according to Michael Broadbent – at 23s a bottle), fabulous Hocks and several vintages of Krug, also devoted a whole page to Australian wines from the 'British Empire'. They included as Ophir Rich Burgundy and Chablis, Perthonia and Melbonia (Irvine) reds, 999 Rich Tawny (Emu) and 'Big Tree' Sauternes.

The Australians annoyed the Spanish by calling their heavy-handed wines Florita, Chiquita, Mantilla, Pepita, Granada and Del Pedro. In England they were considered inferior to South African 'sherries'. The Australian styles were not as easy to identify, with one man's 'amontillado' very different to another's in style, weight and degree of sweetness. With the use of flor and by skilful blending they improved, but the market was shrinking. Their darker types, rich and full flavoured, and with homespun names like Chestnut Teal, Autumn Brown and Fine Old Hanwood, were clearly aiming their sights at British companies like Williams and Humbert, whose brands had a warm, pipe-smoke-and-slippers feel about them.

From the very beginning Australian wines had their begrudgers. C.E. Hawker wrote in the 1920s: 'The Australian climate can hardly be in all respects suited to the successful production of wine.' He advised English consumers not to make the comparison with the European classics, because up to now 'the balance of advantage has not been on the side of the Colonial wines. It does not seem likely that Australian vintners will ever endeavour to enter into effective rivalry with the vignerons of Europe.' Too much Australian wine, he argued, 'was mixed together and sold under the name Australian burgundy. For the unexacting palates of the masses, who are content to ask no questions, so long as a florin or half a crown will purchase a roomy flagon of strong, full-bodied, fruity wine, this policy may serve very well, but the connoisseur must not be expected to show much interest in the matter until he is in a position to compare one region or vineyard with another.'

Maurice Healy wrote: 'On Australian wines I can hardly bring myself to write with patience.' Most of the Australian wine that came his way was 'detestable; its inferior nature was not rendered less obvious by the way in which it borrowed the phrases in which genuine Burgundy was praised. The Australian soil appears to be so rich that it cannot produce a wine. It is stiff with iron; the so-called wine almost goes rusty in your mouth. The grape must be of a very coarse kind; if it is a French vine that has been carried out to Australia, it has degenerated in the new soil. Its produce is horrible; hot, coarse and flavourless; it puzzles me how people continue to drink it.' 'We have done all we can to imitate French wines,' an Australian is said to have told a cynical Maurice Healy. 'We have imported their vines, we have imported their skilled vignerons, we have even imported shiploads of their soil, and we have tried every sort of dressing on it; but it is all in vain.' No Australian is that apolgetic.

André Simon was more positive when he attended a dinner in New South Wales in 1948, hosted by the winemaker Leo Buring, Sir Lawrence and Lady Olivier were among the guests. With oysters, baked snapper, lamb cutlets grilled on the barbecue over smouldering eucalyptus leaves, potatoes roasted in ashes, strawberries, flambées, ice cream and Australian Maczola, a Gorgonzola-type cheese, the following wines were served:

> Quelltaler Granfiesta Flor 'sherry'
> 1944 Drayton's Hunter River Semillon dry
> 1920 White Hermitage, from the late Dame Melba's Coldstream Vineyard,
>   near Melbourne, Victoria
> 1932 Coonawarra Red Hermitage
> 1934 Hunter River Hermitage
> 1893 Great Western (Victoria) Hermitage

Simon commented on the last wine only, which he said 'had retained a beautiful ruby colour, and was a remarkable wine in spite of its fifty-five years'.

Raymond Postgate wrote in 1951 that the Australian public were not interested in wine and could easily be sold a vinous pup. While 'the knowledgeable Frenchman or German will not allow the wine producer to sell bad wine – if they do, he sees they get into trouble – the Australian neither cares nor knows if the wine is good; he prefers whiskey anyway.' Many of the Australian wines sold in the United Kingdom, Postgate argued, were massive in structure and irony on the tongue, 'a natural result of the strong sun and fertile soil'. He remembered one or two very decent Australian wines that crept through the net and escaped to England. 'A 1938 Cawarra [red Claret] a Yolumba [*sic*] hock of the same year and a Penfold's Grange Hermitage 1954 could all stand beside all but the best of French wines. They all had what is very rare outside Western Europe – a bouquet.'

In 1963 John Burgoyne attempted to stem the critical tide. In an article in *House and Garden* he asked: 'Do you drink labels? When you see an imposing bottle, its label decorated with a château-like building, and bearing a name that you feel you should know, you are likely to be prejudiced in favour of its contents, which may fall short of excellence. Those who, unfairly, try to compare Australian wines with the greatest in France and in Germany would have a shock if they could taste the best European products of, say, four centuries ago.'

The man who put an Australian wine right up there on the top table where the great Clarets and Grand Cru Burgundies sun themselves was Max Schubert, a former 'messenger boy and brass polisher' at Penfold's. Schubert is credited with single-hand-edly rescuing Australian wines from the doldrums in the 1950s, when 90 per cent of Aussies drank nothing but beer or home-grown 'port' or 'sherry'. Schubert intended to pay homage to Claret with a young, dark, experimental bone-dry wine he made from ultra-ripe Shiraz. Schubert would rather have used the Cabernet Sauvignon after an eye-opening pilgrimage to Bordeaux, when as a guest of Christian Cruse he tasted great Claret half a century old. Penfold's were not keen at first; Australian wine was not elitist – it was healthy, well honed, but not 'fancy'. Schubert persevered and named his baby wine Grange after a hovel in the Magill vineyard which supplied some of the grapes. The smouldering behemoth was dismissed as tasting of 'crushed ants' by Australians used to sweeter wines. However, Schubert, who had supped at the Médoc, fountain, knew exactly what he was doing.

Schubert's first vintage of Grange Hermitage was the 1952. In 1955 Australia's 'first Grand Cru' – blame Hugh Johnson for that – was greeted with delirious epithets from not easily impressed 'experts'. French plaudits were noticeably muted. Renamed Penfold Grange, the 1998 vintage was described as 'a fruit bomb', a silly expression. Retailing at around £100 a bottle, it is Australia's most expensive wine. Is it worth it? The modest Schubert cannot now tell us, as he passed away aged seventy-nine in 1994.

Michael Broadbent's tasting notes include a few Australian wines like the Sunbury Hermitage 1872, which he described as having 'still enough body, lovely flavour, more Burgundy than Bordeaux and very attractive considering its age.' A Semillon made 'by the great Maurice O'Shea' was dry and lovely, 'a great unsung hero from the less wine-conscious past'. The 1956 Seppelt's Great Western Chasselas M14, tasted in 1977, sounds like something out of a of Monty Python sketch, but in fact it was 'a classic, made by one of Australia's great winemakers Colin Preece in Victoria'. A 1962 McWilliams Show Sauternes had Broadbent's elegant brow furrowed as he searched for poetry. 'Mint-leaf bouquet, rich and yellow, fragrant and fat, Côteaux du Layon or Sauternes, who could tell? Complex? Very. Finish? Lovely!' Tyrrell's Chardonnay was served, and enjoyed, at the André Simon Centenary Dinner at the New South Wales Chapter of the Wine and Food Society.

The man credited by Jancis Robinson with persuading Australians that wine was not 'a poofter's drink' was Len Evans, the Brendan Behan of Australian wine. A swaggering, Napoleonic, congenital competitor, a former glass washer, Krug swigger, hotelier and facilitator, Evans established Rothbury Estate in 1968, with David Lowe as winemaker and hundreds of shareholders financing the venture. Elegant, creamy Semillons, full-flavoured Hermitages, minerally Chardonnays, Cabernets and Pinot Noirs followed. The quality made English critics sit up and write up the wines. Jancis Robinson comments: 'By the 1980s every dinner party in the land, it seemed, was lubricated by bottles and bottles of deep golden Australian Chardonnay.'

Giles Kime wondered if recent Australian success in Britain was less to do with the jolly swagmen image of the Australian wine industry and more to do with pasty-faced English supermarket buyers fancying a few weeks away from their fog-shrouded, icicle-festooned branches, 'seduced by a bit of Anglo-Saxon bonding over a barbie in the Barossa, rather than standing up to their knees in a boggy vineyard in France.' Parker is also gloomy. Accepting that Grange or Bin 707 Cabernet 'are as fine as any red wine in the world', the American says, 'Australia's overall wine quality is barely average, with oceans of mediocre and poorly made wines.'

Say what you like, within a few years the thrusting Australians have battered down the door to the cobwebbed *chais*, grabbed the French by the goolies and dragged them into their brash world, where men are men and pansies are flowers. The French response is commendable. They have thrown open their country to gold-medallioned heathens from Down Under, inviting them onto their sacred soil to make wine from French grapes. Successes at international tastings prove that even a French grandmother can be taught to suck eggs. The French are tucking into portions of their extra-large humble pie. Recently they bowed to their marketing men and have swapped the Syrah for the far better known Shiraz. The Australians have climbed the mountain, heartily cheered along the way by millions of new wine drinkers.

A last word from John Douglas Pringle. In a piece in the *Compleat Imbiber* in 1960 he wrote: 'In Australia you learn not to bother too much about searching for superlative wines. When I think of Australian wine I do not think of an elegant dinner table with men and women slowly savouring each glass. I think of picnics in the bush with the red wine warming in the sunshine or the white wine cooling in the creek and glasses laid out on the rocks where the lizards flick and rustle. At those times and in those conditions it is as good as any wine in the world.' Sometimes one hits upon a wonderful surprise like Maurice O'Shea's 1948 Sauternes. Pringle wrote: 'I swear it was as good as any French Sauternes I have ever drunk. If a trifle past its best, it was still beautiful. I remember drinking it with those huge Sydney prawns on a beach beside the Pacific while the surf dazzled and deafened us and the sun sent us slowly to sleep.'

America

Thomas Jefferson, as governor of Virginia in 1779 planted his own vineyard with native vines. Like the 'prentice poet who cannot believe his trite warblings are less than fantastic', Jefferson put his noted palate on hold and developed a taste for foxy wine, even comparing his home-made hooch to Burgundy. In his dotage Jefferson remembered a clear white wine from the Scuppernong grape from the subgenus Muscadine. It compared to 'Frontiniac', he said, and 'would be distinguished on the best tables in Europe, if it wasn't doused in foul brandy', a practice he said was, 'peculiar to the English'.

In 1769 Padre Juinpero Serra planted the first vineyard at Cucamonga, in San Bernardino County. Commercial growers soon got wind of the success of 'the Padre' and they bought land and sent to Europe for cuttings. The new vines prospered. In 1875 Isaias W. Hellman, who grew Mission grapes in his Cucamonga, mixed the sweet, partly fermented juice with brandy. Hellman made 'Madeira' and 'port', white and red. Although it was described as 'hardly a wine' and 'not highly thought of', when Michael Broadbent tasted a Hellman wine that had quietly slumbered in a cask for eighty-six years and a further eighteen in the bottle, he described it as 'lovely rich, glowing amber, magnificent bouquet, intense, rich, powerful. Great length, perfect condition. Outstanding.'

'Tokay', a wine with not even the flimsiest connection with the Hungarian classic, was made in the nineteenth century in Carolina. As Catawba it was celebrated by Henry Wadsworth Longfellow (1807–1882), a benign, well-travelled man whose 'joy in life, his geniality, and his lovable disposition were all reflected in his face'. By the mid-nineteenth century, Catawba was a nationwide brand that came in many styles, including fizzy. A trickle arrived in England and wound up in the cellars of the inquisitive. The Duke of Sussex's eclectic cellar at Kensington Palace included 'Virginia, USA, 2 bottles, a present from Mr Stephenson, American Minister.' The wine was identified as Catawba. Vizetelly refers to a sparkling version and 'a diabolical (and highly questionable) imitation' made not from New Jersey peaches, or Vermont apples but from a product of the oil-wells of Pennsylvania, the first, and last, 'petroleum Champagne'.

Described as 'dulcet, delicious and dreamy,' Catawba is still made on the banks of Lake Erie. It proves Longfellow was no wine buff. Jefferson's dream of turning the Eastern seaboard into a fountain of delicious wine failed. But pockets of interesting wines still exist. In Virginia keen and knowledgeable growers are making good wines from French varietals. Most are eagerly snaffled up by tourists or drunk in hotels and gastro inns in small towns and villages within commuting distance of Washington DC.

The Napa Valley was crawling with grizzlies, mountain lions and snakes when the explorer Captain J.C. Fremont recruited 'a group of sixty Indian guides' to find a route across the mountains to the Pacific. One of his scouts was the great Kit Carson, the frontier scout with the blond shoulder-length curls, fringed jacket and trousers and a Colt 45 dangling to his knee.

Agoston Haraszthy left America for a vine-finding tour of Europe in 1861 and ordered 100,000 vines featuring 300 different grape types, including it is said Zinfandel, a grape he found in Hungary. Haraszthy planted 660 acres on dusty slopes and built a large, ugly house.

By the 1860s, although there were 142 cellars in Napa Valley. Towle, an American writing in 1869, said good American wine was rare in hotels and even poor wine was expensive by European standards'. Towle recommended Catawba and 'wild grape wine'.

Anthony Trollope wrote in 1862 that wine lists in the average American hotel were poor and the wines expensive. A bottle of average American wine cost 8s, the equivalent of two decent Clarets in London. Champagne, real or imagined, was often served during dinner. Although wealthy Americans liked French wines. In 1830 2.5 million bottles were imported, a figure that doubled in a decade. It was often stretched with home-grown products. Towle refers to young Americans drinking gooseberry and currant wine. By 1863, according to William Younger, 'the United States imported as much Claret as Great Britain'. A year later America returned the compliment by importing phylloxera to France, via France's old enemy, England.

An article in *The Whisky and Trade Review* of 17 February 1898 indicated that Californian growers were aiming their produce at the English market. It referred to 450 acres 'planted in grape vines of the choicest foreign varieties'. Over 200 different varieties of 'the best imported grapes' were tried and the best selected for future planting. The wines made, they said, aped the English taste in sweet wines. They included 'excellent sweet ports, Muscats, Malaga, Tokaur [*sic*] and Angelica', which was described as 'a heavy, very sweet white grape mixture consisting largely of unfermented grape juice and brandy. Not highly thought of'. Dry wines included Riessling (*sic*), which was 'somewhat similar to the Brucelles [*sic*] of Spain', a 'Burgundy' and a dry sherry, 'said by experts and judges thereof to be the best-produced article in California'.

A Frenchman, Charles Lefranc, had a better idea. He quietly planted Cabernet Sauvignon and Pinot Noir. But it wasn't Californian Cabernet that created a stir in London; it was 'Mustang of Texas', a port-style drink that had been on sale in London since 1876. Mrs Beeton was among its fans. 'The Mustang grape,' she wrote, 'yields a wine hardly distinguishable from the best port.'

Although the Victoria Wines list of 1896 was drowsy with twenty-seven ports, two 'Spanish ports', twenty-one sherries and two Montillas, there were four wines from

California. Encouraged by 'a vogue of Californian wines', Grierson, Oldham and Adams began shipping wines from California 'on a substantial scale.' Californian wines were often labelled Claret, Hermitage, Chablis or Burgundy. They relied on their wines' medicinal qualities and lower acidity compared to the French and German equivalents. Victoria Wines listed a Californian No.1 red wine, 'a natural pure Wine, Claret type, with good body, free of acidity, most wholesome and blood-making'. No.3 red wine was 'a fine rich Wine of Burgundy type'; No.5 white wine was a 'Chablis type, very delicate, clean, dry Wine, free from acidity'. A Californian Muscat was 'rich, very fine'.

In Harrods' 1906 wine list, Zinfandel, 'a good table wine', was listed as 17s a dozen. It was the cheapest of the 'Big Tree' brand. Again the medicinal potential was stressed with a reference to 'blood making'. French names were treated as generic, as indeed they were by English bottlers right up to the 1970s. 'Fine rich Californian Burgundy and Claret of the finest quality' were offered at 25s a case. The whites included 'Chablis', 'Fine Sauterne, very excellent, recommended', 'Hock made from the Johannisburg Riesling grape,' was a 'splendid wine with good body, free from acidity,' and at 29s a dozen it was the most expensive Californian wine on Harrods' list. By 1906 California had joined Texas in offering her port to the English, the most fastidious port drinkers on earth. Californian 'port' was offered for 2s 7d a bottle at a time when the genuine article from the Douro, 'a pure sound wine straight from the wood', was only 1s 6d a bottle.

When the Board of Governors of the Wine and Food Society met at the Bohemian Club in San Francisco on 15 June 1948, the 'Baron d'Agneau avec oignons, navets glacés et haricots verts' was not accompanied by a magnum of the excellent Louis Martini's Special Selection Cabernet Sauvignon grown, vinified and cellared a few miles up the valley, but by Château Lascombe 1929 'en Imperiale', which 'won universal praise'.

On a visit to California in 1958 the London wine merchant O.E. Loeb tasted a 'White Riesling' that was 'exceptionally fine and could without fail stand comparison with a great German Riesling'. Loeb also tasted 'Pinot Chardonnays' and even 'a 1948 well matured Cabernet Chardonnay that proved once again that fine Californian red wines needed a long time to develop in bottle'. Although Loeb found it 'rare in California to get hold of older, well matured vintages', he did sample 'a most excellent' 1941 Inglenook Cabernet Sauvignon and 'very fine' 1944 and 1949 Louis Martini Private Reserve Cabernet, a Private Reserve Zinfandel Red and a good 1957 Pinot Noir from the same stable. A more unusual offering was the 1952 Gamay from the Charles Krug winery, where Robert Mondavi began his meteoric career. Loeb described the Gamay as a 'treasure'. Regarding the 'number of quite remarkable wines' Loeb tasted on his short American jaunt, he was gratified to see all vintages 'were clearly stated' on the label, something he attributed to 'how much progress had been made in recent years in Californian viticulture'.

The year 1962 was a landmark in Californian wines, according to Loeb. 'For the first time more table wines were sold than fortified wines of the port and sherry type.'

The Napa Valley was ready to take on the French; not just the minnows, but the big guns from Bordeaux and Burgundy. 'But efforts to develop markets for Californian wines in Britain have so far had little success, mainly for reasons of price.' Loeb concluded that 'the traditional table wines will remain a domain for France'. Another respected English wine trade figure, Harry Waugh, who once said: 'Tested both by time and experience, the vineyards of France and Germany still produce the finest wines in the world.' But when he visited California in the early 1960s, Waugh's eyes were opened. The Napa Valley, he said, 'was to California what the *commune* of Vosne-Romanée is to lovers of fine Burgundy.'

At Beaulieu Vineyards, Waugh met the French-trained André Tchelistcheff. When Tchelistcheff first arrived in California, he was saddened by the way nature's bounty was wasted on clumsy 'port' and 'hock'. Tchelistcheff's first instinct was to hire a bulldozer to level the vineyards and start again.

For Waugh, Tchelistcheff pulled the corks on three or four Cabernet Sauvignons he had made in the 1940s. 'The quality was so exceptional,' Waugh said, 'at once I realised there was much more potential in these vineyards than I had ever imagined.' The director of Château Latour later reminisced: 'The range we tried that morning showed such astonishing quality that they left an indelible mark on my memory.' The bottle he drank with lunch was so rich it reminded him 'of the gorgeous 1947 Pomerols when they were in their prime.' It wasn't just the red wines. Tchelistcheff's 1968 'Pinot Chardonnay', grown in a cooler Carneros vineyard, 'really hit the jackpot'. It was 'an exceptional wine if ever there was one'. The visiting Englishman was slightly less impressed by the Pinot Noirs. Tchelistcheff agreed and told Waugh that in thirty-two years' experience he had managed to produce only two Pinots he was really happy with, the 1946 and the 1968. When Waugh tasted the latter wine in wood he wrote: 'I would like to lay my hands on a case of this!' When he tasted the rare 1946 Waugh described it as 'a powerful, rich, full-bodied masterpiece'.

Tchelistcheff worked his magic for Beaulieu Vineyards for thirty-seven years, culminating in his immense and stylish Georges de Latour Private Reserve Cabernets. It is ironic that Tchelistcheff, who once said 'It is very false of us to steal the Appellations of Europe. I accept it with the bleeding of my heart, but it was a necessity, a compromise I accepted with tears', had such a powerful influence on the winemakers who slaughtered the French at the misguided Paris venture in 1976. To recap: Californian wines received a tremendous fillip by comprehensively defeating some of the finest wines from Bordeaux and Burgundy at a blind tasting in Paris in 1976. The French, who pompously underestimated the opposition, were hammered. The white wine section was dominated by Californian Chardonnays, with only two French wines in the first six. The top placings were: first, 1973 Château Montelena, part-owned by the Croatian Mike Grigich (132 points); second, 1973 Meursault-Charmes Domaine Roulet (126.5 points); third, 1974 Chalone (121 points). The French reds fared slightly better, with two famous Clarets in the first three and four in the top six. Sadly for the stunned French, the top-placed wine was an impudent arriviste from the Napa Valley, a Cabernet Sauvignon which vanquished two legendary, but the French would say

Schramsberg

FOUNDED 1862 ®

RESERVE

NAPA VALLEY
CHAMPAGNE

PRODUCED AND BOTTLED BY SCHRAMSBERG VINEYARDS · CALISTOGA CALIFORNIA
ALCOHOL 12% BY VOLUME   CONTENTS 750 MLS

Deliciously creamy Napa sparkler patiently perfected in cool, dark, cellars dug by Chinese in the nineteenth century. R.L. Stevenson caught the setting sun there with a glass in hand.

'not quite ready', classical Clarets from a cracking vintage. First was 1973 Stag's Leap Cellar's Cabernet Sauvignon, a creation of Warren Winiarski (127 points); second, 1970 Château Mouton-Rothschild (126 points); third, 1970 Château Haut-Brion. It might have been worse. One Napa wine legend, the late Fred McCrea of Stony Hill Vineyards, would not allow his wines to be entered. Blind tasting can be manipulated to prove anything. Sometimes it depends on the judges. Sadly for the embittered and hurt home team, the men who consigned great growers to a vinous hell were all French.

Back to Waugh. With a group of wealthy wine amateurs, he blind tasted 'half a dozen of the finest Cabernet Sauvignons existing in America' from the 1946 and 1947 vintages. The main contenders were from BV, Charles Krug, Inglenook and Louis Martini. Waugh placed the 1947 Beaulieu Private Reserve, 100 per cent Cabernet Sauvignon, 'a masterpiece' ,first and the 1946 second. He put the 100 per cent varietals Inglenook third. The rosy-cheeked amateur tasters unanimously agreed. Sighs of relief all round. Inglenook received another pat on the back from Jancis Robinson at a dinner in London. After tasting a 1943 Cabernet Sauvignon made by Tchelistcheff, who was present, Robinson wrote: 'The Inglenook was quite extraordinary. We were privileged to have our palates exposed to such a historic bottle.' The potential longevity of the best Californian Cabernets is legendary. A 1937 Beringer Cabernet Sauvignon tasted in London half a century later was languidly ripe and fruity.

The re-emergence of Californian wines in the 1960s was driven by men with European ties. The Wentes were originally from Germany, Charles Carpy of Freemark

Abbey was from Bordeaux, Louis Martini was the son of an Italian immigrant. In fact a great number of Italians were involved in the success story that is Californian wines. Robert Mondavi left the family firm Charles Krug to found his empire at Oakville in 1966 nearly a century after Simi started in Sonoma in 1876. Foppiano began in Sonoma in 1896, Pedroncelli in Geyserville in 1904, Franzia Brothers at San Joaquin in 1906 hand, the Gallo empire began at Stanislaus, Modesto in 1933. Joe Heitz and Jerry Luper, former winemaker at Freemark Abbey, both did time at Gallo. Parducci started in Mendocino in 1933, Pesenti at Templeton, San Luis Obispo in 1934. They are still coming. Rafanelli is making stellar Zins and Cabs at Dry Creek. Rochioli began proceedings in the Russian Valley in 1979. Papagni set up in Madera in 1975 and Ferrari-Carano make a Superyank called Siena. Francis Ford Coppola makes an excellent Claret-style wine with his Rubicon Meritage.

The exciting Californian wines shipped by the late Geoffrey Roberts in the 1970s and 1980s helped to dispel Caliphobia among English wine drinkers. Roberts, a Etonian who burned his barrister's horsehair ringlets to became an agent for Robert Mondavi, packed his blue wine-covered lists with great Californian names; Joseph Phelps, the late great and cheerfully eccentric Joe Heitz, Don Chappellet, whose Chenin straight from the cask is as good as anything in the Loire, Paul Draper of Ridge, who is a genius, and Bob Travers of Mayacamas, who once memorably said of his vintages: 'Each one is like sex. When it's good it's really good. When its not so good, it's still really good.' The obsession with smooth fruit wine has pushed Mayacamas into the background. Travers's wines are European throwbacks, wonderfully sinewy, discursive, packed with nose and flavour. They are punished in the 'ratings' because they lack that instant gratification.

39

New Zealand: from Frozen Lamb to Cloudy Bay

In the 1960s all over England men in suits, were performing a sacred Sunday ritual. They were carving a defrosted and roasted shoulder of New Zealand lamb. The yellow butter slowly melting into the new potatoes was Anchor. There was a whiff of mint in the air and a cat called Whiskey sat curled in the sun. There was no chilled Sauvignon Blanc, no Kiwi bubbly leaning in an ice bucket. New Zealand to all practical purposes was then a non-wine-producing country.

But – hang on – wasn't James Busby making wine at Waitangi in 1835? It was good enough to be positively plugged by a French sailor, Dumont d'Urville, who tasted it while on shore leave in 1840. 'Very sparkling, and delicious in taste', the *matelot* trilled. 'I've no doubt that vines will be grown extensively all over the sandy hills of these islands, and very soon New Zealand wine may be exported to English possessions in India.'

Joseph Soler, a Spaniard from Tarragona who settled in Wanganui, 'had his wine placed third at the London Colonial and Indian Exhibition in 1886, in competition from all colonies including South Africa'. Watching the Kiwis' success with keen interest, the Australians entered some of their wines at the Christchurch Exhibition in 1906, fully expecting to sweep the board. To their horror the New Zealand wines, all made by the obviously talented Señor Soler, won three gold medals out of five. The Australians, famed sportsmen that they are, immediately filed an objection, implying – no, stating with jabbing fingers – that the judging was rigged in favour of the home team. The Kiwis calmly apologised and agreed the tasting should be rerun in the interest of fair play. This time the judge would have to be eminent, and approved by the Australians. You can imagine what happened. The New Zealanders won all five golds. The Australians punched holes in the walls.

Early British settlers in New Zealand were, buttoned up and teetotal. As Hugh Johnson puts it: 'The small and strait-laced Anglo-Saxon community did not provide an encouraging market place.' However, a mini rush of planting and winemaking between 1890 and 1910 meant New Zealand was able to wrestle some of the emerging wine sales away from the Aussies. Many of the well-known New Zealand wine estates were established then. Te Mata Estate planted in Hawkes Bay in 1896, Corbans made wine in Auckland in 1902, Collard Brothers Ltd did the same in 1910, Babich and Co. laid down roots in Auckland in 1916, Glenvale Vineyards Ltd in Hawke's Bay in 1933. Another spur to the local vignerons was the invasion of thirsty Yankee troops during Second World War.

The recent renaissance began when gum workers started the ball rolling in and around Auckland. They knew nothing of wine production, they just wanted plain wine to drink so they planted vines and made wine. What they swigged was sweet, revolting and head-spinning. By the 1970s New Zealanders planted Müller-Thurgau and made a sort of cheap hock. Then an Australian, David Hohnen of the decent Cape Mentelle winery, visited Marlborough in the summer of 1985. He searched about until he found a perfect site for Sauvignon Blanc. The wine tasted pure with the refreshing tang of gooseberries. The New Zealanders needed a Grange and they found it in Cloudy Bay, a wine that showed even the French how Sauvignon Blanc should be made. According to Robert Parker, Cloudy Bay started a panic among British wine writers, who, lemming-like, jumped on planes, clutching their free tickets and sleeping socks to visit the area. They fell for the hype. Cloudy Bay apart, according to Parker, New Zealand wines are so-so: 'It is appalling that anyone can find something to praise in these offerings.' Cyril Ray acknowledged how freebies can grease the writing arm and fuel the positive prose. 'Everyone who writes about wine owes a debt of gratitude to the wine trade,' says Ray, 'not only for the gladly shared scholarship of its members, but for the hospitality with which they produce their most precious bottles, as material for the scholarship of others.'

There is no doubt that New Zealand growers, having invested heavily in wine, are worried about the reluctance of foreign markets to drop everything else and drink lots of their widely planted Pinot Noir and Chardonnay. They may have to continue chucking around plane tickets and the free Thai masseuses.

40

Chile: a Wine Paradise

Professor Saintsbury gave Chilean wines no mention in his famous *Cellar Book*, and when Walter Berry researched his *In Search of Wine* he too stuck to well-trodden paths. H. Warner Allen, Maurice Healy, Alec Waugh, William Younger and Ian Campbell all would have shrugged uncomprehendingly at the mere mention of Chile as a wine country. Now Chilean wines, smartly dressed and super-confident, stand shoulder to shoulder with the diminishing French, Italian and German in every cobwebby independent and brash supermarket in the land. The seventeenth-century Berry Bros, that most traditional of wine merchants, where once a bunch of elegant old duffers blearily contemplated pre-phylloxera Clarets over lunch above the din of squeaking handcarts, gladly welcome Chilean wines into a list still packed with classics.

When the Spaniards crossed the Andes in 1541, carrying rosary beads, machetes and bundles of vine cuttings, they need to make something to wash down The Mass. A Jesuit noted in his diary in 1557: 'Today Pais was planted, may the Lord be praised.' Pais survived and it still makes wine that would make even God wince. The Central Valley was discovered and a thriving industry established there when Juan Jufre and Diego García de Cárceres, with viticultural guidance from Father Alonso Ovalle and in 1554 planted Torontel.

When Vice Admiral John 'Foulweather Jack' Byron (1723–1786), grandfather of the poet, was shipwrecked off the coast of Chile, he had time on his hands. With a few damp survivors, he hitched to Santiago and was shoved straight into prison where he spent the next three years cracking lice and licking his parched lips thinking of the rich, sweet Muscatel he once swigged and favourably compared with Madeira. In 1851 a wealthy Chilean with a taste for fine Claret, Don Silvestre Ochagavia Echazarreta, shipped vines from France. They included Cabernet Sauvignon, Merlot, Pinot Noir, Cot and the white Sauvignon Blanc and Semillon. They thrived in the balmy climate and survive still, the Chileans claim, as the only pre-phylloxera clones in the world. A phalanx of wealthy landowners acquired land; a gentleman with a private army just took in those days, and planted more vines.

The people were poor and they drank wine to keep sane and dream colourfully. Most of the wine they made in Chile over the next 300 years was better taken kneeling with a good Latin Mass than with a juicy steak. Wine was an industrial project, with carts towed by mules or horses miserably hunched in the blazing queue, each with its nest of green eggs by its feet, patiently waiting to unload the simmering fruit that leaked streams of red wine into the dusty gutters.

A few wealthier growers launched Chilean wines on to the world market in 1784. No-one noticed. Undeterred, they exhibited again at the Vienna Exposition in 1873 were succesful. They followed up with exhibitions in Bordeaux in 1882, Liverpool in 1885 and Paris in 1889, where to great excitement the 'copiers of Claret', won the Grand Prix. Exhibitions in Chicago and Buffalo, New York were equally encouraging.

Ships piled high with casks of dark, minerally reds were soon sailing out of Chilean ports. By 1889 a quarter of a million acres were planted. The smoke curling up from the valleys was dead strow burning to eliminate the nip of winter frosts. Canals were dug to irrigate the vines. Unusual grapes were tried, like the 'red Cock's Claw with its red pepper-like berries' and juice so thin it was distilled to make pisco, a tempting but leg-dissolving anaesthetic when idling around a pool in Santiago.

When the Spanish were ejected in the 1820s, other European immigrants took their place. The influx went on for another eighty years, injecting a moribund wine industry with Continental verve, enlightened winemaking and proven grapes. Anything French became chic among the more sophisticated Chileans. They recruited French viticulturists. The rush of European talent to Chile was not unconnected with the devastation of French vineyards by phylloxera. Chilean entrepreneurs backed the newly energised wine industry. The wines improved.

Full-flavoured Chilean 'Claret' helped fill the gap caused by the Second World War, elbowing many a bland Bordeaux into the shade. Chilean exports rose, triggering an edict in 1952 'concerning standards and minimum quality requirements'. There was no attempt to challenge the best of the French. Chileans knew their limitations. Their target was at the bottom end, a place occupied by cheap Spanish, Portuguese and Bulgarian. Had the Chileans seriously promoted their wines they would have quickly seen off the vapid, branded wines that filled shelves in the 1950s, '60s and '70s. Instead they marked time and lost ground. When Château snook into English wine lists in the 1970s, comfortably priced at under £4 a bottle. Intelligent wine drinkers soon sniffed out a bargain.

General Pinochet took over and posters of him, bemedalled and imperious, stared from every damp cellar wall. 'If it were not for a great man like General Pinochet,' a well cushioned matron snorted from under a hat, when she heard English accents, 'you would not be staying in such a fine hotel. How dare you have him in prison in England!' At the time the dictator had forsaken his uniform for a cardigan and was honing his swing at Wentworth Gold Club. Chilean wine is now popular and excellent value for money.

Eager to stake their claim in the fine wine market, 'super' Chilean wines recently claimed a hollow victory at the Ritz Carlton in Berlin. A jury of 'experts' from Switzerland, Germany, Austria and Britain awarded first place to Vinedo Chadwick's £35 Cabernet Sauvignon. Sena, a £45 Claret-style wine made jointly by Robert Mondavi and the Chilean firm Errazuriz was second. Completing the podium was an infant Château Lafite from the 2000 vintage and priced at £285. Among the dead and wounded lay Latour, Margaux and the super Tuscans Sassicaia and Solaia. Eduardo

Chadwick, the winning owner, who organised the tasting, said: 'The point was not to try and prove any one wine better than another.' Perish the thought. After the tasting the 'experts' grabbed the unmedalled but expensive French and Italians and leaving the Chilean winners discarded like pouting starlets. 'Did my fellow tasters not believe their notes?' asked Andrew Catchpole of the *Daily Telegraph*.

Chile is a delightful country. South of a relaxed Santiago, miles of immaculate white wooden fencing surround emerald meadows full of tail-swishing thorough-breds. Peasants live in what seems to the casual visitors picuresque poverty, their smiling children running with the chickens and lolloping house pets. Apart from the odd severed pig's head flung into deserted market squares, Chile seems quiet now. Her smiling people deserve it.

Argentina

Chile enjoyed a better class of invader, the wealthy Spanish Basques, while the Argentinians welcomed poor Italians.

The natives drowned their sorrows in cheap wine and became the third highest wine drinkers on the planet. They now swallow less than half that. A lack of interest in gutrot had the effect of forcing wine makers to seek new markets and improve their products. By the 1980s the image of the gap toothed wino was replaced by a growing middle class eating intelligently, and switching to light dry white wines.

In the sixties, Malbec, a French reject, was planted – 125,000 acres of it. Most of it was bonfired when prices nosedived in the 1970s and '80s. País and its sister workhorse Crezea, both making oceans of sandpaper red and flavourless white on arid soil under a burning sun, survived. Ironically when the Malbec crop was reduced to 10,000 acres sales improved, especially in Britain, where the soft, tongue-staining wine became fashionable. The Argentinian climate is not as sure footed as Chile's. Access is still a problem and many of the Italian grapes planted, however good the wine may be, do not sell as easily as French varietals. The introduction of the Syrah and a focus on Cabernet Sauvignon and Merlot have redressed the balance. New optimism in the wine industry has encouraged investment in sparkling labs and shiny cellar equipment. Some growers are buying new oak. The trade, though, is still tied to bulk wines, which Parker, who has tasted more bad wines than anyone, classifies as either 'uninteresting, sterile and fruitless, or if you prefer, clumsy, oxidised and dirty'.

Argentinian wine is good and unpretentious. It brings much-needed revenue to a very large and very poor country. Great Britain, Spain, Switzerland, Italy, Belgium, Germany and the Scandinavian countries drink and enjoy it. Established old-fashioned wineries like Bodegas Lopez, Norton and Flichman continue to send decent and interesting wines to Britain. Bodega Weinert (Parker's house wine, now there's a compliment) consistently make good wine with style and savour. Parker tells the story about the time a 'one of Bordeaux's most famous oenologists' pitted a 1985 Weinert against 'top 1989 Pomerols and Saint-Emilions'. The assembled French 'oenologists and winemakers' disgraced themselves, again, by putting the Argentinian wine first. All of which just proves the French need to get out more.

Wine Merchants

The Worshipful Company of Vintners in the City of London, was founded in 1364, the last of the twelve great City Companies to be granted its Charter. This company was born 'to protect trading practices, maintain standards, educate apprentices, and generally assist their members'. The Vintners' Hall is close to the town house of Alderman Sir Henry Picard, who held the Feast of the Five Kings (of England, Scotland, France, Denmark and Cyprus) in 1363. It is 'an indication of the wealth and importance of a City company'.

The Great Hall is still used by the wine trade to train apprentices and still wearing my total abstainer's pin I enjoyed the hushed atmosphere, the smell of mansion house and the funereal squeaking of polished brogues in the early 1960s. The company has kept swans on the Thames since the early sixteenth century. They 'up' swans, occasionally eat them and have a chap, a direct descendant of the original swanherd who answers to the name Mr Swan. It is not essential to belong to the wine trade and most 'vintners' don't. Tommy Layton, a Vintner himself, remembers a particular clerk to the Worshipful Company of Vintners. His 'black shiny jackboots' gave him a very naval air. He kept a grey parrot in a great cage in his office. His extra shiny bald head and steel-rimmed spectacles gave him a terrifying air when he frowned.

There were fiercely independent wine merchants, strawberry-nosed gentlemen who wore regimental ties and floppy Oscar Wilde hankies in their breast pockets. They were brusque and their knowledge was often patchy, but they spoke with stentorian authority. Berry Bros, who began as a coffee shop close to where Charles II in 1668 purchased a house for the Countess of Castelmaine, as a consolation prize for replacing her with the blowzy rustic Nell Gwynne from Hereford.

Number 3 St James's Street dates from 1730 and is still the head office of Berry Bros and Rudd, England's most illustrious wine merchants. No other English wine merchants, can claim that Emperor Napoleon III of France, during his exile in the 1830s, plotted his return to France in their cellars. Above the shop, for well over two centuries, men 'of high office' sought solace among friends around a great dining table, disfigured, the scratches of diamond rings, and the scars of sliding cut-glass decanters. Soldiers, airmen, ambassadors and journalists, their nerves strained to breaking point, came to Berry's to relax. Colonel Gounouilhou, the proprietor of Château Climens, with his 'enthusiasm and eagerness to kill Germans', was always a welcome guest, and yet when the foreign secretary, an ambassador and their wives came to dinner, the wines were 'Hocks of the highest order'. They 'encouraged light conversation'.

Statesmen were able to 'forget, for the moment, universal catastrophe' and concentrate in 'fathoming the depths of splendour presented by an incomparable sequence of wines of the Rhine 'that could scarcely be beaten for sheer body, sweetness and aroma.' Hugh Rudd introduced a novel way to 'cut' the richness of fine Riesling. He had placed on the table a dish of sliced Cox's Orange Pippins. 'After a mouthful of the apple, the sweetness is gone, killed by the acidity of the fruit, and all that remains is the glorious flavour'.

Another famous London firm was Corney and Barrow. Who would have thought, when a young man named Bland flung back the shutters to a newly painted wine and spirit emporium in Old Broad Street London in 1780, smacked his hands and tipped his straw boater to passers-by, that he would not merely survive into the next millennium but would wax fat, as Corney and Barrow, the only wine merchants to hold warrants to supply wine to the Queen Mother, her daughter Elizabeth and her son the Prince of Wales. Starting with a slim portfolio of sherry, port and Claret, the list is now a full of the fine wines.

In 1794 a vigorous Bristol wine merchants, Messrs John Harvey and Sons, was established. Bristol's wealth was founded on wool, grown, spun and woven in the west of England, and wine, 'a product of sunnier lands. Alexander Pope (1688–1744), as he stood on the dock, described Bristol in the early eighteenth century. 'In the middle of the street, as far as you can see, hundreds of ships, their masts as thick as they can stand by one and other, which is the oddest and most surprising sight imaginable.' Godfrey Harrison, author of *Bristol Cream* in 1955, also describes the city: 'It was a thriving, boisterous, romantic, squaldid place. … The rich had their fine houses and choice wines. For the poor there was plenty of beer and cheap gin. The number of ale houses permitted in 1736 (excluding wine shops, inns and coffee houses) amounted to one for every sixteen private dwellings in the city.'

It was not a good time to start a wine company. It was a time of political instability, of constant wars featuring the belligerent French versus the rest. The Bank of England wobbled, refusing cash payments in 1797. The Irish, their gore-flecked pikes glittering in the moonlight, were rising up. Striking sailors blockaded the Thames in a quest for more pay. In Simon's words, there were 'so many other exciting happenings'. Harvey's of Bristol was founded in the 1790s in Denmark Street, Bristol by William Parry. Harvey's main business was in leather but they sold a range of wines on the side, including the fashionable Madeira, the costliest of all the wines, at £63 in 1794, rising to £65 a pipe for a superior 'Old London Particular'. By 1799 it had climbed to £84 a pipe and by 1800 had crashed through the £100 a pipe barrier for the first time, shooting up to £105.

Mountain from Malaga was a bargain by comparison. From 1794 to 1798 they sold a few crates in bottles but by 1800 they were paying £65 a butt. Tent, more properly known as Tintilla de Rota. The darkest of all Spanish reds as a result of its swarthy pigmentation was used to inject insipid wines with a bit of colour. Sales figures were not spectacular, so Harvey's only shipped a butt every three years. 'Old Tent' fetched 42s a case in 1798. Vidonia, a respected dessert wine, was shipped direct from the Canaries at £65 a pipe.

In a large barn behind the shop animal hides were dried. There were bull and horse skins from the West Country. 'Bassells', 'Cordovian' and 'Body Legs' hung gruesomely alongside the tiny pelts of battered seals. Wine sales were supplemented by a substantial cheese counter, a feature of which were fat yellow 'Old Gloucesters', weighing 27lb each, which were regularly dispatched to, of all places, Caerphilly. When John Harvey, a teenage scion of a seafaring family, joined the business in 1822, sherry dominated the new list.

Harvey's were keener on port than on sherry at the time and shipped 1788 Burmester in pipes. They sold seventy pipes of red port a year and a few cases of white. They did business with the Birmingham-based Beckman and Harris Bros, who in 1801 became Quarles Harris. Professor George Saintsbury, was among its clients. 'My cellars (and even cupboards) have seldom for fifty years been without a certain "Margarita" from some vaults in Bristol City.' Commenting on the completion of his *Notes on a Cellar Book*, Saintsbury said: 'I was, during the keeping of this book, permitted by the kindness of my friend, Mr John Harvey, to be possessed of a small quantity of Romanee Conti '57. ... More than one good judge agreed with me that it was almost impossible to conceive anything more perfect in its kind.'

Avery's of Bristol was established in 1793. Ronald Avery, 'born in the celebrated Bordeaux vintage of 1899' assumed control over the company in 1923. Leaving Cambridge prematurely due to the death of his father, Avery served his apprenticeship with the London based Bordeaux agents, Barton et Guestier. He made frequent trips to Bordeaux to fine-tune his palate and soon became competent enough to select wines in cask for shipping to Bristol. His obituary states that when the barrels arrived, he topped them up 'with another wine altogether'. In the 1930s Avery packed his list with over 100 Clarets, including 1921 Cheval Blanc, a wine virtually unknown in Britain. With friendly rival Harry Waugh of Harvey's, Avery imported an expensive wine from Pomerol called Château Petrus. In a Cabernet-inoculated Britain, there was no rush to batter down the Avery cellar doors. As well as a selection of decent Hocks and Mosels, Avery's listed an eye-catching range of Burgundies. Ronald Avery ran his company in a relaxed but ethical way. His son John sold the family farm in 1987.

When the Essex boys Walter and Alfred Gilbey 'took cellars' at the junction of Berwick and Oxford Streets in London in February 1857, the national taste was for port, Madeira and sweet sherries or their imitators. Commonwealth wines filled that role also. They were cheap, packed with fruit and reassuringly alcoholic. They appealed to the palate and pocket of a new breed of Brit Gilbey's identified as 'steady, middle-class clientele'. The wealthy minority supped Champagne, Claret and Burgundy. Gilbey's pressed on, seeking new wines and soon evolved 'into an all-embracing business purveying every type to millions of customers'.

A truce in the centuries of petty squabbling between England and France in 1860, meant a sharp reduction in the duty on French wines, which made them accessible to the mass of the British drinking public for the first time in 150 years. Shippers immediately cut their orders for Commonwealth wines. Gilbey's enthusiastically embraced the slightly more expensive French wines, but as 'pioneers of low-priced wines they had a certain amount of prejudice to overcome.' The family business prospered and within a decade the Gilbey label 'became a familiar and honoured trademark through-out the country.' Chancellor Gladstone took the unusual step of writing to Gilbey's, 'I have always regarded the proceedings of your firm with a peculiar interest. You have been, as far as I am able to form an opinion, in an eminent sense, and in a degree with which no-one can compete'.

Gilbey's initial foray into the off-licence trade in 1872 via Leverett and Fry, grocers and wine and spirit merchants, 'proved a disaster'. A bid for Foster and Co. in the 1930s was more successful and 'formed the bulk of the 2,000 links in the Gilbey's chain'. They had a strong base in Ireland and I well remember, as a white-coated teenager working in a grocery emporium next door to their rather bookish wine shop in Rathmines, very quiet man in a suit stooped behind the counter reading a book behind ricks of Odds On cocktail, a buyers popular beverage sipped behind lace curtains in respectable Dublin.

In 1875 Gilbey's bought the 470-acre Château Loudenne in the Médoc for £28,000. It was a perfect marriage, a pair of ambitious Essex boys and a pink French château. J.W. Lambert, writing in 1958, reflected after an after-dinner stroll in the Château grounds: 'The wine in the grey cellars sleeps in serried hogsheads. The stone of the house flakes a little, the grass grows longer. The pigeons stir in the darkness, an owl calls. It is time to go in, to leave the shadowed river, the brooding wine-block, to pass through the shadowed house, take a bygone English bestseller from the shelves and, settling under the mosquito nets, which rise like imperial canopies behind our pillows, read ourselves gently into an Anglo-French oblivion.'

Gilbey's spent £64,500 renovating and their extending cellars, cooperage and out-buildings, even sinking an artesian well to 1,600ft. A track was constructed which took a tram from the *chais* to a jetty by the riverbank. Phylloxera, along with the new English obsessions of smoking, drinking whisky, sipping Claret after dinner instead of port and an attachment to drinking Champagne throughout the meal, combined to severely dent sales. By the end of the nineteenth century though Claret had once again assumed its proper place on the English table, with the main course.

Peter Dominic's was a bright flashing light to wine pilgrims in the 1960s. Carafino's slogan, 'Big Value in Big Bottles' came about as a result of the teenage daughter of Paul Dauthieu, the owner going to Bordeaux in the early 1950s to 'exchange' with the daughter of negociants Hubert Lemaire, who specialised in *vins ordinaires*. When in 1952 the containers of wine arrived, 'every empty Vermouth bottle was eagerly seized for the reception of Lemaire's three *ordinaires*, rouge, rosé and blanc.' A wash-ing machine worked by the 'United Nations' – a team of one-time refugee ladies of many nationalities – prepared the bottles for the bottling line. With a simple label in dramatic black and white declaring 'Vin Ordinaire', Carafino took off. It became affectionately known as 'Dominic's Plonk'. Soon afterwards, the company launched a sparkling white Burgundy made by Meulien, a small grower in Rully, and labelled Cristal Dry. 'Later, the realisation dawned that any father bold enough to depart from convention by serving sparkling white Burgundy (then 17s 6d a bottle) at a wedding reception instead of Champagne (23s 6d a bottle) could make a considerable saving to put in his own pocket or to pass on to his daughter if he felt rich enough.' In 1960 Dauthieu was described as 'the private company which has done more than any other to fit wine to the English palate and pocket since the war'.

Peter Dominics organised tastings at their cellars 2–8 Orange Street in London, close to where Samuel Pepys was 'dining very handsomely' at the Cock in Suffolk Street. It was a dark, interesting place with a low-vaulted roof where men and women descended from the hubbub of London to sit on upturned whisky casks, surrounded by good wines and buckets of blood-soaked sawdust, learning a little then mopping the goulash with crusty bread. Dominic's went on to organise the Chelsea Wine Fairs, where guests paid 7s 6d to taste 300 wines. The company lost money on the project but the publicity, with Harold Wilson, Tony Hancock, Reggie Maudling, John Arlott, André Simon, Maigret, Steptoe and the entire cast of *Z Cars* present, did the company no harm and gave wine lovers an opportunity to taste a range of wines in a convivial atmosphere.

The opening of supermarkets in the mid-1960s was predicted to be a calamity for the winetrade. Wine merchants recruited spivs in pin stripes to sell to the new gleaming glass cathedrals. Miffed young Masters of Wine, who were privileged to taste row upon row of great Clarets in the company of wise old buying directors in calm and antiseptic tasting rooms, suddenly felt betrayed. Being a Master of Wine was the Holy Grail and led to a buying job and an opportunity to swank it with French growers and perhaps rush off the odd esoteric little piece for the glossies. Now the crafty old pros of the wine business, who knew enough but were considered several levels below the posh end of the trade, were filling the supermarket shelves. Wine varied and cheap would soon be on sale seven days a week.

The Lord's Day Observance Society, policed by James Joyce clones in wet macs, waved placards but to no avail. Masters of Wine left the upscale shippers and became mini rivals. More wines from more places, eye-catchingly packaged at bargain prices, were offered by the mountain. The British wine industry had the fillip it needed. Soon everyone would be drinking wine. They did not know a Chardonnay from a Sangiovese but they soon would.

The Augustus Barnet chain – unfashionable locations, jemmied-open wine crates, no carpets, garish posters, bearded poets and slow moving philosophers behind the counters – was a yell in the ear that wine could be sold like fish in Billingsgate or cracked Delft in the Portobello Road. Jancis Robinson was a customer. 'The real thrill of this period [the 1970s] was bargain hunting. It would take me ages to to get home at night, because I liked nothing more than to idle in every wine shop I passed, scanning the shelves looking for something unusual or particulary well-priced. August Barnett, owned by a charismatic barrow-boy, was the most exciting group of off-licences at that time. Jancis admits that as she peered into the Soho branch of Augustus Barnett swinging her school satchel, 'the sort of thing that made my heart beat faster was a pink Rioja'.

Tony Laithwaite, who as a Transit van-driving ex-schoolteacher began buying cheap wine at cellar gates in France to sell to friends in the 1970s, has turned his micro-business into a phenomenon. Laithwaite's blistered Bacchanalian grin and bushman's hair pokes through letterboxes offering glossily dressed wines while the traditional trade helplessly, and enviously, looks on. For no-one can touch the publicity-conscious Laithwaite and his cleverly sourced basket of wines, often from obscure grapes and unmapped regions. Dewy eyed, soft-focused pictures of the wine makers, committed Italian or French peasants, wild colonial boy Aussies and impoverished aristocrats give a refreshingly rebel feel to wine buying and make the sleepy-eyed pyjama'd punter get on the phone to order a case before putting on the morning kettle.

The British are now the least parochial wine consumers in the world. Most of what we drink is far better than the average stuff the Frenchman or Italian drinks on a daily basis. The austere Englishman has a touch of the romantic deep inside him and his love for wine is more passionate, and better informed, than it ever was in Chaucer's or Shakespeare's eras. And now, instead of muffling up and risking highwaymen or footpads on his way to the tavern, he can sit by his computer and order it unshaven in his underpants.

43

Food and Wine

Matching wine with food was not a priority of ancient man. As Hugh Johnson says, 'it was not the subtle bouquet of wine or the lingering aftertaste of violets and raspberries', nor was it the *au point* haunch of venison; it was the brutal alcoholic thwack and munching something as fuel. Bread and alcohol were the cocaine of their time. They made short and brutish lives bearable.

When wealthy Egyptians dined, it was a sensual experience. They matched their best wines with food in a colour-splashed scene with intense fragrances, gilt, drapes and wonderful costumes. Large, airy rooms were aglitter with the starry luminosity of lit candles and reeked with the pungency of freshly plucked flowers. The trembling anticipation of casual sex increased the excitement. Only the slimmest beauties wearing the flimsiest of gauzes were selected to serve at table. That image might not have appealed to the dandruffed bachelor sharing his last bottle of 1985 Lynch Bages in his flat in Preston with a 'special fwend', or the flashy property developer with his pointy shoes trying to impress his 'laydee' with Le Pin.

The Romans brought wine and food to gluttonous pinnacles of vulgarity. When a 'degraded' lady arrived late and flustered at Trimalchio's dinner, 'her face on fire with thirst enough to drink off the vessel containing full three gallons which was laid at her feet and from which she tosses off a couple of pints before her dinner to create a raging appetite: then she brings it all up again, and souses the floor with the washings of her insides, drinks and vomits like a big snake that has tumbled into a vat. The sickened husband closes his eyes, and so keeps down his bile.'

William Younger leaps to the Roman's defence. 'The excesses of the few,' he says, 'do not mean all Romans were bestial gluttons who reeled with unsteady lechery through monstrous orgies.' In fact some were so terrified of being seduced into having a good time that Pliny wrote that some took hemlock in case 'a fear of death compelled them to drink'. On the other hand there were trenchermen like Novellius Torquatus, who was proud of his reputation for being able to guzzle 10 litres of wine in one gasping, choking, spraying draught.

When the Romans invaded Britain, homesick centurions, their helmeted heads bent as they guarded windswept Hadrian's Wall, scribbled notes to their families telling them the food was good. Foot soldiers ate bread smeared with fish sauce and fatty pork to keep out the cold. They ate gruel made from roasted barley, but even when reduced to starving, they drew the line at horse meat. They drank low-strength wine, must and vinegar. On special occasions they were given spiced goat's milk, young pig, ham, corn, venison, salt and flour, and vintage wine.

The Romans introduced the pheasant, peacock, guinea fowl and fallow deer to England for something to hunt. They also introduced vines, figs, walnuts, chestnuts, medlars and mulberries. The planted parsley, alexanders, borage, chervil, coriander, dill, fennel, mint, thyme, garlic, leek, onion, shallot, hyssop, rosemary, rue, sage, savory, sweet marjoram and radish. They introduced cabbage, lettuce, endive and turnip. Mallow, orache, corn salad and fat hen failed to survive the Romans' departure as foodstuffs, but they are still growing in disused railway sidings and by the sides of motorways. The industrious Roman gardener and botanist planted damson, plum, cherry, apple and pear.

The Romans loved oysters. A dig at Silchester unearthed over a million oyster shells, as well as evidence of their regard for periwinkles, mussels, whelks, cockles and scallops. Pike, eel, dace, perch and carp were fished from rivers and ponds. Cod, ling, haddock, grey mullet, herring and sea bream were netted from boats or caught on bronze hooks. Crabs and lobsters were attractive delicacies. The Romans flavoured their sauces with garum, a liquid made from the guts of tunny fish, gills, juice and blood. It was extensively used. They poured it into almost all savoury dishes, including snails, suckling pig, partridge, boiled goose, venison and hare, as well as truffles and pottage.

They tempted wild pigeons into tall *columbaria* – dovecotes – and ate them and their eggs. They hunted red, roe and fallow deer and wild boar with hounds, and bred hares in captivity. The barnacle goose was a particular favourite of Pliny, who called it 'the most sumptuous dish known to the Britons'. Tough and rubbery, the peacock had to be hung for weeks. It was pulverised into a kind of burger then boiled in honey and pepper.

Roman chefs were constantly dreaming up new ways to please their masters. They bred dormice in large jars, fattening them on seeds and nuts for the table. They fed snails on milk, wine must and wheat, then fried them in oil and served them with *liquamen* and wine. They ate frogs too. They preferred British beef to all other forms of meat. Both longhorn and shorthorn types were bred for the quality of their meat. British beef was exported to continental Europe long before the Roman invasion of Britain. The humble ox supplied milk, cream, butter and cheese when it wasn't pulling ploughs or heavily loaded drays. Even in death it was useful, supplying dark, nutritious meat, tough and durable leather, bone, glue and horn. It was an invaluable asset for farmers, carters, butchers and cobblers. Veal, made from the delicate flesh of shorthorn calves, was fried and smothered in a rich sauce made with vine fruits, honey, onions and herbs. Mutton and lamb were boiled or roasted.

The pig was another magnificent source of flavoursome meat. The finest were selected for fattening in sties or enclosures as they are today. Suckling pigs were spit or oven roasted and, when tender and crispy, were served with a sauce made with hot fat spiced with lovage, rue, caraway, celery seed, wine must and olive oil. Hams and shoulders were either salted and hung on barn or kitchen beams for months to cure, or they were boiled with figs and spices. The hams were then wrapped in pastry and baked. After they had cooled the shoulders were sliced and eaten with wine and pepper sauce.

Cheese was made throughout the kingdom and wild bees were collected and tamed for their honey. Large tilled gardens were stuffed with vegetables with which we are now familiar – carrots, cabbage, asparagus, cucumber, globe artichokes, leeks and onions. The Romans loved herbs so much so that they were chastised for it by one famous cook, who said: 'Life is so short for men in this world, since they stuff their bellies with herbs even the cows leave alone.' Dried grapes, which were used for cooking and for making homemade wines, were shipped over from southern France in great, hand-woven hampers.

They organised great banquets like those the rulers enjoyed back in Rome. Live pigs, 'muzzled and hung with bells', paraded on a slippery catwalk in a bizarre beauty contest to decide which was to be disembowelled in front of an applauding audience and bloodily dragged to the kitchen to be butchered and boiled. It was unlikely, though, that the between-course entertainment was as much fun as the party arranged for the Emperor Elagabalus (reigned AD 218–222). In his short reign he had a team of chefs prepare a meal made from the brains of 600 ostriches, served with bowls of shelled peas into which grains of gold were sprinkled. The lentils were mixed with precious stones. Side dishes contained whole pearls and polished slivers of amber. Acrobatic ladies did the splits on the tables, young boys had their heads patted by oily hands, clowns clowned, music blared and gladiators wrestled, all between courses. Elagabalus watched it all with a voyeur's smirk as he prodded *foie gras* through the lips of his favourite hounds. It is perhaps unnecessary to relate Elagabalus suffered the pig's fate at the hands and knives of the praetorian guard.

With this splendid array of home-grown food, the Romans had access to a respectable wine list. There was plenty of red wine from Germany, Spain, France and Italy which was shipped over in two-handled amphorae or small wooden casks. The best of its was kept in dry dark cellars but the majority was drunk within three months of arriving. They also had plenty of good brown ale and barn-brewed cider. A substance called 'wyne-cute' was also drunk. This was another version of boiled-down grape juice, similar to the Anglo-Saxon *cæren* or the Latin *carenum*. In medieval times *vinequyt* was a wine mixed with other ingredients.

Old or oxidised wine was not wasted. The Roman loved the tang of vinegar. Soldiers drank it diluted with spring water when on the march. It was also used for cutting and flavouring sauces and for preserving fruit, vegetables and fish. There is evidence that this clever and innovative race made wine from figs, pomegranates and any juicy berry or bitter sloe they could find. After the Romans departed Britain, Warner Allen writes: 'Wine was poor, food tasteless, gastronomy at its nadir and the wine-grower had lost the secret of making the wines which had moved the classic authors to poetic rapture.'

44

What Goes with Stuffed Ass's Head?

When Henry III's daughter Margaret married Alexander III of Scotland at York on Boxing Day 1251, wine was used both in cooking and in celebration. The King's representative visited markets and fairs to find the finest beast for fattening. Thirteen hundred deer were killed, 170 wild boars were slaughtered, 7,000 hens and hundreds of game birds, rabbits and hares were sacrificed. The king's stew pond on the River Foss, as well as other rivers and even the sea, was dragged for fish. The catch included masses of fine fat trout and eels, to which were added 60,000 salted herrings, 1,000 unsalted cod, 10,000 haddock and 500 conger eels, and 68,000 small loaves were baked. Around 150,000 bottles of wine were poured.

When Edward II was replenishing his army's stocks in 1316 for his impending joust with the Scots, he purchased 4,000 casks of wine. In 1327 Edward III bought a mere 300 tuns for his expedition. The biggest spender of all was Henry VIII. In 1543 it took sixteen ships to deliver his wine order. Unfortunately for him, the Scots got wind of the flotilla and swiftly commandeered the lot. But Henry was not without wine for long. At the Field of the Cloth of Gold he took a travelling wine warehouse with him. At a quart per soldier per day, it didn't last long. Fighting on foot, carrying heavy metal armaments and wearing steel hats and chain mail, a garrison of 1,000 men could decimate 60,000 bottles a month.

Richard II of England topped the French monarch with his 300 kitchen staff answering to a Master Cook, author of *The Forme of Cury*. The book was published anonymously and in spite of a sycophantic dedication to 'the best and ryallest viander of all Christian kynges', the author died poor and unknown. The Earl of Northumberland ate everything with feathers or fur on, except puffins. Their flesh was too oily. In 1512 thousands of rabbits were eaten by the voracious nobleman, as well as 49 deer, 123 cows, 667 sheep, 25 pigs, 28 veal calves and 60 lambs. The Earl of Oxford was almost a vegan by comparison – in 1431 he and his friends only devoured 36 deer from his own park and what his hawking brought in, a few grouse, snipe, larks and thrushes. Enormous 'trencher' loves, freshly baked in the Earl's kitchens, were offered to each with their plates of meat for breakfast. On an average day the Earl and his wife each ate a couple of pounds of meat and drank a quart of wine , and the same of home-brewed ale.

'The sixteenth century,' says Peter Brear, author of *Food and Cooking in Sixteenth-century Britain*, 'has bequeathed to posterity a whole series of rich and potent images, full of spectacle and a robust *joie de vivre.*' Men and women dressed lavishly and, fanning themselves, they listened to the music of Morley, Dowland and Campion, the poetry of Spenser and Sidney and watched the plays of Marlowe and Shakespeare. 'A keen interest in wine and food,' Brear says, reflected 'the influence of Renaissance Europe, in addition to providing evidence of the sumptuous entertainments held largely for political reasons both at court and in the larger houses.' The food Englishmen enjoyed in the sixteenth century was local and organic, and there was nothing better than good English beef from a young slab-sided bullock up to his knees in buttercups.

Pig meat was not so fashionable. Andrew Boorde in his *Compendyous Regyment or Dyetary of Health* published in 1542 says: 'Beef is a good meate for an Englysshe man, so be it the beest be yonge and that it be not kowe-fleshe. Bacon is good for carters and plowmen, the whiche be ever labouringe in the earth or dung.' Venison was also served and on occasion it may have been delicately slaughtered by the Queen herself. 'While visiting Viscount Montagu, Elizabeth rode out into the park where a delicate bower had been prepared for her reception. Here a nymph with a sweet song presented her with a cross-bow which she used expertly to dispatch three or four deer driven across her view.'

At Home Lacie, Herefordshire, home of the Scudamores, over Christmas 1639 the festivities raged for '2 weekes and 5 dayes'. Lord Scudamore, 'a thorough gentleman and scholar' who presided over a vast estate, was showered with presents from local dignitaries and tenants. The mayor and the aldermen, 'as a recognition of his services to the city', gave him a hogshead of Claret. The incoming mayor, not to be outdone, handed over a tierce of the same wine. The wife of a former mayor mysteriously donated 'three loaves of sugar', a wealthy occupant of Drinsop Court gave a fat ox and some game, another a brace of salmon caught in the River Wye, which curled around the estate. Occupiers of humble hovels gave their last hen or hand-reared sucking pig. One impoverished peasant from Little Dewchurch gave four blackbirds he had taken the trouble to net that morning. The noble Lord employed a 'Sergeant of the Acaterie' to make sure all donated. He was also instructed that all donations, be they 'beefe, muttons, linges, coddes shall be goode and of the best.'

Over the holiday, among the items eaten were the following: '2,904 Pounds of beefe, 3,391 Pounds of muttons, 12 Brawne collars, 49 Pigs, 13 Neats tongues, 8 Udders, 20 Tripes, 21 Does, 188 Rabbits, 53 Turkyes, 54 Geese, umpteen Ducks, 150 Partriges, 29 Pheasaunts.' Add three barrels of pickled oysters, 100 carps, 30 eels, 1,017 eggs and sundry items like cheese, bread, calves feet, civets, *etc.*, and it was a well-fed occasion. Let us hope the poor peasant with his four blackbirds didn't starve. Wine and beer: one hogshead and 16 gallons of Sack, a hogshead, 31 tierces and 7 bottles of Claret, 17 gallons and 1 pint of 'Muskadine', 1 gallon and 1 pinte of other white wine.

Yuletide guests, who might include everyone from top table equals from other windy old mansions to big-knuckled rustics, were clearly not all Claret drinkers, as the following litany of assorted booze consumed over Christmas indicates. '54 Hogsheads of Beere, 1 Hogshead of Alle and 6 Hogsheads of Cider'. From Lord Scudamore's capacious coffers came gifts for the entertainment and the caterers. 'Musicke' was provided by the cathedral players as a cost of £4 10s and as much as they could eat. Two 'harpurs' played – One 'Walsh' and sighted, one not and blind. They were both given 10s. Miles the Taborer earned 5s for his contribution, and 'ye Singinge Boye' received the same. The hard-working kitchen staff were well recompensed, as much delicious crackling as they could slyly peel off the roasting carcases and some cash. 'Ye Coocks and Others in Ye Kitchinge' were paid £11 10s, 'two Scouringe Women' earned 8s and as much licking of the bowls as they wanted. 'Daves Helping ye Bruer' had 7s in his breeches pocket as he skipped home by the light of the moon.

Lady Mary Wortley noted when visiting Vienna in 1716: 'First people of quality' were offered eighteen different wines at dinner with a wine list provided. Dr Andrew Boorde, a randy Carthusian whose sexual activities led to his unfrocking before and after, suggested wine and food partnerships in his *Dietary of Health* which he published in 1542. 'Mean wines, especially Claret wine; were excellent with meat,' he confided. 'Hot wines', like Malmsey and certain sweet, full bodied Greek wines 'be not so good to drink with meat, but after meat, and with oysters, salads or fruit, a draught or two may be suffered.' William Harrison, another sixteenth-century writer, agreed. 'We use our wines by degrees, so that the hottest cometh last to the table, for the stronger it is, the more it is desired.'

Queen Elizabeth's royal household employed a battalion to feed and water important dignitaries. Working under the stern leadership of the Lord Chamberlain, there were officers, sergeants, clerks and master cooks right down to the humble scullion salivating at the tantalising aroma coming from an enormous brown-fleshed ox slowly revolving on a giant spit, its full grease pan sloshing beneath with scalding fat. Fire-tanned underlings, stripped to the buff, carefully basted the massive carcass. The Sergeant of the Seller took charge of all 'liquid refreshments'. He stalked the wine bins like some great grey heron ready to pounce on the dusty flagons or with chisel and hammer, preparing to broach a cask of Bordeaux or golden Iberian, sniffing the aroma as the wine gushed into pitchers. It was the responsibility of the Yeoman of the Pitcher-house to ensure all drinking vessels, silver mugs, jacks and cups were spotless and properly laid by each place at the great oak table, at which all wines, spring water and fruit drinks would be served by the Yeomen for the Mouthe. The table was laid with embarrassing pomp, even though like a dress rehearsal the main actor was never present. All dishes and drinks were tasted for poison before being served to the Queen.

When James I was a dinner guest at Houghton on Sunday 17 August 1617, he was served capon, duck, veal, roast shoulder of mutton, haunch of venison, turkey, swan, goose, beef, pigs and pies crammed and crimped with chicken, tripe and mince. The cold table was piled with sliced mutton, rabbits, roast heron, curlew pie, tongue pie, soused capon and veal. There were bowls of salads and tubs of custard.

The second course featured a hot fat pheasant and six quails specially prepared for His Majesty, partridge, poults, chicken, artichoke pie, roast curlew, pease buttered, rabbits, ducks, plovers, red deer pie, pig's ears soused, three hot roasted herons, lamb roast, gammons of bacon, pear tart, dried tongue, turkey pie, pheasant pie, hog's cheek dried

The studious Sandrone. A tiny grower with a big reputation.

and cold turkey chicks. The drinks list would have listed good ale, home-made cider and perry, punches and possets. The wines were Spanish, Portuguese and French. For breakfast the next morning the King was offered the same menu with wild boar pie and 'sliced beef humble pie'. The Earl of Bristol said, 'when you were entertained at Houghton Hall you were likely to be up to your chin in meat and over your chin in Claret', the host Sir Robert Walpole's favourite wine.

By the 1550s the large Christmas bird, the turkey, had arrived from America. However, in 1660 Christmas feasts were an opportunity to eat forgotten dishes like 'Patty of Lumber with Trouts about it, Pickled Pullets in Jelly, Lambs Heads Larded and broiled, A Pastry of Venison in Blood, Calves Heads hashed with Livers Larded, A Capon in Ye Bladder Boiled.' The 'Cold Messes' were plenty and imaginative too: 'Collared Eel, Potts of Lampries, Ice Creams, Nuts and Tarts galore.' The menu came to 180 dishes, and the table was 15ft long and 9ft wide, although this was minuscule compared to Lord Nelson's, which ran to 53ft long.

The table seating at the household of the Earl of Dorset at Knowle in Kent in 1613 was 'My Lords Table, occupied by My Lord and Lady and their friends'. At the Parlour Table sat skilled, mainly kitchen staff, such as cooks, bakers, slaughtermen, the house brewer, gardeners etc. Then came the Nursery Table, followed by the Long Table, which comprised mainly equestrian servants, grooms of various descriptions. The Laundry-Maids' Table came next, with the Kitchen and Scullery Table last.

Certain dishes were made for fun, to entertain guests. For example, pies were filled with live frogs which jumped out on the table and horrified women and children. Edmund Wyle, a close friend of John Aubrey (1627–1697), hosted many a famous dinner party. One of his party tricks was to sow 'parsely, purslane and balme' seed in a earth-filled porringer, which was then placed in 'a Chafing dish of coales'. By the time the meal was coming to a close, 'tiny and delicious green shoots were growing in the porringer'. Aubrey liked his wine and was particularly fond of the new, dark 'excellent Portugall Wine'. His philosopher friend Thomas Hobbes (1588–1679) was a messy eater but light, who may have suffered from bulimia as he 'had the benefit of vomiting', which he did easily. 'For thirty or more yeares, his dyet, etc, was very moderate and regular. After sixty he drank no wine, his stomach grew weak, and he did eate most fish, especially whiting, for he said he digested fish better than flesh.' It clearly didn't do him any harm as he lived to celebrate his ninetieth birthday, while his friend Aubrey kicked the bucket at seventy.

Poorly paid servants obediently stood silently for hours as their masters noisily ate, drank and shrieked. In the *Footman's Directory* the author advised footmen: 'While waiting at dinner, never be picking your nose, or scratching your head or any other part of your body.' Senior kitchen staff helped themselves, sometimes overdoing it. A Northumbrian gentleman admonished 'the butler and his cronies for indulging too freely' in his wine. It was, he said, hardly possible to find a 'more drunken establishment'. On grand occasions servants ate very well. In fact the fifteenth Earl of Derby complained his servants generally ate better than he did.

The Monk's Tale

Monasteries, from the Greek *monos*, 'alone', meant 'men living alone'. They existed in Egypt in the fourth century. The monks enjoyed wine and in their isolation were glad to hand a beakerful of vinegar to any passing nomad as an act of friendship. Superstitious barbarians avoided attacking any monastic building marked with a cross. It is said that the fearsome Tortula, an Ostrogoth, was reduced to jelly by the mere sidelong glance of St Benedict, a man who insisted every brother was allotted his daily *hemina* (0.27 litre) of wine.

The contribution made by French, German, Austrian, Italian and Spanish monastic orders was crucial to the development of the wines we drink today. A 'league table' of Crus created and established by monks puts France on top with 109, followed by Germany (45), Austria (27), Italy (17), Switzerland (12), and Portugal (9). There are others in the USA, Israel, Lebanon, Algeria, East Africa, Australia, New Zealand, Chile and Argentina. Being sporting, we should add to that list Nyetimber, an Anglo-American fizz made from Chardonnay with a smidgin of Pinot Noir and Meunier grapes grown on once Cluniac-owned land in West Sussex. Religious orders, which 'piously acclimatised European vines and assured the survival of an art they had perfected', would be very proud.

The abbeys of Saint-Denis and Saint-Germain, having conquered Paris with the freshly delivered wine from their vineyards at Saint-Germain-des-Prés (which made more than 50,000 litres a year), cast covetous eyes at the white cliffs of Dover. Even before the Hundred Years' War, which raged fitfully from 1337 to 1453 and carried on intermittently during the reigns of five English kings, wealthy Englishmen were happy enough with the light reds from Bordeaux. Besides, the English had heard that if a man were to drink one pint of thin monks' wine from Saint-Germain, often consisting of tannic acid and oily second pressings, he would piss half a gallon of acid. To protect their interests in Bordeaux and discourage exports to England, English vineyard owners taxed wines from the Perigord, Tarn and Quercy.

Apart from the religious orders, which made wine because they had to, a few English landowners tried because they enjoyed the challenge. But a London red? Pepys refers in his diary to 'a very good red wine made by Lady Batton in Walthemstow.' It is highly likely grapes played no part.

Cooking, Art and Literature

Cookery books tumbled off printing presses but the recipes dealt mainly with stodgy puddings and pies. John Partridge published *The Treasury of Commodious Conceits and Hidden Secrets* in 1580. It ran to several reprints. *The Good Housewife's Jewel*, a possibly misleading title, was published by Thomas Dawson in 1585. *The Good Housewife's Handmaid for the Kitchen* followed in 1594. A deep knowledge of wine was not considered essential.

The connection between art and cooking was exemplified by minor poets, playwrights and painters donning their bibs to work in kitchens. Claude Gelée, a flour-dusted pâtissier, is credited with creating the feather-light pastry known today as 'feuillage'. Gelée painted landscapes in his spare time. Although his early work drew encouraging and sympathetic comments from his friends, his later work attracted the admiration of the great British artist J.M.W. Turner (1775–1851).

In England during the reign of Charles II, assisted and advised by 'the Merrie Monarch's' French friends, a culinary renaissance began. With fine food came a clamour for the finest wines. Evremond saw to it that his favourite wine was poured

PENGETHLEY

James the Gardener

ENGLISH TABLE WINE
Reichensteiner
Produced by and bottled for
Pengethley Manor Vineyard
Ross-on-Wye, Herefordshire, UK

11% vol   *Produce of the United Kingdom*   75 cl e

Grown in an old walled garden, the grapes ripe, the wine, crisp and light, is eagerly despatched by guests.

in volume at every great party attended by those mythical 'men of noble birth and remarkable wit'. Evremond dragged his scented carcass to every polite breakfast, splendiferous dinner and twee soirée where the beautiful (for which read tiresome) gathered to flaunt their elegance, wealth and 'wit'. One positive thing that came out of all this irritating posturing was that the quality of the fare was raised a notch or two. This new-found interest in food and wine as something to be tasted, savoured and enjoyed, rather than shovelled into one's stomach as one would fill a pig's trough with slops, 'was not limited to the Court and the nobility but was shared by all classes'.

The country tavern, where the farmer and his parlour maid gathered with the pongy drover and the straw-chewing labourer, offered organic food and real ale and pints of the new ruby wine from Portugal. In the threadbare inns of Elizabethan London 'stale bachelors and thrifty attornies' met to bore one another to death as they scooped their soup and fingered their bread rolls, while in the posher pubs 'gallants rubbed shoulders with templars and country squires' on wide-eyed visits to the capital. In the gastro pubs of the day the cooks aped the French, just as they do today, adding fancy names but not flair. M. Pontac, an immigrant from Bordeaux, opened Pontac's in the City of London in 1688. The trendy flocked there to sample his 'famed ragouts and new-invented salads'. Almost needless to say Pontac's became not only famous for his creative cooking, but also 'for the excellence of his wines and the extravagance of his charges'. It all helped to make Pontac's *the* place for writers, artists and actors. Steele, Congreve and Swift sallied there to discourse over a tasty dinner for five bob. If they felt flush after a book deal or an opening night, they blew two guineas a head on a really sumptuous meal with Champagne for pipe openers, good Claret with the main course and port to finish. This was phenomenally expensive at a time when a poor, worn-out working man and his broken wife brought up a hovel of dishevelled kids on a few shillings a week.

In Queen Anne's reign the quality of food and wine, the style and the content improved. Aristocrats and 'men of letters' approved. The dining rooms in fine houses expanded. Cellars went deeper, bins and racks went in. Tasting apparatus were installed. Cellar books were filled with happy squiggles. A Dr Lister published at his own expense a translation of the *Apicius Cookery Book*, while another doctor, Dr King, 'made himself responsible' for a compendium of recipes entitled *The Art of Cookery*, which was prefaced with an invitation to drink Palm and Anjou as aperitifs, followed by fine Bordeaux and Champaigne(*sic*) by the 'flask'. The success of this book triggered a small avalanche of books on cookery. One featured a recipe for the Countess of Rutland's legendary Banbury Cake, while another published by John Middleton in 1734 bore the catchy title *Five Hundred Receipts in Cookery, Confectionery, Pastry, Preserving, Conserving and Pickling*.

English cooking took a step backwards with the passing of Queen Anne. 'Gastronomy,' André Simon writes, 'never received any encouragement at court during the reigns of the first three Georges', although the Earl of Sandwich did put two slices of bread together but forgot to patent the idea, and the Duchess of Devonshire employed a French chef, Vincent de la Chapelle, who in his quiet moments wrote *The Modern Cook*, which was published to acclaim in 1733.

In spite of the best efforts of the Prince of Wales, later George IV, interest in cooking declined in England during the latter part of the eighteenth century. Citizens, 'from the most exalted to the lowest', were too drunk on cheap gin to eat and the taverns were making too much money serving Blue Ruin to chalk up a simple menu. Such dark times were in contrast to the sunny disposition of a tiny cabal of monstrously wealthy and arrogant French. Supported by royal patronage, gastronomy flourished, according to Simon. 'Courtiers and courtesans, financiers and church dignitaries paid lavishly for the services of gifted chefs.' From the choicest of ingredients, the best chefs prepared, cooked and served in the most imaginative way sumptuous dishes, while the poor wandered the alleys of the big cities eating their sleeves. In back gardens and in broken-down workshops starving men got busy sharpening scythes, making crude bombs and oiling the wheels of tumbrels. The Revolution was not far off.

Thomas Love Peacock (1785–1866), who published *Crochet Castle* in 1831, was keenly interested in wine and food, sharing his enthusiasm with his many friends, some famous. Many of the great poets of the day, including Coleridge, Shelley and Byron, were recipients of his sharp wit. Love Peacock threw them together at real or imagined dinners in the vast country seat of a newly rich *parvenu*, Mr Crochet, a miserable Jewish Scot.

Dr Johnson's recipe for a pleasant evening – 'no competition, no vanity, but a quiet interchange of sentiments' – certainly did not appeal to Mr Crochet. He wanted to see his famous guests lower their masks under the influence and settle old scores. He hadn't gone to the trouble and expense of putting together an A-list of guests and some expensive wine not to see some skin and hair flying. His coterie of 'ill assorted and violently opposed intellects' duly obliged. English gentlemen to a man, and lacking 'the stimulus of feminine society, proper, or improper', they brayed, bragged and dizzily passed the bottle.

Crochet's cellar was a 'temple of Bacchus, a beautiful spectacle, and a model arrangement'. In it lay 12,000 bottles of fine wine. His dinners were painstakingly planned and skilfully executed. Some guests would have enjoyed a good glass of Madeira with the soup; even the great Brillat-Savarin embraced Madeira with soup. But they had to wait until the fish course for a glass of wine. With fish Crochet poured Rhenish – not a disagreeable combination as long as the Hock wasn't too sweet.

The wines that followed were a haphazard parade of Champagne, followed by Graves, Sauternes and Hermitage, then after palates were thickly coated and deadened with food and Sauternes, a 'matchless Claret', the wine of Waterloo (1815 was considered the first widely celebrated Claret vintage in England). Crochet purred as he poured, smiling at his oneupmanship. The Waterloo wine, 'a remarkable year in every respect, was agreeable and perfumed, having both body and richness'. It was the sort of wine the *nouveaux riches* like Mr Crochet would haul into his cellars by the wagonload to prevent other snobs getting their hands on it. A man's wine merchant was more important than his banker if he wanted to groom the right sort of important and influential friends. It was ever thus, from the time of the Egyptians. Madeira was a popular wine and many a trencherman walked around the table to grab his favourite

Malmsey. Older men like the seventy-six-year-old Thomas Love Peacock eschewed strong, earthy, liverish wines like port, Madeira and Mountain at the end of the meal and instead sipped a gentle old Claret between puffs of a good cigar.

The inferior quality of the wines – sweet Spanish, ordinary port and obscure table wines from Portugal and Spain – reveal that English taste and knowledge was still in its infancy. Advertisements in *Tatler*, a magazine for the 'leisured classes', suggested there was a market for fine French wine, but Spanish wines were still popular. On 20 March 1710 bids were invited for 'Thirteen Pipes of excellent red Barrabas and Thirteen Pipes of new white Carcavella', a firmly established Portuguese wine. There was a huge stock of 'rich, racy and delicate Passadella' – sixty pipes of it – and others called 'White Bottoms', 'Oporto Stum' and 'Zant, a white wine of very fine flavour from Cadiz'. There were also 'new white Chesillion', 'Canary, neat and fit for draught and crackling' and '17 Butts of Bene Carlos from Barcelona', and there was an entry in *Tatler*'s small ads: 'Fifty-one casks of new excellent Pale Wine of Neufchatel'.

By the end of the eighteenth century a more varied British wine list was taking shape. A dinner at Stationers' Hall on 23 April 1778 featured wines from France, Germany, Spain, Portugal, Madeira and South Africa. In 1790 Messrs Edward and William Cox of Derby listed a wide choice of wines. Among the usual Florence, Canary, Sack, Madeira and red and white port was an unusually eclectic range of French wines, including Champagne, Hermitage and a spectacular coup for a Midlands merchant; '14 Doz. fine old Hautbrion Claret at £25 18s'.

Lord Byron's weekends at Newstead Abbey were at times both indolent and hyperactive. After a late breakfast – Byron was 'esteemed a prodigy' for rising between eleven and twelve – the afternoon was packed with reading, boxing, fencing, single-stick or shuttlecock in the great room; practising with pistols in the hall; walking, riding, cricket, sailing on the lake or 'teasing the wolf'. Dinner was at 7 p.m. and often lasted until breakfast. 'After revelling on choice viands, and the finest wines of France', the tablecloth was removed and a human skull filled with burgundy was passed round. If cheese was served it was not accompanied by wine. In certain houses, the wine glasses were removed when the brick of soapy cheese arrived. Ale or cider were the normal partners; otherwise it was soda water and sermons. Luckily, today, with delicatessens, farm shops and supermarkets offering as many home-grown cheeses as they do in France, no meal is complete without an hour or two getting fat and drunk on port or good strong red wine, and a fragrant plate of delicious British and Irish cheeses.

The French introduced aperitifs in the nineteenth century but the fashion did not catch on in England. 'Victorians and Edwardians,' says William Golding, 'displayed an almost total lack of interest in aperitifs', sweet, fizzy or bitter. Sherry diluted and destroyed with soda was sipped uncomfortably by a few, but the majority of diners glumly made small-talk with both hands in their pockets, choking on saliva.

While the French drank their poorest wine with the soup, and introduced their best with the meat or even at the end of the meal, some English, intent on making a gesture to their peers, drank their finest throughout the meal, though it was not unusual for men of otherwise impeccable taste to wait until their guests were beyond caring to pour home-made blackberry or nettle hock. English ale was popular with the cheese course. It was low in alcohol, thirst-quenching and better for the liver than half a dozen bumpers of young port.

When Boswell was a guest at Sir Alexander Dick's dinner and dance in Edinburgh he remembered the 'boiled beef and greens, the large turkey and the fine chickens and the 250 [who counted them?] asparagus, fresh from his host's hothouse, and a fine pig.' Wine from the farm was served. The wine list was eclectic as well as elastic. With the jugs of currant and gooseberry came 'Greek wine from the Consul at Leghorn', Claret, port and punch. Boswell, a noted sponger, brought his own cache of ales wherever he went, then stayed on for several days wearing out his welcome as he hoovered up everything in sight.

The ruddy and sturdy yeomen who stood with pikes and tin hats outside St James' Palace in the early nineteenth century drank a gallon of good English ale per head per day, with a couple of pounds each of home-grown beef, pork or lamb. The *Epicure's Year Book*, published in 1868, was more 'anal', suggesting Madeira, sherry and Vermouth with soup, Sauternes with *hors d'oeuvres*, iced Rhenish with sorbets, Claret with hot and cold *entrées*, Romanée-Conti or Laffite (*sic*) with roasts and sherry with dessert.

Meat was hugely popular among all classes. The poor risked hanging or, worse, a one-way, vomity cruise to Tasmania, in order to poach a hare, rabbit or knock a pheasant on the head. Horse or hedgehog meat was essential. During the Siege of Paris in 1870 deprived gourmands tucked into the contents of Paris Zoo, accompanying an unusual selection of animals with fine wines. Guest at Voisin's, 'under the command of the chef, M. Bellanger', enjoyed a small glass of sherry, tucked their napkins into their collars and started with elephant soup, eagerly followed by stuffed ass's head, roast camel, bear chops, haunch of wolf, kangaroo stew, cat (appropriately garnished with rats) and antelope with puréed red beans, mushrooms and watercress salad on the side. It was meat of all descriptions, furred, feathered or naked. Sardines and fried fish made a token, almost apologetic appearance.

The assembled foodies honoured the dead denizens of jungle and African plain with very superior wines. Château Palmer 1864 (a five-star vintage), was followed by Mouton Rothschild 1846 and Romanée-Conti 1858. To enable the sticky-fingered guests to draw breath, refreshing saucers of Bollinger frappé were served and, for those who preferred white with their stuffed ass's head, Château La Tour Blanche 1861, arguably the first sweet white Bordeaux and at the time rated second only to Château d'Yquem, was poured. A light vintage port, 1827, sent diners replete and fearful back to the lethal streets and morbid reality of a city in chaos.

When George Meredith and the poet Dante Gabriel Rossetti (1828–1882) were entertained by Sir William Hardman they ignored the axiom that sherry and Madeira went best with soup, white with fish, red with meat, port with cigars, *etc.* Sir William briskly matched Chablis with oysters and salmon: fine, but Amontillado with fillet steak, lamb and guinea fowl? Chicken, omelettes and macaroni was biliously sluiced with sparkling Hock. The dinner over, the gentlemen shuffled to the drawing room to smoke cigars, drink coffee and liqueurs – and open the Chambertin.

When Lord Culpin invited Samuel Taylor Coleridge and his wife to dine, he wiped out a bevy of delicious Clarets with decanters of Madeira, port and sweet Frontignac, old Hock, Malaga, sweet Champagne and for chasers, more of that elderly Hock. He then served jugs of sweet punch with sliced cucumber bobbing on top, then presumably ordered his staff to stand by with mops, pails and lots of Jeyes fluid.

At Edwardian picnics, elegant affairs with neither primus stove, Ikea deckchair nor billy can in sight, lolling toffs and their parasoled ladies sipped Champagne with *mayonnaise de saumon, médaillons de homard à la russe, poulet rôti, pâté de foie gras, truffe, suprèmes de volaille Saint-James, salade de coeurs de laitue, gateau princesse* and *blancmange aux amandes,* followed by a gentle stroll in a not-too-distant bee-loud glade.

When André Simon met Maurice Healy and a few intimates for lunch in 1931 they opted for simplicity – plain food and fine wine with old friends. It was 'an excellent lunch,' Simon said, 'hard to improve upon; an omelette, a tender steak and a bit of cheese.' With it they drank Château Margaux 1920, Château Ausone 1904, '05 and '09, and Château Haut-Brion 1874.

Simon was also present on a less satisfactory occasion. He was invited to a wartime lunch in a 'luxury London hotel'. Exotic food was understandably scarce but the order went out 'that the best must be found, whatever the cost for the occasion'. An off-form kitchen produced a meal that was too heavy and far too rich. Simon gagged. With the 'very good but rather rich *truite saumonée*', Forster Jesuitengarten Trockenbeerenauslese 1921 was served. It was a magnificent wine, 'filling the room with its wonderful scent', but it was far too luscious, smothering at birth the magnum of Mouton-Rothschild 1929 that followed. The 1929 Mouton, one of the truly great wines of the century, was seriously sought after by collectors. 'It was the idol of the salesrooms,' Michael Broadbent said; 'Like Marlene Dietrich, it was ineffable, unattainable, full of mystique and star quality.' The magnum was ruined, so was the wonderful Hock. No wonder the little Frenchman was asterisking.

While numerous taverns served hearty roasts and glutinous stews, hotels and restaurants offered greater variety, but they often printed their menus in pidgin French. Predictably this enraged the fully paid-up Frenchman André Simon. After seeing haggis advertised on the Savoy menu in the 1940s as 'Pouding de Saint André', Simon's fluffy white moustache twitched menacingly. 'The language of the country must always be best for the food of the country', he rasped. He was equally unimpressed when he saw *pâté de foie gras* advertised on a pre-war 'all-English Menu' as 'Pie of liver fat'.

47

The Wine and Food Society

The Wine and Food Society did much to stimulate an interest in wine and food between the wars. It was born in 1933 out of a fortuitous meeting between the editor of the *Observer*, A.J.A. Symons, founder of the First Edition Club and publisher of the *Book Collector's Quarterly*, and an unemployed fifty-five-year-old André Simon. Their mission was 'to bring together and serve all those who took an intelligent interest in the problems and pleasures of the table'. It was also intended to press for the raising of standards of cooking in the United Kingdom, to use its voice to try to improve the deplorable state of country inns, to set up local wine and food circles and to issue good hotels and restaurants with a badge of approval. They never got round to the last bit.

The new society's mouthpiece, a gastronomical quarterly edited by Simon, price 2s 6d, first saw the light of day in spring 1934. Michael Broadbent, when called upon to deliver the André Simon Memorial Lecture at Christies in 1971, said that while society members 'organised excellent tastings, luncheons and dinners, their influence on commercial establishments or on public taste in general was virtually nil.' Tommy Layton, a contempory of Simon, called the Frenchman 'our most enigmatic man, our most knowledgable man, and a man who has done more to popularise wines in this century than anyone else.'

A bias towards French cuisine and wines was established from the start with the Chairman's Memorable Meals. A typical Memorable Meal was the one held on board the *Queen Elizabeth* at Southampton on 25 July 1947. With *canapés, délices de sole Véronique, tournedos sauté, bouquetière, pommes soufflées* and a *corbeille de fruits* the society served coffee, Amontillado, Bâtard Montrachet 1937, Château Gruaud Larose Sarget 1933 and Château d'Yquem 1937.

The first meeting of the Bedford branch opened at the Bridge Hotel on 20 June 1947. Simon was present so naturally the food and wine spoke with a French accent. The *contre-filet de boeuf périgourdine* was served with *petits pois à la menthe* and Sylvaner d'Alsace and Châteauneuf du Pape Reserve, neither with a vintage. The seventh meeting of the Birmingham branch at the Hotel Rembrandt on 16 May 1947 also had Simon in the chair. Again the menu was determinedly French, as were the wines, except for a 1934 Rüdesheimer Berg. The red was exceptional, a Château Rausan Gassies 1929. Simon again popped up when the Merseyside Branch held their thirty-first meeting at the Exchange Hotel in Liverpool on 2 May 1947. The fare was modest and the wines uninspiring. *Vol-au-vent* with peas and new potatoes was accompanied by a medium-sweet 1934 Liebfraumilch and a very sweet 1944 Château Rieussec, a poor vintage. Fancy serving the fussy, professional Frenchman with Liebfraumilch! Not a memorable meal, then. Simon's diary was probably full next time they asked him.

By the 1960s menus and wine lists were a little more adventurous, with some societies weaning themselves off the obligatory French menu. When the society kicked off its 478th meeting in London in January 1966, they were positively rebellious. The theme was 'Classic Greek'. The food was an uneasy mix of taramasalata, *keftedes, loukmades* with *hymettus*, and roast duckling *farci au Bourgourie*. When it came to choose the wines, the society suffered a collective loss of bottle. No Greek wines appeared; instead they chose Champagne, dry sherry, Richebourg and d'Yquem, then spoilt the effect by pouring a humdrum Piesporter.

A Creole Luncheon at Nick's Diner in March 1966 was proceeded by a tasting of mediocre Californian wines: Christian Brothers Chenin Blanc, Louis Martin Zinfandel, Buena Vista Pinot Noir and Almaden Blanc de Blanc. The branches may have wanted to be more adventurous, but finer, more interesting wines had yet to arrive in the United Kingdom. After this unimaginative tasting, things improved over lunch. With daube of beef à la Créole, with Carolina saffron rice and herb gumbo, Charles Krug Traminer, Buena Vista Johannisberg Riesling and Beaulieu Private Reserve Cabernet were served.

In May 1965 the Marquis of Bath flung open the doors of Longleat House to the unwashed when he hosted an Italian tasting, followed by 'an excellent fork supper of Italian food'. On 24 September, Goldeny House in Bristol was the venue for a tasting of South African wines hosted by the South African Wine Farmers' Association. For the Christmas dinner, held at Fortes Restaurant in Bath, the boat was well and truly pushed out and the French culinary dictionary vigorously thumbed. With the *consommé royal, blanchailles diables, faisan Romanoff, céleri bordelaise, choux de Bruxelles, pomme croquette, canapé Corburg, meringue américaine au Kirsch* and *Charlotte russe aux fraises*, the wines were Château Olivier 1962, Château Liversan, Haut-Médoc 1955, Château St Sauveur 1955, Château Coutet 1955 and Delaforce 1950.

Soldiering bravely on without their founding chairman, the Wine and Food Society held their March Dinner at Lambert Court on the Hagley Road under the new chairmanship of Mr A.W. Jeffs, who supplied the Taylor 1912 port. The fare began, cheekily, with *petite marmite Henri VI* followed by *scallopes de rousette à la Provençale, tournedos Béarnais* and *pointes d'asperge au beurre*, and triumphantly culminated with *soufflé à la reine*. The whites were Château Filhot 1960 and Château Coutet 1949; the sole red was Corton 1952. Apart from the *marmite* everything was French. Simon's ghost would have been pleased. The evening finished with a bang – the unleashing of the new chairman's impressive magnum of Taylor's 1912.

Hugh Johnson has divided 'the infinite variety of wine into ten categories', and associated each category with a selection of dishes which gave the green light to experimentation. There were only a few dishes which in his opinion destroyed the flavour of wine. One was salad dressed with vinegar and another was chocolate.

'Chocolate dominates and spoils the taste of any wine', Johnson avers. He goes on to say that 'most desserts are better served without wine. Some creamy, highly perfumed concoctions fight rather than complement wine. Citrus fruit is particularly guilty.' Johnson takes a sensible and relaxed view about wine with food, leaving it to the host to decide, but warns: 'A more formal meal with a succession of wines is the great opportunity of gastronomy. To achieve a graduated harmony of successive flavours it is worth taking pains.'

To Oz Clarke, 'most wine rules date from another era when cooking cultures didn't overlap, and we drank the relatively few old classics like red Bordeaux and white Burgundy.' Clarke says its not just the menu that has changed. Modern wine, he said, is 'unrecognisable from the wine of a generation ago'. Now be it white, red or rosé, 'it is now likely to be an utterly enjoyable drink ... based on ripe fruit expertly vinified, rather than a difficult, frequently fruitless beverage that required sympathetic understanding and a plateful of complimentary food to enjoy.' Is he getting at the French? He concludes: 'Drink what you like. If it is well made from decent grapes grown in a good vineyard, it'll get on pretty well with virtually any food you decide to marry with it.' What would André Simon say to that?

When André Simon died in his mid-nineties after a wonderful, wine soaked existence, Michael Broadbent was asked to select the wines for his last supper. It was tricky: what do you serve a dead man who has tasted so much fine wine? After some head-scratching, Broadbent came up with Pommery and Greno Blanc de Blancs Avize 1962 (who were Simon's first employers in 1895), Hugel's Riesling Auslese, Reserve Exceptionelle 1966, Beaulieu Vineyard's Cabernet Sauvignon, Reserve Georges de Latour 1965 and Château Latour 1929. The late French-born doyen of British wine writers was appropriately toasted with 1950 Château d'Yquem.

48

A Bunch of Grapes

Bearing sweet and flavoursome grapes, the *Vitis vinifera* wriggled, climbed and wound its way into our conciousness, yielding wines that either sun themselves in noisy supermarkets or gather dust in tranquil cellars. The *Vitis vinifera*, according to Jancis Robinson, accounts for 99.998 per cent of all wine-making vines. The full and fascinating story of thrusting tendrils, climates, people with their corporeal and heavenly desires and needs has yet to be written. Let's not linger on the muddled minutiae and instead let's focus on what we know about the main grapes which have emerged from the mass of wiry climbers and made a name for themselves. Some are still reaching for the light in poverty and ignorance like a potential great novelist in the back streets of Dublin or Cairo. Adaptable, durable, disease resistant, the vinous stars have taken aeons evolving. Others, given the chance, will do the same.

Black

PINOT NOIR
The Pinot Noir claims a connection with the Roman *Vitis allobrogica*, an ancient vine referred to by Pliny and Columella. It is certainly believed to be the oldest of the classic grapes. Jancis Robinson whose *Vines, Grapes and Wine* is well thumbed essential loo reading, says the Pinot Noir 'is thought to be one of the first refinements of wild vines made by man on his route to civilisation'. It is a fecund and promiscuous berry. Experts widely disagree on its clonal variation. Some say it has 1,000 siblings, others say 200. It may be cousin to the 'Pinot vermeil', which was mentioned in Burgundian tracts in 1375. It has sired the Pinot Gris and the Pinot Blanc. It is difficult to find a good bottle that is also cheap. Even the Burgundy Grands Crus, fabulous in great years when they make some of the finest wine on earth, can be hideously expensive and downright filthy when it rains. Perhaps the nineteenth-century trick of inoculating weedy musts with a churn or two of rich, dark Hermitage should return. The Pinot has proven staying power. Michael Broadbent gave four stars to an 1892 Inglenook Californian Pinot Noir. When he tasted it in 1979 it was tawny but far from deceased, possessing an 'amber brown rim' with a lovely 'distinctly old Pinot' nose. It proved two things – how wonderful old, well-made wines can be regardless of their country of origin, and the stickability of the Pinot.

CABERNET SAUVIGNON

Its history is short and sketchy. As with a great many viticultural advances, monks were involved. When the Abbé Bellet listed the grape types around Cadillac in the Graves, he recorded eighteen black varities and twenty white. Among the former were Cabernet's hoary antecedents, the Vidures, grande and petite. Both were hard, durable vines, not widely planted but highly respected for the quality and the longevity of their wines. When Baron Hector de Brane acquired land in the newly tilled Médoc, it was the Vidures he chose, not the soft and quick-to-rot varieties, among which was the still-to-be-identified Merlot. The estate would eventually become Château Mouton-Rothschild, which still makes its wine from the two Vidures, now Cabernets with a lop-sided nod to Merlot. Sadly by the end of the twentieth century the eccentric but stingy Cabernet, giver of momentous wines requires ageing. Impatient consumers now drown in a jammy sea of Merlot which is easier to grow, ripen and drink. Bank managers like to see empty cellars.

SYRAH/SHIRAZ

The Syrah or Shiraz may also be the oldest grape known to man. It thrives in the heat, produces fat bunches of sweet grapes and makes heady wines. Phoenician traders are among those suspected of taking it from Iran to France where in the terraced vineyards of the northern Rhône the most elegant Syrah is made with a squeeze of fragrant Viognier. Even so, it is under-used in France. The grape's journey to Australia and subsequent success first with 'port' then with body-builder's table wine is well documented.

MERLOT

Merlot was once the blackberry of Bordeaux, grown by men in cottages rather than châteaux. Now it makes the most expensive red wine in the world, much to the chagrin of Claret drinkers. The emergence of a hitherto unknown blending grape with limited potential has been startling. Its undoubted appeal is to the new drinkers, those who like to hoover up their wines in infancy while they are fresh and luscious. Merlot was mentioned by Faurveau in 1784, so it has been around in the Saint-Emilion and Pomerol for over two centuries. Its flagship is the pampered Petrus, half a century ago virtually unknown and worth a quarter of the price fetched by a Médoc Grand Cru. 'Because Petrus is fat, fleshy, not rigorous and penetrating like a Médoc,' Hugh Johnson writes, 'it appears to be "ready" in ten years or less. Cigar smokers … drink it in full vigour. To my mind it takes longer to become Claret. In a sense the great vintages never do.' Chilean Merlot, often the 'house red', is the place to go on the gastro pub's list. It is ridiculously easy to drink and cheap. Merlot is now the most-planted red wine grape in Bordeaux.

CABERNET FRANC

Known for at least two centuries for its dry, slaty reds, the Cabernet Franc, with its evocative smell, is the most memorable of picnic wines. But as Jancis Robinson points out, any grape that can contribute 66 per cent to the success of the sublime Cheval Blanc, not to mention the 35 per cent it donates to Château Ausone and Château Figeac, the 40 per cent to Château Canon and the 45 per cent to Château La Conseillante, has to be taken seriously.

NEBBIOLO

Nebbiolo is reputed to date from Roman times. According to legend so much did the locals admire the road menders' taste, they tarred the inside of the barrels. Nebbiolo was mentioned in the fourteenth century and in 1514 a grape called 'Nebiolium' made wine at La Morra. An acidic late ripener and mean producer, Nebbiolo demands the best land on south-canted hills. Growers like Luciano Sandrone can be seen, with family in tow, picking off the rotten grapes and removing leaves by hand as harvest approaches. The thinly fleshed grape is too subtle for some and the Cabernet is now lurking threateningly in the wings. The first battle for the heart of Barolo in the 1970s was a trite skirmish, when the young Bordeaux-trained sons of fossilised fathers demanded limited *barrique* ageing instead of pouring the tawny wines into old vats and burying the cellar key. Modern wines are fatter and fuller Barolos. But should we be celebrating the castration of this awkward individual?

SANGIOVESE

Sangiovese can be reliably traced to the sixteenth century when it was variously known as Sangiovese di Lamole or Sangiovese Grosso. It was more than likely the principal ingredient in the cheap red Florence poured in London taverns in the seventeenth century. It is a magnificent grape, but its character is often nullified by blending.

AGLIANICO AND OTHER ITALIANS

Aglianico implies Greek influence, but if this is so, why are modern Greek growers blind to its brilliance? The Romans embraced it and it is said to have played a leading role in the lauded Falernian. There are enough good examples of this grape around today to help us make up our own minds as to its place in history. It makes a strapping wine in the hands of a Mastrobernardino or an Angelo.

The excellent Negroamaro, a sturdy, sun-resistant grape is a real find. From Calabria or what the Greeks called Enotria, a place where the food and wine were good and the living was easy, the Gaglioppo makes Ciro, a mahogany wine 'with international standing', it has more than casual Greek connections and it made sparingly. It is descended from the heralded Krimisa, a wine once used to toast early drug-free Olympiads and therefore the oldest wine in the world. You can take that with a pinch of salt. Ciro Rosso, though, is a real comer, which after three years in wood and weighing in at 13½ per cent alcohol can be called Riserva. There is an old Calabrian saying: 'wine, like women, ages too quickly'. In order to prevent premature ageing the wine at least is put into Bordeaux-style *barriques*.

In England a taste for sweet reds died out years ago, but the Italians still love the smarmy Aleatico, it ages well and develops a porty elegance. In Roman strongholds like Latium and Apulia, grockles sip it in the sunny squares, their backs to a venerable wall. If it were French it would be famous.

TOURIGA NACIONAL

Touriga Nacional is a ragged trousered Cabernet, waiting nervously to leap out, top hat raised, cane a-twirl. A modest bearer of top quality fruit, the juice is now being sold as an expensive port varietal. We have yet to see great Nacional table wines but it is surely only a matter of time.

TINTA CÃO

Tinta Cão helped make the Etonian's Blackstrap, a wine of which it was said: 'It's black and it makes you drunk. What more can you ask for?' The fact that what little wine the Tinta Cão makes is nectar is failing to save it. Sadly it's not Cão but *au revoir* for this one. Not many have a good word to say about the Tempranillo. In that case why does Spain make so much lovely wine from the Cencibel, Ull de Llebre or Tinto de Toro? After all, it helps make most of the good high-grown Riojas, and the Spanish obsessive Jan Read calls it 'the Rioja grape *par excellence*'. It also adds its pennyworth to both Navarra and Ribero del Duero.

White

PINOT GRIS

Historians have Emperor Charles IV taking Pinot Gris cuttings to Hungary in 1375 for the Cistercians to plant at Badascony. The Hungarians still call it *Szurkbarat*, or Grey Monk. In 1375 they sent cuttings via Colonel Baron Lazare de Schwendi to Alsace where it became known as Tokay (the colonel had tangled with the Turks in Tokay), before whence it trickled into Germany where in 1711 it was renamed Rulander after the wine merchant Johann Seger Ruland. The Pinot Gris is known in Burgundy as Beurot, after bure, the rough material worn by monks. In the Côte de Nuits, planted in a suntrap by the grizzled Bacchanalian Yves Chaley, the Beurot makes a creamy wine. 'Waitrose want it all but I am not selling', the grower growled through a forest of stubble.

RIESLING

Riesling was identified at Russelsheim near Frankfurt in 1435, which makes it the oldest of the great white wine grapes. It is suspected it might even be a direct descendant of the wild *Vitis vinifera silvestris*. Bassermann-Jordan, growers in the Rheinpfalz since 1718, are of the opinion that the Riesling could be related to a vine mentioned by Pliny in the first century AD. In the ninth century King Louis ordered the destruction of the Trollinger, the fat black Hamburg often seen in crumbling English glasshouses, to plant Riesling. It is impossible to say if the Riesling is wholly or in part responsible for the wonderful seventeenth-century Steinweins, or the old Rhenish that at one time was the most expenisive wine of any hue sold in English taverns. It is easily Germany's key grape, making wine so different from the more popular Chardonnays and Sauvignon Blancs. Modern methods help make Spatlesen and Auslesen wines of astonishing freshness. They have a fragrance and a blade-sharp sweetness about them. It is a bewitching style that no-one outside a handful of Germans can touch. 'A teasing, tingling lusciousness', Hugh Johnson calls it.

CHARDONNAY

The Chardonnay is an ancient grape, related some say to the Muscat, the mother of all white grapes. It is said to come from the Middle East and there are native vines in Lebanon which bear a family resemblance. The Crusaders are supposed to have taken time off decapitating heathens to bring it back to Burgundy, where it settled in a village spookily called Chardonnay. 'Chardonnet, which yields the famous wine of Montrachet,' is said by Vizetelly, presumably after much intemperate gargling to be kin to the widely unknown Epinette, 'a variety of Pineau [sic] Blanc'. A hardened traveller, Chardonnay yields skinny wines in rainy Chablis and bleak Champagne, and full leaded in Californian, Australia, South Africa and Chile. It is compliant and adaptable. Can the best, and optimistically priced French Chardonnays, see off the pretenders? At a London Chardonnay tasting, featuring some serious white Burgundies, a haggle of Masters of Wine and 'press and trade representatives', confidently placed an 1983 Acacia from Carneros in California, a 1985 Cook's New Zealand and a Jean Leon's Spanish Chardonnay in the top three places. The nearest French was Leflaive-Clavoillon's Puligny-Montrachet in seventh position.

The French did the same thing in Braune. This time the judges should have known what they were about. Fourteen of them were winemakers. Acacia was again first. A French wine was second, but it was only a 1985 bog-standard Bourgogne Blanc. What did it prove? That the French are not very sophisticated tasters. Well we know that. However, they did get the Acacia, which in spite of their soul searching, wet hankies and whingeing, must have been the best wine. What is more interesting is how poorly the expensive French wines fared in both tastings.

SEMILLON/SAUVIGNON BLANC

Semillon's history is skimpy. It grows everywhere, struggling anonymously. Its main claim to immortality is the 80 per cent of nobly-rotted raisins it contributes to Château d'Yquem. But it needs the prickly gooseberry of the Sauvignon to leaven the dough. Like the Merlot it needs nursery education, lavish care and vicious pruning. Even then the wine is often as yellow and bland as margarine; it is capable of developing complexity if imprisoned in a barrel for a year or two. Cheap versions are as oily and inept as a Greek gigolo after a litre of retsina. Semillon has been trumped by the Sauvignon Blanc and now languishes in its wake. Gravesmakers are diluting its cloying sugars with more and more acidic Sauvignon Blanc. It is at its best as sweet wine, and Château Climens, who make one of the sweetest Sauternes, use up to 98 per cent of this grape. Château Lafaurie-Peyraguey and Château Siglas Rabaud use 90 per cent. Sauvignon Blanc, the least versatile of the so called great grapes, makes delicious, zippy dry wine that should be drunk young.

MUSTCAT BLANC À PETITS GRAINS

The yellow, pink or brown Muscat Blanc à Petits Grains has filled gold-scrolled goblets and chipped clay mugs for countless centuries. It is easy to see how in its wild untamed version it brought a gummy grin to the face of the first goatherd who plucked and ate it. A honey-flavoured, energy-giving fruit was perfect picnic food for nomads, so the grape became an easy travelling companion. It refreshed and rejuvenated the Phoenicians, Greeks and Romans, who swigged it on their boats and their mules; it took root in whatever warm place they planted it. Its friendly sweet wine needs no explanation. Raucous men drank it in London taverns as easily as the Egyptians did in their reed huts. Crowds in Roman amphitheatres drank it with the wrestling. Chaucer, Shakespeare and Pepys drank it. Sweet, fruitily flavoured, as scented as a nosegay, dowagers and virgins at bottle parties all loved it.Modern growers can make it unctuous or effervescent. It should always be sweet.The Aussies make brilliant Muscats as thick as marmalade and as sleep-inducing as a right hook.A necklace of golden islands in the Mediterranean make wonderful yellow versions to sip at sunset while muttering contentedly.

CHENIN

The Chenin's spiritual home is not in California, where superb examples have to be doused in oak to pretend they are Chardonnay, or in South Africa, where it is a sweating workhorse. The Chenin Blanc belongs on the banks of the great River Loire or on one of its tributaries, where it has been making honey-flavoured wine for 1,000 years. Once again, the secretive monks must take the credit, as they paid homage at Chenin's birth at the Abbaye de Glanfeuil in Anjou. The glorious history of French wine is not just the grape or the *terroir*, it's the sombre abbeys, the quiet monks, the culture of dedication to God, to unpaid slavery, study and severe dieting. These can never be replicated. At the pace of an indolent snail it took another 500 years for Chenin to find its way up the green lanes and dusty goat tracks to the castle belonging to the Squire of Chenonceaux, via his brother-in-law, the Abbot of Cormery. Word was passed around tables and taverns, helping the Chenin to speed along the middle Loire and its tributaries. Today it makes good sparkling wine but brilliant sweet and sour dessert wines and elegant bone-dry dinner wines. What other grape is as versatile? 'The Chenin Blanc is one of the world's most undervalued treasures', says Jancis Robinson.

MALVASIA

The Malvasia goes back to the Greeks – to Cyclades, Naxos, Heraklion, Candia and to Monemvasia. The Venetians dealt with Greek exporters, so unsurprisingly the grape is most often seen in Italy. It is also met with in Corsica, in the Canaries and around Rioja. Portugal, Yugoslavia, Austria and Germany also have some planted and, of course, Madeira. The jug-banging English taverns in the seventeenth century would have been downing rich, brown wines that owed some of their agreeable softness to Malvasia in the blend. It is still appreciated on Italy's islands of Lipari and Sardinia. It makes a guest appearance, at 30 per cent, in Frascati. Another Latium wine, Montecompatri, uses 70 per cent. Sadly this old vine is slowly disappearing, in spite of the fact it makes delicious big-bellied wine, especially when late ripened and drooping. A number of lesser grapes are stealing its clothes. Avoid Malvoisie, one of the cuckoos whose eggs are in fact Pinot Gris, and another Malvoisie, which is in fact the modest Maccabeu, which in turn masquerades as Vermentino, Bourboulenc and Veltliner.

PETIT MANSENG

Late harvested and rotted nobly, the Petit Manseng makes some of the most delightful sweet wine in France. Old coves and their parchment-skinned biddies have been so tremendously lit up after a few glasses of Jurancon Moelleux that the label should warn them of potential heart attacks. Jancis Robinson finds 'an exciting cocktail of fruit and spices, very ripe peaches and cinnamon toast' in the wine. The Petit Manseng is another grape threatened because it cannot make bulk wine for the masses. Sex maniacs should hurriedly unite to protect this 'prince' that turned the French novelist Colette into a writhing temptress.

49

Tasting Terms

Tommy Layton, a London wine merchant, started the Circle of Wine Tasters in 1946. It was really intended to publicise wine and kick-start its consumption after the gloom of the Second World War. A tasting sponsored by Danish food producers was held in Cyril Ray's London flat. 'There was not much wine-tasting,' Layton later recalled, 'but it sounded like a really good binge.' The place was packed with journalists and politicians, including Tom Driberg and Hugh Gaitskell. It was too dreary for Layton, so for the next tasting he introduced 'dancing girls in Portuguese costumes and some Portuguese music on gramophone records'. After a meal of dried codfish, chicken with rice, pineapple cake, Portuguese sparkling white wine and red Portuguese, the evening exploded in a swirl of Portuguese legs and 1927 port. It was 'raucously good', Layton recalled.

Most English tastings are funereal, po-faced affairs where mourners in suits stare at samples. Layton tried to inject a bit of fun, as well as introduce some new wines to a tired 1950s selection. A trade gathering, where the first few tables are groaning with pub wines is not the place to learn about wine tasting. Tasting fine wine is expensive and exclusive. That is where wine shines, if it is a finely polished thing full of quirky flavours, smelling of the people, the food, the tradition and the dirt it oozed from. No PhD, only a little sensitive appreciation is necessary. As Hugh Johnson puts it great wine 'flows over tongues and down throats of people who are not attuned to it, not receptive to what it has to offer'. 'Nothing the winemaker can do dispenses with the need for a sensitive and interested drinker,' Tommy Layton wrote. 'While the art of tasting wine can be thought, and while people can have what they call "natural" palates, these can never be as useful or perceptive as the palate which has been trained by the professional taster.'

Tasting notes were once straightforward. Sir Guy Fison, Bart., one of the first Masters of Wine, made the following tasting notes when he tasted his company's stock of fine Clarets from May to September 1966. They are models of unvarnished brevity:

Château Calon Segur 1961: Fine nose and flavour, full, long will take many years.
Château Cheval Blanc 1952: Deep colour, good nose, big wine, plenty of body but still a marked firmness.
Château Haut-Brion 1952: Dull nose and flavour, rather heavy and without character. Does not seem to match last year's tasting.

Château Leoville Poyferre 1957, UK bottled: Fair nose, lacks fruit, very severe tannin finish. Not too hopeful of it softening up.

Château Batailley 1945: Pretty nose and flavour, very well advanced, slight sweetness with tannin. Should last but it will be a bit dry.

Château Leoville Poyferre 1955, UK bottled: Lacks grip, though a certain softness and some fruit. Needs drinking.

Château Palmer 1955:Very good nose, fine flavour, fruity, long ready to drink but will be even finer.

Château Mouton Rothschild 1961: Superb nose and flavour, great balance, probably needs 10 years or more.

Sir Guy's quiet charm belied his stature in a trade where his palate was considered second to none. Though within arm's reach of all the great wines, Sir Guy liked nothing better than to drink the firm's inexpensive Rioja at home. As a youth I carried the weekly crate and stowed it in the boot of his shiny old Lagonda. He was often seen on sunny Saturdays playing golf on Richmond Park public golf course with his son, carrying an old canvas golf bag rattling with old cleeks and mashies.

The wine journalist Giles Kime writes with reference to the large number of wines gaining high marks at the International Challenge, a taste-athon annually held in London which attracts a daunting number of wines up to 9,000. A myriad of tasters of varying ability and experience sniff and spit over several days before handing out 3,600 medals. The 'liberal' marking, says Kime, 'gave the impression that the only people not to totter out of the event happily clutching a gong were the cloakroom attendants.' He went on: 'The wines that do best at blind tastings are those with pronounced flavours and aromas, rather than the more delicate, subtle examples from Bordeaux, the Loire and the Rhône.' No wonder the French are suicidal. 'Perhaps there is something about tasting ninety wines a day that encourages the judges of wine competitions to develop rose-tinted spectacles,' Kime concludes. Evelyn Waugh in his little book *Wine in Peace and War*, which he wrote for Saccone and Speed circa 1950 recalled a Bordeaux-blind tasting that was won by a man who hated wine so much he would not permit a single tannic drop to pass his lips. He merely sniffed each wine and when he came to the test he was able to name the chateau and year of a dozen clarets. He was, Waugh wrote, 'like a sanitary inspector smelling drains'.

The blind tasting terrifies everyone, especially the professional. One reason may be, as Michael Broadbent says, that 'the more one has tasted, the less clear-cut one's reactions and the less dogmatic one's pronouncements. The seasoned taster, almost always a professional, has experienced such a wide range of closely related smells and tastes, and has met with many exceptions to the rule.' The triumphant novice, on the other hand, 'having fresh perception and uncluttered vinous memory, is frequently more accurate in identification.' Broadbent, surprisingly for a professional, is in favour of the professional exposing himself to derision by taking on the dreaded blinder, even when performing in front of 'a hideously expectant audience'. The room goes quiet while the poor pro's head is on the block. He knows his fellow diners are hoping he will fluff grape, country, vineyard and vintage. It is 'most useful and salutary discipline that that any self respecting taster can be given', Broadbent says sweetly. 'It should not embarrass the professional, even if he or she gets it wrong.'

Old wine men of breeding would take a stern, polished monocled view of today's pretentious whippersnappers showing of their ill manners and pretended knowledge, especially in front of venerable old casks who had tasted more wine than they could even wet dream about. At a wine trade golf match recently a nerdish, newly crowned Master of Wine had the cheek to take the bottle of wholesome claret he had been bought by his opponent, briskly pour himself a tasting sample and proceed to ostentatiously snort, sip, smack his lips, adopt a quizzical pose, grimace and make a long, wearisome, and negative pronouncement. Unamused elders were more interested in getting down to the real business of savouring their roast and two veg and chatting to old friends. To make matters worse the MW slid away without buying the Kummel, the putting juice no wine trade golfer can manage without after a good lunch.

It is said women are better tasters than men – according to the chauvinists, this is because they get more practice sniffing babies, locating hidden cat poo, tasting soup and casting their nostrils like metal detectors over meat and fish in the supermarket. Another theory is that their heads are uncluttered with stuff from wine books. They come to the subject fresh and jargon-free, and they have the balls to say what they really think instead of beating about the bush like men do. Smokers have a real disadvantage. André Simon said there might have been smokers who could tell a Cabernet Sauvignon from a Chardonnay but he never met one. Then a lifeline was thrown to all the smokers. Fritz Hallgarten, shipper of fine and delicate German wines, always smoked a huge cigar before beginning his evaluation of the subtleties of a row of fine Rieslings. However, it seems age rather than a thick coating of nicotine is the biggest barrier to accurate tasting. Scientists have concluded that people over forty are wasting their time tasting. By then, sadly, the palate, like the teeth and the sex drive, is seriously diminished.

Then there was old Tom Davies (Dr Thomas Davies, Senior Fellow of Jesus College, Oxford between 1803 and 1844), the finest judge of wine in Oxford, who could tell a vintage accurately by the smell. 'Joyous was the Common Room steward who could call in his judgement to aid in the purchase of pipe or butt. He lived and died in his own room, consuming meditatively, a daily cob-webbed bottle of his own priceless port.'

50

A Whiff of Oak

An obsession with oak is often an attempt to bolt on a little spurious complexity to an otherwise dull wine. It is not new. Armenian merchants sent their wines down the Tigris in palmwood barrels nearly 3,000 years ago. However, it was not until the third century AD that trees were felled wholesale to ferment, age and transport wine. It was customary in the early nineteenth century to leave white wine in wood for almost as long as red. In 1809 Warre's were selling port to the Duke of Wellington that had spent a dozen years in cask. Alexander Henderson, author of *A Classic History of Wines* in 1824, refers to Château Haut-Brion spending six or seven years in wood before bottling. He also said sherry was kept in wood for four or five years and in exceptional cases up to twenty years.

Writing in 1876, Cyrus Redding thought that white Hermitage, which he considered the finest white in France, could be cellared for a hundred years without the least deterioration. This is unlikely if the wine was made from an elderly forebear of Marsanne, which Jancis Robinson says makes a 'brown-tinged wine … with a smell not unpleasantly reminiscent of glue.' On the other hand, if Redding's wine was made from the Rousanne, it does have an ageing potential and it 'can emerge as a well-preserved ten or even twenty-year-old'.

Some white wines with sufficient fruit can benefit from a year or two in cask as long as the cask again is done with the light touch the French bring to their cooking. Old tar-treated barrels are still used by the majority of non-millionaire wine makers. They allow a little oxidation to occur while reducing the woodiness in the wine. Given the choice most drinkers prefer to taste grapes. I recall a cravated French gentlemen grower shouting from the seat of his smoking old Fergie tractor as he tilled his monastic soil: 'If I want my wine to taste of oak I will use trees instead of grapes.'

The New World is curtailing its love affair with oak. Now the grape has a chance to express itself. A visit to a coopery in Meursault recently conforms that the heavy toasting demanded by some Australian growers is more delicate than before. A Chilean grower was delighted to show off his novel way of giving his wine that authentic oakiness. He strung oak lattices he had shipped from France onto lengths of wire and dangled them in the wine. 'You cannot tell the difference,' he said. The wines of Rioja white and red are the most oaked of all European wines. The oaking is delicately done. In the bad old days it was achieved by adding a phial of pure oak essence to each vat.

No-one knows what exactly happens to wine in a sealed wooden cask, though the wood in which it is imprisoned can influence the flavour and the development of the wine. Coconut-flavoured lactones give wines a taste some wine makers find indispensable. The familiar vanilla flavour is due to phenolic aldehydes. Burning the insides of the barrel on a large gas ring can increase the vanilla smell and taste. The singeing of the oak can also introduce new flavours to the wine. The oils in American oak are terpenes, present in fruits, tea and cosmetic fragrances, and would, one imagines, detrimentally affect the taste of wine. A jury of white-coated scientists are still mulling over their findings. If the wood is seasoned, good cask makers allow up to two years in the open air, the flavour of cloves is diminished and the cask more expensive. At around £500 a pop, not all winemakers can justify the expense. Amphorae added little and took little away. A cask that introduces foreign flavours to wine cannot be justified. The answer seems to be to restrict oak-ageing for the better wines and use the finest, most carefully seasoned French oaks from Allier, Nevers, Troncais and Limousin.

While over oaking can destroy the delicacy of a wine lacking fruit; Corinne Rousseanu, Scion of a Venerable Burgundy grower support the idea that hugely concentrated wines, like a 2003, benefit from 100 per cent new oak.

51

Blending, Stretching and Plain Fraud

A decree was passed in the City of London in 1419 which forbade the mixing of sweet 'Romeney' with 'wyne of Spayne, Rochell, and other remenauntz of brokyn, sodyn, reboyllid and other unthrifty wynes of other contrees'. The addition of wax 'and other horrible and unwholesome things' was also condemned. Under threat of public humiliation in the stocks, 'no man wythin the Citee may coloure nor medle with wine.' White wine was not supposed to be mixed with red nor 'Renysshe with Rochel'. Nevertheless, fraud continued and William Harold, a cooper, was convicted of attempting to resuscitate his 'feble old Spaynissh' plonk by adding gums, powdered bay leaves and other powders to 'dying wyne'. A chronicler of the time wrote: 'There is in this city a fraternity of chymical operators who work underground in holes, caverns, and dark retirements to conceal their mysteries from the eyes and observation of mankind. They can squeeze Bourdeaux out of a sloe and draw Champagne from an apple.'

In 1594 London vintners were accused of adulterating their wines with a purple dye called turnsole, alum and various 'aromatics'. Inspectors were recruited to visit cellars, warehouses and taverns to inspect all wines and condemn them if required. During Edward IV's reign a wine merchant was accused of mixing Garçon with the dregs of old casks. He was convicted at the Chancery and asked for an offence of diluting 100 tuns of wine to be considered. Taverners still sold wine that was 'unwholesome for man, in deceit of the common people, to the shameful disgrace of the officers of the City'. John Penrose, a taverner, was forced to drink a draught of his bad wine. The remainder of the cask was ladled over his head and he was banned from selling wine in London.

Unscrupulous wine shippers no longer deemed it necessary to buy wine abroad. Who needed the expense of travel, language, papers and shipping when all blenders needed was a copy of the *Treasure of Euonymus*, which was published in 1559 and advocated mixing spices with boiling water and adding alcohol?

In the eighteenth century a *Lexicon of Deceits* was published, in which the author accused publicans and wine merchants of adding sugar, sultanas, fruit juice, syrup, water, brandy, sulphur, herbs and slaked lime to Spanish, Hungarian, Italian and German wines. Books were published on how to make Madeira Malaga, Claret, Champagne and port without fretting about sun-kissed hills and ripening grapes. The peasantry couldn't care less. With their shallow pockets and sandpaper palates, they drank anything they could get hold of, including the foul rinsing of casks, according to Joseph Addison (1672–1719) in the *Tatler*, No.131, on 9 February 1709.

Sir Edward Barry reported in 1775 that 'large quantities of nominal Port Wines are made in England without any Port Wine in them at all.' William Golding wrote: 'These distortions may seem to us improper but when we look back and see the things that had been mixed with wine throughout the Middle Ages, the Renaissance and in the Puritan century, we cannot be surprised.'

P.G. Crosley reported in 1765 that in England most port sold in taverns was a blend of aloes, blackberries and turnip juice mixed with wild fruit beer and monoxide of lead, which could be lethal. In 1696 it was added to a sweet wine that killed 'more than fifty persons'.

In the late eighteenth century, while wealthy wine enthusiasts took to the newly fashionable light Bordeaux, some still hankered after the soft caress of rich fruit on the Johnston palate and the fiery kiss of alcohol which port gave. After a tongue-shrivelling tasting of the 1801 Claret vintage, Nathaniel Johnston, one of 'the most conscientious of wine merchants', sent a recipe to his Bordeaux partner, advising him to add 'three to four gallons of Spanish and three gallons of Hermitage' to the First Growth and good Second Growth wine, and 'five gallons of Spanish' to the lesser Clarets. The Château Lafitte (*sic*) of 1795, an excellent vintage, after being baptised with liberal doses of Hermitage, was considered 'the best liked wine of any of that year'.

'Parliament was petitioned', André Simon wrote, 'doctors were alarmed, and poets were despondent.' Stendhal (1783-1842), the novelist and confidant of Napoleon wrote; 'Today I saw a wine factory. Out of wine, sugar, iron filings, and some flower essences, they make the wines of every country. A personage wrapped up in dignity assured me that no injurious substances were used in the factory. I took that with a grain of salt.'

As a worrying proportion of wines shipped to England 'went off', shippers added 'stum', 'cute', or 'soot'. They were all names for boiled-down must. Honey, liquorice, 'long almonds', herring roes, Gascon wine, even port and sherry were also tried. Wines which were 'stummed' could 'trigger a loosening of the bowels, or result in barrenness in Women.'

Warner Allen states that the Château Latour 1800, a poorish year, was blended 'with an equal quantity of the passable Kirwan 1801. Lafite 1800 was mixed with Château Rausan 1801, and Margaux 1800 with double the quantity of 'an unspecified second growth'. Johnston liked his Claret young with the whiff of crushed blackcurrants on the nose. He had little time for the ripe pong of ancient wines and dismissed the 1802, less than a decade old at the time, as 'unfit for nothing but cutting port'.

When Michael Broadbent tasted the 1803 Lafite, a similar style of vintage, in 1979, he described it as 'very appealing, sound as a bell' and gave it five stars. However, a bottle of 1784 lovingly poured for him by a starry-eyed American was dismissed as 'undrinkable, with a nose like balsamic vinegar'.

Nathaniel Johnston was overwhelmed with orders for Châteaux Margaux, Latour and 'Lafitte'. Château Haut-Brion was not among the most desirable of wines at the time. One client wrote: 'I want the fullest and finest of wines.' He refused Château Latour, which he felt was inferior to Château Margaux. Johnston responded through gritted teeth. 'I assure you Sir, the liking of one of the First Growths more than another depends a good deal on fancy.' Johnson wrote to H. Guestier, his partner in Bordeaux, telling him to go easy on the adulteration, especially for First and Second Growths. Guestier was accustomed to 'helping' well-known Clarets with Hermitage, Benicarlo and Alicante. 'I think they ought to be made up very lightly this year – the first and even good seconds with no more than three to four gallons of Spanish wine and about three gallons of Hermitage,' Johnson insisted. 'The other wines need not to have more than five gallons of Spanish wines.' Even the excellent 1802 came in for a little pepping up. Johnston advised Guestier to 'make up 20 or 30 Tuns of a good Claret by mixing them with Spanish Benicarlo and good Hermitage'. One Bordeaux shipper unashamedly advertised his 'Claret' blend as 'Eight tuns of Red Vienne, made up strong and deep with new Alicant one third.'

'M. Chapoutier told me,' Warner Allen says, 'that in his grandfather's time practically the whole yield of Hermitage and Châteauneuf du Pape was destined to give colour, alcohol and body to feebler wines grown elsewhere, Hermitage being earmarked for Bordeaux, Châteauneuf for Burgundy.' 'The product called Claret in England,' Cyrus Redding wrote, 'is a mixture of several sorts of wine.' The English, with their tastuds clogged with port, could not abide 'real' Claret. It was neither strong enough nor full bodied enough. John Croft wrote that in Queen's Anne's day it was fashionable to do the reverse, temper good port with light Claret. 'When two friends met in a tavern they ordered a bottle of port and a bottle of Claret and mixed the two' he said cheerfully. Philip Percy Carnell writing in 1814 suggested a novel ingredient for revitalising sick Claret. 'Add two pecks of Claret vine leaves, powdered red tartar, rosemary leaves, six juicy oranges, brandy and sugar.'

Dubious practices are not always confined to grubby warehouses on brown factory sites. Fritz Hallgarten's *Wine Scandal*, published in 1986, shows that reputable merchants are also tainted. Transgressions are quickly forgotten and the guilty party sympathetically ushered back into the fold. Working in the cellar of a very large company in the 1970s, I well remember a trio of joyous West Indian women who did nothing else all day but scrape labels off bottles and replace them with something vaguely similar. 'Sometime we label them so often no-one knows what the hell's in them', one of the women recalled with a belly laugh. They were of course responding to a missive from an unseen hand of authority high up in his oak-panelled office.

52

Wine and Health

In 1740, a Dr Shaw penned an optimistic homily to wine. 'Wine is a light, clean, beautiful fluid of a fragrant scent and delicious flavour. It has the power to warm the stomach, stimulate the fibres, promote digestion, raise the pulse, rarify the blood, and open up all obstructions and forwarded excretions. It promotes perspiration, increased natural strength, and enlarges the faculties of both of body and mind.' Red port was good for diarrhoeas and gleets, Rhenish cleared the kidneys of stone and gravel, Mountain cured colic, but for 'a sudden flush of animal voracity', it had to be Champagne.

Before the discovery of the means to purify water, wine was safer. During the reign of Elizabeth I, the Queen, like many of her subjects, began her day with a draught of ale. For lunch or dinner she quaffed the light wines of Bordeaux and Charentes, shipped from La Rochelle, a pink and watery wine at tuppence a bottle. The royal cellars also housed Rhenish, Malmsey, Muscadine and Bastard.

In the scabrous hospitals of the eighteenth century the swill patients were fed was dispatched with gin. Dr Pringle, a medic ahead of his time, preferred wine. 'There is nothing compared with it,' he chortled manically. 'Convalescents should have a quart a day of French wine'.

The advent of the theriac was a boom for quacks. It could be a blend of anything, the more bizarre the mix the better chance of bamboozling a superstitious and ignorant public. However, to convince the educated the blend had to include a great number of ingredients – some contained up to 250. Salvatore Lucia wrote: 'The more numerous, rare and costly substances the theriacs claimed to contain, the greater the power they were believed to possess.' One of the more exotic, prepared by Pietro Andrea Mattiolo (1501–1577), contained emeralds, red coral and 'the powdered parts of vipers', mixed with very old white wine. Matthiolus's theriacs were highly respected and some were included in the *London Pharmacopoeia* of 1618 – they were in demand as official remedies until 1746. Kenelm Digby (1603–1664) had his own cure for everything; it was a powder containing ground flesh and moss from a dead man's skull marinated in white wine ether.

During an outbreak of plague, Queen Elizabeth suggested the Lord Mayor make available to the dying masses her favourite theriac made from sage, rue, elder leaves, red bramble leaves and ginger in white wine. The recommended dose was a spoonful morning and evening for nine days. Thomas Lodge, a 'Doctor in Phisicke', who published a *Treatise of the Plague*, was so out of touch with reality he advised impoverished plague sufferers to drink plenty of good Claret. Whilst incarcerated in the Tower of London from 1603 to 1616, Sir Walter Raleigh invented his own theriac from forty roots, seeds and herbs, macerated in brandy and distilled. He instructed Le Febre, his French apothecary, to put into the blend bezoar stones, pearls, coral, deer horn, amber, musk, shavings of a brittle silvery alloy, several kinds of soil and sugar.

The lucrative business of theriacs was hijacked by conmen who focused on the rich and gullible. *Theriaca Diatessaron* was specifically prepared for the less wealthy but still gullible. It contained only six ingredients – easily available berries and herbs, gentian, laurel berries, birthwort, juniper berries and honey – all compounded in wine. It 'was warranted an excellent remedy for all fevers and poisons'. The very poor gathered a few weeds from the roadside or made do with a prayer from a warty wise woman.

A famous English physician, Dr William Heberden (1710–1801), having tested some the more outlandish theriacs, both ancient and modern, came to the conclusion they were all bunkum and that the poor man with his few simple herbs was a wiser fellow after all. 'I think,' Heberden concluded, 'the intentions would surely be much better answered by giving opiates and aromatics without loading a sick man's stomach with so many other useless things.' When Heberden delivered his findings in front of a full house at the College of Physicians, his fellow doctors, many of whom had a vested interest in theriacs, dismissed his findings. In spite of loud opposition, he narrowly carried the vote to outlaw 'alexipharmic nostrums' by fourteen to thirteen. It was effectively the end of theriacs in England, but the French continued to make them up to the end of the nineteenth century.

53

Wine Taverns

Monasteries were the original bed and breakfast stops. Brewing and winemaking took place there and some religious establishments offered overnight accommodation with wine, ale and food all made on the premises, organically, too, before the term became sullied by the supermarkets. According to Frederick Hackwood in his *Inns, Ales and Drinking Customs* of *c.*1904 the tired and bewildered traveller could choose from 'the Ale-house, the Wine-house or an Inn'. Drinking lots was encouraged, particularly in Saxon times, when the last man standing upright and looking dazed was 'the most admired'. Sounds like a wine trade golf day.

The tavern was an early form of town centre wine bar, with customers going back to their own beds after a night's drinking and conversation. There was a little food to accompany the basic wines, a slab of cheese, a boiled egg or a pork pie perhaps, but no accommodation. Its origins go back to around the twelfth century. It was designed by vintners and wine merchants to serve wine, which was dearer than ale, to a better-off clientele in a more salubrious place than the numerous alehouses had to offer. Taverns were often below street level, with snugs and casks of wine on scantlings. Unlike the alehouses, many of which were iniquitous and anonymous 'holes in walls', the tavern was confident enough to have a name nailed up outside and a rush light over an open door. Although King Edgar of England (reigned 959–975) attempted to set a standard size for ale-drinking vessels in a futile effort to stamp out short measures, wine measures were not enshrined in law until the Magna Carta over two centuries later.

Walter Mapes, nicknamed the 'jovial archdeacon' and chaplain to Henry II, wanted to die in a tavern. His poem translated from the Latin makes this very clear:

> Well, let me jovial in a tavern die,
> And bring to my expiring lips the bowl,
> That quiors of angels, when they come, may cry,
> God be propitious to the toper's soul.

After a furore in 1556 about the increasing number of taverns opening up in Oxford, a defender of taverns briskly responded: 'Poor scholars will have wine, whatever the cost.' He was referring especially to Gascony, Sack and Malmsey, most of the latter from Crete and and Malaga, which were the backbone of the sixteenth wine list in the better class of tavern. A list in 1577 gave only 339 taverns in the whole country, compared to thousands of alehouses. Taverns were limited to two per small market town, up to eight for provincial towns and forty for London.

The tavern reached its zenith in the seventeenth century. It offered comfortable beds, more elaborate food, a slightly more adventurous wine list and private rooms. Before the advent of the coffee house, which sold more wine than coffee, the tavern was a comfortable and safe place for a gentleman banker, landowner or eminent physician to socialise and discuss business. The Olde Cheshire Cheese in Fleet Street, London, which date from the seventeenth century and retains many old fixtures and fittings, is said to be the nearest thing to an ancient English wine tavern in existence.

In 1285 King Edward put his signature to a roll of parchment regulating the price of wines sold in taverns. Eight pints of wine were to cost 'threepence and not dearer' and it had to be sold by the gallon, pottle or quart, 'not by the hanap', a wooden goblet of ill-defined capacity the taverner supplied. Failure to comply with the new laws, which were to be tested by highly unpopular mounted inspectors every quarter, would cause the erring innkeeper to 'play bo-peep through the village pillory'.

Besoms or 'alestakes', sometimes fully grown trees so long and thick they knocked drunken men off their horses, stuck out across the muddy streets to announce the pub was open and a new brew was ready to serve. Sometimes their great weight pulled the sides off the pub. In 1375 an Act was passed to restrict any pole that hung over the King's highway to 7ft under 'pain of paying a 40 pence fine'.

This encouraged the mounted inspectors to rein in and enjoy a leisurely time ascertaining the beer's strength and quality, and to set a price per pint based on the cost of grain. Wine and ale was to be sold in accurate pots and mugs, not by gryskin, a small drinking cup seen in taverns. A first offence meant three days in prison and a 40d fine. For a third offence a man had to leave the city. In the fourteenth century, for an outlay of one penny, a traveller could drink two 'pottles', or 8 pints of the best ale. A gallon of Claret cost six times that.

The sale of wine was regulated, with taverners permitted to sell only one sort of wine to prevent mixing. In 1353 sweet wine had to be sold exclusively sweet wine merchants, who were forbidden licences to sell any other kind. Very few citizens except tavern keepers were permitted to keep more than 10 gallons on their premises unless they were gentlemen with an income of £66 13s 4d, and a house worth at least ten times that. The popularity of the new wine meant that the old was considered *passé*, and was either dumped or given to the poor. Royal cellar clearance sales to make room for new wines were well attended, which suggests there was still a demand for more mature wines.

By the fifteenth century the tavern had become more respectable. A Venetian envoy reported to the Doge in Venice with reference to inns in and near London. 'Few people keep wine in their houses, but buy it for the most part in taverns; and when they mean to drink it a great deal they go to the tavern and this is done not only by the men, but also the ladies of distinction.' It seemed good English ale was preferable to poor imported wine, for the report adds: 'At an entertainment where there is plenty of wine, they will drink ale and beer in preference to it.' Established inns like the 'taverne of the Sonne', where Sir John Howard sipped his ale in 1464, or the Mermayd in Bread Street, were known as polite eating houses where gentlemen could play dice, smoke and eat.

In the *Canterbury Tales* Chaucer records the jolly goings-on in the Tabard:

'Our Host gave us great welcome; everyone
Was given a place and supper was begun.
He served the finest victuals you could think,
The wine was strong and we were glad to drink.'

Edward VI established the first licensing laws in 1552, with unrestricted opening hours. The Act limited the number of inns selling wine. Mill owners who wanted their men to commence work at first light supported the decree. Landlords of crumbling 'ale only' shebeens were forced to close at 9 p.m. Candle-lit snugs were ideal places to plan crime. Philip Stubbs, a sixteenth-century teetotaller who despised shady inns and the scum who 'haunted them like malt-worms' before 'disgorging their filthy stom-achs', would heartily agree with that. Unfortunately the owners of muddy back-street provincial taverns where unlikely to obey laws made in London.

'Nobody drank water because it was bilge,' André Simon said. 'It was beer and ale for breakfast and at midday, with wine in the evening. Only a peer of the realm, a qualified vintner, or a licenced innkeeper could cellar and sell wines.' The streets were broken and muddy, beggars sat on their haunches with their palms upwards. Rabid dogs sniffed lampposts, bawds offered their tainted wares, thieves slid about moon-lighting. The gold light from the tavern's candles were like a guiding star. Taverns were large and noisy, with snugs upstairs were men could 'exchange ideas on politics and religion'. Fat barrels squatted on scantlings in the lower bar. Buxom country girls filled jugs and carried them sloshing to every room. As they climbed stairs they felt the callused fingers of old men feel their bare knees as if they were testing a mare for the spavins. Men ate noisily and heartily, belching and picking their teeth with straws. Robbers might be hanged and heretics burned during the day, but at night visitors with opinions made their way to the inns where men who could neither read nor write could talk with charm and wit. Farmers exchanged market day stories, gentlemen travellers avoided the rabble and, top hats in hand, jockey-booted and with claw-hammered tailcoats, they strode upstairs to eat in peace.

The quantities of wine sold in Elizabethan taverns were gargantuan: it was all young wine, not sipped, but swilled in bumpers and at leisure. 'Although the population of England was a tenth of what it is today,' Simon said, 'more wine was imported into England than at present. In terms of wine, as of so much else, it was a golden period. Elizabeth did not overtax her subjects; she believed in their right to happiness. With the accession of James I, the State began the interference with the rights of the individual.'

In 1556 Oxford University undergraduates, who had a huge number of taverns to choose from, drank Gascon, Malmsey and Sack, 'in spite of the cost'. The labourer in his favourite dive watched cockfighting while clutching his tankard of watery ale with his toothless friends, unaware he was being frowned upon by Fynes Moryson, an early wine snob. Dabbing his nostrils with a floppy lace handkerchief, Moryson sighed: 'Clownes and vulgar men only use large drinking of Beere or Ale. Gentlemen garrawse only in Wine, while many mix sugar … And because the taste of the English is thus delighted with sweetnesse, the Wines of the Tavernes (for I speake not of Merchants or Gentlemen's Cellars) are commonly mixed at the filling thereof, to make them pleasant.'

Elizabethan Oxford University undergraduates drank like fish but when stony broke and unable to afford to visit a tavern, they had to survive in their lodgings on a diet of strawberries, oranges and glasses of Rhenish. Muscadine, Bastard and Sack were served at the better country taverns, and at yeoman farmers' rafter-shaking parties. In more sophisticated homes, guests were served wine in cups or mazers, a stemless drinking vessel, or drank it straight from the ewer it came in, the server making sure to wipe the rim of the jug first. Sweet wines were popular and were served with everything.

The Elizabethan housewife added to her endless chores that of cellar mistress. An early chronicler of the time wrote: 'It is necessary that our English Housewife be skilful in the election, preservation, and curing of all sorts of wines, because they be usually charges under her hands, and by the least neglect must turne the Husbands to much losse. Therefore, to speak first of the selection of sweete Wines, she must be careful that her Malmseys be full Wines, pleasant, well hewed, and fine; that Bastard be fat, and if it be tawny it be sweet, for the tawny Bastards be always the sweetest. Muskadine [often a blend of Bastard and Malmsey with ginger and skimmed milk added] must be great, pleasant, and strong, with a swete sent, and amber colour. Sacke should be, you shall know it by the marke of a corke burned on one side of the bung. The longer they lye the better they be.'

The sixteenth-century playwrights Beaumont and Fletcher met and collaborated in the famous writers' and actors' inn, the Mermaid Tavern, a lively place also frequented by Ben Jonson (*c.*1573–1637). John Gay (1685–1732), whose *Poem on Wine* is almost a complete wine list of the wines available at the time, was another habitué of the Mermaid. Jonson immortalised Raph, the landlord of the 'Swanne tavernne by Charing-crosse, who drew him good Canarie'. When Jonson regaled the King with such stories, 'for this drollery his majestie gave him [Jonson] an hundred poundes'.

In a pamphlet entitled *Discovery of London Monster called the Black Dog of Newgate* published in 1612 Charneco, from Lisbon, made an appearance with the usual sweet and syrupy suspects from Spain, and dry French wines called Orleance, Bourdeaux and Gascoine. An inventory of the stock held by the Mouth Tavern, Bishopsgate, London, reveals a bias towards French and Spanish wines.

	£	s	d
Fower pipes of white wine	20	0	0
Two hogsheads of old Graves wine	2	0	0

Seven hogshead of Orliance [Orleans] wine	17	10	0
One butte of Maligo wine	17	0	0
One ranlett of Sherry Sacke, contayning sixteene gallands	1	12	0
Three quarters of a pipe of old Malmsey	1	10	0
Three gallands of Alligante	0	9	0
Halfe a pipe of Malligo	6	0	0
One hogsheade of old Clarett	0	16	0
One hogshead of Graveswine	3	0	0
Halfe a hogsheade of white Orliance wine	2	10	0
Halfe a hogsheade of Graves Clarett	0	10	0
One thyrd part of a hogsheade of red wine	1	10	0
Three tunne and a halfe of emptye hogsheads, at 6s per tunne	1	1	0
Three Rochelle pipe, emptye	0	9	0
One Alligante pipe, emptye	0	3	0
One cane and funnelle for wyne	0	5	8

James Boswell (1740–1795), Samuel Johnson's biographer, while visiting the Shakespeare Inn 'to entertain ladies by whom he hoped to be entertained', ordered 'choice sherry' until he had drunk 'quite a lot'. Boswell drank so much dubious 'port' it 'boiled in his veins' for several days. It did not prevent him 'in a flow of animal spirits, and burning with fierce desire' picking up pretty girls and returning to the tavern where he introduced them to the knockout delights of sweet sherry. William Powell Frith, RA (1819–1909), whose painting of Derby Day in 1858 is one of his best, tells the story of his trip to London with his mother in 1837/38. She ordered him to stop at a likely tavern, handed him an empty bottle and told him to get the landlord to fill it with his best sherry from the cask. Innkeepers also delivered wine to nearby shops and houses. To guarantee the return of their bottles they 'had their names scratched on a glass lozenge welded to the bottle neck'.

The Hon. John Byng (1742–1813), later the fifth Viscount Torrington, criss-crossed England on the back of a horse between 1770 and 1790. He invariably holed up at taverns and liked to crack a *bon mot* or two with the local wall-eyed denizens after a plain dinner with a good bottle of wine. In the frequent absence of Claret, Rioja or anything else, this usually meant port or Madeira, both of which every dive in the land stocked. When Byng trotted on to Worksop he stopped at the Red Lion, which advertised multifarious wines and good home-made food. When the wine list was produced it offered Claret and Lisbon, as well as various ports and Madeiras. But the food was ordinary and the wine disgusting. Byng, who preferred bread and cheese to a feast and bad wine, condemned the Red Lion as 'pretentious'. At Grantham, after drinking two bottles of foul Claret, he rode away muttering that money spent on wine in such places was money thrown into the sea. One might as well ask for Champagne in Wapping, Byng muttered. On a return visit he foreswore dodgy Claret and stuck to port, which was so hallucinatingly excellent Byng was inspired to write an excruciating poem:

'Grantham, the nurt'ring school of Newton's mind,
That deals out good Oporto to mankind.'

Bumping along in wind and rain is never conducive to fine wining and dining. It was generally a case of chewing on rubbery pork chops and drinking puckering port, but Byng finally struck oil at the posh Castle Hotel in Brighton. He enjoyed 'a very good dinner of stuffed wheatears' (how many wheatears constitute a good dinner is not recorded). He crunched the miniscule birds and washed them down with decent Claret and a damn good port, the most reliable type of wine he encountered on his travels.

When James Woodforde, whose *Traveller's Diary* is described by William Younger as both 'a bedside book and a nightmare', dined at the King's Head, Norwich on 1 June 1787, he ate 'fryed soals, boiled beef, a Pudding, a fore-quarter of lamb, with cucumber and lettuce garnish', all for a shilling. At another inn Woodforde gagged on 'Roasted tongue and udder'. His diary entry was: 'I shall not dine on either again very soon.' Woodforde was a hearty eater, who dispatched the following on a Christmas Day at New College, Oxford: 'Two fine Codds boiled with fryed Souls round them and oyster sauce, a fine sirloin of Beef roasted, some peas soup, and an Orange pudding.' For the second he devoured 'a wild duck rosted, a fore Qu. of Lamb, Sallad and mince pies.' What he drank is not known.

Finding comfortable and clean bed and board was a matter of luck. John Farringdon records an unhappy experience in his 1803 *Diaries*. 'At 5 o'clock we dined and were not very pleased with our entertainment. The fowls were tough and the wines very bad. At Ross our dinners were charged at 2s 6d each – Wine 4s 6d a bottle [quite steep in a small provincial town at the time] and Brandy 6s a bottle.' Breakfast was 1s 3d with 1s for the use of the bed. Farringdon sniffed: 'The Landlord never made his appearance to us, and on the whole we were glad to shift our quarters.'

PUNCH AND NEGUS

When the Georgians mixed their 'memorable quintiles of Punch and Negus', named after Colonel Francis Negus (d.1732), the recipe was nutmeg, lemon, water, sugar and wine – they reached for anything in the cellar. According to Turberville (Vol.1, p.183), in 1741 in St James's in London Negus had a morning drink made of 'one-third Spanish wine and two-thirds milk fresh out of the cow which was milked on the spot'. The habit continued under Queen Victoria, when port and sherry were diluted with hot water and flavoured with spices. It was served to 'accompany the dancing and the card games of lower middle-class parties'. By the 1870s the hot water was replaced with a mixture of 'Chablis' syrup, lemon juice, the whites of eggs, meringue and Champagne. 'One notes with surprise,' Golding says, 'that even as late as Edwardian times, this punch had become part of the formal dinner' and was served between courses and often with roasts. It was also served with toast as a cure for a hangover.

54

Coffee Houses and Tea Gardens

The first of many coffee houses opened London in 1652. They were tranquil alternatives to rumbustious taverns and their unfragrant clientele. Bewigged businessmen, lawyers and politicians sat on soft chairs and cracked open newspapers or talked. Of course they drank coffee, as much as they could stomach without getting dizzy, 'all for a penny a day'. The coffee houses became so popular that tavern owners tried to close them down. Henri Misson de Valbourg, a visiting Frenchman, wrote: 'Making coffee annoyeth neighbours by evil smells.' There was also a fire risk. 'By keeping fire for the most part night and day, whereby his chimney and chamber might set on fire, to the great danger and affrightment of his neighbours.'

According to Hugh Johnson, 'a catalogue of coffee houses, and the groups who gathered in them, would show almost every shade of political sentiment, of literary taste, and even of commercial activity in London in the later years of the seventeenth century.' Writers, dandies, Whigs, clergy, stockbrokers and aristocrats all had their favourite coffee houses.

Coffee houses were followed by tea gardens in the eighteenth century. Andrew Barr writes: 'Their appeal was limited principally to warm, or at least dry, days in summer… They provided flowered walks, shaded arbours, a room with music for dancing, skittle grounds, bowling greens, and various entertainments.'

The English equivalent of the French *auberge*, the 'ordinary', opened in London out about the same time. Sir Walter Scott (1771–1832) wrote: 'An ordinary is a late-invented institution, sacred to Bacchus and Momus, where the choicest of noble gallants of the time meet with the first and most ethereal wits of the age, where the wine is the very soul of the choicest grape, refined as the genius of the poet, and ancient and generous as the blood of the nobles.' The best-known ordinary was Pontack's Head, established in 1666 next to the Old Bailey by a scion of the Pontac family, who owned Château Haut-Brion. It was a 'gastro tavern', with French-inspired food. The family flagship, Château Haut-Brion, at 7s a bottle, dominated the wine list. Gross-bellied lawyers crowded into the raucous atmosphere with their favoured clients, chubby, beringed fingers erect for a wine waiter. Pontac's success triggered a minor invasion of French chefs. Their presence inspired the first edition of *The Epicure's Almanac* in 1815. It was a thin volume. The French were soon matched for quality and inventiveness by Locket's, with its 'Dainties' and 'Rich Champaign' for £2 a head. The poorer citizen visited an eighteenth-century version of the burger bar, a cook shop, where for a shilling he could eat as much meat as could shovel into his guts. Beer was the only alcohol served.

The chop house was a superior cook shop. Among the best were Betty's Chop House and Dolly's Steak House, where Boswell licked his lips when he espied 'a jolly profusion of smoking, juicy beefsteaks'. The sporting gentlemen who did not mind mixing with the rabble as long as he could place a bet, ogle a spilling cleavage or watch young boxers stripped to the buff thumping seven bells out of one another in training, often frequented such places. Pierce Egan (1772–1849) eulogised: 'In this delightful place of amusement and convenience there is provender for philosophers or fools, stoics or epicureans; contemplation for genius of all denominations; and it embraces every species of science and art having an especial eye to the important art of cookery. The name, the very name alone, is sufficient to excite all that is pleasant to our senses.'

At the royal palace of Westminster normal licensing laws do not apply. Some of the seven bars are open for business as long as Parliament sits. It was near the end of the eighteenth century before provision was made to supply food and drink to MPs, when a caterer and vintner called Bellamy was recruited in 1773. Bellamy became friendly with Fox, Sheridan and Pitt the Younger and these connections helped spread the word about Bellamy's wine list. Some MPs preferred his cooking. On his deathbed, Pitt the Younger sighed before passing away: 'Oh, for one of Bellamy's pies!' Charles Dickens in *Sketches by Boz* further cemented Bellamy's place in history. According to Dickens, Bellamy's assistant, Nicholas, supplied MPs with very strong mixed drinks. This resulted in more than one drunken member draining tumblers then popping up and down swearing. When Lord Brougham spoke for three-and-a-half hours on the Reform Bill in 1831, he slugged copious quantities of mulled wine. Claret then was a whopping 10s a bottle and port and sherry both cost 6s a bottle.

MPs also gathered in Alice's Coffee House in Westminster Hall, where a sandwich and a pitcher of chilled wine cost half a crown. Some preferred to frequent 'one of the taverns that clung like limpets round the precincts of the old Palace'. MPs preparing for a long, butt-numbing sitting returned to the house clutching brown bags of food. As ministers droned, backbenchers nibbled and peeled. Those with their own teeth cracked cobnuts, the sound reverberating around the chamber like assassination attempts. Gorging members were soon up to their silver-buckled footwear in 'the nuts shells and orange peel that littered the legislature'.

Soup and fish were added to the menu in 1852 and meat in 1864, when a saddle of mutton was served at one o'clock, roast beef at two, another saddle of lamb at five, and forequarters of lamb at six. At seven o'clock members were offered lamb, beef, mutton and salmon with lobster sauce. The house Claret was a shilling a bottle. By the beginning of the First World War it had come down to 10d, with a 'light hock or Graves' at a shilling. Champagne from the plentiful 1893 vintage was 6s to 8s 6d a bottle. The exceptional 1884 was 15s.

The tradition of heavy-drinking politicians carried on into the 1960s, when MPs and their guests anually dispatched 6,680 bottles of Claret, 4,680 bottles of Burgundy, 3,300 of Graves, 3,066 of Hock, 2,800 of sherry, 2,700 of white Burgundy, 1,936 of

Champagne, 1,146 of Mosel, 863 of brandy, 640 of port (of which 490 were tawny), 3,124 of whisky and 2,600 of gin. Today those members not totally brainwashed by dead-eyed 'spinners' can carry a Nebuchadnezzar of Krug into the house like giggling schoolboys without hindrance. Not that they would dare, sadly.

55

Trenchermen and Topers

Samuel Pepys (1633–1703) described a Lord Mayor's Feast he attended in 1663. He was allocated a place among the 'merchants-strangers' with no knife, fork or napkin, just a mug and a salt cellar. At a signal to begin, the poorer guests reached into their pockets for spoons and knives. Pepys ate 'ten good dishes' and drank 'wine of all sorts'. The wine list reflected the popular choices of the day, bolstered by good ale and a mead so thick with honey and spices 'it could support an egg'.

Samuel Johnson (1709–1784) was a trencherman of gargantuan proportions. With him there were no half measures. He could either 'abstain from wine or get hugely drunk'. His friend Boswell observed: 'When at table, he was totally absorbed in the business of the moment: his looks seemed rivetted to his place; nor would he, unless when in very high company, say one word, or pay the least attention to what was said by others, till he had satisfied his enormous appetite: which was so fierce, and indulged with such intenseness, that while in the act of eating, the veins of his forehead swelled, and generally a strong perspiration was visible.' Johnson, who thickened his port with Capillaire, a heavy cane syrup, either drank himself senseless or sat moping at table not touching a drop because he was convinced alcohol would drive him mad. 'He had found that resolving to drink moderately was useless, for by the time he had drunk moderately, he no longer cared.' In old age Johnson lost all interest in wine. Like a delicate old duchess, he sipped tea because of its agreeable paraphernalia – the elegant cups and brass-bound tray, 'the necessity to be made afresh as the night advanced and as often as Mrs Thrale could be persuaded'. Johnson did not miss alcohol in his dotage. Boswell observed: 'No person ever enjoyed with more relish the infusion of that fragrant leaf.'

In the mid-eighteenth century Van Horn, a Hamburg-born merchant who had settled in the City, belonged to a drinking club which convened at the Bull in Bishopsgate. He was a committed toper, who, in spite of swallowing prodigious quantities of alcohol, only missed two meetings of his drinking club. Once was for his wife's funeral, the other for his daughter's marriage. He died hale and hearty at ninety.

At the Lord Mayor's banquet in 1782, trenchermen disposed of the following bottles: port, 438; Lisbon, 220; Madeira, 90; Claret, 168; Champagne, 143; Burgundy, 16; Malmsey and Sack, 4; Hock, 66. Napoleon Bonaparte (1769–1821) enjoyed Burgundy and his liking for Chambertin is well chronicled, even though his chef, M. Chandelier, said the Emperor preferred Bordeaux, both white and red. While in captivity on St Helena, Napoleon and his retinue drowned their sorrows with 240 bottles of red Bordeaux, 60 Graves, 30 Madeira, 150 Tenerife, 5 Champagne, 15 Constantia and 630 Cape, the wine given to the lower orders. Napoleon died in 1821. It was said that 'he ruined his stomach and his stomach killed him.'

George IV's banquets were boisterous, wine-spraying affairs with many toasts taken and much drink spilt. Dyott (1781–1845), a diarist of the time, reported: 'We had a good dinner, the very best Claret I have ever tasted. We had the Grenadiers drawn up to fire a volley in honour of the toasts.' The Prince Regent tossed back twenty-three bumpers of Madeira 'without a halt'. All present clambered onto their chairs to drink toasts to their host. Soon the immaculately braided and bemedalled governors, generals and commodores 'were so drunk they could scarce stand on the floor', let alone climb onto a rickety chair. 'It was the most laughable sight I ever beheld,' Dyott reported. 'His Royal Highness stood at the head of the table. I never saw a man laugh so in my life. Twenty men drank sixty-three bottles of wine.' It was mainly fine Bordeaux donated by the Prince.

George was a corset-stretching consumer of beef, veal, lamb, game and poultry. At his wedding his guests devoured 7,442lb of beef, 7,133lb of mutton plus the contents of his parks and henhouses. Remarkably, his other hobby was sex and he flopped his gaseous carcass over any female foolish enough to come within trapping distance. His only exercise was blundering from the table to the water closet, although he had hunted in his youth. Although he was about to meet his maker at a very acceptable sixty-seven years of age, true to type George IV weakly ordered his last supper. Staff rushed to the kitchens and returned with two pigeons, three steaks, a bottle of wine, a glass of Champagne, two glasses of port and a glass of brandy. As he lay sweating, a throbbing amoeba in his voluminous night shirt, on a fine June morning in 1830 the King opened a rheum-filled eye and whispered to his doctor 'My dear boy, this is death.'

The Duke of York was such a renowned toper that 'six bottles of Claret after dinner scarce made a perceptible change in his countenance'. Except when he fell under a passing phaeton. An equally hapless descendent of Duke of Clarence, the no brainer who drowned in a vat of Malmsey (it was more than likely Canary), when invited to dine at the Royal Household of Windsor got so legless on Champagne he was 'utterly incapable of keeping his promise to open the ball that evening with his sister Mary'.

The Sublime Society of Beefsteaks, formed in the early nineteenth century, lasted for a hundred years. 'Its members included royalty and were a model of deportment, using wine as a means to congenial discussion for its own sake.' They ordered decent port from the nearest tavern and any member demanding something different was fined 40s, unless it was toddy or punch, which were allowed. Less formal societies recruited racy gentlemen eager 'to spend most of their time drinking a muddy kind of beverage, red wines and other sophisticated liquors with a fury and intemperance which consumed many noble estates.'

Lords Dufferin, Panmure and Blayney could effortlessly swallow half a crate of port each at a sitting. John Mytton was the best-known tragic buffoon of all, thanks to a biography of him by his friend Nimrod, also known as Charles James Apperley. Mytton was almost weaned on port and had three pipes sent to Cambridge. Throughout his life he had a bottle of port within reach, beginning with one while shaving with a cut-throat razor in the mornings. A loyal and generous soul, Mytton was continuously drunk for twelve years. He had more bottom than Cyril Smith and would tackle any insane caper, usually with disastrous results. One attempt at jumping a seven-bar gate in a gig pulled by two skittish thoroughbreds resulted in injured horses, a smashed gig and a seriously injured friend. Among the sporting eccentrics of the nineteenth century Mytton was a hero. His life was short but dripping with adrenalin. He even managed to be elected to parliament as the member for Shrewsbury in 1819 with a huge majority. He repaid the electorate by visiting the house once. He died at thirty-eight, having 'contrived to live out his short span with as much good humour as the ravages of drink and the importunities of his creditors allowed.'

Atop a windy Dublin mountain sits the gaunt remains of the local branch of the Hellfire Club. It is grizzled and grey like the skull of a pathetic giant. For two and a half centuries they terrified small snotty boys gazing from their bungalow windows and secretly thrilled colleens in headscarves pedalling home from Legion of Mary meetings. John Wilkes, also known as John of Aylesbury, a professed 'votary of Venus before Bacchus', and his hedonistic brethren were serious drinkers gamblers, and womanisers in the mid-eighteenth century. They frequented isolated houses and partied until they collapsed, as wrung out as old dishcloths. Records show that one bottle of Claret per man, less than half what is expected of the modern rebellious teenager, was enough to gain respect in the Hellfire Club, but some chaps were quite capable of putting away as much as six bottles, switching from Claret to port to Carcavelos.

Irritating as it may be to total abstainers, or pussy-footers as George Saintsbury called them, insane indulgence in wine did not always mean an early and painful death. On the contrary, Lord Chaplin was just one of a number of prodigious drinkers and diners who lived well beyond his Biblical expectation. Chaplin was still hunting with the Cottesmore five days a week at eighty years of age and weighing over eighteen stone. When he wasn't hunting, Chaplin was trudging over the Sutherland hills. He was pursuing foxes with the Pytchley until a year before he died penniless at the age of eighty-two.

When Peter the Great (1672–1725) visited England he stayed with his party at Godalming. Thirteen sat down to supper. They ate five ribs of beef weighing three stone, a sheep, three–quarters of a lamb, a shoulder and a loin of veal, eight pullets and eight rabbits. With this they drank thirty bottles of Sack, twelve bottles of Burgundy, unlimited beer and twelve pints of mulled Sack before retiring for the night. Did they wake chaste, ill and guilty? Come on, they were Russians. Next morning breakfast they had six bottles of brandy, half a sheep, 19lb of lamb, seven dozen freshly laid eggs, ten pullets and a dozen chickens.

56

Wine and Sex

Opinion is divided as to the aphrodisiacal powers of wine. It certainly bulldozes priest-built walls and levers upward the heavy metal manhole covers that lead to many a forbidden and fragrant garden. 'Where there is no wine,' said Euripides, 'there is no love.' However, Aristotle warned that, 'too much drinking makes one very improper for the acts of Venus.' Ovid (43 BC–c.AD 17) said wine 'warms the blood, adds lustre to the eyes, gives courage and makes men apt for passion'. Plutarch (c.AD 46–after 120) warned women off wine, as it led to loose behaviour. It was okay for men and though. Augustus (Emperor in AD 475) brought in the death penalty for women who drank and then committed adultery. He became so fed up with his daughter's drinking he had her sent into exile.

What constitutes the correct amount of wine? That area between feverish expectation and snoring? Herbert Bass writes: 'Besides loosening inhibitions, wine slows the male orgasm, to the enduring gratitude of both parties.' Arnald the Catalan (c.1235–1311), a pioneer in the use of wine for medicinal purposes, had a recipe to make female partners more beautiful and give them 'a white, subtle and pleasant complexion. Put ginger and cinnamon bark into wine, distil it like rose-water', then ladle it into them.

In our knackered and complicated times, only tasting notes get saucier. Olivier Lapidus, a Frenchman, navel-gazed in 2002: 'The glass of Bordeaux in front of me is posing like a size-6 model. My eyes touch it but do not go through it. The glass creates a certain sensuousness. One might even say it imbues taste with sexuality. I watch the wine as it swirls. I taste it, taste it again. I wait for it to oxygenate. I await that state of ecstasy. I am no longer the same, nor completely another. I love Bordeaux wine – I understand it.' What cobblers.

Andrew Barr is on a similar tacky tack. 'In order that the taste of fine wines should be enjoyed most fully, it is necessary to suck in air in order to aerate the wine in the mouth. This is done by wine-tasters at professional tastings, but if they were to extend this practice into a social context it would be condemned – because sucking is a sexual act.' Little wonder then that the spottier breed of wine scribblers, brought up on a diet of late night porn and lavatory-obsessed 'comedians', are more lightly to grope for the description 'sexy' when they have nothing more interesting to say about a wine. Liquid Viagra. Pure sex in a glass, yawn, yawn, zzzz....

Hugh Johnson and Michael Broadbent, as you would expect, are more elegant and subtle. With reference to the early Egyptians and their sensuous attitude to wine and women, Johnson writes: 'Painting after painting expresses with brilliant vitality the pleasure they took in it. Scenes of feasting are sometimes serene, elegant, decorative, sometimes boisterous and licentious… They are scenes so graphic, of girls gossiping, … of serving girls, who are usually all but naked, that one feels like an eavesdropper on their perpetual partying.' Broadbent commented after tasting Cheval Blanc 1929: 'ripe, delicious, charming. Like Marlene Dietrich, as I remember her in *Cabaret* in the 1950s.' Broadbent returns to the sexy but tantalisingly fridgid image of the German *chanteuse* in more than one tasting note.

The Talmud warns: 'One glass of wine makes the woman pretty; two glasses and she become hateful; at the third glass she lusts invitingly; at the fifth she becomes so excited that she will solicit an ass upon the streets.' According to the Shastas of the Hindus, wives were allowed only to smell wine but mistresses were encouraged to drink it.

57

The Decanter

Nowadays, with screw caps for instant access, even pulling a proper cork is too much of a chore for the impatient wine guzzler igniting his caravan-sized barbecue. It is, however, still a prerequisite in Surbiton. The auction oddment with its artfully tatty label and unknown provenance has sat for a week in the fitted kitchen. The cork glistening with wine diamonds is drawn slowly. With gynaecological tenderness, the host in stiff and funny Napa Valley bib begins the breathtaking business of decanting. The decanter is immaculate and stench free, the antique funnel and muslin are in place, the hand is steady, the browning stream starts. Dry mouthed, the pourer watches it fall. Oops! too late, the bleeding sediment has beaten him to it. The wine is cloudy, but it will fall if he keeps it a week. Can't wait: they won't notice. A small tasting is poured. Is it good, bad or terrible? Sniff. It is worth the fifty quid, isn't it? They are at the door. Quick chuck it down the sink and unscrew a Aussie. Who can resist the mystery of decanting?

The earliest mention of of a decanter, or 'decantor', is in a 1690 pottery advertisement in the Ashmolean Musuem. John Kersey, in his *New English Dictionary* of 1701, describes a decanter as 'a bottle made of clear flint glass for the holding of wine to be poured off into a drinking glass'. They were more elegant than the jet-black knobbly jugs wenches used to take wine from the barrel to the tavern table.

As so much good wine was still shipped in bulk, and bought by wealthy gentlemen with cellars, something more interesting than a ewer was required. Glassblowers and engravers got to work. The decanter changed shape at the will of fashion and its maker. The balloon shape arrived in and around 1730, to be followed by the short shoulder, and the tall shoulder emerged between 1750 and 1770. Some 'decantors' were lavishly decorated with scrolls, curliques, grapes and vine leaves. They changed shape again, becoming narrower, more elegant. The barrel shape was fashionable between 1775 and 1825, with the cylinder appearing near the end of the eighteenth century.

The early use of clear decanters was to show off the colour and clarity of the wine. Then with the invention of the bottlescrew, a primitive cousin of the corkscrew, when wines were swamped in peaty sediment, the decanter came into its own. Decanters in many shapes and designs were hand-crafted in factories in Bristol, London, Stourbridge and Waterford in Ireland from the mid-eighteenth to the mid-nineteenth centuries. The French were slow to take up the idea and even today there is no word in the French language for decanter, only the rather plebeian *carafe*. The

French are still not keen on decanting. André Simon said even for unstable old Clarets and venerable Burgundies, the French won't decant, whatever the wines birthright majesty. The opposite is the case with the English. They decant Piat d'Or. A nice idea is to decant, then rinse out the old bottle and pour back the cleaned up wine. Dusty old bottles with faded labels look good. 'When decanted, Claret is best served in perfectly white stemmed glasses, unadorned, slightly in-curved and large enough to hold a generous measure,' Simon says.

But Samuel E. Morrison writing in 1938 said decanters of Port were traditionally slid clockwise around the table 'with the sun' because 'Port will take offence at being circulated against the sun, and go sour on you'. He also suggested 'a light Sherry as a mouthwash' after a couple of goes at the circulating decanter. The 'victim' who finished the last dregs the 'buzz', before another full decanter slid ominously towards him was entitled to an extra glass.

Glasses with a dishwater gleam are very recent in wine's timespan. Shiny glasses are not necessary. Remember the little flat-capped French grower taking a Woolie's tumbler from under the roof of his cellar, wiping out the spiders with a dirty hand, and then filling it with wine foaming from the cask. The *Sunday Times* coach party might recoil.

The Egyptians, Greeks and Romans used wood, horn, onyx, silver and gem-encrusted gold. According to Thomas Haywood in his *Philocothonista, or the Drunkard Opened* in the seventeenth century 'receptacles were hewn from elme, some of box, some of maple, some of holly.' There were 'mazers, broad-mouth'd dishes, moggins, whiskins, piggins, cruizes, ale-bowles, wassell-bowles, court-dishes, tankards, kannes, from a bottle to a pint, from a pint to a gill. Others had leather, but they are most used among the shepherds, and harvest-people of the countrey; small jacks we have in many ale-houses, of the citie and suburbs, tip't with silver, besides the great black jacks and bombards at the court. When the Frenchmen first saw them, they reported at their return into their countrey, that the Englishmen used to drinke out of their Bootes. We have besides, cups made of the horns of beaste, of cocker-nuts, of goords, of the eggs of ostriches, others made of the shells of divers fishes brought from the Indies, and other places, and shining like mother of pearl. Come to plate, every taverne can afford you flat bowles, prounet cups, beare bowles, beakers and private householders in the citie, when they make a feast to entertain their friends, can furnishe their cupboards, with flagons, tankards, beere-cups, wine-bowles, some white, some partly gilt, some gilt all over, some with covers, some without, of sundry shapes and qualities.'

58

Wine Writers: Necessary Parasites

Before Michael Broadbent, Hugh Johnson and Jancis Robinson, books on wine were scarce. Classical scholars, water engineers, retired judges, redundant schoolteachers and out-to-grass diplomatic correspondents penned most of what was available. A few were written by wine men; Charles Walter Berry, Hugh Rudd, Ian Campbell, André Simon, Harry Waugh and Tommy Layton, while others were self-indulgent memoirs about fantastic food and amazing wines shared with beautiful friends. They were teeth-grittingly useless if you were a penniless apprentice sucking your pencil at the Vintner's Hall trade exams in the 1960s.

One book that changed hands quicker than *Lady Chatterley's Lover* at the time was *The Science and Technique of Wine*, by Lionel Frumkin, a fourth-generation wine merchant. His editor wrote: 'There is a complete lack of the printed word in English on the subject of the science and technology of wine, and students are handicapped because of it.' Frumkin's book was cheaply produced and illustrated with drawings of insects with names like Rhynchite. The only other useful material at the time were the wafer-thin series of lectures written by strawberry-nosed old shippers, and book-lets by Luke Bayard, not as you'd think a consumptive Country and Western singer from Nashville, but the *nom de plume* of the plump and ruddy-faced John Mahoney, secretary to the Wine and Spirit Association of Great Britain.

Wine writing was unromantic and plain then. No-one used 'mid-palate', 'tobacco leaf', 'lead pencil', ' wild raspberries', 'Maraschino cherries', or least of all 'leather', 'vibrant', 'muscular' or 'sex on a stick'. Old wine merchants hung their noses over a glass primed with mature Claret, sniffed and said nothing. They may have been knocked out by the quality, but they were more likely to be pleased the wine they had purchased in a cold cellar in Bordeaux as an inky mouthful was developing nicely because they had a few several hundred cases of it.

Hugh Johnson comes across as the Corinthian golfer who plays with hickory-shafted clubs tied with string, uses scarred Pinnacles and still plays to five. His books have been hugely influential in introducing beginners to bottles, labels, grapes and flavours. His simply asks: would you drink another bottle? Johnson, without pomp, pointed the way, leaving the nonsensical stuff to a tribe of foot soldiers who came after him. Although the nearest he got to working in the trade was helping out on a van at Christmas, Johnson's series of books, starting with *Wine* in 1966, marked him out as a man with a knack for research and getting the fruits of it over in a tasty way. In a country starved of attractive, down to earth digestible, information it was an immediate bestseller. *Wine* encouraged thousands to leave the reliable but boring branded wine on the shelf and try that obscure Italian from Calabria, or the hand-crafted Riesling made by some old lederhosened baron in a fairytale Schloss on the Rhine. Johnson's *Pocket Wine Book*, which sells around 400,000 copies annually, has made millions of ordinary people think they are wine experts. It has made him the most widely read writer on wine in the world. Stuffed with cogent one-liners on every wine worth seeking out, it is the one to slyly palm when bemused by a phalanx of bottles, or confronted by an uppity waiter.

Johnson's *Atlas of Wine*, which followed in 1971, was another triumph, an essential tool which enables wine lovers to organise their holidays in the wine regions and walk among the vines. My own first edition was so abused it ended up in shreds and covered in wine stains. Johnson doesn't hector, he gives information. Now with the bus pass beckoning, it's no more 'mister nice wine guy'. Sick of the modern bunch of pseuds with more bull than you'd meet at a *corrida*, Johnson, the Eric Cantona of wine writing, asks mysteriously: 'Do we need to know the water levels of the Andes?' He is more likely; 'Think of a paper-white glass of liquid, shot with greeny gold, tart on your tongue, full of wild-flower scents and spring-water freshness. And think of a burnt-umber fluid, as smooth as syrup, as fat as butter and sea-deep with strange flavours. Both,' Johnson intones with the reverence of an old priest slipping First Communion wafers into mouths of white-veiled children, 'are wine.'

Michael Broadbent (b.1927), began his blessed career as a 'spud basher, bottle label-ler and van driver' with the eccentric Tommy Layton. It was Layton who, 'spurred on by Broadbent's enthusiasm', encouraged the lad to keep a tasting book, which the young trainee 'accurately and without prodding, kept written up, in the modern italic calligraphy so popular in Public Schools'. Broadbent went on to publish *The Great Vintage Wine Book* in 1980, a salivating feast of wonderful old wines he tasted, mostly at Christie's, but also around the world. In America, he is welcomed as a Messiah.

Twenty years later another big beast entered the jungle: Robert Parker Junior, an American lawyer. Continuing the golfing analogy, Parker seemed the sort of chap who arrives early on the practice range and sweats buckets moving the driving range sod by sod. He will have the latest Tiger Woods bigheaded driver, with a woolly squirrel's-head cover. If Johnson doesn't do narrow-eyed earnestness, Parker Junior invented it. The American is undeniably industrious and the trade uses his exhaustive application to tasting and re-tasting young wines to sell their *en primeur* wines. In this area he is influential, a fact that winds up Brits.

We do despise his much-criticised marking system, but the French growers love it, but only if they agree with his evaluation of their wines. With Parker's 100-point rating system, 'the most repugnant wine of all' gets 50 points just for turning up. Why not start at 50 then? And what was wrong with the little plastic vintage charts André Simon invented and Gordon's Gin gave out in the 1950s? Wine then was judged out of 7. 'Repugnant' got 3, light quaffers 4 and 'the most glorious, perfect gustatory experience', 7. The English wine trade was skewered when Simon's plastic wind-screen scrapers achieved wide distribution. No longer could wine merchants palm off ropey wines. Even the small, out-of-the-way country hotel in the Highlands was able for the first time to 'wave away such duds as 1925 Clarets, 1930 Burgundies, and 1936 Rhine wines'. 'Celluloid', Layton wrote, 'is a most inflammable material. It is doubtful if so small a strip can ever have generated so much heat.' Parker can probably identify with Simon.

Stung by the criticism, especially from Hugh Johnson, Parker retorted: 'An unhealthy legacy of English critics is the fallacious belief that for a wine to be considered serious and profound it must have the ability to improve in the bottle.' Hang on, try telling that to those who have drawn the cork on a great wine that has been allowed to develop the beautiful, complex, multi-faceted traits only long and sensitive cellaring can bring. Good wine must not be drunk when it is consumed too young, acne-spotted and wearing a thong. Rebellious old growers might as well chuck their great-grandfather's traditions on the bonfire and recruit Michel Rolland, if they can afford him. Wine should not be allowed to go the way of Coca-Cola. Jancis Robinson resents trends in Bordeaux that 'without any shadow of a doubt is making more and more wines in the Parker mould, rather than being absolutely true to their geographical origins.' The British, Robinson says 'who of all nations have managed to establish a reputation for connoisseurship' are being 'transformed into a satellite of zombies, buying what someone else tells to.' No wine enthusiast wants Barolo, to be made like raspberry jam.

Jancis Robinson is the most widely read female writers. She adds a touch of logic to an otherwise feverish and self-opinionated male activity. Apart from her savvy and straight-talking columns in international magazines and in trade journals, Robinson has produced a series of books. Her *Vines, Grapes and Wines* is a fascinating study of a bewildering subject and a joy to dip into, while the magnificent doorstop, the *Oxford Companion to Wine*, which she edited, gathers so much information between covers it has become the anorak's bible. Robinson's big and startlingly red-rimmed glasses on television put her in the category previously occupied by those icy librarians in 1950s films and made half blind women sexy. Attacked by the barbarous Parker over some reasoned remark she made about Château Pavie, the usually cool and self deprecating Robinson, with nails spread, went for the American's ample jugular, much to the delight of her supporters.

Among the current batch of wine writers there are an encouraging number of Masters of Wine who are also wine merchants, David Peppercorn and Serena Sutcliffe among them. To see the plethora of wine books now on the market covering every aspect of wine, often in nose-bleeding depth, it is hard to imagine the dearth forty years ago. Hugh Johnson jemmied open the sluice gates. Now the wine consumer thinks he know more about wine now than those who make it.

59

The Future

In spite of black clouds ominously positioning themselves over the world's wine growers and unbuttoning their flies, growers are frenetically planting from France to Chile, Mexico and Dorking. But the fact is that for the past thirty years or so we have been drinking less. Sure, the British, Danes, Japanese, Indians and Chinese are unscrewing a few more metal caps but the French and Italians are no longer the heroic gully emptiers of yore and, with the Spaniards, drink litres less than they used to. French children, who once slid easily from nipple to *vin de pays*, now go straight to Bacardi Breezers via Coke. Lunching in a back alley bistro in Reims recently, I was the only punter drinking wine. The place was packed with worried Gillette sales-men smoking and clutching their filofaxes. In suits and eye-watering neckties they sat upright at the bar, nervously sipping Badoit and gazing at their balance sheets, while abstractedly forking vegan salads. Stringent new drink-drive laws, diet concerns and jogging have made the French teeter on the teetotal. One can understand why embattled growers are marching in protest. The French wine industry is convinced the government is determined to stamp out wine altogether. No longer do we see lorry drivers enjoy three-hour lunches with a carafe apiece in Relais Routiers before hitting the roads, not to mention the tourists.

Enraged French growers paraded noisily in Bordeaux, Burgundy and the Loire, grovelling for financial help. Many are staring into the abyss of bankruptcy. No-one appears to want French wines. They are out of fashion, leaving growers hurt and confused. Ambitious growers from the New World are pushing the French into the gutter. Too conservative and too pompous for too long, the French are on the run. The problem of collapsing wine sales and the resultant overproduction is not just French, it's a worldwide problem. The Australians, so cocky and successful in England, are among the worst hit. Huge harvests from newly planted vineyards are sold. New wineries opened on a wave of Aussie fizz and misguided optimism. Now growers are sitting on their verandas sipping XXXX's, while contemplating acres of ripe grapes rotting with no-one interested in buying them, not even at a quarter of their normal price. In the Riverland region growers who trousered £340 a ton only twelve months ago were recently offered an insulting £60 a load. 'Some growers are heading towards bankruptcy', said Chris Green of the Riverland Winegrape Growers Association. New Zealanders and Californians will soon be in the same boat, fol-lowed by the Chileans and Argentines, who are both building vast new wineries and planting new ground. Their wines are delicious and they are seeing off the French, but it is a shrinking market. The French make better Pinot Noir, Cabernets, Syrah,

Merlot, Chardonnay, Semillon and Chenin Blanc than anyone on earth. We all enjoy Chilean but when we want to pretend we are millionaires we drink French. Slowly drawing long, bloody corks on fine Burgundy or great Claret thrills like no other wine can, no matter how good.

The survivors must turn to making wines the public want and at the right price. But they must also continue to make wines with bite, flavour and an alcohol level that does not put the drinker in a coma. Many small growers, who have been making ordinary wine for generations to pay off the bank manager, will meekly walk cap in hand to the blood spattered wall, their wive's aprons billowing in the cold breeze, their children amused and mystified.

In Britain we are returning to the mediocre ad-man's plonk of the 1960s. Mateus Rosé, Blue Nun and Black Tower have been revamped and sales are up. Conglomerates reflect the vulgar excesses of our time with wines like 'Old Git Red' and 'Old Tart's White', 'The Scraping of the Barrel' and 'Gnat's Piss'. Names have got nastier. In the past there were lots of nuns, bishops and kind old monks. Now the shelves yell 'Fat Bastard' at some inoffensive pensioner trying to find something that goes with Complan. After all the years of Oz, Serena, Gilly, Jancis, Hugh, Robert and the rest, the poor old punter gets no assistance from the pimpled shelf stacker.

For the first time in history, France is reduced to distilling some of her better wines. By 2006 Americans may be getting their own back by filling their gas guzzlers with petrol that includes a pichet of French Chardonnay or Pinot Noir. Olivier Gibelin, (a troubled grower in the over-productive Costieres de Nimes),' tilts a glass of deep red wine, sniffs and sips at a table set between the 15ft-tall concrete vats of fermenting grape juice in is rustic winery. 'Do you want to try what will be going into your tank?' he asks ruefully, pouring a visitor a glass. 'If my father could taste what I am turning into alcohol, he'd turn over in his grave.'

But regardless of the machinations of the marketing men, Luddites will continue to savour the smooth elegance of Claret, the tarry subtleties of a Barolo, the wood-polished silkiness of a mature Rioja and the meaty rusticity of old Burgundy. What genuine wine lover will not grin idiotically as he or she finds an arthritic, shoulder-level red in a mixed case of Soave and Emva Cream purchased for a fiver at a farmhouse auction? Easing out the crumbling cork crumb by crumb they sniff a fetid nose and gargle on faded charms before deciding the old wine has enough left to stimulate discussion among good friends.

Acknowledgements

I am indebted to Bill Mason, wine buyer of Bentall's of Kingston for getting me started in the wine trade, and giving me my first foreign assignment, a dismal, grape picking trip to Chablis in 1963. The grapes melted on the vine, but the wine maker performed a miracle. He turned dish water into limpid Chablis. Since then I have enjoyed a fascinating adventure, travelling, tucking into interesting food and making lots of lively, red nosed friends. I want to raise a schooner of sack to Ellis's of Richmond and Charles Kinloch of park royal. We were behind Guinness' brewery at the time and shared yeasts when we were both bottling.

Credit is due to Sir Guy Fison, Bart, M.W. and his team for many enchanting opportunities to skive and eavesdrop in the tasting room, and 'high fives' to Charles Sanderson, my erstwhile and unbeatable golfing partner and oldest wine trade mate, for so many inspired after-lunch matches.

Via my ouija board I send felicitations to the incredible eccentrics of the 'sixties wine trade, and, fittingly, to the Wine & Spirit Association of Great Britain, for their lectures and exams. I salute wine growers everywhere and every wine drinker with whom I have shared a bottle. I am especially grateful to writers, artists and poets from the dead to the near dead, whose works I have unashamedly pillaged.

For help in sourcing illustrations and other material, I thank my wife Heather, my son Lawrence Hurley, Brian Joy, John Williams, Tanner's and Berry Bros., and a phalanx of librarians and archivists. Finally, to Holly Bennion and James Howarth at Tempus Publishing, who have worked wonders to bring this blind and groping infant into the world. Any mistakes are mine.

Bibliography

Books

Ainslie, M. *An Outline History of the Wine Trade*, c.1960

Anderson, B. *Vino, The Wines and Winemakers of Italy*, London, 1982

Apuleius, L. *The Golden Ass*, Penguin Classics, 1990

Arbiter, T.P. *The Satyricon*, This Edition, London, 1986

Arlott, J. *Krug, House of Champagne*, London, 1976

Avery, P. & Heath-Stubbs, J. *The Ruba'iyat of Omar Khayyam*, London, 1979

Ball, A. (ed.) *Food of Love*, London, 1971

Barr, A. *Drink, A Social History*, London, 1998

Baus, H.M. *How to Wine Your Way to Good Health*, New York, 1973

Benson, R. *Great Winemakers of California*, California, 1977

Berry, C.W. *In Search of Wine*, London, 1935

Bespaloff, A. *The Fireside Book of Wine*, 1977

Black, J. *Eyewitness, The Who*, London, 2001

Boswell, J. *The Life of Johnson*, London, 1906

Bradford, S. *The Englishman's Wine*, London, 1969

Brandwood, G., Davidson, A. & Slaughter, M. *Licensed to Sell*, 2004, London

Brears, P., Black, M., Curbishley, G., Renfrew, J., & Stead, J. *A Taste of History: 10,000 Years of Food in Britain*, London, 1993

Briggs, A. *Haut-Brion*, London, 1994

Briggs, A. *Victoria Wine and the Liquor Trade*, London, 1985.

Brillat-Savarin, J.-A. *La Physiologie du Gout*, London, 1994

Broadbent, M. *The Great Vintage Wine Book*, London, 1980

Broadbent, M. *Wine Tasting*, London, 1968

Brook, S. *Bordeaux, People Power and Politics*, London, 2001

Burke, T. (ed.) *The Book of the Inn*, London, 1932

Busby, J. *Journal of a Tour*, facsimile edition, London, 1979

Busby, J. *Manual for Vineyards and Making Wine*, facsimile edition, London, 1979

Busby, J. *Treatise on the Culture of the Vine*, facsimile edition, New South Wales, 1979

Butler. R. & Walkling, G. *The Book of Wine Antiques*, 1995

Carcopino, J. *Daily Life in Ancient Rome*, London, 1941

Carr, J.G. *Aroma and Flavour in Winemaking*, London, 1974

Chaucer, G. *The Canterbury Tales*, modern prose rendering by David Wright, London, 1965

Chesterfield, Lord. *Letters*, World Classic Edition, Oxford, 1992

Christie's Wine Companion, ed. P. Matthews, London, 1987

Clough, A.H. (ed.) *Plutarch's Lives*, vol.1, London, 1864

Cocks, E. *Feret, Bordeaux and its Wines*, 15th edition, Bordeaux, 1998

Cooper, G. *Your Holiday in Spain and Portugal*, 1957

Dawes, F.W. *Not in Front of the Servants*, London, 1973

Dayagi-Mendels, M. *Drink and be Merry, Wine and Beer in Ancient Times*, Jerusalem, 2000

Deighton, Len (ed.) *Drinks-man-ship*, London, 1964

Delaforce, J. *The Factory House at Oporto*, London, 1979
Dervenn, C. *Madeira*, London, 1955
Debuigne, G. *Larousse des Vins*, Paris, 1984
Elderfield, E. *Kings and Queens of England and Great Britain*, Devon, 1966
Faith, N. *Latour*, London, 1991
Faith, N. *Victorian Vineyard*, London, 1983
Forbes, P. *Champagne, The Wine, the Land and the People*, London, 1979
Francis, A.D. *The Merchant Venturers, The Wine Trade*, London, 1972
Frumkin, L. *The Science and Technique of Wine*, London, 1964
George, R. *The Wines of Chablis*, London, 1984
Gibbon, E. *The Decline and Fall of the Roman Empire*, London, 1985
Ginestet, B. *Sauternes*, Paris, 1990
Girouard, M. *A Country House Companion* , *c*.1980
Gwynn, S. *Burgundy*, London, 1930
Halasz, Z. *Hungarian Wine Through the Ages*, Budapest, 1962
Hallgarten, F. *Wine Scandal*, London, 1986
Hamblyn Book of Wines, The, London, 1975
Hammond, P.W. *Food and Feast in Medieval Engand*, Gloucester, 1993
Harrison, G. *Bristol Cream*, London, 1955
Hawker, C.E. *Chats about Wine*, London, *c*.1920
Healy, M. *Claret, and the White Wines of Bordeaux*, London, 1934
Healy, M. *Stay me with Flagons*, London, 1941
Hogg, A. *Traveller's Portugal*, Chichester, 1986
Hogg, A. (ed.) *Wine: My First Anthology*, London 1970
Howkins, B. *Tokaji*, London, 1999
Hinkle, R.P. *Central Coast Wine Book*, USA, 1980.
Hinkle, R.P. *Napa Valley Wine Book*, USA, 1979
Hurley, H. *The Pubs of the Royal Forest of Dean*, Herefordshire, 2004
Hurley, J. *A Ross Anthology*, Herefordshire, 1999
Hurley, J. *Wine for Game and Fish*, London, 1986
Jeffs, J. *Sherry*, London, 1992
Johnson, H. (ed.) *The Pan Book of Wine*, London, 1964
Johnson, H. *The Story of Wine*, London, 1989
Johnson, H. *Wine*, London,1966
Johnson, H. *The World Atlas of Wine*, London, 1994
Johnson, H. *Wine Companion*, London, 1989
Kazantakis, N. *Zorba the Greek*, London, 1952
Latimer, P. *Sonoma, Mendocino Wine Book*, 1979
Lausanne, E. *The Great Book of Wine*, 1970
Layton, T.A. *Winecraft*, London, 1959
Layton, T.A. *Wine's my Line*, London, 1955
Liger-Belair G. *Uncorked, the Science of Champagne*, Princeton, 2004
Livingstone-Learmonth, J. & Master, M. *The Wines of the Rhône*, London, 1978
Lloyd-Hughes, T. 'The Queen's Pub', *Wine and Food* magazine, Autumn 1967
Love Peacock, T. *Gryll Grange*, Gloucester, 1984
Lucia, S.P. *A History of Wine as Therapy*, USA, 1963
Maxwell Campbell, I. *Reminiscences of a Vintner*, London, 1950
Maxwell Campbell, I. *Wayward Tendrils of the Vine*, London,1948
Mendelsohn, O. *The Dictionary of Food and Drink*, London, 1966
Monimpex, *Wines from Hungary,* Budapest, *c*.1970
Morny, C. (ed.) *A Wine and Food Bedside Book*, London, 1972
Morton Shand, P. *A Book of French Wines*, London, 1964
Ordish, G. *The Great Wine Blight*, London, 1972

Parker, R. *The Wine Buyer's Guide*, London, 1993
Paronetto, L. *Chianti, The Story of Florence and Its Wines*, London, 1970
Pellucci, E. *Antinori, Vintners in Florence*, Vallecchi, Florence, 1981
Penning-Rowsell, E. *The Wines of Bordeaux*, London, 1969
Pepys, S. *Diary of Samuel Pepys*, Vol.2, 1665–1669, London, 1930
Picard, L *Dr Johnson's London*, London, 2000
Picard, L. *Restoration London*, London, 1998
Postgate, R. *A Plain Man's Guide to Wine*, London, 1963
Rainbird, G. *Pocket Book of Wine*, London, 1963
Ray, C. *In a Glass Lightly*, London, 1967
Ray, C. *Lafite*, New York, 1971
Ray, C. (ed.) *The Compleat Imbiber* No.2, London, 1958
Ray, C. (ed.) *The Compleat Imbiber* No.3, London, 1960
Ray, C. (ed.) *The Compleat Imbiber* No.6, London, 1963
Ray, C. (ed.) *The Compleat Imbiber* No.7, London, 1964
Ray, C. *The House of Warre, 1670–1970*, London, 1970
Ray, C. *Mouton-Rothschild*, London, 1980
Read, J. *Spanish Wines*, London, 1983
Read, J. *Wines of Portugal*, London, 1987
Reis, R. *Route of Port Wine*, Portugal, 1989
Riders, Schardanus. *Brittish Merlin*, 1669, London
Robertson, G. *Port*, London, 1978
Robinson, J. *Confessions of a Wine Lover*, 1997, London
Robinson, J. *The Great Wine Book*, London, 1982
Robinson, J. *The Oxford Companion to Wine*, Oxford, 1994
Robinson, J. *Vines, Grapes and Wines*, London, 1986
Rudd, H. *Hocks and Mosels*, London, 1935
Saintsbury, G. *A Last Vintage*, London, 1950
Saintsbury, G. *Notes on a Cellar Book*, London, 1939
Sandeman, G. *Port and Sherry*, London, 1955
Seward, D. *Monks and Wine*, London, 1979
Stewart, D. *Early Islam*, Nederlands, 1967
Simon, A.L. *Bottlescrew Days*, London, 1926
Simon, A.L. *Drink*, London, 1948
Simon, A.L. *A Concise Enclopaedia of Gastronomy*, London, 1960
Simon, A.L. *Guide to Good Food and Wines*, London, 1960
Simon, A.L. *The Gourmet's Weekend Book*, London, c. 1950
Simon, A.L. *Know Your Wines*, London, c.1950
Simon, A.L. *The Wines, Vineyards and Vignerons of Australia*, London, 1967
Simon, A.L. (ed.) *A Wine and Food Bedside Book*, Devon, 1972
Smithes, M.F. *Portugal*, Plymouth, 1930
Soto y Molina, J, de *Sherry*, Jerez de la Frontera, 1958
Spenser, E. *The Flowing Bowl*, London, 1925
Stern, G.B. *Bouquet*, London, 1931
Sutherland, D. *The Mad Hatters. Great Sporting Eccentrics of the Nineteenth Century*,
     London, 1987
Taylor, J. (ed.) *The Wine Quotation Book*, London, 1989
Thomas, H. *The Slave Trade 1440–1870*, London, 1997
Thorpe, D. *Vin Rude*, London, 1980
Todd, W.J. *Port: How to Buy, Serve, Store and Drink it*, London, 1925
Toussant-Samat, M. *The History of Food*, London, 1994
Vandyke Price, P. *Woman of Taste*, London, 1990
Vigne et Vin, Cahors, 1981

Ward Lock & Taylor, *The Complete Etiquette for Gentlemen*, *c.*1900

Warner Allen, H. *A Contemplation of Wine*, London, 1951

Warner Allen, H. *A History of Wine*, London, 1961

Warner Allen, H. *Number Three, Saint James's Street*, London, 1950

Warner Allen, H. *Through the Wine Glass*, London, 1954

Watney, J. *Mother's Ruin, The Story of Gin*, London, 1976

Waugh, A. *In Praise of Wine,* London, 1959

Waugh, A. *Merchants of Wine*, London, 1957

Waugh, E. *Wine in Peace and War*, London *c.*1950

Waugh, H. *Diary of a Winetaster*, New York, 1972

Waugh, H. *Wine Diary, 1982–1986*, London, 1987

Younger, W. *Gods, Wine and Men*, London, 1966

Booklets, leaflets, newspapers and magazine articles

Bickerton, L.M. *English Drinking Glasses, 1675-1825*

Black, M. *Food and Cooking in Medieval Britain*, London 1985

Brears, P. *Food and Cooking in sixteenth-century Britain*, London, 1985

Brears, P. *Food and Cooking in seventeenth-century Britain*, London, 1985

David, E. *The Use of Wine in Italian Cooking*, London, *c.*1960

Davis, S.F. *History of the Wine Trade*, London, 1969

Deighton, L. (ed.) *Drinks-man-ship*, London, 1964

Bannell, L. 'Get Drunk Quicker', *The Sunday Telegraph Magazine*, 5 August 2001

British Chronicle, The. 'Vidonia of the Madeira Flavour', 7 January 1789

Broadbent, M. 'Cape Wines at Christie's', *Capewine*, No.3, 1976

Broadbent, M. *The André Simon Memorial Lecture*, London, 18 October 1971

Budd, M. *The Little Book of Honey*, London, 1984

California's Wine Wonderland, Wine Advisory Board, 1970

Cape Cavalcade, London, *c.*1960

Chapman, D.R. (ed.) *Scudamore Papers , 'Home Lacie' Christmas Festivities*, Hereford, 1639

Christie's *Corkscrews* catalogues, London, 1999 and 2001

Cook's Wine Co. *A Short History of the New Zealand Wine Industry*, *c.*1988

Crawford, A. *Bristol and the Wine trade*, University of Bristol 1984

Cyprus Trade Centre. *Cyprus Wines*, London, 1970s

Galard, G. *Great Bordeaux Wines of the nineteenth Century*, Pessac, 1981

Graham, W.G. *An Introduction to Port*, Portugal, 1996

Hallgarten, P. *Côtes du Rhône*, London, 1976

Hereford Journal, The, 'Cheap Port Wine', February 1824

Hereford Journal, The, 'Wine Drinkers', 31 January 1824

Hereford Journal, The, 'Fraudulent Claret', June 1824

Hedges, A. *Bottles and Bottle Collecting*, Bucks, 2000

Hugel, J. *And Give it My Blessing*, Alsace, 1982

Institute of Masters of Wine. International Symposium: *Alternatives to Cork and Glass*, Oxford, 1982

Jefford, A. *Curious to Say*, Decanter 2003

Jones P. & Youseph, R. *The Black Population of Bristol in the eighteenth Century*, Bristol, 1994

Johnson, H. (ed.) *Pan Book of Wine*, London, 1964

Johnson, H. (ed.) *Wine*, House and Garden Special Edition, 1963

Johnson, T. *The Story of Berry Bros and Rudd*, London

Junta de Andalucia. *Malaga and its Wines*, Spain, 1989

Lallemand (ed.) *Champagne, Vin de France*, Paris, 1968

Lechmere, A. *Growing Pains, The Australian Wine Industry in Paralysis*, Decanter 2003

Long Ashton Research Station. *Wine Research*, Bristol, *c.*1980

'Portugal and Madeira', Christmas edition of *Wine and Food*, 1965

Niehaus, C.J.G. Lecture on South African Sherry, Vintner's Hall, London, 1963

Perry, E. *Corkscrews and Bottle Openers*, Aylesbury, 1980

Renfrew, J. *Food and Cooking in Prehistoric Britain*, London, 1985

Renfrew, J. *Food and Cooking in Roman Britain*, London, 1985

Slessor, K. T*he Grapes are Growing*, New South Wales, *c.*1960

South African Wines of Origin, Cape Town, 1976

Stead, J. *Food and Cooking in eighteenth Century Britain*, London, 1985

Van Den Toorn, F.J. *The Cork Oak*, Holland, *c.*1960

Whiskey Trade Review, The. 'A Description of a Californian Vineyard', 17 February 1893

Wilkinson, I. *British Families Raise a Glass to 300 Years of Port*

Wine International, 'Corks versus Alternatives', 2003

Woolhope Transactions, 'English Rhubarb into "Best Champagne" ', p.296, 27 August
        1897

Worshipful Company of Vintners, The. *A Present for an Apprentice*, London 1939

Wine and Food, No.53, Spring 1947

Wine and Food, No.55, Autumn 1947

Wine and Food, No.59, Autumn 1948

Wine and Food, No.60, Winter 1948

Wine and Food, No.85, Spring 1955

Wine and Food, No.130, Summer 1966

'Wine and The Wine Trade', Five Lectures delivered at Vintners Hall, London and at
        Birmingham, 1946, 1949 and 1950

Wine and Spirit Gazette, 'Turn the Back Page', Harpers, 22 October 1965

Wine lists

Army and Navy Stores, 1934

Cheltenham and Hereford Breweries Ltd, 1957

Fortnum and Mason, 1989

Harrods, 1906

Hay and Sons, Sheffield, 1933

Perrett, A., Hereford, 1937 and 1958

Pulling, W., Hereford 1887 and 1922

Rookes, C.A., Stratford-upon-Avon, early 1950s

Southam, Thomas, Shrewsbury, 1905

Tanners of Shrewsbury, 1914

Winter, G. and Son, Yorkshire, *c.*1920

Index

If you are interested in purchasing other books published by Tempus, or in case you have difficulty finding any Tempus books in your local bookshop, you can also place orders directly through our website

www.tempus-publishing.com